Particles

OXFORD STUDIES IN COMPARATIVE SYNTAX

Richard Kayne, General Editor

Principles and Parameters of Syntactic Saturation
Gert Webelhuth

Verb Movement and Expletive Subjects in the Germanic Languages
Sten Vikner

Parameters and Functional Heads: Essays in Comparative Syntax
Edited by Adriana Belletti and Luizi Rizzi

Discourse Configurational Languages
Edited by Katalin É. Kiss

Clause Structure and Language Change
Edited by Adrian Battye and Ian Roberts

Dialect Variation and Parameter Setting: A Study of Belfast English and Standard English
Alison Henry

Parameters of Slavic Morphosyntax
Steven Franks

Particles: On the Syntax of Verb-Particle, Triadic, and Causative Constructions
Marcel den Dikken

The Polysynthesis Parameter
Mark C. Baker

Particles

On the Syntax of Verb-Particle,
Triadic, and Causative Constructions

Marcel den Dikken

New York   Oxford
OXFORD UNIVERSITY PRESS
1995

Oxford University Press

Oxford   New York
Athens   Auckland   Bangkok
Calcutta   Cape Town   Dar es Salaam   Delhi
Florence   Hong Kong   Istanbul   Karachi
Kuala Lumpur   Madras   Madrid   Melbourne
Mexico City   Nairobi   Paris   Singapore
Taipei   Tokyo   Toronto

and associated companies in
Berlin   Ibadan

Published by Oxford University Press, Inc.,
200 Madison Avenue, New York, New York 10016

Library of Congress Cataloging-in-Publication Data
Dikken, Marcel den, 1965–
Particles: on the syntax of verb-particle, triadic,
and causative constructions / Marcel den Dikken.
p.   cm.   —   (Oxford studies in comparative syntax)
Rev. and updated version of the author's thesis—Leiden, 1992.
Includes bibliographical references.
ISBN 0-19-509134-5 (cloth).
ISBN 0-19-509135-3 (pbk.)
1. Grammar, Comparative and general—Particles.
2. Grammar, Comparative and general—Verb.
3. Grammar, Comparative and general—Syntax.
4. Causative (Linguistics).
I. Title.   II. Series.
P283.D55   1995   415—dc20   94-41274

9   8   7   6   5   4   3   2   1
Printed in the United States of America
on acid-free paper

For Evelien

Preface

When, in 1989, I started doing research on the syntax of English verb-particle constructions — especially of the "complex" type, instantiated by such sentences as *They made John out a liar* — I could never have imagined that this would prove to be an extremely rich domain of investigation, both empirically and theoretically. In the course of the execution of my research on complex particle constructions, it gradually started to dawn upon me that, once having gained proper insight into the workings of these constructions, we would be able to shed fundamental new light on the analysis of triadic constructions and the phenomenon of Dative Shift, and that, with a novel approach to these in hand, we would be in a position to take a fresh look at the structure of transitive causative constructions. An in-depth investigation of such small and apparently insignificant elements as particles turned out to teach us quite a lot about secondary predication. The present study, which is a fully revised and updated version of my 1992 Holland Institute of Generative Linguistics (Leiden) dissertation, reports the outcome of this investigation.

It was Richard Kayne's (1985) study of particle constructions that first aroused my interest in the subject. Although — if what is argued in this study is correct — his particular analysis of particle constructions is incorrect in detail, the overall approach to verb-particle constructions taken by Kayne, in terms of small clauses, lies at the heart of the proposals to be developed in what follows. Kayne's analyses, of particles as well as of countless other issues, have been a continuous source of inspiration throughout my work. I feel deeply honoured to have been invited by him to publish my work on particles in his Oxford Studies in Comparative Syntax series.

Closer to home, Teun Hoekstra and his ground-breaking work on (secondary) predication and small clauses have always had a profound influence on my work. Studying English and linguistics in Leiden and doing graduate research there, under the supervision of Hans Bennis, Frits Beukema and Teun Hoekstra, never failed to be extremely inspiring and challenging.

Of the many people who have helped, encouraged and challenged me, I must make special mention of David Pesetsky. Although we disagree on virtually everything that is discussed in this book, his research on especially the syntax of zero elements (see Pesetsky 1993) has been of immense value to me.

I am very grateful to Hans Broekhuis, Eric Hoekstra, René Mulder, Ad Neeleman, Rint Sybesma, Guido Vanden Wyngaerd and Jan-Wouter Zwart for showing great interest in my work from its very beginnings. Their comments and suggestions, as well as the written comments on my dissertation that Maria Teresa Guasti, Eric Reuland and Jan Voskuil sent me, have led to substantial improvements in virtually all departments.

I thank Oxford University Press for the opportunity to publish this book in the Oxford Studies in Comparative Syntax series, and Cynthia Read for her editorial assistance.

Finally, my warmest thanks are due to my parents, to Alma Næss and especially to Evelien Keizer, for reasons that they know best.

Amsterdam, September 1994   Marcel den Dikken

Contents

Particles

I lately lost a preposition;
It hid, I thought, beneath my chair
And angrily I cried, 'Perdition!
Up from out of in under there.'

Correctness is my vade mecum,
And straggling phrases I abhor,
And yet I wondered, 'What should he come
Up from out of in under for?'

Morris Bishop
The New Yorker, 27 September 1947

This is the sort of English up with which I will not put

Winston Churchill
quoted in Gowers (1954:137)

1

Preliminaries

1.1 Introduction

This book presents a study of various secondary predicative constructions featuring a verbal *particle*. A simple initial example of such constructions is given in (1), in which the particle is italicised:

(1)   John looked (*up*) the information (*up*).

Taking the development of an analysis of English complex particle constructions of the type in (2), containing an additional (boldface) secondary predicate, as its point of departure, this study addresses in detail the structure of triadic constructions and the Dative Shift transformation, and the relationship between dative and transitive causative constructions, all of them built on the basic structural template proposed for complex particle constructions.

(2)   a.   They made John *out* **a liar**.
      b.   They painted the barn *up* **red**.
      c.   They put the books *down* **on the shelf**.

The analyses to be presented have their roots in the principles-and-parameters theory of generative syntax, developed in Chomsky (1981, 1986). A key role throughout this study is played by the notion of a SMALL CLAUSE, a tenseless subject-predicate structure (cf. Stowell 1981; Kayne 1984; T. Hoekstra 1984, 1988a, 1991; and references cited there). Small clauses will be found to be pervasive in the analysis of the secondary predication constructions to be discussed in what follows.

In section 1.2 of this introductory chapter, a number of theoretical assumptions which are instrumental to the analysis of particle constructions and related phenomena are spelled out and, wherever possible, supported on the basis of independent considerations. No general introduction to the principles-and-parameters framework or the small clause analysis will be presented here. I refer to Chomsky (1981, 1986) for the overall structure of the former, and to T. Hoekstra (1988a, 1991) for a survey of the major arguments for the small clause analysis of secondary predications.

3

Readers not specifically interested in the theoretical preliminaries addressed in section 1.2 (to which cross-references will be made at the relevant points later in the book) may wish to skip ahead to section 1.3, where the object of study, *particles*, will be delimited.

1.2 Some theoretical assumptions

1.2.1 A modular theory

The principles-and-parameters theory of generative grammar is a *modular* approach to grammar, in two respects. First, it looks upon the various sub-domains of linguistic investigation (syntax, phonology, semantics etc.) as independent but interrelated components or modules of the grammar. An influential perspective on the organisation of generative grammar is Chomsky & Lasnik's (1977) "T-model", reproduced in (3):[1]

(3)

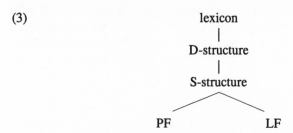

Secondly, within the syntactic component (constituted by D- and S-structure and LF in (3)) several modules conditioning the well-formedness of syntactic constructs are distinguished as well:

(4) a. *X-bar Theory* (structure-building conventions).
    b. *Theta Theory* (Theta Criterion).
    c. *Government Theory* (head-dependent relations).
    d. *Trace Theory* (proper government; ECP).
    e. *Binding Theory* (coindexation relationships).
    f. *Bounding Theory* (locality conditions; Subjacency).
    g. *Control Theory* (distribution of PRO).

---

[1] Chomsky (1993) considerably simplifies the conventional T-model in (3), abolishing the D- and S-structure levels of representation. In this study, I shall on the whole not be concerned with this "minimalist" approach to the organisation of the grammar. In section 1.2.7 I shall address the place of the lexicon in the grammar.

The list in (4) gives a representative sample of the various modules of the syntactic component of the principles-and-parameters framework. Quite possibly, some of these modules can or in fact should be dispensed with. Since this is not a study of the relevance of the modules of the theory, however, I shall not be concerned with issues pertaining to this.

In addition to the module-governed conditions on syntactic constructs, a small number of ubiquitous principles, among which most notably the Projection Principle (which decrees that the lexical properties of heads remain constant throughout the derivation), regulate the output of the single rule Move α (or Affect α; cf. Lasnik & Saito 1984).

1.2.2 A conjunctive ECP

Whenever, as a result of a movement process instantiating Move α, a constituent does not appear at S-structure in the position in which it was base-generated, the Projection Principle ensures that a token associated with the extracted constituent occupies the D-structure position of this constituent at post-D-structure levels of representation. Since it is clear that movement is not possible from just any position in the syntactic tree structure, the distribution of these empty tokens of extracted constituents, labelled *traces*, should be subject to constraints. In particular, the distribution of traces is conditioned by a licensing constraint known as the Empty Category Principle (ECP), which requires traces to be *properly governed*, proper government being a more restricted instance of the general configurational relationship of government.

In Chomsky (1981), the ECP was defined in a disjunctive fashion — a trace was taken to be properly governed if it was either lexically head-governed or locally bound by an A'-antecedent (antecedent-government). In more recent developments of the theory, however, the disjunction in Chomsky's original formulation of the ECP is generally replaced with a conjunctive formulation according to which traces must meet two requirements: (i) formal licensing and (ii) identification (which continues to be disjunctively formulated). Rizzi (1990) is a prime example of this conjunctive ECP:[2]

(5)   *Empty Category Principle*   (Rizzi 1990:32)
        A nonpronominal empty category must be
        (i)   properly head-governed (Formal Licensing)
        (ii)   antecedent-governed or Theta-governed (Identification).

---

[2] Notice that a disjunction remains in (5ii). Also note that in section 1.2.3 NP-traces will be argued not to be subject to the ECP. The definition of the ECP should be revised accordingly; i.e. "nonpronominal" in (5) should presumably be replaced with "nonpronominal, nonanaphoric".

Of particular importance to the analysis of (complex) particle constructions to be presented in this study is the precise formulation of the proper head-government requirement in (5i). From the account to be developed the conclusion ensues that the formal licensing condition on traces should be stated as in (6):

(6)   *Formal licensing*: A trace must be *lexically* governed.

In this regard I essentially follow Chomsky's (1981) original insight, and adopt the position taken in Rizzi (1982), Lasnik & Saito (1984) and Carrier & Randall (1992) that lexical government does not require θ-marking.

It is interesting to note that in the recent literature, English VP-topicalisation figures prominently in the context of the question of whether lexicality should be relevant with respect to formal licensing or not, and is presented as evidence for both an affirmative (Law 1991) and a negative (Rizzi 1990:30–31) answer to this question. Let us consider the example in (7) in some detail:

(7)   I said that I would win the race, and [win the race] I *(*did*).

Rizzi (1990) argues that Infl, the governor of VP, must apparently be able to formally license the trace of the fronted VP in (7) in spite of the fact that Infl is not a lexical category, which he then presents as an argument against the view that only lexical governors can be formal licensers. Law (1991), by contrast, capitalises on the fact that the auxiliary *do* is obligatorily present in examples of VP-fronting of the type in (7), and construes this as an argument in favour of the relevance of lexicality in the definition of formal licensing. If θ-government alone is insufficient, the obligatory presence of *do* in (7) can be accommodated, Law argues, if *do*, a *lexical* (non-functional) category, is needed to provide the VP-trace with a lexical governor so that its formal licensing requirement can be met.

Law (1991) presents further evidence in favour of the view that lexical government is crucial for formal licensing. He notes that, if a DP-analysis of nominal constituents is adopted (cf. a.o. Abney 1987), the fact that examples of the type in (8b) are ungrammatical can be directly made to fall out from the plausible assumption that determiners, being functional elements, are non-lexical and hence do not qualify as proper governors. The impossibility of fronting IP-complements of the complementiser *that*, illustrated in (9b), can be captured in much the same way, given that Comp is not a lexical governor.[3]

---

[3]   Extraction of the subject from the SpecIP position is rendered compatible with the Formal Licensing clause of the conjunctive ECP in (5) by having the verb raise to Comp at LF, as a result of which V comes to lexically govern SpecIP.

(8) a. $[_{DP}$ The $[_{NP}$ books written by John]]$_i$, I like t_i.

    b. *$[_{NP}$ Books written by John]$_i$, I like $[_{DP}$ the $t_i]$.

(9) a. $[_{CP}$ That $[_{IP}$ Mary left]]$_i$, John believed t_i.

    b. *$[_{IP}$ Mary left]$_i$, John believed $[_{CP}$ that $t_i]$.

Functional categories, then, do not qualify as proper governors and, as a consequence, do not allow their complements to be extracted. In the light of the discussion of the examples in (7)–(9), I hence opt for a formulation of the formal licensing condition of the ECP as in (6), in terms of *lexical* head-government. Two questions arise in this context, one concerning the definition of the notion "lexical", and the other pertaining to the argument/adjunct distinction. Let me address these questions in turn.

From the above discussion it should be evident that "lexical" cannot be taken to mean "having a phonetic matrix" — in spite of their being endowed with a phonetic matrix, determiners and complementisers should nonetheless not be taken to belong to the class of lexical governors. A more adequate characterisation of the distinction between lexical and non-lexical governors capitalises on the difference between lexical and functional heads. I assume, with Law (1991), that all and only lexical categories can be proper head-governors.[4]

With respect to the argument/adjunct distinction and formal licensing via lexical government, let me point out that in Rizzi (1990:Ch. 2) VP-adjuncts (manner adverbials) are shown to meet the formal licensing condition by being properly head-governed by the verb (probably after V-movement to the functional head position immediately dominating VP, T on Rizzi's assumptions (cf. Belletti 1990), has taken place), while sentence adverbials are argued to be directly inserted in their S-structure position and hence do not leave a trace in need of formal licensing.[5]

---

[4] Since there is no particular reason to assume otherwise, we may take the auxiliary *do* in (7) to head its own (lexical) VP. For the class of English modal auxiliaries (which are also capable of properly head-governing the trace of a fronted VP; cf. ... *and win the race, he will/can/should/ must*) a similar assumption can be made. Notice that (as Teun Hoekstra points out) the standard assumption that modals are base-generated under Infl is hardly more instructive with regard to the peculiar properties of these auxiliaries than the alternative view that modals head their own VPs. After all, given that there are both finite and non-finite Infl nodes, the fact that modals only have finite forms does not in and of itself fall out from the assumption that modals are Infl elements. Only if modals are restricted to be inserted under *finite* Infl will the claim that modals are Infl elements be able to shed any light on the modals' morphological properties. But clearly, an alternative statement to the effect that modals head VPs which may only be governed by finite Infl would do just as well.

[5] Rizzi (1990:47–48) supports this latter assumption with the aid of French *wh-in-situ* data. He notes that while overt *wh*-"movement" of the sentence adverb *pourquoi* 'why' is perfect (ia), *wh-in-situ* of this adverb (in contrast to manner adverbs) yields an ill-formed result (ib). This follows if no trace is present in (ia), while the forced presence of a trace in (ib) after LF movement of the

1.2.3 NP-traces and the ECP

In the previous subsection I confined my attention to instances of A'-extraction (i.e. movement to a non-argument position). Alongside these, the grammar also features cases of NP-movement to an A-position, as in passive and subject-raising constructions:

(10) a.   John$_i$ was killed t_i.
      b.   John$_i$ seemed t_i to be t_i afraid.

The analysis of the properties of complex particle constructions to be developed in chapter 2 of this study leads me to conclude that NP-traces (i.e. traces left by NP-movement) are not subject to the ECP. It hence forces me to reject Chomsky's (1986) ECP account of "superraising" phenomena, in which illicit NP-raising across an intervening expletive subject takes place. A standard case of "superraising" is given in (11):

(11)   *John$_i$ seems that it is certain t_i to win.

adverb to SpecCP yields an ECP violation on the assumption that this trace cannot be formally licensed for want of a suitable head-governor. (A similar argument is based on French complex inversion; I shall not discuss it here.)

(i)   a.   *Pourquoi* a-t-il parlé?
            why has he spoken
       b.   *$^?$Il a parlé *pourquoi*?
            he has spoken why

   Notice, with respect to Rizzi's assumption that manner adverbs are governed by the (moved) verb, that several languages allow such adverbs to incorporate into the verb. Thus, Lonzi (1991) argues that Italian *ben* (the reduced form of *bene*) left-adjoins to the participle in an example like (iia). Similarly, for Modern Greek (iiia) Rivero (1990) points to the fact that that the adverb (*siga* 'softly', mutated to *sigo*) is directly preceded by the future tense morpheme *tha*, which may only precede verbs, to show that the adverb is part of a complex verb. And in Dutch, manner adverbs may form part of compounds of the type in (iv), something which, if compound formation is subject to the ECP (the non-head part being incorporated at some level of representation), also supports Rizzi's view that manner adverbs are (properly) head-governed; also cf. 1.2.4, below.

(ii)   a.   Ha *ben* capito la questione.
            (he) has well understood the question
       b.   *Ha (*bene*) capito la questione (*ben*).
(iii) a.   To fagitó tha *sigovrási*.
            the food FUT soft-boil
       b.   To fagitó tha vrási *sigá*.
(iv)   *snel*wandelaar 'fast-walker'; *schoon*springer 'beautifully-diver'

Chomsky (1986:18) derives the ill-formedness of examples of this type from the ECP by assuming that '*certain* governs but does not properly govern *t*, the trace of *John*, and antecedent government is blocked (at least) by CP'.[6] It is dubious, however, that *certain* does not properly govern *t*. For clearly, if it did not, then (12) should violate the ECP as well — an unfortunate result in view of the impeccability of the example. Moreover, the head-government requirement is clearly met in a "superraising" construction like (13) (*told* being the proper head-governor of *t*). Yet (13) is just as bad as (11).

(12)   John$_i$ is certain t_i to win.

(13)   *John$_i$ seems that it was told t_i that Mary loves him.

These problems can be averted with the adoption of a conjunctive formulation of the ECP, (11) and (13) then being ruled out as a consequence of the fact that the identification requirement (5ii) (antecedent-government) is not met. Consider, though, what the assumption that NP-traces must be antecedent-governed leads to in the *Barriers* framework, and, in particular, how this assumption could accommodate the well-formedness of an example like (12). Before turning to this example, let me first of all address the case of a simple passive like (10a), repeated here, with some structural details, as (14) (cf. Chomsky 1986: 76):

(14) $[_{IP}$ John$_i$ $[_\alpha$ be$_j$-I] $[_{VP'}$ t_j $[_{VP}$ killed $t_i]]]$

As it stands, (14) violates the ECP — *John* cannot antecedent-govern its trace across the VP projected by *killed*, which is a barrier excluding the purported antecedent of the trace, *John*. In order for the identification requirement on traces to be met, therefore, this ECP violation must somehow be lifted in (14).

To achieve this, Chomsky (1986:76) capitalises on the featural non-distinctness of the VP headed by *be* and that headed by *kill*, and the Specifier-Head agreement relationship within IP. He notes that the "stacked VP" structure that is a subpart of (14), repeated here in (15), can be viewed as a special, base-generated case of the adjunction structure in (16). Invoking May's (1985) notion of a "segment", Chomsky argues that in adjunction structures of the type in (16), the outer ß-projection counts as a "segment" of a multi-segment ß-projection.

(15) $[_{VP'}$ t_j $[_{VP}$ killed $t_i]]$

(16) $[_ß$ α $[_ß$ ...]]$

---

[6] Notice that, at least at this stage in *Barriers*, Chomsky presupposes a disjunctive ECP.

In this way, Chomsky achieves the desired effect that α in (16) is not dominated by ß since it is not dominated by every segment of ß, so that hence α is extractable from ß in this adjunction structure. In this way, intermediate adjunction of a category to a projection can be seen to be a means to void the barrierhood of this projection.

Transposing this segment approach to the base-generated double-VP structure in (15), Chomsky now manages to have t_i governed by t_j. After all, if VP counts as a segment of VP', VP does not exclude t_j and hence no barrier intervenes between t_i and t_j.[7] This provides a partial answer to the question of how (14) can be grammatical if NP-traces must be antecedent-governed. The remainder of the answer lies in the fact that in this structure index i equals index j, as a result of the Specifier-Head agreement relationship between *John* in SpecIP and $[be+I]$ (which receives the index j through percolation from *be*). In this way, t_j in (14) can be identified as the antecedent-governor of the NP-trace in the participle's complement.

Now let us turn to our earlier example in (12), whose partial structure can be represented as in (17):

(17) $[_{IP}$ John$_i$ $[_\alpha$ be$_j$-I] $[_{VP}$ t_j $[_{AP}$ certain $[_{IP}$ t_i to win]]]]

How can the NP-trace t_i in (17) be antecedent-governed? Clearly, no recourse can be had to a "base-generated adjunction structure" account of the type employed in the case of (14), since VP and AP are not categorially identical. AP hence counts as a barrier for antecedent-government of t_i by t_j, and an ECP violation is expected to arise, as Chomsky (1986:78) also notes. The fact that (12) is grammatical must then be accommodated with the aid of 'some special stipulation, perhaps marked coindexing of *be* and [*certain*] (a kind of restructuring), so that chain coindexing (hence, proper government) holds of the extended chain ([*certain*], *t*)'. Chomsky defends invoking an *ad hoc* stipulation to account for the grammaticality of (12) by suggesting that raising constructions of this type are cross-linguistically marked. However, if Cinque (1989, 1990) is right that there exists a substantial class of *ergative adjectives*, NP-raising from the complement of adjectives is far from exceptional. It seems, then, that the core grammar, rather than some peripheral stipulation, should cater for the possibility of NP-raising from AP.

Similarly, it should presumably allow for NP-movement out of CP-barriers, depending on one's analysis of the infinitival complement of raising predicates. In (17) I assumed the *to*-infinitival complement of *certain* to be an IP, but a case can be made, on the basis of facts concerning the licensing of negative polarity items, that such infinitives in fact project CPs. Consider (18):

---

[7]   A category α is excluded by ß iff it is excluded by *all segments* of ß.

(18) a. *John denied *anything*.
      b. John denied that he had won *anything*.
      c. *John is uncertain of *anything*.
      d. John is uncertain to win *anything*.

An inherently negative verb like *deny* can license negative polarity items (NPIs) like *anything* in its complement clause (18b), but NPIs cannot show up in the object position of such a verb (18a). Progovac (1988) and Laka (1990) account for the contrast in (18a,b) by postulating an element in the inherently negative verb's CP complement which takes care of NPI-licensing — an operator in SpecCP (Progovac) or a negatively specified Comp (Laka). NPI-licensing with inherently negative predicates thus being contingent on the presence in the predicate's complement of a negatively specified CP, we may now take the facts in (18c,d) to show that *uncertain* in (18d) selects an infinitival CP complement containing the licenser of the negative polarity item *anything* embedded in it.[8] This being the case, and CP being a barrier (by inheritance from IP) for government of the trace of the raised subject of the infinitival clause, what we have here is another case of NP-raising which apparently violates the ECP but which the theory should allow for.

It does once we exempt the ECP from applying to NP-traces,[9] and appeal to some other mechanism to accommodate the locality conditions on NP-movement, for instance — in conjunction with the strict cycle condition (Chomsky 1993) — Principle A of the Binding Theory.[10] Whatever the exact means of restricting NP-movement, the thing to bear in mind in the context of this study is that NP-traces are not to be taken to be subject to the ECP.

---

[8] But see Frank (1992:212) for a different conclusion. Pesetsky (in prep.) and Ormazabal (1994) argue that the infinitival complement of ECM-verbs is a CP. Given a minimalist approach to Case-feature checking in ECM-constructions, according to which the ECM-subject undergoes NP-raising out of the infinitival clause to a SpecAgrOP position in the matrix clause, this would also constitute a case for NP-movement across a CP boundary.

[9] Also cf. Davis (1984), and Lasnik's (1993b:fn. 8) conclusion that 'the ECP may be entirely irrelevant for A-movement'. I shall continue to subject A-movement of *non-referential* constituents to the ECP (cf. chapter 3 on predicate inversion).

[10] For recent discussion of the idea that NP-movement is constrained by Principle A of the Binding Theory, cf. Freidin (1992:235–45, 310–13). Kayne (1991b) argues that anaphors and pronouns should not be distinguished by characterising the former as [+anaphoric, −pronominal] and the latter as [−pronominal, +anaphoric]. Instead, anaphors (particularly monomorphemic ones) should be considered a special subclass of pronouns; no category corresponds to the feature set [+anaphoric, −pronominal]. If this is correct, NP-trace cannot be characterised in these terms either. Kayne hence suggests that NP-trace is completely featureless, so that its locality constraints must be attributed to the ECP. Kayne's proposal is clearly incompatible with what is argued with respect to NP-trace in the present study.

1.2.4 Incorporation and the ECP

Apart from A'-movement of maximal projections, and NP-movement, the grammar also distinguishes a class of instantiations of Move α affecting heads. In this study, I shall be particularly concerned with one instance of head movement (or *incorporation*) — particle movement. Consider the word-order alternation in the English verb-particle construction, illustrated by the example in (1), repeated here:

(1)   John looked (*up*) the information (*up*).

Of the various ways of looking at this word-order alternation from a theoretical perspective, one is to assume that the particle is optionally incorporated into the verb in the course of the derivation. In essence, this is the approach that will be taken in this study. The details of the analysis will be spelled out in chapter 2. What is relevant in the context of this introductory chapter, however, is to address some theoretical issues arising in connection with head incorporation phenomena, whose properties were first studied extensively in the principles-and-parameters framework in Baker (1988).

Head movement is constrained by the ECP (under which, as Chomsky 1986 has shown, Travis' 1984 Head Movement Constraint can be subsumed). Incorporation is hence predicted to be impossible from ungoverned positions, a prediction which, Baker (1988) argues, is appropriately reflected by the empirical restrictions on head incorporation. Thus, while the head of a complement are readily incorporated, incorporation from ungoverned subject positions is disallowed. Heads of ECM subjects or of lexically governed adjuncts (cf. section 1.2.2) will be seen to be incorporable into their governors.

The latter two incorporation configurations (ECM subjects and lexically governed adjuncts), which are crucially invoked at various points in this study, give rise to some theoretical discussion. As they stand, they apparently violate the Subject Condition (or Kayne's 1984 ban on extraction from left branches) and the Adjunct Condition: subjects and adjuncts are generally opaque to sub-extraction.

Arguing specifically against the possibility of incorporation of the head of a specifier, Hale & Keyser (1992) have suggested that this would result in an ECP (Minimality) violation. They obtain this result by assuming that in a configuration of the sort in (19), the lower head Y governs its specifier (ZP), and hence counts as a closer governor for the trace of the head of this specifier, thereby preventing the complex head X created by incorporation from antecedent-governing the incorporate's trace.

(19) $[_{XP} [_X X + Z_i] [_{YP} [_{ZP} \ldots t_i \ldots] [_{Y'} \ldots Y \ldots]]]$

Hale & Keyser's suggestion seems to go through neither theoretically nor empirically, however. Theoretically, it is crucially dependent on the assumption that heads of projections govern their specifiers, a view that is at the very least debatable.[11] Moreover, there is direct empirical evidence that incorporation from specifier positions should not be ruled out on a principled basis. Consider, for instance, the Mohawk example in (20), taken from Baker (1988:90):

(20)   Wa'-hati-*nawatst*-a'rho' ka'-nowa-ktatie'   Rania'te'kowa.
        AOR-3MPL-mud-placed   PREF-carapace-along   Great Turtle
        'They placed mud along (the edge of) the Great Turtle's carapace.'

What we have here is a resultative locative construction featuring incorporation into the verb of the head of the "locatum" argument, *nawatst* 'mud'. T. Hoekstra (1988a, 1991) has argued in detail that resultative constructions involve SC complementation. The verb in (20), then, takes a SC complement headed by the affixal P *ktatie'* 'along'. It is the head of the subject NP of this SC, *nawatst*, which undergoes incorporation into the verb in (20). Schematically:

(21)   [$_{VP}$ mud$_i$–place [$_{SC}$ [$_{NP}$ t_i] [$_{PP}$ along the Great Turtle's carapace]]]

In view of the grammaticality of this Mohawk example, we must hence conclude that it is empirically possible to incorporate the head of a specifier into a governing head. This is further corroborated by the distribution of reflexive incorporation in Old Norse.

Old Norse reflexive anaphors come in two guises, a free form and a suffix on the verb. The properties of the Old Norse suffixal reflexive at once support the view (propounded in Miller 1993:ch. 9, to which I refer for original data sources) that syntactic incorporation is at stake, and the claim that incorporation from lexically governed subject positions should be allowed by the ECP:

(22)   Hann veit   *sik*   vanfær-an   til at skipt-a
        he   know.3SG.S   REFL.ACC   unable-ACC.S   of to divide-INF
        orð-um   við konung-inn.
        word-DAT.PL   with the-king.ACC.SG
        'He knows himself incapable of vying with the king in words.'

(23)   mað-r   þót-tu-*mk*   (ek) mennsk-r.
        person-NOM.SG think-PAST.1SG-REFL I   human-NOM.SG
        'I thought myself a human being.'

---

[11] It would, for instance, render all PROs (particularly, PRO subjects of adjunct-SCs) governed. Notice, furthermore, that it is not obvious that Y will still set up a Minimality barrier if (as in the specific case that Hale & Keyser address) it is itself incorporated into X (cf. also Büring 1992:53; Büring postulates a whole class of cases of incorporation from specifier position).

The things to note about (23) — the reflexive incorporation construction — are the Case form of the SC predicate (nominative rather than, as in (22), accusative) and the function of the affixal reflexive (subject of the verb's SC complement). The former supports the view that syntactic incorporation is involved in (23), the Caselessness of the incorporate (cf. Baker 1988) explaining why the SC predicate cannot Case-agree with it and must take on the Case of the root subject. And once we have established on this basis that (23) features reflexive incorporation, the fact that the reflexive in question is the subject of the SC in the complement of the incorporating verb then identifies (23) as another example of incorporation from a governed specifier position.[12]

Incorporation from specifier positions must hence be a theoretical option. The same holds for incorporation of the head of a lexically governed adjunct into the governor. We already encountered cases of incorporation of manner adverbs in fn. 5, above, where — among other things — I cited Modern Greek examples of the type in (24) (from Rivero 1990) as evidence for the view that manner adverbs are lexically head-governed by the verb:

(24)   To fagitó tha *sigo*vrási.
            the food FUT soft-boil

---

[12] If antipassivisation in Chamorro and cliticisation in Romance involve head movement (cf. Baker 1988 on the former and Kayne 1991a on the latter; but cf. Sportiche 1992 for an interesting alternative approach to Romance cliticisation), the examples in (i) (featuring the Chamorro ECM verb *ekspekta*; Gibson 1980, Baker 1988:135–36) and (ii) are further illustrations of such incorporation.

(i)   Kao   *man*-ekspekta hao   pära un ma'-ayuda?
           Q   APASS-expect   you(ABS)   IRREAL-2SG-PASS-help
           'Do you expect *someone* to help you?'

(ii)   Je *le* crois [$_{SC}$ [$_{NP}$ [$_N$ *t*]] fidèle].
           I him(CL) believe honest
           'I consider him honest.'

As Hans Bennis points out, noun incorporation from specifiers seems to be impossible in Dutch. This is shown by the ill-formedness of (iiib), on the assumption that complex verbs like *pianospelen* 'play the piano' are derived via incorporation. Plausibly, however, Dutch complex verbs like *pianospelen* are lexically rather than syntactically derived. If so, the deviance of (iib) follows from the fact that, given the SC analysis, *piano* in (iiib,c) is not an argument of the verb *spelen*. Mohawk (20) and Old Norse (23) show that noun incorporation in these languages is a syntactic process (*contra* Grimshaw & Mester 1985; Di Sciullo & Williams 1987; Broekman & Den Dikken 1988).

(iii)   a.   dat Jan wil pianospelen.
              that Jan wants piano-play
        b.   *dat Jan [$_{SC}$ *t* stuk] wil *piano*spelen.
              that Jan broken wants piano-play
        c.   dat Jan [$_{SC}$ de piano stuk] wil spelen.
              that Jan the piano broken wants play

How do we explain the fact that heads are apparently exempt from the Subject and Adjunct Conditions on extraction? The facts of head movement dictate the following descriptive generalisation:

(25)   If a head X lexically governs a projection YP (in the sense of 1.2.2), it can incorporate the head Y of this projection.

The theory can accommodate this generalisation in the following way. First note that (as a result of percolation along the projection line) heads of projections are identical with their maximal projections in all relevant respects. Hence if a head X lexically and antecedent-governs some YP, hence assigns a γ-mark to it (cf. Lasnik & Saito 1984), this γ-mark will percolate to YP's head Y, which ends up γ-marked as a result. In this way, the theory allows heads of lexically governed constituents (including ECM subjects and a subclass of adjuncts; cf. section 1.2.2) to incorporate into their lexical governors.[13]

Extraction of *non-heads* from ECM subjects and adjuncts, on the other hand, continues to be ruled out by the Subject and Adjunct Conditions. This follows from Subjacency on the assumption that subjects and adjuncts are not L-marked, hence inherent barriers, and that successive cyclic extraction via adjunction to the subject or adjunct (to void barrierhood) is impossible.[14] This theoretical difference between heads and non-heads as far as extraction from lexically governed adjuncts and subjects is concerned is empirically justified. It can be illustrated particularly nicely on the basis of two instances of incorporation of empty dative prepositions which figure prominently in chapters 3 and 4 of this study. At this point, I can only present the rough outlines of the analyses to be developed, focusing on the main point of current interest.

In chapter 3 I argue that Dative Shift, illustrated in (26), involves movement of a dative PP containing an empty dative preposition and the indirect object NP. The landing-site of the moved PP is the subject position of a SC governed by the verb into which the zero dative P incorporates, as is shown in the simplified structure of the double object construction (26b) given in (27).

---

[13] The apparently problematic case of *ne*-cliticisation in (i), in which *ne* is not itself the head of the SC subject, could be made compatible with the above if *ne* is extracted from the SC subject via intermediate adjunction to the *head* of the SC subject. The fact that the phrase *di quali libri* cannot adjoin to the head of the SC subject on its way up explains the deviance of this variant of (i).

(i)   *Ne*/*Di quali libri* hai mandato [$_{SC}$ [$_{NP}$ un carico *t*] via]?
        of-them(CL)/of which books have-you sent a load away

[14] The latter follows, in the case of subjects, from the theoretical impossibility of adjunction to arguments (Chomsky 1986:6); in the case of adjuncts, this is a stipulation in *Barriers*. By assuming that subjects of lexically θ-marked constituents are not L-marked, hence inherent barriers, I differ from Chomsky (1986). Chomsky assumes that L-marking can proceed via Spec-Head agreement, and thus renders L-marked all subjects of constituents governed by a lexical θ-marker.

(26) a.   John gave a book to Mary.
      b.   John gave Mary a book.

(27) $[_{VP}$ V $[_{SC}$ $[_{PP}$ P$_\emptyset$ NP$_{Goal}]_i$ ... NP$_{Theme}$ $t_i]]$

Incorporation of the head of the moved PP, a left-branch constituent, is licit, in view of what was argued above. Extraction from the indirect object NP, on the other hand, yields a left branch effect:[15]

(28)   *Who did John give friends of a book?

Movement of the head of a left-branch constituent is hence legitimate, while extraction non-heads from subjects yields a Subject Condition violation.

The same dichotomy between head movement and XP-movement recurs in the domain of extraction from adjuncts. In chapter 4, I argue that, in certain languages and under certain conditions, the empty-headed dative PP of a double object construction is prevented from moving to the SC-subject position in (27), and instead is *scrambled* to a VP-adjoined position. From this position, the head of the moved dative phrase is incorporated into a verb governing the adjoined dative PP, in accordance with the conditions on head movement discussed above. Again, however, extraction of a non-head from the scrambled dative PP is impossible. This can be illustrated on the basis of the examples in (29). While in (29a) the empty head of the scrambled dative PP can be licensed by incorporation, (29b) shows that *wh*-extraction from the scrambled PP is impossible:

(29) a.   Wat$_j$ heeft Jan $[_{PP}$ P$_\emptyset$ Marie]$_i$ waarschijnlijk t_j t_i gegeven?
            what has Jan Marie probably given
      b.   *Waar$_j$ heeft Jan $[_{PP}$ t_j aan]$_i$ waarschijnlijk een boek t_i gegeven?
            where has Jan to probably a book given

Just as in the case of subextraction from subjects, we see that head movement is permitted while non-head extraction yields a deviant result. The facts of dative and double object constructions (as analysed in chapters 3 and 4 of this study) hence empirically vindicate the theoretical conclusion that we drew earlier on.

The upshot of the discussion in this section is that extraction from subjects (left branches) and adjuncts should not be categorically excluded. While extraction of XPs contained in these constituents is indeed impossible, the *heads* of

---

[15] In chapter 4, I shall argue that extraction of the entire indirect object NP from the position in (27) is also illicit, as expected. Empirical illustration of this is not straightforward, for reasons that I shall address in detail in chapter 4.

lexically governed adjuncts and subjects must be permitted to leave their maximal projections. Subjects and adjuncts, then, are not barriers for extraction of their heads. This can be made to follow from the theory by exploiting the identity between maximal projections and their heads.

1.2.5 Incorporation, indexation and c-command

Li (1990) has recently argued that head movement is subject to the Binding Theory. He seeks to provide an explanation for the well-known fact that complex heads created by incorporation as a rule do not contain inflectional material. Thus, in noun incorporation constructions, the incorporated noun is always a bare N root; it is never accompanied by a determiner. If, as Abney (1987) has argued, determiners are heads taking NP as their complement, there is no *a priori* reason to expect things to be like this. After all, a derivation whereby N first incorporates into D, the D+N complex subsequently undergoing incorporation into V, would appear to be perfectly compatible with the theory, in the sense that it involves strictly local head-movement steps.

(30) $*[_{VP} [_V V + [_D D + N_i]_j] [_{DP} [_D t_j] [_{NP} [_N t_i]]]]$

By distinguishing between two types of heads (A- and A'-heads, the latter comprising the functional heads) and extending the scope of the Binding Theory into the domain of heads, Li can accommodate the fact that complex heads created by incorporation typically do not contain inflectional material. Since movement from a lexical (A-)head position through a functional (A'-)head to another lexical (A-)head position would instantiate "improper movement", the theory (specifically, Principle C of the (extended) Binding Theory) correctly rules out the incorporation of inflected forms. In the specific case of (30), "improper movement" results from raising of N, an A-head, via D, an A'-head, to V, an A-head.

I shall make important use of the binding-theoretic restrictions on successive-cyclic head movement introduced by Li (1990) in my account of the properties of complex particle constructions and the dative alternation. One theoretical consequence of incorporating Li's (1990) "improper head movement" scenario is worth pointing out at this stage — the fact that (contrary to Li's own claims) it is crucially dependent on a definition of c-command in terms of the first branching node (cf. Reinhart 1976). Let us see why this is so. In order for "improper movement" to arise in a case of movement of an A-head via an A'-head to another A-head, the three head positions must all be part of the same chain, and must hence all bear the same index. It is crucial, then (as Li states explicitly), that an incorporate *transmits* its index to an incorporation complex (i.e. a complex head created through head incorporation).

Suppose now that, following Li (1990:408), we were to adopt a definition of c-command in terms of domination, as in (31):

(31) α c-commands β iff α does not dominate β and β is not excluded by the node immediately dominating α.

Since an element α is dominated by node γ iff α is dominated by *every segment* of γ (cf. Chomsky 1986:7), the definition of c-command in (31) will allow an incorporate in an incorporation structure of the type in (32), below, to c-command its trace directly. The incorporate is not dominated by the complex head created through incorporation since it is not dominated by all segments of this complex head, which instantiates a multi-segment adjunction structure. Given the definition of c-command in (31), then, an incorporate can antecedent-govern its trace *directly* without having to percolate its index to the incorporation complex (cf. also Borer 1991 for the same conclusion).

(32) $[_\gamma \; \alpha_i \; [_\gamma \; \gamma]] \; ... \; [_\beta \; t_i]$

But if transmission of an incorporate's index to the incorporation complex is not required, there will be no "improper movement" in a case of A-A'-A head movement. There will be two *independent* (i.e. non-coindexed) chains. One links an A-head to an A'-adjunction position to an A'-head; the other connects the trace of the complex A'-head to an A'-position adjoined to an A-head. Both these chains are perfectly licit, and no Binding Theory violation ensues.[16]

If, by contrast, we base ourselves on a definition of c-command in terms of the first branching node, the ECP will force the incorporate to percolate its index to the complex head into which it is moved. After all, on a "first branching node" definition of c-command, the incorporate α in (32) will c-command only its host head, γ, and will be capable of antecedent-governing its trace in β only if it transmits its index i to the complex γ-node resulting from incorporation. The conclusion to be drawn from this discussion, then, is that, if Li's (1990) "improper head movement" account is to be maintained (see sections 2.3.6 and 3.10.2, below, for evidence supporting Li's proposal), we should adopt a "first branching node" definition of c-command rather than one in terms of domination, as in (31).

The same conclusion ensues from a consideration of another property of head incorporation phenomena, Baker's (1988) observation that incorporation extends the governing domain of the incorporating head, codified in (33):

---

[16]   Chomsky (1993) (cf. esp. his fn. 20) effectively assumes that successive head movement creates a series of independent chains. Li's "improper head movement" cases can no longer be captured on this assumption.

(33)   *The Government Transparency Corollary* (GTC)
            A lexical item which has an item incorporated into it governs
            everything which the incorporated item governed in its original
            structural position.   (Baker 1988:64)

In the course of this study, concrete instantiations of the GTC will be discussed.
For the moment, let me just point out that the GTC can in effect be viewed as
a corollary of the theory if and only if c-command is defined in terms of the
first branching node.[17] For only if we adopt this definition of c-command do
we force an incorporate to transmit its index to the incorporation complex, and
only if index transmission takes place do we derive the desired result that the
complex incorporation structure bears the index of the trace of the incorporate,
which then comes to be a part of the chain headed by the incorporation complex.
    Since both Li's (1990) extension of the Binding Theory to heads and Baker's
(1988) Government Transparency Corollary seem well-motivated ingredients of
the theory of head movement (which I shall be making essential use of in the
remainder of this study), and since they are both crucially dependent on a "first
branching node" definition of c-command, I conclude that, in any event in the
domain of head movement phenomena, this definition of c-command should be
preferred to any others. Since it would clearly be undesirable from the point of
view of the principles-and-parameters framework to assume a different definition of c-command to be operative in the "macro-syntax", the null hypothesis
must then be that minimal c-command should also be the relevant structural
notion above X^0-level.

1.2.6 Uniformity of Theta Assignment

In the words of Pesetsky (1993:7), 'hypotheses about language should put as
small a burden as possible on the child's linguistic experience and as great a
burden as possible on the biologically given system, which we call *Universal
Grammar* (*UG*)' (original italics). In the specific domain of the *lexicon*, no
doubt a fair amount of lexical learning from experience takes place, but, as
Grimshaw (1990:3) puts it, '[t]he position taken in much earlier work, that the
lexicon is idiosyncratic and is acquired piece by piece, simply cannot be maintained. It fails to explain the high degree of regularity of the lexical system as
well as how children come to acquire lexical information.'

---

[17] Chomsky (1993), dispensing with the concept of government, sketches the outlines of a
"minimalist" alternative to the GTC. He claims that 'the GTC is not strictly speaking a corollary'
(1993:18). It seems to me, however, that it *is* (at least in the *Barriers* framework), provided that
government is defined in terms of minimal c-command, as argued here.

With the objective of capturing the regularities in the relationship between lexical thematic information and initial, D-structural representations, scholars in two generative frameworks, Relational Grammar and the principles-and-parameters framework, have formulated the *linking* hypotheses in (34) (from Perlmutter & Postal 1984) and (35) (from Baker 1988):

(34)   *The Universal Alignment Hypothesis* (UAH)
        Principles of UG predict the initial relation borne by each argument
        in a given clause from the meaning of the clause.

(35)   *The Uniformity of Theta Assignment Hypothesis* (UTAH)
        Identical thematic relationships between items are represented by
        identical structural relationships between those items at the level of
        D-structure.

Of these two hypotheses, (35) is weaker in one respect than (34) in that it is concerned only with specific lexical items, while (34) is formulated in general terms, abstracting away from concrete predicate-argument relationships. Taken as is, then, Baker's UTAH does not have anything to say about the question of whether the relationship between *John* and *hit* in (36a) should be represented syntactically in the same way as that between *John* and *kicked* in (36b) or not — all UTAH says is that in all tokens of constructions involving the predicate *hit* and a Patient argument, the structural relationship between *hit* and this Patient argument should be represented identically, and a similar account applies to *kick* constructions, but entirely independently.

(36) a.   Bill hit John.
      b.   Bill kicked John.

UAH, due to its being formulated in an item-independent, general fashion, generalises across the examples in (36). It is weaker than UTAH, however, in not requiring identical D-structural representations for thematically identical relationships, but merely decreeing predictable patterns of argument linking, as Pesetsky (1993:15) points out.

Precisely in this domain where UTAH makes a stronger claim than UAH, recent work has tended to weaken the original UTAH, thereby bridging the gap between the two hypotheses in (34) and (35). Thus, Larson (1990:601) suggests that (35) should be relativised to the statement in (37).[18]

---

[18] Also cf. Speas (1990:90) and Holloway-King (1993:129) for similar modifications of UTAH. As implied by the formulation, Larson's relativised UTAH is based on the view that thematic roles are hierarchically organised (cf. Jackendoff 1977; Carrier-Duncan 1985; Belletti & Rizzi 1988; Grimshaw 1990). All that UTAH prescribes on Larson's assumptions is that the universal hierarchisation of θ-roles be respected.

(37)   *The Relativised Uniformity of Theta Assignment Hypothesis*
         Identical thematic relationships are represented by identical relative
         hierarchical relationships between items at D-structure.

Larson's prime motive for relativising UTAH is to address Jackendoff's (1990)
objection to his analysis of the dative alternation, which is incompatible with a
strict formulation of the hypothesis. The analysis of Dative Shift to be presented
in chapter 3 of the present study, however, is fully reconcilable with Baker's
(1988) original UTAH. Since I aim for the strongest possible formulation of
UTAH, I hence dismiss (37).

Baker (1989a) himself has also proposed a revision of his original UTAH,
substituting *similar* for *identical* in (35) and presenting the formulation in (38):

(38)   *The Revised Uniformity of Theta Assignment Hypothesis*
         Similar thematic relationships are assigned at D-structure in similar
         structural configurations within (and across) languages.

With regard to this revised UTAH, we should note that, while constituting an
obvious retreat from (35) in one respect (viz. the weakening of *identical* to
similar), (38) simultaneously strengthens (35) considerably in two other respects. First, it no longer makes reference to "items" and hence is significantly
more general than the item-specific formulation of the original UTAH. Moreover, while (35) generalised neither across items nor across languages, the
parenthesised part of the revised UTAH in (38) now also forces us to carry over
an analysis motivated for one particular language to thematically similar
constructions in other languages. In these two respects, then, UTAH has gained
considerable force in the formulation in (38). It is now basically identical with
UAH as stated in (34).

In this study I shall essentially base myself on the revised (c.q. generalised)
Uniformity of Theta Assignment Hypothesis in (38), with the proviso that, since
nothing in what follows leads me to believe that a retreat from strict identity is
required, *similar* should be changed back to the original *identical*.[19]

---

[19] Borer (1991) argues against UTAH, presenting an argument to the effect that, while morphological inchoatives like *widen* in *The canal widened* can be both pre-syntactically and syntactically
derived, morphological causatives like *widen* in *The flood widened the canal* can only be pre-syntactically derived. In the latter, then, the adjectival base of the verb, *wide*, does not project and hence
does not assign its θ-role in the same structural position as in constructions in which it does project
syntactically. Borer further points to the well-known difference between verbal and adjectival passives, and the problem it poses for UTAH. While recognising that UTAH may well face problems
in some domains (further research of which is clearly called for), I maintain that UTAH is the most
viable constraint on the relationship between theta-semantics and initial syntactic structures. Note
also that many (if not all) of Rosen's (1984) objections to a strict lexicon/syntax mapping are based
on dubious assumptions, misanalyses and mistakes in the data (cf. Martin 1991 for discussion).

(39)   *The Strongest Uniformity of Theta Assignment Hypothesis*
            Identical thematic relationships are assigned in identical D-structure
            configurations within and across languages.

1.2.7 Modularity and syntactic word formation

An important question which has been the focus of much research throughout
the development of the theory is the question as to where in the overall
structure of the grammar word formation processes should be taken to apply.
In his concise historical survey of the views taken with regard to the relationship between morphology (or word formation) and syntax, Schultink (1988)
quotes De Saussure (1916:186) as stating that '[l]inguistiquement, la morpho-
logie n'a pas d'objet réel et autonome; elle ne peut constituer une discipline
distincte de la syntaxe'. It was not until Chomsky's (1970) rebuttal of the
practices of the Generative Semantics movement (cf. Lakoff 1970; McCawley
1968a,b, 1976) that the generative framework radically extended the significance of the lexicon as a syntactic component from being a mere repository of
idiosyncrasy into being the sole locus of word formation. The theory of Lexical
Morphology and Phonology (cf. Kiparsky 1982) developed this *lexicalist*
approach into a full-fledged theory of lexical word formation. Recent years,
however, have witnessed a steady and ongoing return from the lexicalist framework to a theory in which word formation is carried out mostly or even wholly
in the syntactic component of the grammar.

The introduction of the category Infl, which hosts the Tense and Agreement
features of clauses, already meant a departure from strict lexicalism, in that
different parts of morphologically complex words (inflected verbs) are generated
in different syntactic positions, the actual word not being composed until at a
post-lexical stage.[20] Recent developments in the wake of Pollock (1989), Belletti (1990) and Chomsky (1991) recognise the syntactic head status of a wealth
of other functional elements beyond the original Tense and Agr features.

At the same time, radical executions of alignment hypotheses such as those
discussed in the previous subsection have led to the postulation of abstract
syntactic heads corresponding to (θ-)semantic primitives such as CAUS (cf. e.g.
Pesetsky 1993), and have rendered it possible to deny morphology its status as
an independent module of the grammar. They have at least opened the door to
exclusively syntactic formation of morphologically (and semantically) complex
constructs.

---

[20] Chomsky's (1993) *checking* approach to inflection no longer assumes that the terminal nodes of
inflectional phrase markers are the actual inflectional morphemes; instead, inflectional heads
dominate sets of features, the affixes against which these are checked being base-generated on the
inflected lexical item.

It is important in this context to realise the dual role that the concept of "module" or "component" plays in current theory. As Grimshaw (1986:148) has noted, a component can either be (i) a set of rules or representations defined over a certain vocabulary and governed by principles of a certain type, or (ii) a set of rules and operations which act as a block in the organisation of the grammar, and are linearly ordered with respect to other such blocks. The success of analyses which hold that word formation can (at least partly) take place in the syntax (cf. Baker 1988 and much related work) has made it clear that ordering all word formation before the application of syntactic transformations (cf. (ii)) would be ill-advised. Whether there is no word-formation module in the sense of (i) either has turned out to be a debatable issue. Sproat (1985:505) cautiously concludes that 'there is no separate word-formation *component* [in the sense of (ii)], what has come to be termed the "Lexicon" in recent years [but that] the well-formedness of various aspects of word structure is taken care of by principles applying in the various components of the grammar'. These principles governing the well-formedness of morphological constructs might well constitute a *module* in the sense of (i), much like the modules (3). This morphological module would then be sequentially unordered in relation to the syntactic component(s) of the grammar.

It is this concept of *parallel morphology* which has been developed in recent work of Borer (1991, forthc.), who emphasises that '[g]iven this notion of autonomy it is clear that there is no particular need to maintain that two autonomous modules interact with one another at a fixed unique point' (1991:135). To illustrate this point with reference to the central topic of this study, let me briefly mention the fact that in a language like Dutch, verb-particle combinations, whose constituent parts are syntactic atoms (as will be argued in chapter 2), can form the input to derivational morphological processes, as illustrated in (40) (where in each case the particle is italicised and the additional derivational morpheme is printed in boldface; the base verb is unadorned):[21]

(40) a. *op*-merken 'up-notice'
        op-merk-**zaam** 'up-notice-ive' (attentive)
     b. *toe*-laten 'to-let' (ad/permit)
        toe-laat-**baar** 'to-let-able' (admissible)
     c. *over*-geven 'over-give' (vomit–V)
        over-geef-**sel** 'over-give-SFX' (vomit–N)
     d. *uit*-sterven 'out-die'
        uit-sterv-**ing** 'out-die-ing' (extinction)

---

[21] The examples are taken from Neeleman & Weerman (1993:439). What follows is a sketch of an account of (40) in a parallel morphology approach, which should be perfected by future research so that it accommodates the fact that English verb-particle combinations do not normally undergo derivational word-formation processes (except for non-productive cases like *onlooker* and *bypass*).

Although for some of the derivational morphemes in (40) it can perhaps be argued that they are *syntactic affixes* which are attached in the syntactic component (cf. Fabb 1984; this may be particularly likely in the case of *-baar* '-able'), this does not seem to be the case in general. Examples of the type in (40) can easily be dealt with on the assumption that the morphological, word-formation component works in tandem with the syntactic component, and that, in principle, there is unlimited two-way traffic between the two modules, such that 'the relevant aspects of the output of each syntactic operation are available to the word formation component' (Borer 1991:135).

For the purposes of this study it is largely immaterial whether morphology is denied independent status as a component of the grammar (as in De Saussure's 1912:186 contention quoted at the beginning of this subsection), so that all affixation is syntactic, or whether the principles governing the formation of complex words constitute a module in the sense of, for instance, Theta Theory or Binding Theory. What is worth emphasising is that, with the adoption of alignment hypotheses of the type discussed in 1.2.6 and other general principles of the grammar, the theory is driven to the postulation of abstract syntactic D-structures which, particularly via incorporation processes, are developed into concrete surface representations in the course of the derivation. A major guiding force in the development of initial syntactic structures in especially chapter 5 will be the fact that apparently simplex constructions can be shown to feature syntactic regularities characteristic of syntactically more complex constructions, particularly those involving *small clauses*.

1.2.8 Small clauses and subject-predicate relationships

Subject-predicate relationships may come in many guises. Semantically, their hallmark is the fact that they involve the ascription of a property to a subject. This is most transparently the case in copular constructions of the type in (41a), and also in verbless predications embedded under *consider* type verbs (41b). In resultative constructions, too, the clause-final secondary predicate ascribes a certain property to its subject. Thus, an adjectival resultative construction such as (41c) can be paraphrased as 'there was a hammering event which resulted in the state of affairs of the metal being flat'. The same goes for prepositional resultatives, including prepositional dative constructions. Thus, (41d) is paraphrasable as 'there was a putting event such that the books ended up on the shelf', and the meaning of (41e) can be appropriately (albeit rather clumsily) rendered by the clause 'there was a giving event which resulted in the books being "to" (i.e. in the possession of) Mary'. Subject-predicate relationships hence all share the semantic aspect of property ascription.

(41) a. John is a fool/foolish.
    b. They consider John a fool/foolish.
    c. They hammered the metal flat.
    d. They put the books on the shelf.
    e. They gave the books to Mary.

Structurally, too, subject-predicate relationships are one. They are all formally represented by a small clause (SC) constituent:

(42)   SCs are the sole incarnation of subject-predicate relationships.

This is the strongest possible (hence most attractive) view to take in varieties of the principles-and-parameters framework incorporating the structural construct of a SC (Stowell 1981; Kayne 1984; T. Hoekstra 1984 and much recent work). I shall take (42) as given. For extensive discussion of a radical implementation of the SC analysis along these lines, I refer to T. Hoekstra (1991).

Adopting (42) naturally commits me to the view that the subject of the clause is base-generated within a SC headed by the finite verb — the "SC-internal subject hypothesis". The recent literature (particularly Sportiche's 1988 influential study of floating quantifiers in French) has come up with a good deal of evidence in favour of the view that the base position of the subject should be taken to be lower than SpecIP.

Where exactly is the subject generated, though, and what is the structure of a SC? Stowell's (1981, 1983) "subjects across categories" proposal assumed that the SC is a projection of the lexical head of the SC (which may be of any category), with the subject being generated within the maximal projection of this lexical head. The fact, however, that predicates of SCs can undergo syntactic movement processes of their own is difficult to reconcile with a structure of the type in (43a), in which the node exclusively dominating the SC predicate is a first-bar projection. Given a restrictive view according to which movement processes can affect only heads and maximal projections (cf. Chomsky 1986), the structure in (43a) would wrongly exclude movement of SC predicates.[22]

(43) a. $[_{XP}$ subject $[_{X'}$ predicate$]]$ (where $X \in \{A, N, P, V\}$)
      b. $[_{Xmax/XP}$ subject $[_{XP}$ predicate$]]$
      c. $[_{FP}$ subject $[_{F'}$ F $[_{XP}$ predicate$]]]$

---

[22] Proponents of the structure in (43a) may argue that what actually moves in cases of SC predicate fronting is the entire SC, containing a trace of the SC subject (which is moved out prior to movement); cf. Huang (1993) for arguments for such an approach. Combinations of (43a)/(43b) and (43c) are possible; that is, XP in (43c) may contain the subject of X (as in the a- and b-cases) at D-structure.

In response to this problem posed by (43a), several scholars have argued for a modification of Stowell's original proposal according to which the subject of the SC continues to be base-generated within the maximal projection of the SC-head, but the X-bar structure of the projection of the lexical head of the SC is manipulated in such a way as to render it possible to identify the SC predicate as a maximal projection in its own right. These analyses, which essentially come in two slightly different guises, are schematically represented in (43b). Manzini (1983), among others, suggests that the SC subject is *base-adjoined* to the maximal projection of the SC predicate (cf. the "iterated XP" variant of (43b)), while Koopman & Sportiche (1988, 1991) argue that the X-bar schema should be extended to contain a new node type dominating the SC predicate and its subject, labelled X^{max}.

An alternative way of reconciling the mobility of SC predicates with restrictive views on movement of the type expressed in Chomsky (1986) is to assume that there is more to the structure of SCs than meets the eye. In particular, in line with the recent inflation of the functional structure of clauses, one may well take SCs to contain a projection of some functional head "F", as in (43c). Proposals to this effect can be found in Hornstein & Lightfoot (1987), Den Dikken (1987), Hoekstra & Mulder (1990), Cardinaletti & Guasti (1991), Chomsky (1993:8) and Den Dikken & Næss (1993). The exact nature of the functional head (or even heads) involved need not concern us here; a likely candidate is Agr(O). On the plausible assumption that this head is *categorially non-distinct* from the lexical head of the SC, Stowell's (1981) claim that verbs select SCs of specific category types does not discriminate between (43c) and the XP-analyses in (43a,b).[23]

Let me just briefly link up the discussion of the categorial status and internal structure of small clauses to an issue arising in the context of the object of study of this book — the verb-particle construction. As already noted in section 1.2.4 above (p. 12), one of the striking properties of the English verb-particle construction is the fact that the particle is generally freely placeable either to the left or to the right of the object NP. The word-order alternation in English verb-particle constructions being analysed in this study as abstract, LF-incorporation of the particle into the verb, this incorporation process must apparently be *optional*. In the light of recent theoretical developments according to which an

---

[23] In (43c) the trace of the extracted SC predicate cannot be formally licensed by the functional head "F" by itself, which does not qualify as a lexical governor. But if "F" is reanalysed with or incorporated into the lexical head governing the small clause, the Government Transparency Corollary (33) will ensure that the complex lexical head created by incorporation then comes to govern the predicate's trace. Note that, even though "F" qua functional head is an A'-head in the sense of Li (1990), incorporation of "F" into V does not instantiate "improper (A-to-A'-to-A) movement"; A'-to-A movement (unattested in the domain of XP-movement for independent reasons) arguably does not violate Principle C on the assumption that the initial trace in this case is not a variable (given that variables by definition are A'-bound); also cf. chapter 2, fn. 51.

application of Move α is either obligatory or impossible (cf. Chomsky 1993), apparent optionality raises serious questions. I shall briefly outline a way of accommodating the surface optionality of verb-particle reanalysis in English without assuming optional application of particle incorporation, by making crucial use of the structure of small clauses.

The essential difference between (43a,b) on the one hand, and (43c) on the other, lies in the presence outside the projection of the SC predicate of a functional projection. The head of this functional projection, "F" in (43c), counts as an A'-head in the sense of Li (1990) (cf. section 1.2.5). The structure in (43c) will hence render it impossible for the predicate head X to incorporate into the verb governing the SC given Principle C of the (extended) Binding Theory ("improper movement"). Whenever the SC complement of a particle verb hence features FP, particle incorporation is barred. If, on the other hand, the verb selects a "bare" particle phrase as its complement, incorporation will be possible — obligatory, in fact, if it is assumed that the head of a lexical projection in the complement of a lexical head cannot survive on its own and must incorporate into the higher lexical head (cf. T. Hoekstra, class lectures HIL). The surface optionality of particle incorporation then reduces to the lexical selectional freedom of particle verbs to select either FP or particle phrase complements; incorporation is barred in the former case and forced in the latter. By exploiting the theoretical options regarding the structure of SC we can thus accommodate the word-order alternation in English verb-particle constructions.

This theoretical consideration aside, however, it is generally immaterial to my specific concerns in this study what the categorial status and internal structure of SCs may turn out to be.[24] For purely expository purposes, I shall, in the structural representations to be provided in what follows, consistently assign SCs as a whole the conveniently neutral label "SC" (where it should be borne in mind that no claims about the independent existence or necessity of such a label are intended). Small clauses, then, will be represented here as in (44):

(44)   [$_{SC}$ subject [$_{XP}$ predicate]]

1.2.9 Small clauses and abstract syntactic structure

A systematic implementation of the small clause analysis is conceptually well-motivated because it leads to a strictly binary branching tree geometry, which is more restrictive — hence yields us more insight into (the speed of) the process of language acquisition — than non-binary branching analyses. The

---

[24] In Den Dikken & Næss (1993) it is argued that the functional head of SC in (43c) can function as the landing-site of the head of the SC predicate, which would support a SC structure of the type in (43c). For additional support for (43c) from a minimalist perspective, see Den Dikken (1994).

burden of proof in matters of syntactic structure hence *a priori* resides with those who advocate more-than-binary branching structures. Striving to abolish SCs would seem fairly counterproductive. For not only are SCs directly allowed by X-bar theory, but the widely held view (expressed in Fukui & Speas 1986; Kuroda 1988; Sportiche 1988; Koopman & Sportiche 1988, 1991, among others) that the subject of S originates VP-internally has effectively introduced SCs into every single syntactic structure.[25]

Small clauses, then, are available at no cost whatsoever. The same goes for abstract syntactic structure, and the *decomposition* of apparently atomic lexical items into two or more syntactic heads. An example of such decomposition is an analysis of causative psych verbs like *annoy* according to which this verb is underlyingly treated as a bimorphemic verb consisting of a zero causative morpheme CAUS and a non-causative root, which (following Pesetsky 1993) we may represent as √annoy. These morphemes can be assigned independent syntactic head status, the surface verb *annoy* arising as a result of a predicate raising operation amalgamating the two constituent parts of the decomposed verb. This is depicted (in a simplified way) in (45) (cf. Lakoff 1970, Mulder 1992b:ch. 5 and Pesetsky 1993 for different implementations of this idea):

(45) a.   [the newspaper article CAUS [John √annoy]]
      b.   [the newspaper article [CAUS+√annoy$_i$] [John t_i]]

In this study, abstract syntactic structures play an important role. Chapter 3 argues that the possessive verb *have* does not exist as a lexical unit but instead is the spell-out of the complex verb created by the incorporation of a dative preposition into the copula *be*. This structure of possessive constructions is an integral subpart of the structure of *triadic verb* constructions, which features *two* verbs, the lower verb being an abstract token of the copula. In chapter 5 this structure is transposed to the analysis of transitive causative constructions, in which both the matrix verb and the embedded verb can phonetically realised.

In each case of abstract syntactic structure, the concrete surface result is obtained via the amalgamation of the various (abstract or, in part, concrete) heads through the application of *head incorporation*. The postulation of abstract structures, then, is constrained by the theory of head movement. Only if an abstract underlying structure can be turned into the appropriate surface output via legitimate applications of Move α can this abstract, decomposed structure be adopted. The present state of the theory of movement in the principles-and-parameters framework is such that relapses into the excesses that the Generative Semantics framework has led to can likely be avoided.

---

[25] Note that for the point at hand, it is irrelevant whether all "small clauses" are treated as VPs (as in Larson's 1988 work; cf. section 3.2, below) or whether SCs range over all lexical categories.

1.3 Particles

This is a study of particles and particle constructions. The obvious question to start out with, then, would be: What is a particle? Let me, in this section, briefly review the variation among the class of particles and intransitive prepositions which has been noted in the literature (cf. esp. Van Riemsdijk 1978), and delimit the domain of investigation of this study on the basis of this inventory.

Emonds (1972, 1976) has classified English particles of the type used in our initial example in (1), above, as *intransitive prepositions*. This study will adduce direct support for the view that particles are prepositional in nature. They are also quite obviously intransitive in the sense that they take no more than a single argument. In at least one respect, however, particles are different from intransitive prepositions of the type illustrated in the Dutch example in (46) (cf. Van Riemsdijk 1978:54):[26]

(46) dat Jan *boven* wil wonen.
  that Jan upstairs wants live
  'that he wants to live upstairs.'

The difference between "genuine" particles and intransitive prepositions such as *boven* 'upstairs' in (46) lies in the fact that, while the former are freely incorporable into the verb cluster in Dutch, the latter often are not. Van Riemsdijk (1978:55) illustrates this point with the aid of the example in (47). In its non-incorporated variant, this example is ambiguous between a particle reading ('be in the lead') and an intransitive preposition reading ('stand in front of e.g. the house'). The incorporation construction in (47b), by contrast, can only have the particle reading.

---

[26] Several questions come up in connection with "intransitive prepositions" like *boven* 'upstairs', *buiten* 'outside' and *binnen* 'inside'. One concerns their morphological complexity — a P like *buiten* should presumably be analysed as consisting of the prefix *be-* (which chapter 5 analyses as an affixal *particle*), the preposition *uit* 'out (of)' and the suffix *-en* (which is presumably an inflectional morpheme); looked upon this way, these Ps have the same structure as perhaps more perspicuously complex *be+N+en* Ps like *bezijden* 'beside, wide of', *bezuiden* '(to the) south of' and *benoorden* '(to the) north of'. Whether and, if so, how these morphological observations translate into a more complex syntactic analysis of *boven* etc. is a question that I cannot answer here.

Another issue arising in the context of "intransitive Ps" like *boven* is whether these really are intransitive, or whether, instead, they should be analysed as transitive Ps taking a null (*pro*) complement (cf. Koopman 1993:13). The latter approach seems plausible in the light of the fact that in an example like *De wagen staat voor* 'the car stands in front', there is always an understood location in front of which the car is situated (and the same, *mutatis mutandis*, holds for (46) and similar examples). A transitive approach to "intransitive Ps" like *boven* in (46) gains further support if these turn out to be unergative (cf. below), given that, as Hale & Keyser (1993) and Kayne (1993a) (among others) have argued, unergatives are really transitives with a zero object.

(47) a.   dat hij *voor* schijnt te staan.
            that he(it) in front seems to stand
            'that it (the team) seems to be in the lead.'
            'that it (e.g. the dustbin) seems to stand in front.'
      b.   dat hij schijnt *voor* te staan.
            that he seems in front to stand
            'that it (the team) seems to be in the lead.'
            *'that it (e.g. the dustbin) seems to stand in front.'

Whether the difference in incorporability really calls for a robust structural distinction between particles and intransitive prepositions is far from clear, however. As Bennis (1991:fn. 2) points out, the possibility of incorporation seems to depend on aspectual rather than lexical factors. This is shown most clearly by the minimal contrast between (48a,b):

(48) a.   dat Jan (*boven*) wil (**boven*) wonen.   (cf. (46))
            that Jan (upstairs) wants (upstairs) live
      b.   dat Jan (*boven*) wil (*boven*) komen.
            that Jan (upstairs) wants (upstairs) come

While in (48a) the verb denotes a state, in (48b) it denotes an activity resulting in the state of Jan being upstairs. Apparently, this aspectual difference between (48a,b) conditions the incorporability of the intransitive preposition.

It may nonetheless be that, even though lexical factors do not exhaustively govern the incorporability differential between intransitive prepositions and particles "proper", these two preposition types are lexically distinct. In chapter 2 of this study, I shall argue in detail that particles "proper" are to be analysed as *ergative* prepositions. Intransitive prepositions, by contrast, might be looked upon as *unergative* non-Case-assigning representatives of the category P — an obvious theoretical possibility in view of the typology of head types (transitive, ergative and unergative-intransitive; cf. also fn. 26). Since I have no arguments that would allow me to settle this issue, however, I shall leave this a moot point.

Another question in the context of the demarcation of the object of study concerns the relationship between particles and *postpositions* in a language like Dutch (cf. Van Riemsdijk 1978:sect. 3.7 for detailed discussion). Postpositional phrases are frequent as the predicates of resultative SCs specifying the end point of motion. Whenever there is an alternation between a prepositional phrase and a postpositional phrase with one and the same P, the postpositional phrase typically has resultative semantics. This is evident from the contrast in (49), where (49b) is resultative while (49a) is not, witness the fact that (49a) selects *hebben* 'have' as its perfective auxiliary whereas (49b) takes *zijn* 'be' (cf. T. Hoekstra 1984, 1988 on auxiliary selection in Dutch).

(49) a. dat Jan [(*op*) de berg] heeft/*is (*op*) gereden.
that Jan (on) the mountain has/is (on) driven
'that Jan drove on the mountain top.'

b. dat Jan [de berg (*op*)] is/*heeft (*op*) gereden.[27]
that Jan the mountain (up) is/has (up) driven
'that Jan drove up the mountain.'

Postpositions are like particles in that they easily incorporate into the verb cluster (cf. (49b)).

One might speculate that postpositional phrases are derived from prepositional phrases by movement (either internal to the SC, or all the way up to the governing verb) of the P-head to the right, across its complement. Though perhaps initially plausible, such a view is rendered dubious by the fact, noted by Van Riemsdijk (1978:94), that postpositional phrases can undergo PP-over-V (i.e. PP-extraposition) as a unit, as in the b-examples in (50) (adapted from Van Riemsdijk 1978) and (51):[28]

(50) a. dat hij **de berg af** (*mee*) wilde (*mee*) rijden.
that he the mountain down (along) wanted (along) drive
'that he wanted to drive along down the mountain.'

b. dat hij (*mee*) wilde (*mee*) rijden **de berg af**.
that he (along) wanted (along) drive the mountain down

(51) a. dat hij **de heuvel op** (*door*) wilde (*door*) lopen.
that he the hill up (on) wanted (on) walk
'that he wanted to walk on up the hill.'

b. dat hij (*door*) wilde (*door*) lopen **de heuvel op**.
that he (on) wanted (on) walk the hill up

Full SCs do not undergo movement (cf. Den Dikken 1987). Hence the maximal constituent that can have undergone PP-over-V in these examples is the PP-predicate of SC. Since, however, the postposition is still physically part of the extraposed phrase in the b-examples in (50) and (51), hence has not moved out of the predicate of the resultative SC, these examples are hard to reconcile with an account of postpositional phrases in terms of P-movement (which would of necessity remove P from the moved PP). Movement of P's NP-complement seems equally incompatible with the facts in (50) and (51), for similar reasons.

---

[27] (49b) with *hebben* 'have' seems grammatical (if no incorporation of *op* obtains) on a reading in which *de berg op* is construed as an adjunct: on the way up, Jan was the driver (while on the way down, somebody else was). This is irrelevant in the context at hand.

[28] In section 3.11.2 below I shall address the nature and distribution of Dutch PP-over-V (cf. Koster 1973; Hoekstra 1984) in some detail.

Presumably, then, the base rules of Dutch construct postpositional phrases; there is no transformational relationship of sorts between prepositional PPs and postpositional ones.[29]

One other thing to note about the examples in (50) and (51) is the role played by the particles. Clearly, *mee* and *door* in these examples do not have any effect on the argument structure of the sentences in (50) and (51). Rather, they seem to play an essentially adverbial or aspectual role (comitative, continuative). A question that arises with regard to these particles is whether they should be assigned the same analysis as argument structure changing particles. Should all and only particles affecting the argument structure of the base verb with which they are combined be analysed in terms of SC complementation?

There does not seem to be a simple answer to this question. While in some contexts, aspectual particles do not seem likely candidates for SC-predicatehood, it would appear to be ill-advised to follow Bennis (1992b) in denying such particles predicative status throughout, since other contexts suggest that they do project SCs in the verb's complement. As Den Besten (1992) observes, there is a contrast in this respect between motional and non-motional verbs. Adding *door* to the non-motional verb *werken* 'work' does not bring about an *ergative shift* (that is, the verb continues to be an unergative verb, as is evident from the fact that its past participle cannot be used attributively in nominals; T. Hoekstra 1984), whereas addition of this particle to the motional verb *lopen* can (but need not) result in an unaccusative construction:[30]

(52) a.   Jan heeft gewerkt.
            Jan has worked
      b.   Jan heeft *door* gewerkt.
            Jan has on worked
      c.   *de (*door*) gewerkte man
            the (on) worked man

---

[29] Many questions are raised by postpositional phrases and their relationship with prepositional PPs (cf. Koopman 1993 and — from the "antisymmetric", uniformly head-initial perspective of Kayne 1993b — Rooryck 1994 and Zwart 1993:359ff.). I ignore them in this study, however, since they are tangential to my concerns.

[30] The two variants of (53b) are not semantically equivalent. While the ergative alternant with auxiliary *zijn* 'be' means that Jan walked on/continued walking, the unergative *hebben* 'have' perfect is roughly paraphrasable as 'Jan kept up a pace', and can be made more felicitous by the addition of an adverb specifying the extent to which this is the case (cf. *Jan heeft/*is flink door gelopen* 'Jan kept up a stiff pace'). This second, unergative construal of *doorlopen* is unavailable for the attributive participle in (53c); that is, **de flink door gelopen man* is ungrammatical, as expected. (Eric Reuland, p.c., tells me that for him, *Jan is flink doorgelopen* and *de flink doorgelopen man* are acceptable; I have no suggestions to offer with respect to this variation of judgements.)

(53) a.　Jan heeft gelopen.
　　　　　Jan has walked
　　　b.　Jan heeft/is *door* gelopen.
　　　　　Jan has/is on walked
　　　c.　de *(*door*) gelopen man
　　　　　the (on) walked man

The ergative shift in the pertinent variant of (53b) and in (53c) can be accounted for with the aid of the assumption that the particle *door* projects a SC in the verb's complement (cf. Hoekstra & Mulder 1990 for other instances of ergative shift analysed in SC terms).

Apparently, in non-motional constructions like (52) *door* does not head a complement SC. It seems more like an adverbial modifier. Why there should be a difference between motional and non-motional verbs in this respect is not immediately obvious. Eschewing a discussion of this question,[31] let me finish this section by briefly skipping ahead to two later sections of this study, in which further considerations are presented which suggest that aspectual particles can head complement SCs. One such consideration is the fact that the presence of a particle, regardless of whether it is an argument structure changing or aspectual one, facilitates extraposition of predicative PPs in Dutch (cf. (50b) and (51b), which are ungrammatical if the particle is dropped). In section 3.11.2 it will be argued that only particles in complex particle constructions of the type discussed in chapter 2 (i.e. particle constructions in which the particle is the head of a SC in the verb's complement) can have such an effect on the placement of predicative PPs. Another indication that aspectual particles can be SC heads is the blocking effect that they — just like argument structure changing particles — have on head movement. This blocking effect on head movement will be the topic of section 2.3.6.

Having laid bare certain differences and similarities between particles "proper" on the one hand, and intransitive prepositions, postpositions and aspectual particles on the other, I shall largely set aside this latter, hetero-geneous set of P-type elements in the remainder of this study. Whenever I use the term PARTICLE, it is meant to designate the class of prepositional elements characterised by the statement in (54):

(54)　　　In this study, the term PARTICLE refers to the class of non-Case-assigning, argument-taking prepositional elements.

---

[31]　See also Den Dikken (1993) for discussion of questions relating to the effect of (affixal) particles on the argument structure and transitivity/(un)ergativity of the verbs with which they are combined.

Particles in the sense intended by (54) will be argued to be *ergative* SC heads. In some wider sense of the term, the class of particles might well include (some of the members of) the heterogeneous set of P-type elements which I briefly introduced in the above. Some of these might then instantiate unergative representatives of the (wider) class of particles. As said, however, no specific claims are made with regard to prepositional elements other than particles "proper", as delimited by (54). This is merely a practical delimitation of the object of this study, no necessary theoretical implications being intended.

1.4 Preview

We are now fully equipped to face the intricacies of complex particle constructions, which I shall unravel in chapter 2. With the results of the study of complex particle constructions in mind, I then proceed, in chapter 3, to the analysis of triadic constructions and Dative Shift, arguing for a transformational approach to the latter. A number of S-structure phenomena associated with double object constructions are addressed in chapter 4, which as one of its major results defends the view that not all double object constructions are actually the output of the Dative Shift transformation. Chapter 5 then investigates the status and syntactic position of applicative and causative morphemes, and examines the relationship between dative and transitive causative constructions, arguing for a structural assimilation of the two. Chapter 6 sums up the major findings of this study.

2

The Structure of Particle
Constructions

2.1 Introduction

Particle constructions are an important probe into the structure of various secondary predicative constructions, as I shall try to show in what follows. Chapter 3 argues that the properties of particle constructions shed light on the analysis of triadic constructions. Before proceeding to this discussion, however, we should first of all establish the structure of particle constructions in general. To this end, I shall present in the pages to follow an in-depth investigation of the structure of COMPLEX PARTICLE CONSTRUCTIONS in English. The central claim to be defended is that, in any event in complex particle constructions, the particle is an *ergative* small clause (SC) head, selecting another SC as its complement. Towards the end of this chapter, the results of our case study of English complex particle constructions will be considered against the background of similar constructions in Dutch, and simplex particle constructions in both languages.

2.2 Complex particle constructions: Preliminaries

Complex particle constructions are constructions featuring both a verbal particle and an additional secondary predicate. In English several types of complex particle constructions can be distinguished. In (1), some representative examples are given (cf. a.o. Jackendoff 1977; Kayne 1985):[1] [2]

---

[1]   In each example, the particle is italicised and the additional secondary predicate is printed in boldface.

[2]   That the dative PP *to the stockholders* is indeed predicative will become evident in chapter 3, where this is shown to play a criterial role in the analysis of triadic constructions. Déchaine (1993:228ff.) and Bowers (1993:636) agree that dative PPs are predicative. Reinhart & Reuland (1993:688–90) deny Ps *syntactic* predicatehood, arguing that Ps are at the most only *semantic* predicates; they do not, however, necessarily oppose a SC approach to predicative PPs (cf. their fn. 31). See also chapter 3 (section 3.3 and fn. 8) for more discussion of PP's predicativity.

(1)   a.   They made John *out* (to be) **a liar**.
       b.   They turned *out* (to be) **intelligent**.
       c.   They painted the barn *up* **red**.
       d.   They put the books *down* **on the shelf**.
       e.   They sent a schedule *out* **to the stockholders**.

Complex particle constructions of the type in (1) are an interesting challenge to the theory. Given some assumptions that I shall motivate presently, the principles-and-parameters framework leaves us with very few ways of approaching constructions of this type.

2.2.1 The clause-final constituent as a SC predicate

An initial claim that I would like to make and support here is that the boldface constituents in (1) are predicates of SCs. To argue this effectively involves (i) showing that these phrases pass independently established tests for predicativity, and (ii) arguing that subject-predicate relationships of the type featured by (1) are to be structurally represented in terms of a SC.

The claim that in a complex particle construction like *They made John out a liar* the clause-final NP *a liar* entertains a relationship of predication with the NP sandwiched between the verb and the particle *out* is semantically well motivated — it is *John* to whom the property of being a liar is attributed. Similarly, in a prepositional complex particle construction such as (1d), it is the books which end up on the shelf as a result of the activity denoted by the verbal predicate. Apart from semantic plausibility, however, we may mention at least one straightforward syntactic predicativity test which confirms the hypothesis that the boldface constituents in (1) are predicative — Locative Inversion.

Hoekstra & Mulder (1990) provide evidence to the effect that the English stylistic phenomenon known as Locative Inversion, illustrated in (2b), is restricted in its application to *predicative* constituents. Specifically, only predicates of SCs in complement positions may trigger Locative Inversion by being moved to clause-initial position; PPs which, though they may well be predicative, are not predicative *complements*, such as the clause-initial PPs in (3), may not invert with the finite verb, as the ill-formedness of the examples shows:

(2)   a.   The baby carriage rolled *down the hill*.
       b.   *Down the hill* rolled the baby carriage.

(3)   a.   *At great speed* rolled the baby carriage.
       b.   *On a leash* ran the dog.

Hoekstra & Mulder (1990) accommodate this restriction on Locative Inversion by noting first of all that the post-verbal NP in Locative Inversion constructions bears nominative Case (as is evident from the fact that it is this NP which triggers number inflection on the finite verb), even though the post-verbal subject apparently does not occupy the canonical nominative Case position, SpecIP. Since nominative Case cannot be directly assigned to the post-verbal NP, then, it must somehow be transmitted to it in Locative Inversion constructions. Hoekstra & Mulder (1990) present an analysis of Locative Inversion according to which A-movement of the fronted constituent into SpecIP takes place, as schematised in (4):

(4) $[_{IP}$ PP$_i$ Infl $[_{VP}$ V $[_{SC}$ NP$_i$ $[_{PP}$ $t_i]]]]$

Nominative Case is assigned to the fronted PP in SpecIP, in the familiar fashion.[3] This PP is coindexed with its trace in the predicate position of SC, and this trace, in its turn, is coindexed with the SC-subject by virtue of the Specifier-Head agreement relationship (a coindexation relation; cf. Chomsky 1986) between the two. Along this chain of identical indexations, the nominative Case feature assigned by Infl can be transmitted to the post-verbal subject NP, which remains *in situ* in the SC subject position. Now notice that it is crucial that the post-verbal subject entertains a Spec-Head agreement relationship with the fronted phrase, for otherwise the two would not be coindexed, and nominative Case transmission would fail to apply. The need for a coindexation relationship between the clause-initial phrase and the post-verbal subject NP, forced by the Case Filter, thus explains the fact that Locative Inversion is restricted to apply to *predicative* complements only.

With this in mind, we may now construe the grammaticality of applying Locative Inversion in the (prepositional) complex particle constructions in (5) as support for the hypothesis that the post-particle phrase in the sentences in (1) is predicative.

(5)   a.   *On the shelf* were put down some books.
        b.   *Under the table* sat down a big fat cat.
        c.   *Under the table* turned up a big fat cat.

---

[3]   In Bresnan (1990) and Den Dikken & Næss (1993) it is argued that PP, after touching down in SpecIP, undergoes topicalisation in Locative Inversion constructions of the type in (2b). I shall largely ignore this additional step in this study (but cf. chapter 4, fn. 36).

Locative Inversion as analysed in Hoekstra & Mulder (1990) violates Chomsky's (1993) principle of Greed, according to which movement of one constituent (here PP) to "help" another constituent (the SC-subject NP) is prohibited. I relegate problems concerning the compatibility of proposals made here and elsewhere with Chomsky's Greed to future research.

This in and of itself does not prove my second hypothesis, that the post-particle phrase in (1) is a *SC* predicate. In line with much recent research (cf. e.g. T. Hoekstra 1988a, 1991, and references cited there), however, I would like to assume that predication is the exclusive property of SC constructions, small clauses being the sole incarnation of subject-predicate relationships (cf. section 1.2.8, above). Given this assumption, which I shall adopt here without further argument, the conclusion that a particular constituent is predicative is equivalent to the conclusion that the constituent in question is the predicate of a SC.

2.2.2 The particle as a SC head

The theoretical status of particles has been and still is subject to considerable debate in the generative literature. A rough initial distinction can be made between analyses based on the premise that the particle forms a lexical unit with the verb that it combines with (some recent instantiations of which are Johnson 1991; Pesetsky 1993 and Neeleman 1994), and accounts which take the particle to be an independent syntactic head (cf. a.o. Kayne 1985; Aarts 1989; Guéron 1990; Koopman 1991, 1993).[4] I subscribe to the latter line of research. The analysis of complex particle constructions to be developed in what follows is an extended argument in favour of this view of particles. Not wishing to make this theoretical choice solely on the basis of the success of the analysis of complex particle constructions to be based on it, however, let me mention one initial consideration which, to my mind, pleads in favour of an analysis of particles as syntactic heads belonging to the category P(reposition).

Prepositional phrases differ from verbal constituents in being modifiable by adverbs such as *right* or *straight*.[5] The examples in (6) and (7) testify to this:

(6)   John threw the ball *right/straight* through the window.
(7)   *John *right/straight* threw the ball through the window.

---

[4]   For a brief survey of the literature, with particular reference to Dutch verb-particle construct-ions, I refer to Bennis (1992a). Aarts (1989) lists several verbless absolute constructions in which particles occur (e.g. *with the heater off*), which cast doubt on a complex verb analysis of verb-part-icle constructions and lend support to a SC approach. Hyams, Schaeffer & Johnson (1993) and Broihier *et al.* (1994) have recently brought data from the domain of the acquisition of verb-particle constructions to bear on the choice between the analyses of these constructions. Specifically, these papers have argued that the acquisition facts of English and Dutch/German verb-particle construct-ions support Johnson's (1991) complex verb analysis, and cannot be accommodated on a small clause analysis of particles. However, Bennis *et al.* (1994) show that their arguments either do not hold water or can in fact be construed as evidence in favour of the SC approach.

[5]   Other such modifiers include *way*, *all* and *the hell/the heck* (cf. Fraser 1974:26–27).

We hence seem justified in characterising *right* and *straight* as PP-modifiers. Now it is significant that particles pattern with PPs with respect to modification by these adverbs (cf. Emonds 1976; also cf. Van Riemsdijk 1978:52 for Dutch *pal* and *vlak* 'right'):[6]

(8)   John threw the ball *right/straight* back/up/down.

The grammaticality of (8) distinguishes between the two approaches to particles mentioned above. Irrespective of the categorial label assigned to particles, an analysis treating particles as parts of complex verbs (from which the verbal head can be *excorporated* by verb movement; cf. Johnson 1991, and Roberts 1991 on the general properties of excorporation) cannot capture the well-formedness of (8). After all, the particle not being the head of the V–Prt complex, and the non-head being unable to percolate its categorial features to the complex X^0-node that dominates it,[7] at no point will the categorial specification of the particle be able to play any active role outside of the dependent (non-head) portion of this complex X^0-node. Given that, as suggested by the data in (6) and (7), the distribution of the adverbial modifiers *right* and *straight* is determined by the categorial feature set of prepositional elements, and given that the constituent dominating the particle is *verbal* on a complex verb approach to verb-particle constructions, such an analysis would predict (8) to be ungrammatical, contrary to fact.

The above line of thought is built on the premise that the adverbial modifiers *right* and *straight* find themselves outside the complex verbal head consisting of the base verb and the particle. Suppose, however, that one were to assume that these modifiers are adjoined directly to the particle, inside the complex X^0-node, as in (9):[8]

(9) $[_{VP} [_V V [_P \text{ } right/straight [_P \text{ Prt}]]] \text{ NP}]$

---

[6]   I thank René Mulder for drawing my attention to the significance of this fact.

Two brief remarks with regard to the generalisation that *right* and *straight* are PP-modifiers are in order. First, Emonds (1987:623) notes that 'a stigmatized variant of American English' allows *right* to modify APs (as in *right pretty, right seldom, right soon, right worrisome*). For our purposes, this usage of *right* can be ignored. Secondly, *right* can be used to modify so-called "bare-NP adverbs" (cf. *right that way, right this minute*). Following Emonds (1987) (also cf. Bresnan & Grimshaw's 1978 original proposal to this effect), I take this to indicate that bare-NP adverbs are PPs with an empty preposition (against Larson 1985, of which Emonds 1987 is a detailed critique).

[7]   Percolation of Prt's categorial features is barred due to the fact that the head has categorial specifications of its own. Non-heads may only percolate features that the head is unspecified for (cf. Di Sciullo & Williams 1987; Williams 1994).

[8]   I thank Hans Bennis for pointing this theoretical option out to me.

An analysis of the type in (9) would enable one to steer clear of the categoricity problem: *right* and *straight* directly modify a prepositional element. However, once we allow for a base structure of the type in (9), we are at a loss explaining why the surface output corresponding to this structure, given in (10), is ungrammatical, since there is no obvious theoretical motive to force the complex verb in (9) apart in the course of the derivation.[9]

(10)   *John threw *right/straight* back/up/down the ball.

Another possible rebuttal of the modification argument against a complex verb analysis of verb-particle constructions might read as follows. Suppose that, in order to capture the fact that modification of the particle is possible just in case the "object NP" separates it from the verb (cf. (8) *vs.* (10)), one were to assume that the particle can percolate its categorial features to the complex X^0-node dominating it only if the verb is excorporated from this complex X^0-node. This assumption, coupled with the idea that the "object NP" (*the ball*) undergoes (Case-driven) movement to some higher specifier position (cf. Johnson 1991 for a concrete proposal), could then draw the desired distinction between (8) and (10).[10] The suggestion that percolation of the particle's categorial features is possible only if V-excorporation takes place could in fact be made to fall out from Di Sciullo & Williams' (1987) percolation apparatus (cf. fn. 7) if a V-trace (or a trace in general) is featureless.

A suggestion along these lines would allow for an account of one of the recalcitrant properties of English verb-particle constructions which it seems very difficult for the SC analysis to accommodate.[11] Consider the contrast between (8), repeated here as (11a), and (11b), and compare this with the pair in (12), both members of which are perfectly grammatical:

(11)   a.   John threw the ball *right/straight* back/up/down.
        b.   *John threw the ball *quickly* back/up/down.

(12)   a.   John threw the ball *right/straight* through the window.
        b.   John threw the ball *quickly* through the window.

---

[9]   The contrast between (8) and (10) is not an isolated quirk of English — Collins & Thráinsson (1993:164) show that Icelandic exhibits the same modification and particle placement properties:

(i)   a.   Jón hefur rétt hamarinn *beint* niður.
              Jon has handed the-hammer right down
        b.   *Jón hefur rétt *beint* niður hamarinn.

[10]   I leave technical details aside here, referring the reader to Johnson (1991).

[11]   Johnson (1991) introduces these facts and presents a rather less straightforward analysis based on his particular complex verb account of verb-particle constructions.

The deviance of (11b), in contrast to the well-formedness of all other examples in (11) and (12), might be accounted for in the following way. Suppose that *quickly* and other manner adverbs are designated to modify verbal projections only, and suppose (as hypothesised in the previous paragraph) that, after excorporation of the verb from the complex V + Prt head in particle constructions, the projection headed by the complex X^0-node comes to be prepositional in nature. Then the ungrammaticality of (11b) would follow from the conjunction of the requirement imposed by manner adverbs on their host projections that they be verbal, and the non-verbal nature of this projection in "outer particle constructions" (featuring verb excorporation from the complex X^0-node). The contrast between (11b) and (12b) would follow in turn from the assumption that the transitive PP in the latter example defines its own projection, while particles are subparts of complex X^0-categories.

While an approach incorporating what we might refer to as "dynamic category membership" may hence have something to recommend it, it should be noted that if we subscribed to this line of thought, we would effectively make the claim that the selectional properties of the head selecting the complex X^0-node harbouring the verb and the particle can vary between D-structure and S-structure. After all, at D-structure, the head in question would invariably select a verbal complement, the verb being present under X^0 at this point. By S-structure, however, the higher head will either still select a VP, or, if the verb is excorporated from the complex X^0-node, take a prepositional complement. If categorial selection means anything in the theory, a "dynamic" approach like the one resulting from the above constellation of hypotheses does not seem particularly appealing. In view of this, I conclude that a complex verb analysis of the verb-particle construction yields no obvious account of the modification data in (6)–(8).

By contrast, an account of verb-particle constructions according to which the particle is an independent syntactic head of the category P (as originally proposed in the work of Emonds 1976; also cf. Kayne 1985; Van Riemsdijk 1978 for Dutch) easily accommodates the well-formedness of (8) (as well as the deviance of (10), to which I shall return in section 2.4.6, below). The fact, then, that typical PP-modifiers like *right* and *straight* can combine with particles is evidence against a complex verb analysis of verb-particle constructions, and in favour of the alternative view, which holds that particles are syntactic atoms of the category P.[12]

---

[12] The contrast between (11b) and (12b), and also Jackendoff's (1977:80) observation that *We painted the house (*completely) up red* is bad with the modifier in place, remain mysterious though.

Guéron (1990) argues that particles '*acquire* the syntactic and semantic status of a verb in the course of the derivation, as a function of T-marking' (my italics). In view of the above, and also in the light of the analysis of complex particle constructions to be developed in what follows, however, particles must be prepositional (non-verbal) throughout.

Having reached this conclusion, I propose that particles are heads of SCs in the complement of the verb. That this is a sensible move can be gathered from a comparison of (6) and (8), above, against the background of T. Hoekstra's (1988a) conclusion that *resultative constructions* — of which (6) and (8) are both instantiations — involve SC complementation.

Well-known empirical arguments for the SC analysis of particle construct- ions, due to Kayne (1984), are the fact that subextraction from the "object NP" in constructions of the type in (13a) is ungrammatical, just as subextraction from SC subjects in general yields an ill-formed result (cf. (13b,c)),[13] and the correspondence between particle constructions and other SC constructions with regard to the impossibility of nominalisation, as shown in (14).

(13)   a.   *What did they look [[the information about *t*] *up*]?
       b.   *Who do they consider [[the brother of *t*] *a fool*]?
       c.   *What did they paint [[the door of *t*] *black*]?

(14)   a.   *our looking of [[the information] *up*]
       b.   *our consideration of [[John's brother] *a fool*]
       c.   *our painting of [[the door] *black*]

Svenonius (1992) further substantiates the view that the particle forms a (SC) constituent with the "object NP" by capitalising on the observation (cf. Stillings 1975; Hudson 1982) that in English gapping can leave behind no more than two constituents. Gapping with retention of three constituents yields an ill-formed result, as shown by the contrast between (15a,b) and (15c):[14]

---

[13]   The deviance of (13) (but cf. Carrier & Randall 1992) follows from Kayne's (1984) Connected- ness Condition; from the perspective of Chomsky (1986) (who extends L-marking into the realm of Specifier-Head agreement), it is quite mysterious.

[14]   See Bowers (1993:604) for a recent endorsement of the requirement that gapping leave behind no more than two constituents, which, it should be noted, has been called into question in the literature (cf. Sag 1976; Ross 1976; also cf. Sag *et al.* 1985:157) on the basis of the acceptability of such examples as:

(i)   a.   Peter talked to his boss on Tuesday, and Betsy to her supervisor on Wednesday.
      b.   John talked to his supervisor about his thesis, and Erich to the dean about department politics.

While (ib) might perhaps be reanalysable so that it complies with the restriction on gapping (*to the dean about department politics* possibly being a constituent), (ia) seems a genuine counterexample to the above requirement. Thanks to Marjan Grootveld for bringing these cases, and the relevant literature, to my attention.

(15) a. John eats with chopsticks, and [Mary]₁ [with a fork]₂.
   b. John eats spaghetti, and [Mary]₁ [chop suey]₂.
   c. *John eats spaghetti with chopsticks, and [Mary]₁ [chop suey]₂ [with a fork]₃.

Interestingly, now, the following gapping constructions featuring, in the gapped conjunct, an "object NP", a verbal particle and an additional adjunct are grammatical:

(16) a. Turn the oxygen off when I say to, and
       [the acetylene *on*]₁ [a moment later]₂.
   b. Turn the oxygen off with your knee, and
       [the acetylene *on*]₁ [with your elbow]₂.

In view of what (15) led us to conclude, the conjuncts in which gapping obtains in (16) should contain at most two constituents. Since joining the particle in one constituent with the temporal/instrumental adjunct makes no sense, the only remaining bracketing of the examples in (16) is as indicated. The particle, then, forms a constituent with the "object NP". The constituent in question is a small clause.

2.2.3 Conclusion

In this section, I have briefly considered the motivation for my adopting the two basic premises in (17) and have contrasted them with possible alternative views.

(17) a. Particles are heads of complement-SCs.
   b. The post-particle constituents in (1) are predicates of complement-SCs.

In the next section, I shall put these hypotheses to use in an analysis of English complex particle constructions.

2.3 The structure of English complex particle constructions

2.3.1 Introduction: The theoretical options

Returning to the challenge that complex particle constructions like (1) pose for the theory, let us bear in mind that, in line with the conclusions drawn in the previous subsection (cf. (17)), the structure of these constructions will have to contain *two* SCs in complement (A-)positions. The specific case of (1a) (without the infinitival copula) unites both SCs found in the examples in (18) in a single clause. One of the SCs in (18) (*John a liar*) moreover is not a surface constituent in (1a).

(18) a.   They called [$_{SC}$ John *a liar*].
      b.   They found [$_{SC}$ John *out*].

Following Kayne (1984) (and cf. section 1.2.9, above), I shall assume a strictly binary branching phrase structure. Given the combination of strict binarity, the premises in (17), and the plausible assumption that *John a liar* is a D-structure constituent, there are precisely two conceivable D-structures for a complex particle construction such as (1a).[15] These are given in (19)–(20):

---

[15] Two logically possible alternative analyses compatible with strict binarity and the essence of (17) should be rejected. One is an analysis according to which the SC [*John out*] is the subject of a SC with *a liar* as its predicate (in a way the mirror-image of (19), depicted in (i)).

(i)   [$_{IP}$ They [$_{VP}$ made [$_{SC1}$ [$_{SC2}$ John out] [$_{NP}$ a liar]]]]

This analysis makes little semantic sense. Moreover, even though an analysis along these lines would directly generate the appropriate surface word order, it would wrongly lead one to expect there to be no differences between (18a) and (1a) with regard to the extractability of *a liar*; on these, cf. further below in the main text.

Another logical possibility would base-generate *John* in the subject position of the particle-headed SC and would have this NP control a PRO in the subject position of the nominal SC. Kayne (1985) essentially ends up with a structure of this sort, after applying extraposition to *a liar* in his structure in (19) (cf. below for details) — in order to comply with the demands of the Extended Projection Principle after extraposition, Kayne adds a PRO subject to the extraposed predicate nominal at S-structure. On the basis of evidence provided by Lasnik (1993a:168) and Takahashi (1994), any approach to complex particle constructions involving PRO (hence control) can be eliminated. The contrast between (iia) and (iib) shows that VP ellipsis is possible in control constructions but not in ECM constructions. Applying this as a diagnostic for control, we can conclude from the deviance of (iii) that complex particle constructions featuring the particle verb *make out* are not control constructions.

(ii)   a.   John tried to be courageous, and Mary tried to [$_{VP}$ *e*] also.
       b.   ?*I believe John to be courageous, and I believe Mary to [$_{VP}$ *e*] also.
(iii)   ?*I made out John to be a liar, and I made out Mary to [$_{VP}$ *e*] also.

Kayne (1985) makes important use of the postulated S-structure control relationship in his account of the ill-formedness of (iva,b) (cf. also Safir's 1992 *They prevented there from being a riot* vs. **They held there back from being a riot*) — since *there* and idiom chunks are unsuitable controllers, they cannot show up in the "object position" of complex particle constructions. In the light of (iii), however, an approach to (iv) along these lines must be rejected. The analysis of complex particle constructions to be presented below offers no ready alternative account; I leave this problem open.

(iv)   a.   *They made (out) there (out) to be no solution to this problem.
       b.   *They made (out) advantage (out) to have been taken of John.

(19)   [$_{IP}$ They [$_{VP}$ made [$_{SC1}$ [$_{SC2}$ John a liar] [$_{PP}$ out]]]]

(20)   [$_{IP}$ They [$_{VP}$ made [$_{SC1}$ [$_{Spec\theta'}$ *ec*] [$_{PP}$ out [$_{SC2}$ John a liar]]]]]]

In what follows, I shall first adduce evidence against the analysis in (19), adopted in Kayne (1985), in which the particle *out* is an unergative SC predicate, taking the nominal SC [*John a liar*] as its subject. Then I shall proceed to motivating the one remaining option, (20). In this structure, the particle is taken to be an *ergative* (or unaccusative) SC head (cf. Guéron 1986, 1990) which selects the nominal SC as its complement.

In order to be able to proceed to an evaluation of the pros and cons of the alternatives in (19) and (20), we should first of all have a closer look at the properties of the English *make out a liar* construction. As Kayne (1985) points out, the construction in (1a) without the infinitival copula *to be* exhibits a very rigid word-order pattern within VP: the particle may only be positioned in between *John* and the predicative NP *a liar*:[16]

(21)   a.   They made John *out* a liar.
        b.   *?They made *out* John a liar.
        c.   *They made John a liar *out*.

Moreover, the ungrammaticality of (22) shows that the *make out a liar* construction does not allow the predicative NP to be *wh*-extracted (regardless of where the particle is positioned). In this respect this construction contrasts with a semantically parallel example that lacks a particle, such as the impeccable *What kind of a liar did they call John?*.

(22)   *What kind of a liar did they make (*out*) John (*out*)?

It is interesting to note that once we add the infinitival copula *to be* to (21a), verb-adjacent particle placement and *wh*-extraction of the predicative NP yield grammatical results, as shown in (23b) and (24):

(23)   a.   They made John *out* to be a liar.
        b.   (?)They made *out* John to be a liar.
        c.   *They made John to be a liar *out*.

(24)   What kind of a liar did they make (*out*) John (*out*) to be?

These two differences between (21)/(22) and (23)/(24) will turn out to be crucial in determining which of the structures in (19) and (20) is correct.

---

[16] The fact that (21b) is apparently somewhat less bad than the totally unacceptable (21c) is explained neither by Kayne (1985) nor by the analysis to be developed in what follows. Like Kayne, I have chosen not to differentiate between (21b) and (21c) in the main text.

2.3.2 On Kayne's (1985) analysis of complex particle constructions

Kayne (1985) reconciles the underlying constituency of the SC *John a liar* with its surface discontinuity by generating this SC in the subject position of the particle-headed SC (cf. (19)). In the mapping of D-structure onto S-structure, the predicate of the subject-SC undergoes movement into an adjunction position to the particle-headed SC, as is illustrated in (25):[17]

(25) $[_{IP}$ They $[_{VP}$ made $[_{SC1}$ $[_{SC1}$ $[_{SC2}$ John $t_i]$ $[_{PP}$ out]] a liar$_i]]]$

Case Theory is held responsible for the obligatory extraposition of the inner-SC predicate. The subject NP of SC2 must receive Case, but is separated from the Case assigner, V, by two SC boundaries. One of these boundaries must hence be removed. Kayne (1985) assumes a definition of a barrier in terms of L-containment (cf. Chomsky 1973:section 6), which can be roughly stated as in (26) (taken from Kayne 1985:113):

(26)   In $[_\alpha \ldots Y \ldots]$, α can count as a barrier to government for Y only
           if … … contains lexical material.

Given this approach to barrierhood in terms of L-containment, extraposition of the predicate of SC2 will in effect render the inner SC transparent, so that the Case which is assigned by the matrix verb can now reach the inner-SC subject. This explains the obligatoriness of the movement operation displayed in (25), and at the same time captures the ungrammaticality of (21c) as a violation of the Case Filter.

Kayne's account of the impossibility of verb-adjacent particle placement (cf. (21b)) is heavily dependent on his analysis of the word-order alternation in the verb-particle construction. Kayne assumes, in line with (17a), above, that particles are SC heads. Specifically, he assumes that particles are unergative, and that, hence, (27a) represents the underlying structure of the English verb-particle construction. The alternative word order in (27b) is derived from this D-structure, on Kayne's assumptions, via *extraposition* of the NP-subject, as indicated:

(27)   a.   John looked the information *up*.
       b.   John looked t_i *up* the information$_i$.

---

[17] Aarts (1989:288–89) presents an analysis of complex particle constructions that is identical with Kayne's (1985), without, however, referring to the latter in this context. Rightward movement of *a liar* is obviously no longer a theoretical possibility in the light of Kayne (1993b), as Kayne notes.

Given this approach to the word-order alternation in the English verb-particle construction, the word order in (21b) could only be derived from the underlying structure in (19) through rightward movement of the entire inner SC. This, however, would leave unaffected the violation of the Case Filter, since the barrierhood of SC2 is not voided, its predicate not being removed from the SC.[18] Besides, SCs in general appear to resist being the input to syntactic movement transformations (cf. Den Dikken 1987 for relevant discussion):[19]

(28) a. *[John a fool]$_i$ I do not consider t_i.
     b. *[Who foolish]$_i$ do you consider t_i?

The obligatory adjunction of the predicate of SC2 to SC1, in conjunction with a specific definition of a variable, furthermore provides Kayne with an explanation for the fact that the presence of the particle in the *make out a liar* construction renders *wh*-extraction of the predicate of SC2 impossible, as is shown by (22). If we assume that the predicate of SC2 is *wh*-moved to SpecCP from the adjunction position to SC1, problems arise since the trace in the (A'-) adjunction position to SC1 does not qualify as a variable, given that variables by definition stand in A-positions. The initial trace in the D-structure position of the inner-SC predicate in (29) cannot function as the necessary variable either, since a variable must be locally operator-bound. The local binder of the deepest trace in (29) is the intermediate trace in the adjunction position to SC1, t_i'. This trace, however, is not an operator on Kayne's assumptions. SpecCP does contain an operator; this, however, does not locally bind the most deeply embedded trace.

(29)   [$_{CP}$ *wh*$_i$ did [$_{IP}$ they [$_{VP}$ make [$_{SC1}$ [$_{SC1}$ [$_{SC2}$ John t_i] [$_{PP}$ out]] t_i']]]]

Notice that Kayne's account of the ill-formedness of (22) is crucially dependent on the assumption that intermediate adjunction of the inner-SC predicate to SC1 is mandatory in this *wh*-extraction construction. It is quite unclear what should force adjunction in (22), however, given that direct *wh*-extraction

---

[18] Additional movement of the SC predicate subsequent to extraposition of SC2 would appear to be a theoretical option which, if applied in the case at hand, would lead us to predict that (21b) should be acceptable after all. Apparently, this option should be barred in the *make out a liar* construction in (21). That this is an essentially *ad hoc* move is evident from the fact that Kayne crucially invokes this additional movement operation in his account of the well-formedness of the *make out to be a liar* construction in (23b); cf. the discussion further below in the main text.

[19] Apparent cases of SC movement instantiated by "Honorary NPs", as in *Workers angry about the pay was just the sort of situation that the ad campaign was designed to avoid* (cf. Stowell 1981; Safir 1983), should be analysed as ACC-*ing* constructions with a covert copula, not as "bare" SCs (cf. Den Dikken 1987).

without the intermediate adjunction step would also void the barrierhood of the inner SC.[20] On a fell-swoop analysis of *wh*-extraction, nothing would appear to rule (22) out on Kayne's assumptions.

Even if intermediate adjunction could somehow be forced (for reasons other than the voiding of the inner SC's barrierhood), we should be wary of the fact that Kayne's account of (22) is based on a hypothesis about operator-variable relationships which, in the light of recent developments in the principles-and-parameters framework, is in need of qualification. Kayne assumes that variables must be locally operator-bound, and that a local variable binder which is itself bound by a higher operator does not qualify as a suitable binder for the variable. In the *Barriers* theory (Chomsky 1986), however, successive cyclic *wh*-movement via intermediate adjunction to a maximal projection (notably, VP) is common practice. And even if Chomsky's VP-adjunction strategy for the elimination of potential barriers should turn out to be superfluous (cf. T. Hoekstra 1988b; Lasnik & Saito 1992 as representatives of the view that VP is never an inherent barrier), the option of a variable bound by an "intermediate variable" which in its turn is bound by a higher operator does not appear to be eliminable from the theory as it stands. Indeed, it would seem to be counterproductive to dispense with it. Consider, for instance, the analysis of parasitic gap constructions in Frampton (1990). On this account, the intermediate IP-adjoined trace establishes the necessary link between the "real" and "parasitic" chains in a typical parasitic gap construction like (30):

(30)   [$_{CP}$ *what* did [$_{IP}$ *t* [$_{IP}$ you [$_{VP}$ file *t* [$_{PP}$ without [$_{CP}$ *e* reading *e*]]]]]]

The intermediate adjunction to IP prevents the variable left in the position of the "real" (licensing) gap from being locally bound by the operator in SpecCP. Nonetheless, the example is grammatical. This leads us to conclude that "intermediate variables" like the IP-adjoined intermediate trace in (30) do qualify as licensers of variables in A-positions.[21] This being the case, we must now also conclude that Kayne's specific view of operator-variable relationships should be abandoned, and that, as a result, his account of the deviance of (22) can no longer be maintained.

---

[20]   Thanks to Jan Voskuil for raising this point; but cf. also fn. 23, below.

[21]   A similar argument can be made on the basis of the reanalysis of Frampton's (1990) account of parasitic gap constructions presented in Mulder & Den Dikken (1992). The case of Frampton's analysis is more striking, however, given that it makes use of intermediate adjunction, just as in Kayne's purportedly ungrammatical derivation of (22).

Kayne (1985:fn. 22) points out that '[a] successive cyclic trace in COMP must count as a surrogate operator phrase'. Successive cyclic operator movement via SpecCP is thus distinguished from successive cyclic movement via intermediate adjunction, only the latter being ruled out. Notice that T. Hoekstra (1988b), on independent grounds, also bars movement-via-adjunction.

This account has a number of problematic aspects anyway. In the first place the A'-movement operation displayed in (25) is potentially problematic in view of the Empty Category Principle (ECP) (or Kayne's 1984 Connectedness Condition): extraction takes place out of a left branch. Kayne circumvents this problem by adjoining the predicate of SC2 to SC1, so that the moved predicate can function as a local antecedent for its trace. Adjunction to SC1 is not a theoretical option in the *Barriers* framework, however, if we bear in mind that SC1 is an argument of the verb, and that adjunction to arguments is not allowed (cf. Chomsky 1986:6).

Secondly, Kayne's assumption that extraposition of the predicate of SC2 is crucially involved in the derivation of the correct surface word order of complex particle constructions faces some non-trivial problems. Consider first the word-order alternation in (31):[22]

(31)   a.   They loaded the hay onto the wagon green.
       b.   They loaded the hay green onto the wagon.

In Den Dikken (1987) I have argued that the word-order pattern in (31a) is basic (cf. (32a)), (31b) being derived from it via extraposition around the VP-adjoined SC headed by *green* of the prepositional predicate of the SC in the verb's complement, as in (32b):

(32)   a. $[_{VP} [_{VP}$ load $[_{SC1}$ the hay onto the wagon] $[_{SC2}$ PRO green]]
       b. $[_{VP} [_{VP}$ load $[_{SC1}$ the hay $t]$ $[_{SC2}$ PRO green]] *onto the wagon*

A similar word-order alternation is found in parallel constructions featuring a nominal complement-SC predicate, as is shown in (33).

(33)   a.   They consider Sue an ugly woman nude.
       b.   They consider Sue nude an ugly woman.

This is all in perfect accordance with Kayne's (1985) analysis of the *make out a liar* construction in (21a). Notice, however, that, in contrast to prepositional and nominal complement-SC predicates, APs resist being extraposed around a VP-adjoined secondary predicate, as is shown by the ill-formedness of (34b) (cf. Emonds 1976:109):

---

[22] Déchaine (1993:193) (referring also to Rothstein 1983) reports the judgements in (i), and states that the order "object depictive > resultative" is 'uniformly bad'. The speakers that I have consulted consistently confirmed the judgements on double small clause constructions given in the text.

(i)   a.   ??Jan hammered the metal into shape hot.
      b.   *Jan hammered the metal hot into shape.

(34) a. They painted the house red unsanded.[23]
      b. *They painted the house unsanded red.

The problem that arises now concerns the grammatical adjectival complex particle construction in (1c) (from Jackendoff 1977:67, also noted in Kayne 1985),
which is fully on a par with the *make out a liar* construction with regard to
particle placement:

(35) a. They painted the barn *up* red.
      b. *?They painted *up* the barn red.
      c. *They painted the barn red *up*.

Kayne (1985) assimilates his account of (35) to that of the *make out a liar*
construction in (21), a strategy for which I shall provide support in section
2.3.5.2. Concretely, then, the S-structure in (35a) must have been derived from
the D-structure underlying complex particle constructions on Kayne's assumptions via extraposition of the adjectival predicate of the SC in the particle's
subject position, much as in (25). There is severe friction between this result
and the conclusion ensuing from our investigation of (34) as opposed to (32)–
(33). The fact that extraposition of predicative APs is obligatory in Kayne's
analysis of complex particle constructions such as (35), while it seems impos-
ible otherwise, renders an extraposition approach to complex particle constructions based on (19) highly dubious.
    Kayne's analysis of the *make out a liar* construction also fails empirically
since it cannot adequately differentiate between (21) and the minimally different
example in (23), whose particle-placement and *wh*-extraction properties differ
significantly from those of (21) (cf. (21b) *vs.* (23b) and (22) *vs.* (24)). The
contrast between (22) and (24) is not mentioned by Kayne, and it is unclear how
a solution for it based on his analysis would read. Kayne (1985:114) does notice
the contrast between (21b) and (23b), and suggests by way of a solution that the
latter example could be derived from a D-structure as in (36a) (in which *John
to be a liar* finds itself in the subject position of the particle-headed SC; cf.
(19)) by first of all adjoining the entire ECM infinitival *John to be a liar* to the

---

[23] The fact, noted by Roberts (1988), that in double SC constructions of the type in (34) *wh*-
extraction of the resultative phrase is impossible (while in similar constructions lacking the object
depictive such *wh*-extraction is fine) — cf. (i) — might indicate that being extraposable around the
depictive is a precondition on *wh*-movement of the resultative, hence that *wh*-extraction of the
resultative takes place via intermediate extraposition. This would then eliminate one of the objections to Kayne's (1985) analysis of complex particle constructions made on pp. 47–48, above
(though it would remain quite unclear what would explain extraposition as a prerequisite for *wh*-
movement); it leaves the other arguments against it intact, however.

(i)   How smooth did John iron his trousers (*wet*/*naked*)?

particle-headed SC, after which *to be liar* is then moved rightwards yet another time (in order to render the extraposed infinitival clause transparent for Case assignment by V to its subject, *John*), as depicted in (36b) (where the precise landing-site of the *to*-infinitival phrase — adjunct to S or SC — is left open):

(36) a.   [$_{VP}$ make [$_{SC}$ [$_S$ John to be a liar] [$_{PP}$ out]]]
       b.   [$_{VP}$ make [$_{SC}$ [$_{SC}$ t_j [$_{PP}$ out]] [$_S$ John t_k]$_j$ [$_{XP}$ to be a liar]$_k$]]

As Kayne (1985:fn. 26) himself also acknowledges, however, there is no *a priori* reason why the predicate of the extraposed inner SC (*a liar*) in the ungrammatical example in (21b) should not be allowed to also move rightwards a second time, making the inner-SC subject accessible to Case assignment by V in the same way as in (36). Apparently, an analysis of the type in (36) must be unavailable in the case of copula-less complex particle constructions, but the theory gives us no clue to establishing why this should be so.[24]

It should be emphasised that the *make out to be a liar* construction is not an isolated case with respect to the possibility of verb-adjacent particle placement. It is fully on a par with the prepositional complex particle constructions in (1d,e), which Kayne does not discuss:

(37) a.   They put the books *down* on the shelf.
       b.   They put *down* the books on the shelf.
       c.   *They put the books on the shelf *down*.

(38) a.   They sent a schedule *out* to the stockholders.
       b.   They sent *out* a schedule to the stockholders.
       c.   *They sent a schedule to the stockholders *out*.

---

[24] Also note that it is not immediately obvious whether the constituent labelled "XP" in (36b) is a constituent. In a simple, pre-Pollock (1989) IP structure, no maximal projection can be isolated which uniquely dominates *to* + VP. Recent developments in the domain of VP-external functional projections would probably enable us to identify "XP" as Chomsky's (1993) TP. Since in such an inflated VP-external functional structure the base-position of the subject is no doubt lower in the tree than SpecTP, however, the extraposed "XP" in (36b) would in that case also contain the NP-trace of the raised ECM subject *John*, a trace which, in any event at S-structure, fails to be c-commanded by its antecedent. The well-formedness of the resulting structure would then depend on the question of whether reconstruction is capable of moving "XP" back into a position c-commanded by *John* at LF.

As a matter of fact, irrespective of whether the extraposed constituent in (36b) contains a trace of the embedded subject, questions with regard to c-command and reconstruction naturally arise on Kayne's analysis in cases of anaphor binding such as (i), in which, at S-structure, there presumably is a c-command relationship neither between *John* and *himself* nor between *John* and the PRO subject of the extraposed *to*-infinitival clause (cf. fn. 15) if (36b) is the correct analysis (though this may depend to some extent on XP's precise position and the definition of c-command adopted).

(i)   They made *John* out to be proud of *himself*.

I shall return more fully to the properties of prepositional complex particle constructions, which play a central role throughout this book. In the context at hand, one particular fact about these constructions may serve as a final argument against Kayne's (1985) analysis.

In prepositional complex particle constructions, it is possible to *wh*-extract the particle and the transitive PP together, as in (39) (adapted from Sag 1982 and Stowell 1981:339):

(39) a.   *Down* on which shelf did they put the books?
      b.   *Out* to whom did they send a schedule?

On an analysis à la Kayne (1985) no constituent which exclusively contains the preposed material can be identified, since the only projection that comprises both the particle and the transitive PP in the post-adjunction structure in (40) (i.e. the upper SC1) also necessarily includes the subject NP of SC2 (*the books*, *a schedule*), which is not preposed in (39). The alternative structure in (20), by contrast, readily accommodates the examples in (39). On this analysis, the particle and the transitive PP form a constituent ("PP1" in (41)) which, after NP-movement of the subject of SC2 to SpecSC1, does not also include the subject of the transitive PP.[25]

---

[25] Fronting the particle and the transitive PP together is also possible in Locative Inversion constructions (cf. Mulder 1992a), as shown in (i):

(i)   a.   Down on the shelf were put some books.
       b.   Out to the stockholders was sent a schedule.

This can be made to follow from the analysis in (20) if we can ensure that the post-verbal subject of (i) undergoes NP-movement to the specifier position of the particle-headed SC prior to movement of the particle's projection. Examples of the type in (ii) might be taken to suggest, however, that the post-verbal subject of Locative Inversion constructions may never undergo any NP-movement. That such a conclusion would be too strong is shown not only by (i), but also by inversion constructions such as (iii). The example in (iii) features an *ergative* adjective (cf. Cinque 1989, 1990), whose argument originates in the adjective's complement. This NP must hence vacate its base position prior to AP-fronting.

(ii)   Down the hill seemed (*a baby carriage) to be (*a baby carriage) rolling (a baby carriage).

(iii)   Most unlikely would seem to be a Republican landslide victory.

The difference between (ii) and (i)/(iii) can be traced back to the Case Filter. In (ii), *a baby carriage* receives nominative Case in the position to the right of *rolling*, so further NP-movement is prohibited by Economy (Chomsky 1991). In (i)/(iii), nominative can only be transmitted to the Case-dependent NP if this NP first establishes a relationship of Spec-Head agreement with the fronted constituent. NP can only accomplish this by moving into the specifier of the SC projected by the fronted constituent.   (*continued overleaf*)

(40) $[_{VP} V [_{SC1} [_{SC1} [_{SC2} NP t_j] [_{PP1} Prt]] PP2_j]]$ (cf. (25))

(41) $[_{VP} V [_{SC1} NP_i [_{PP1} Prt [_{SC2} t_i PP2]]]]$

A different argument for the constituency of the particle and the post-particle predicative PP (though not against Kayne's 1985 analysis of complex particle constructions) is presented in Svenonius (1992). Starting out from the observation that gapping allows no more than two constituents in the elliptical conjunct (cf. section 2.2.2; note the qualification mentioned in fn. 14), Svenonius notes the following instance of gapping featuring prepositional complex particle constructions:

(42)   Send the documents back to the CIA by mail, and the secret memos up to the White House by courier.

This example is an unequivocal case of gapping — the presence of the manner adverbials *by mail* and *by courier* indicates that (42) must minimally involve VP-coordination. Suppose, now, that *to the White House* did not form a constituent with the particle. Then the requirement that in a case of gapping the elliptical conjunct contain no more than two constituents would lead one to predict that (42) should be ungrammatical, contrary to fact. The conclusion ensuing from gapping constructions of the type in (42), then, is that the transitive PP in complex particle constructions must form a constituent with the particle. In fact, (42) gives rise to an even stronger conclusion: not only must the particle and the transitive PP form a constituent, but the "object NP" must be part of this constituent as well. This is in perfect accordance with the structure of complex particle constructions in (20)/(41).

In this subsection I have collected and discussed a variety of arguments against an account of English complex particle constructions based on the underlying structure in (19), proposed in Kayne (1985). In the next subsection I shall develop in full detail an analysis of complex particle constructions based on the only remaining structure made available by the overall theory, given in (20).

I note in passing that (i) and (iii) argue against Rizzi's (1990) Relativised Minimality in the domain of A-movement, even if modified in the way proposed by Guasti (1993) (who suggests that only θ'-specifier positions count as interveners): the post-verbal subject in these examples would wrongly be classified as an intervener since it occupies a non-thematic A-specifier position in between the extraction and landing sites of the A-moved SC predicate.

2.3.3 The alternative

The structure in (20), repeated here in a "delexicalised" form as (43) (cf. also chapter 6 for an arboreal representation, which some readers may feel more comfortable with), is not just the default option left to us after giving up the analysis in (19). On the contrary, in this section I shall present a range of evidence in support of this approach to complex particle constructions.

(43) $[_{IP}$ NP $[_{VP}$ V $[_{SC1}$ $[_{Spec\theta'}$ *ec*$]$ $[_{PP}$ Prt $[_{SC2}$ NP Pred$]]]]]]$

2.3.3.1 The ergativity of the particle

The structure in (43) gains considerable initial appeal from a consideration of the example in (44), which differs from (21) and (23) in that the SC/infinitival clause in these sentences has been exchanged for a finite CP. What is striking about the example in (44) is that this finite clause obligatorily follows the particle without there being a dummy argument (*it*) in the position preceding the particle. In this respect (44) contrasts sharply with an example such as (45), in which *it* is obligatorily present:[26]

(44)   They made (*it) out that John is a liar.
(45)   They find *(it) painful that John is a liar.

This contrast was originally noted by Vanden Wyngaerd (1989:16). He concludes from it that the finite clause in (44) is base-generated as the complement of the particle *out*, which must hence be *ergative*. On this analysis (44) features no CP extraposition, which explains the absence of *it*. In (45), on the other hand, the unergative adjectival SC predicate *painful* takes the finite CP as its external argument, and obligatory CP extraposition with concomitant insertion of the dummy pronoun *it* obtains.[27]

---

[26] The relevant point here is that *it* is obligatory in (45) but not in (44) (cf. also German (46)–(47)). That *it* is actually impossible in (44) is unaccounted for; one would expect it to be optional, just as in *They made (it) clear that he was wrong*, which features the ergative adjective (Cinque 1990) *clear*. Williams' claim (made in an oral presentation at Utrecht University, January 1994) that the adjective in this kind of example must be bare in order for *it* to be droppable, and that *They made it as clear as they could that he was wrong* is deviant without *it*, is not subscribed to by other speakers that I have consulted. I shall leave details regarding the distribution of "dummy" *it* open.

[27] Zaring (1994) discusses extraction differences between constructions with an extraposed CP subject of an unergative head and constructions with an *in situ* CP object of an ergative head:

(i)   a.   *How does it prove his innocence $[_{CP}$ for John to treat his children $t]$?
       b.   How does it appear $[_{CP}$ he got lost $t]$?

The contrast in (44)/(45) parallels that between (46), featuring an *ergative* adjective (cf. Cinque 1989, 1990), and (47), containing an unergative adjective:

(46)   Jetzt ist (*es*) klar daß wir ihm helfen müssen.
         now is (it) clear that we him help must

(47)   Jetzt ist *(*es*) peinlich daß wir ihm helfen müssen.
         now is (it) painful that we him help must

It motivates the analysis of *out* as an ergative preposition (cf. also Guéron 1986, 1990), and at the same time gives us an argument in favour of the analysis of the *make out a liar* construction in (43), which is also proposed by Vanden Wyngaerd (1989).

2.3.3.2 *The particle-placement differential*

Now let us return to the examples in (21)–(24). In the D-structure of the *make out a liar* construction the subject of SC2, *John*, is generated in a non-Case-marked position: the particle is ergative and hence, given Burzio's generalisation, unable to assign Case to its complement. In order to avoid a violation of the Case Filter, *John* should hence be moved into the θ'-subject position of the particle-headed SC in the mapping of D-structure onto S-structure. In this position, *John* can receive Case from the matrix verb in the familiar fashion. This derivation is illustrated in (48):

(48) $[_{IP}$ They $[_{VP}$ made $[_{SC1}$ $[_{Spec\theta'}$ John$_i]$ $[_{PP}$ out $[_{SC2}$ t_i a liar]]]]]

Once we can ensure that NP-movement as depicted in (48) is obligatory in the *make out a liar* construction, we immediately explain the rigid word-order pattern exhibited by this construction. How do we prevent the Case-dependent subject of SC2 from remaining *in situ*? Put in more theoretical terms, how do we ensure that Case cannot somehow be transmitted to the specifier position of SC2 in nominal and adjectival complex particle constructions (in which the V–Prt–NP–Pred order is ill-formed; cf. (21b) and (35b)), while Case apparently *can* be so transmitted in *to*-infinitival and prepositional complex particle constructions (cf. the grammaticality of (23b) and (37b)/(38b); all pertinent examples are repeated and renumbered here for ease of reference)?

(49) a.   They made John *out* a liar.   (= (21))
     b.   *?They made *out* John a liar.
     c.   *They made John a liar *out*.

(50) a.   They painted the barn *up* red.   (= (35))
      b.   *⁷They painted *up* the barn red.
      c.   *They painted the barn red *up*.

(51) a.   They made John *out* **to be** a liar.   (= (23))
      b.   ⁽⁷⁾They made *out* John **to be** a liar.
      c.   *They made John **to be** a liar *out*.

(52) a.   They put the books *down* on the shelf.   (= (37))
      b.   They put *down* the books on the shelf.
      c.   *They put the books on the shelf *down*.

(53) a.   They sent a schedule *out* to the stockholders.   (= (38))
      b.   They sent *out* a schedule to the stockholders.
      c.   *They sent a schedule to the stockholders *out*.

Let us start out answering these questions by first of all considering the nominal and adjectival complex particle constructions in (49) and (50). I would like to argue that Case can under no circumstances reach the specifier position of SC2 in these constructions due to the fact that SC2 in these cases is a *barrier* for government from outside. SC2 is a barrier for want of L-marking. Although it receives a θ-role from its governor, the particle, I shall assume that the particle, just like Infl, is not sufficiently lexical to function as an L-marker:[28]

(54)   Particles are non-lexical prepositions, hence do not L-mark their complements.

Since SC2 in nominal and adjectival complex particle constructions is hence impenetrable by outside (Case-marking) governors, the Case Filter forces NP-movement of the subject of SC2 into the specifier position of SC1. NP-movement is licit despite the intervention of a barrier since, as I argued in section 1.2.3, NP-traces are not subject only to the ECP. The obligatoriness of NP-movement straightforwardly accounts for the ungrammaticality of the b-examples in (49) and (50).

Now what is the difference between (49) and (50) on the one hand, and the *to*-infinitival and prepositional complex particle constructions in (51)–(53) on the other, that is responsible for the particle-placement differential that we find (cf. the b-examples)? In view of what was argued with regard to nominal and adjectival complex particle constructions in the preceding paragraph, it is clear that we should somehow ensure that the complement of the particle in *to*-infinitival and prepositional complex particle constructions does *not* constitute a barrier to outside government.

---

[28]   Van Riemsdijk (1990) similarly — but on different grounds — reaches the conclusion that particles are ''functional prepositions''.

T. Hoekstra (1991) argues that, in prepositional and *to*-infinitival complex particle constructions, extraposition of the transitive PP or *to*-infinitival takes place. This assumption, in combination with a definition of a barrier in terms of L-containment (cf. (26)), according to which the barrierhood of the particle's complement is lifted whenever its predicate is removed from it, and with the (implicit) assumption that nominal and adjectival SC predicates cannot undergo the extraposition process, allows Hoekstra to make the desired distinction between the examples in (49) and (50) on the one hand, and those in (51)–(53) on the other.

Three remarks are in order. First, it should be noted that the fact that on Hoekstra's analysis, as on Kayne's (1985) approach to *to*-infinitival complex particle constructions, extraposition of the *to*-infinitival phrase obtains may raise binding-theoretic problems in constructions in which the extraposed infinitival contains an anaphor bound by the infinitive's subject (cf. fn. 24, above). Secondly, and more importantly, Hoekstra's implicit claim that nominal SC predicates fail to undergo extraposition is rendered dubious by examples of the type in (33), above, which show that predicative NPs do extrapose around an adjunct-SC. Finally, his appeal to a definition of a barrier in terms of L-containment to capture the data in (49)–(53) leads Hoekstra to predict that *all* of these complex particle constructions should allow for verb-adjacent particle placement in examples involving *wh*-movement of the predicate of the particle's SC complement. Since predicative NPs generally undergo *wh*-movement, *wh*-extracting *a liar* in (49) should yield a grammatical result (with the particle in V-adjacent position). That this prediction is false is shown by the ill-formedness, regardless of the surface position of the particle, of the example in (22). Considerations like these prevent me from adopting Hoekstra's account of the particle-placement differential in complex particle constructions. Let us proceed, then, to devising an alternative account.

I have assumed throughout (cf. the discussion in section 2.2.2) that particles belong to the category P (also cf. Emonds 1976; Van Riemsdijk 1978; Kayne 1985). In the prepositional complex particle constructions in (52) and (53), the particle takes a prepositional SC as its complement:

(55) $[_{IP}$ NP $[_{VP}$ V $[_{SC1}$ $[_{Spec\theta'}$ *ec*] $[_{PP}$ Prt $[_{SC2}$ NP PP]]]]]

We may now prevent the SC in the complement of the particle in (55) from becoming a barrier by capitalising on the notion of a *segment*, which figures prominently in Chomsky's (1986) definition of a barrier. In the prepositional complex particle construction, the predicate of the SC complement of the particle is *categorially non-distinct* from the predicate of the higher SC, of which the particle is the head:

(56)   ... $[_{PP}$ Prt ... $[_{PP}$ P NP]]

This structure can be looked upon as a base-generated instantiation of the multi-segment structure that is obtained through adjunction.[29] In this structure the lower PP is a *segment* of the entire, multi-segment PP. Since the outermost segment of this PP is L-marked by the verb, and since — as Chomsky (1986) and more recently also Lasnik & Saito (1992) have argued — L-marking percolates down to the head of a projection, we are led to the desirable conclusion that the complement of the particle in the structure in (55) is not a barrier since it is L-marked. Only if the syntactic category of the particle's complement is non-distinct from that of the particle itself can we thus prevent the lower SC from being a barrier.

This does not yet answer the question that we started out addressing: how is it possible for the subject of SC2 to remain *in situ* in prepositional (and *to*-infinitival[30]) complex particle constructions? Now that we have managed to lift SC2's barrierhood if its predicate is categorially non-distinct from the head of SC1, we should proceed to finding a way of transferring the verb's objective Case feature to the specifier position of SC2. Case is assigned under government and/or Specifier-Head agreement. As things stand, the verb neither governs nor agrees with the specifier of SC2 in the structure of complex particle constructions. That it does not entertain a Spec-Head agreement relationship with SpecSC2 is obvious; a government relationship between the two is rendered impossible by the Minimality Condition (Chomsky 1986), due to the intervention of a "closer governor", the particle.

A way of circumventing this minimality effect is to eliminate the intermediate head which blocks a government relationship between V and SpecSC2. This can be accomplished by *reanalysing* the particle with the verb. Verb-particle reanalysis, which I assume takes place at LF in English (cf. section 2.4.3 for some more discussion), is an instance of the general process of *head incorporation* (Baker 1988) — it is what Baker refers to as "abstract incorporation". Being an instantiation of incorporation, reanalysis of the verb and the particle exhibits all the properties of head incorporation. In particular, it will feature the effects of Baker's (1988) Government Transparency Corollary, given in (57) (repeated from section 1.2.5, to which I refer for relevant general discussion):

(57)   *The Government Transparency Corollary* (GTC)
         A lexical category which has an item incorporated into it governs everything which the incorporated item governed in its original structural position.

---

[29] Cf. Chomsky (1986:76) and section 1.2.3, above, for another implementation of this idea in a different context.

[30] These will be addressed on p. 60, below.

On the basis of the Government Transparency Corollary in (57), then, we predict that, if verb-particle reanalysis takes place and the complement of the particle is not a barrier to outside government, the matrix verb (or, more accurately, the reanalysed V–Prt complex) comes to govern the subject of SC2 in the structure of complex particle constructions. Government being one way in which Case is assigned, we can thus accommodate the fact that in prepositional complex particle constructions the subject of SC2 may remain *in situ*, to the right of the particle (cf. the b-examples in (52) and (53)).[31] Whenever V–Prt reanalysis obtains (and the particle's complement is transparent), Case will reach the subject of SC2 in its D-structure position. By Chomsky's (1991) Economy principle, according to which the least complicated derivation is always to be preferred, we then predict that NP-movement to SpecSC1, being unmotivated, is barred in this context. The Case-dependent NP in the complement of the particle hence passes the Case Filter either by NP-moving to a position directly governed by the Case-assigning verb (in which case V–Prt reanalysis is prevented from applying, by Economy), or by having the verb's Case feature transmitted onto it as a result of the application of V–Prt reanalysis (in which case NP-movement of the pertinent NP is barred, again by Economy; on the surface optionality of verb-particle reanalysis, cf. section 1.2.8).

Note again that, irrespective of whether V–Prt reanalysis obtains or not, Case-assignment to the specifier position of SC2 is strictly impossible in nominal and adjectival complex particle constructions, as a consequence of the fact that in these cases the complement of the particle is a barrier: it is neither L-marked nor categorially non-distinct from the particle. Reanalysis of verb and particle will not, of course, be able to change this. In particular, it will not be able to get SC2 L-marked. L-marking is defined as θ-marking by a lexical element. SC2 in the structure of complex particle constructions is θ-marked by the particle. The Projection Principle ensures that θ-relations remain constant throughout the derivation. At all stages in the derivation, then, SC2 is θ-marked by the particle. Now, while incorporation of a lexical element into a non-lexical θ-marker will turn the latter into an L-marker (as in the case of V-to-I movement, which causes Infl to L-mark its VP complement; cf. Chomsky 1986), the reverse does not occur. That is, incorporation of a non-lexical θ-marker into a lexical element will never turn the former into an L-marker. The trace of the

---

[31] If, as assumed in this study (cf. 2.4.3 for explicit argumentation), V–Prt reanalysis is LF particle incorporation, one may wonder how it can have any effect on Case assignment, which is often held to apply at S-structure (also cf. Baker 1988:462, fn. 37 on the interplay between reanalysis and Case assignment, in the context of V–V reanalysis in Romance causatives). In the *Barriers* theory, a way out of this problem would be to assume (cf. Den Dikken 1990a; Müller & Sternefeld 1993: 463) that LF incorporation is foreshadowed in overt syntax by cosuperscripting, whereby the effects of LF incorporation can already be felt prior to LF. In the minimalist programme of Chomsky (1993), there is no issue at all, Case Theory — like all other constraints on representations — being an *interface* condition, and Case being *checked* at LF (and no sooner than LF, in English).

incorporated head continues to be responsible for θ-marking, and it continues to be non-lexical. I should emphasise that L-marking is defined in Chomsky (1986:13) as a property of *heads*, not of chains. This is crucial in the context at hand since, if L-marking were a chain property, verb-particle reanalysis would always render the SC complement of the particle L-marked. For clearly, the head chain linking the particle and the verb contains a lexical element (viz. V). L-marking being a relationship between a lexical *head* and its θ-marked complement, however, only the terminal element (foot) of this chain could ever L-mark the SC in its complement in complex particle constructions. Since this element, the trace of the incorporated particle, is non-lexical at all levels of representation, at no point will SC2 in the structure of complex particle constructions be L-marked. Since the alternative way of lifting SC2's barrierhood (i.e. categorial non-distinctness) is clearly inapplicable in the case of nominal and adjectival complex particle constructions, we correctly predict that the V–Prt–NP–Pred word order is ungrammatical in these constructions (cf. the b-examples in (49) and (50)).

Let us finally discuss the fact that *to*-infinitival complex particle constructions pattern with prepositional complex particle constructions with regard to the possibility of V-adjacent particle placement. I would like to argue that the account of the well-formedness of the b-examples in (52)–(53) can be directly transposed to the example in (51b). The only thing that we need assume in addition to what we have assumed already is that the English infinitival marker *to*, which is homophonous to the preposition *to* to begin with, has the categorial status of a preposition. On this plausible assumption, which is also made in e.g. Reuland (1983), Rigter & Beukema (1985) and Guéron & Hoekstra (1988), the IP complement of the particle in (58) is identical in all relevant respects to a PP, so that (58) is another instance of the substructure in (56).

(58) $[_{IP}$ They $[_{VP}$ made $[_{SC1}$ $[_{Spec\theta'}$ $ec]$ $[_{PP}$ out $[_{IP}$ John to be a liar$]]]]]$

In this subsection I have presented an account of the particle-placement differential found in the various types of English complex particle constructions. A summary of the major points is given in (59):

(59) a.   Particles are non-lexical ergative prepositions which hence do not L-mark their complements;
      b.   As a result, SC2 in the structure of complex particle constructions is a *barrier* in principle;
      c.   The barrierhood of SC2 is lifted, however, iff SC2 is *categorially non-distinct* from SC1 (i.e., iff SC2 has a prepositional head, including the infinitival marker *to*);
      d.   If (59c) applies, the subject of SC2 can be Case-marked *in situ* iff verb-particle *reanalysis* takes place.

2.3.3.3 The ban on clause-final particle placement

In the discussion of the particle-placement differential I have so far ignored the fact that in all types of complex particle constructions, clause-final particle placement is consistently impossible, as shown by the c-examples in (49)–(53), above. The ill-formedness of these examples can now be shown to fall out straightforwardly from the analysis of complex particle constructions presented above.

Recall that at D-structure, the particle precedes both the subject and the predicate of SC2 — it governs SC2, and government is from left to right in English. Depending on the categorial status of SC2's head, the subject of SC2 either may or must move to a position to the left of the particle (cf. the previous subsection). The theory does not, however, provide us with any tools that could conceivably make the particle surface to the right of both the subject and the predicate of SC2.

Consider the three strategies of deriving this word order: (i) leftward movement of SC2 as a whole; (ii) rightward movement of the particle; or (iii) NP-movement of the subject of SC2 to SpecSC1 and adjunction of the predicate of SC2 to the projection of the particle (below SpecSC1). I already noted in section 2.3.2 that SCs are generally immobile (for reasons that need not concern us here; cf. Den Dikken 1987 for relevant discussion). In this way, option (i) can be eliminated. The alternative in (ii), rightward particle movement, is clearly blocked by the ban on adjunction of heads to maximal projections (cf. Chomsky 1986), which may be reducible to Emonds' (1976) Structure Preserving Hypothesis. Finally, (iii), apart from involving an adjunction step that would have no obvious trigger, would result in a structure in which the NP-trace of the moved subject of SC2 wrongly ends up being locally A'-bound by the moved predicate of SC2 (which is coindexed with its subject via Spec-Head agreement). Thus, no *a priori* conceivable derivation of the word order V–NP–Pred–Prt on the basis of the underlying structure in (43) is compatible with the theory. We hence correctly predict that the c-examples in (49)–(53) are ungrammatical.

2.3.3.4 Extraction of and from the predicate of SC2

Apart from the problems posed by the different particle placement possibilities found in the various English complex particle constructions, for which we have now furnished an explanation, these constructions also pose a second cluster of problems, having to do with the restrictions on extraction of and from the predicate of SC2. These will be the topic of this subsection.

From section 2.3.1 the reader will recall the contrast between (22) and (24), repeated (in a somewhat more perspicuous fashion) below:

(60)   a.   *What kind of a liar did they make *out* John *t*?
       b.   *What kind of a liar did they make John *out* *t*?

(61)   a.   What kind of a liar did they make *out* John [**to be** *t*]?
       b.   What kind of a liar did they make John *out* [**to be** *t*]?

Why does *wh*-extraction of the predicative NP yield an ungrammatical result in (60), while (61), and also a sentence as closely related to (60) as *What kind of a liar did they call John?*, are perfectly acceptable?

In our quest for an answer to this question, it is instructive to consider the behaviour of prepositional complex particle constructions in the domain of *wh*-extraction. I give the full paradigms in (62)–(65). For the moment, we need not be concerned with the a-examples in (62) and (64). I turn to these further below.

(62)   a.   On which shelf did they put *down* the books *t*?
       b.   *⁷On which shelf did they put the books *down* *t*?

(63)   a.   Which shelf did they put *down* the books [on *t*]?
       b.   Which shelf did they put the books *down* [on *t*]?

(64)   a.   To whom did they send *out* a schedule *t*?
       b.   *⁷To whom did they send a schedule *out* *t*?

(65)   a.   Who did they send *out* a schedule [to *t*]?
       b.   Who did they send a schedule *out* [to *t*]?

A generalisation that is consistent with the data in (60)–(65) is the following:[32]

---

[32] Two notes on the data are in order. First, T. Hoekstra (1991) claims that (63a) and (65a) (and also (61a)) are unacceptable, and contrast sharply with the corresponding b-examples. This would follow from his extraposition approach, outlined in section 2.3.3.2. No such contrast has been reported to me by any of the native speakers I consulted, however.

Secondly, it should be pointed out that (62b)/(64b) seem somewhat less bad than (60b). Richard Kayne and Ur Shlonsky (p.c.) note furthermore that the former improve if the particle is followed by additional lexical material, e.g. an adverb:

(i)   a.   ⁽⁷⁾On which shelf did they put the books down *yesterday*?
       b.   ⁽⁷⁾To whom did they send a schedule out *yesterday*?

This may well be related to the apparently independent fact that quantifier stranding in post-verbal position is generally impossible in English (cf. (iia)), but becomes noticeably less deviant once an adverbial adjunct is added to the right of the QP (cf. Johnson 1992):

(ii)   a.   *I read the numbers all.
       b.   I read the numbers all *quickly*.

(66)   *Wh*-extraction of the constituent immediately following the particle
         is impossible; subextraction from this constituent is grammatical.

This empirical generalisation can be given formal substance by once again making use of our earlier assumption that particles are *non-lexical* prepositions. This lexical defectiveness of particles can now be held responsible for the fact that extraction of the predicate of SC2 in the structure of complex particle constructions results in ungrammaticality. As the particle is not a lexical governor, the trace left by *wh*-extraction in (60b), (62b) and (64b) is not lexically governed, in violation of the ECP, given that (cf. section 1.2.2) lexical government is a *conditio sine qua non*.

The ungrammaticality of the b-examples in (60), (62) and (64) can hence be viewed as a consequence of the ECP. In the examples in (61), (63) and (65), by contrast, the ECP's demands are met, the *wh*-trace being lexically governed by the copula *be* or the prepositions *on, to*. These examples are therefore ruled grammatical, as required.[33]

Apart from subextraction from the predicate of SC2, as in the examples in (61), (63) and (65), the prepositional complex particle constructions in (62) and (64) allow for an additional way of rescuing the ungrammatical b-variants, by placing the particle in verb-adjacent position, as in the a-examples of (62) and (64). This strategy is unavailable in the nominal complex particle construction in (60), which is unacceptable irrespective of the surface position of the particle. A descriptive generalisation covering these facts is given in (67):

(67)   In prepositional complex particle constructions, verb-adjacent part-
         icle placement renders *wh*-extraction of the predicate of SC2 possible.

The crucial difference between the b-variants of (62) and (64), with clause-final particle placement, and the a-examples, with verb-adjacent particle placement, is the fact that in the latter *reanalysis* of the verb and the particle has taken place, which allows the verb's Case to be transmitted to the subject of SC2 *in situ*. Recall that verb-particle reanalysis is an abstract (LF) instance of head incorporation, and exhibits the effects of Baker's (1988) Government Transparency Corollary in (57). The GTC entails that as a consequence of V–Prt reanalysis the matrix verb will come to govern everything that the particle

---

[33] In the nominal complex particle construction in (60), extraction from the predicate nominal is predicted to yield a Subjacency violation, since the particle's complement SC is a barrier for want of L-marking. Concretely, then, we expect (ia) to be worse than (ib), a prediction which is borne out (Kyle Johnson, p.c.):

(i)   a.   ??Which county did they make him out the count of *t*?
        b.   Which county did they consider him the count of *t*?

governed at D-structure. In the specific case of the grammatical a-variants of
(62) and (64), the trace of the *wh*-moved PP thus ends up being governed by
the matrix verb (or more adequately, by the reanalysed V–Prt complex), which,
in contradistinction to the particle, is a lexical governor. As a result of
reanalysis a *wh*-extraction case like *On which shelf did they put down the
books?* hence satisfies the ECP, which explains its well-formedness.[34]

So far I have confined my attention to cases of *wh*-extraction. The influence
of particle placement on the extractability of the predicate of SC2 in prepositional complex particle constructions can also be illustrated on the basis of PP-
extraposition, however. Consider examples (68)–(69):[35]

(68) a.   They carried *up* the hay onto the wagon green.
      b.   They carried the hay *up* onto the wagon green.
(69) a.   They carried *up* the hay green onto the wagon.
      b.   *They carried the hay *up* green onto the wagon.

The sentences in (68) reflect the underlying relative order of the resultative SC-
predicate *onto the wagon* and the VP-adjoined adjectival SC headed by *green*.
The fact that particle placement is variable here is not surprising (cf. section
2.3.3.2 on particle placement in prepositional complex particle constructions).
The interesting case is the contrast between (69a,b). Here, extraposition of the
predicate of SC2, *onto the wagon*, to a position to the right of the adjunct-AP
green has taken place. Extraposition, like *wh*-movement, leaves a trace which
should meet the demands of the ECP. In particular, it should be lexically
governed. The fact that extraposition yields a grammatical result if and only if
the particle is adjacent to the verb now falls out immediately from the analysis
developed above — verb-particle reanalysis is obligatory in (69).

Finally, let us return to the difference between nominal and prepositional
complex particle constructions, reflected in (60) *vs.* (62) and (64). Why is it
that the surface position of the particle has no influence on the extractability of
the predicate of SC2 in nominal complex particle constructions? In my analysis
of the various types of English complex particle constructions one assumption

---

[34] On the fact that V–Prt reanalysis entails non-application of NP-movement of the subject of SC2
to the specifier of the particle-headed SC, cf. the discussion below (57), on Economy.

[35] I thank Robin Smith (p.c.) for providing the judgements. On the structure of "double SC"
constructions, cf. Den Dikken (1987). Note that the grammaticality of (68a) is problematic for T.
Hoekstra's (1991) extraposition approach to verb-adjacent particle placement in prepositional
complex particle constructions. On this analysis, (68a) must involve extraposition of *onto the
wagon*. The PP does not end up to the right of the VP-adjoined SC headed by *green*, however.
Adjunction of PP below VP, to either of the two SCs in the verb's complement, being barred by
Chomsky's (1986:6) ban on adjunction to arguments, there does not seem to be a possible derivation for (68a) on Hoekstra's analysis.

plays a key role: the idea that particles are non-lexical prepositions. This assumption has two important implications. In the first place the particle's lexical defectiveness causes the complement of the particle not to be L-marked. Hence it is a barrier (unless it is categorially identical with the particle). Secondly, the non-lexical status of the particle implies that the particle is not a lexical governor, so that extraction of a constituent governed by the particle is not allowed. In the examples in (62) and (64) we only had to reckon with the second implication, the complement of the particle being exempt from barrier-hood by virtue of its categorial identity with the particle. In (60), by contrast, there is no such categorial identity. As a consequence the complement of the particle will always be a barrier by lack of L-marking. Reanalysis of particle and verb will not change this (cf. the discussion at the end of section 2.3.3.2; pp. 59–60). Even after reanalysis of V and the particle SC2 will not be L-marked. Being a barrier, this SC will hence block transmission of the verb's structural Case to the subject of SC2, and prevent the *wh*-trace from being properly (i.e. lexically) governed. The example in (60), regardless of the surface position of the particle, hence violates both the Case Filter and the ECP. The contrast between (60) on the one hand, and (62) and (64) on the other, is hence explained on the present analysis.[36]

2.3.3.5 Further support for the analysis: The Norwegian parallel

With respect to the prepositional complex particle construction, there is a remarkably close correspondence between English and (some dialects of) Norwegian. Thus, Alma Næss (p.c.) informs me that in the example in (70), verb-adjacent particle placement is allowed, while clause-final particle placement is not (cf. (52)), and that for many speakers A'-extraction of the predicate of SC2 is not allowed *unless* the particle is in verb-adjacent position, *sub*extraction from the predicate of SC2 being perfect for all speakers irrespective of the surface position of the verbal particle *ned* 'down' (cf. (71) and (72) to (62) and (63)):

(70) a. Han satte katten *ned* på gulvet.
he put the-cat down on the-ground
   b. Han satte *ned* katten på gulvet.
   c. *Han satte katten på gulvet *ned*.

(71) a. På gulvet satte han *ned* katten *t*.
on the-ground put he down the-cat
   b. *På gulvet satte han katten *ned* *t*.

---

[36] Notice that lack of L-containment cannot be sufficient to lift SC2's barrierhood if the present theory (which thus differs from Kayne's 1985 and T. Hoekstra's 1991) is correct.

(72) a. Hva satte han *ned* katten [på *t*]?
what put he down the-cat on
b. Hva satte han katten *ned* [på *t*]?

The same parallelism is found between the English examples in (53), (64) and (65) and their Norwegian counterparts in (73)–(75):[37]

(73) a. De sendte møteprogrammet *ut* til aksjonærene.
they sent the-schedule out to the-stockholders
b. De sendte *ut* møteprogrammet til aksjonærene.
c. *De sendte møteprogrammet til aksjonærene *ut*.

(74) a. Til aksjonærene sendte de *ut* møteprogrammet *t*.
to the-stockholders sent they out the-schedule
b. *Til aksjonærene sendte de møteprogrammet *ut* *t*.

(75) a. Hvem sendte de *ut* møteprogrammet [til *t*]?
whom sent they out the-schedule to
b. Hvem sendte de møteprogrammet *ut* [til *t*]?

Also with regard to the constituency of the particle and the post-particle transitive PP, Norwegian complex particle constructions are fully on a par with their English cognates, as is shown by a comparison of English (39) and Norwegian (76):

(76) a. *Ned* på gulvet satte han katten.
down on the-ground put he the-cat
b. *Ut* til aksjonærene sendte de møteprogrammet.
out to the-stockholders sent they the-schedule

The properties of English complex particle constructions, then, are no isolated oddities to be taken care of by highly language-specific statements. On the contrary, the fact that Norwegian is exactly like English in all relevant respects in the domain of complex particle constructions shows that the theoretical machinery accommodating the properties of these constructions should be an integral part of the core theory. The analysis of complex particle constructions propounded here meets this criterion.

---

[37] I thank Arnfinn Vonen for constructing and judging these sentences.

2.3.3.6 Conclusion

In this subsection I have presented and motivated an analysis of English (and Norwegian) complex particle constructions based on the structure in (43), repeated here for ease of reference:

(77) $[_{IP}$ NP $[_{VP}$ V $[_{SC1}$ $[_{Spec\theta'}$ *ec*$]$ $[_{PP}$ Prt $[_{SC2}$ NP Pred$]]]]]$

This structure involves a SC–in–SC substructure, the verb selecting a SC headed by an *ergative* particle which in its turn takes a second SC containing the additional secondary predicate. I have shown that with the aid of this analysis of complex particle constructions, the properties of the various instantiations of this schema with regard to particle placement and extraction from SC2 can be accommodated, and that this account is to be preferred to the alternative presented in Kayne (1985).

In the next section, I shall discuss and reject a possible alternative to the analysis of (especially prepositional) complex particle constructions built on the structural template in (77). After presenting an inventory of complex particle construction types in section 2.3.5, I then proceed to a discussion of the ergativity of particles (section 2.3.6), and the analysis of simplex particle constructions (section 2.4).

2.3.4 Another possibility?

In the preliminaries (section 2.2) to the discussion of English complex particle constructions presented above, I presented evidence for the two basic hypotheses underlying my analysis of complex particle constructions:

(78) a.   Particles are heads of complement-SCs.
      b.   The post-particle constituents in complex particle constructions are predicates of complement-SCs.

I have shown (section 2.3.3) that on the basis of these hypotheses, an account of the properties of English (and Norwegian) complex particle constructions can be given. Specifically, I have argued that the differences between nominal/ adjectival complex particle constructions on the one hand, and prepositional/*to-*infinitival complex particle constructions on the other, with respect to particle placement and extractability of and from the particle's complement, can be accommodated while assigning completely identical underlying structures to the entire class of complex particle constructions.

It might be suggested, however, that these empirical differences between the various types of complex particle constructions are evidence that the structures underlying these various tokens of the basic construction type are *not* identical. In fact, in earlier work (cf. Den Dikken 1989) I myself took this tack rather than the "uniform D-structure" approach. In particular, one might suggest that, while the analysis of nominal and adjectival complex particle constructions is as given in section 2.3.3, in prepositional cases the particle takes an argumental PP complement. The particle-placement and extractability differentials might then be relatable to the postulated structural distinction, which is represented in (79).[38] In this section I shall briefly consider and reject this possibility.

(79) a. $[_{VP} V [_{SC1} [_{Spec\theta'} ec] [_{PP} Prt [_{SC2} NP \{NP/AP\}]]]]$
  b. $[_{VP} V [_{SC} NP [_{PP1} Prt [_{PP2} P NP]]]]$

Turning to prepositional complex particle constructions shortly, let me first address the minimal pair in (80). It seems perfectly obvious that both in (80a) and (80b) the "object NP" *John* originates internal to the complement of the particle, a nominal SC in (80a) and an infinitival clause in (80b). Since all θ-roles assigned in the two variants are identical, the conclusion is inescapable that the D-structures of (80a,b) must be completely analogous in all relevant respects, given the plausible assumption that the range of possible D-structures is severely curtailed by alignment hypotheses of the type discussed in section 1.2.6. Even abstracting away from the specifics of possible ways in which postulating a structural difference between (80a,b) might accommodate the particle-placement differential, then, conceptual considerations argue strongly against taking such a tack in the case of (80).

(80) a. They made (*out*) John (*out*) a liar.
  b. They made (*out*) John (*out*) **to be** a liar.

For prepositional complex particle constructions, too, it would be ill-advised to assume that the transitive PP is a non-predicative complement of the particle, as I shall try to show in the remainder of this subsection. One immediate objection to this line of thought concerns the fact that the transitive PP passes the Locative Inversion test for predicativity (cf. section 2.2.1, above):

(81)   On the table were put down some books.

---

[38] Mulder (1992b) essentially follows this line of thought. Svenonius (1992) also assumes a complement-PP approach to prepositional complex particle constructions (without considering the SC alternative, and without addressing other types of complex particle constructions).

Perhaps, however, the grammaticality of (81) could be reconciled with an analysis along the lines of (79b) on the assumption that it is the predicate of the particle-SC that is fronted in Locative Inversion cases of this type. The particle would then move out of its own SC (and incorporate into the verb) prior to the application of Locative Inversion:[39]

(82) $[_{PP1}\ t_i\ [_{PP2}$ on the table$]]_j$ were $[$put$+down_i]\ [_{SC}$ some books $t_j]$

Notice, however, that, as the structure in (82) indicates, an analysis of Locative Inversion constructions based on prepositional complex particle constructions along these lines commits one to the view that English features *overt-syntactic* particle incorporation into the verb. In section 2.4.3, I shall present evidence against this view. If it is correct that English has no overt-syntactic particle movement, an analysis of prepositional complex particle constructions incorporating the assumption that the post-particle transitive PP is non-predicative cannot accommodate Locative Inversion constructions of the type in (81).

Moreover, an analysis along the lines of (79b) would run into serious trouble concerning the Theta Criterion when establishing the relationship that obviously exists between a complex particle construction like (83a) and a particle-less but otherwise identical resultative like (83b):

(83) a.   They put the books *down* on the shelf.
      b.   They put the books on the shelf.

For resultative constructions of the type in (83b), T. Hoekstra (1988a) has argued convincingly that they involve SC complementation. The transitive PP *on the shelf* is the predicate of a SC in the verb's complement, and is responsible for θ-role assignment to the SC subject *the books*. In (83b), then, *on the shelf* is a predicative, θ-assigning PP. If we were to adopt the analysis of prepositional complex particle constructions in (79b), however, the very same PP would *not* assign an external θ-role in (83a). Here, it is the particle-*cum*-PP complex which is responsible for θ-marking *the books*. Since, as (83b) shows, PP is a potential θ-role assigner, and since there is no θ-semantic difference between (83b) and (83a), denying PP predicative status in the latter example seems to entail a violation of the Theta Criterion — PP has an external θ-role to assign, but it apparently fails to be satisfied in complex particle constructions, if analysed as in (79b).

---

[39] The trace of the incorporated particle is presumably licensed at LF after reconstruction of the fronted PP1 into its base position. Notice, though, that if Locative Inversion is indeed an instance of *A*-movement, as Hoekstra & Mulder (1990) convincingly argue, it is not obvious that it undergoes LF-reconstruction: A-movement typically does not feature connectivity effects.

To be sure, a proponent of the structure in (79b) might object to the above line of reasoning in one of the following ways: (i) assignment of the PP's external θ-role to an invisible PRO in the subject position of an adjunct-SC projected by PP; (ii) satisfaction of this role via Higginbotham's (1985) strategy of θ-identification by the particle; or (iii) percolation of the external θ-role to the projection of the particle, as a result of which this projection assigns the composite of this θ-role and the particle's own external θ-role (cf. compositional θ-role assignment). As a general remark pertaining to all three strategies, let me point out that whichever tack one were to take, there is no intrinsic reason why such a move should not also be applicable to other (specifically, nominal and adjectival) complex particle constructions, so that there would again be no structural difference between the various types of complex particle constructions. This would be an unfortunate result (from the perspective of the non-uniformity approach) in view of the empirical differences between the various types of complex particle constructions discussed earlier in this chapter. In addition, each of the above strategies gives rise to some additional comments as well.

Of these options, the first commits one to the view that the transitive P in a prepositional complex particle construction heads a SC generated in an *adjoined* position. This is necessary since the PRO subject of this SC (the recipient of PP's external θ-role, controlled by the particle's argument) must be shielded from outside government. Now recall that A'-extraction of the transitive PP in prepositional complex particle constructions is possible if the particle finds itself in V-adjacent position:

(84)   On which shelf did they put down the books?

An analysis of prepositional complex particle constructions according to which the transitive PP is the predicate of an adjunct-SC would wrongly predict (84) to be ill-formed. After all, as Chomsky (1986:81–83) originally pointed out, extraction of the predicate of an adjunct-SC (regardless of whether its PRO subject is controlled by the subject or by the object) is impossible in English, as the ungrammaticality of (85b) and (86b) bears out. In this respect, adjunct-SCs differ markedly from complement-SCs, whose predicates are generally extractable in English (cf. (87b)).

(85)   a.   John$_i$ left the room [$_{SC}$ PRO$_i$ angry].
        b.   *How angry did John leave the room?

(86)   a.   John ate the meat$_i$ [$_{SC}$ PRO$_i$ raw].
        b.   *How raw did John eat the meat?

(87)   a.   John painted [$_{SC}$ the door green].
        b.   How green did John paint the door?

Several suggestions have been made in the literature to account for the deviance of the b-examples in (85)–(86) (cf. esp. Roberts 1988; Rizzi 1990:48–50).[40] In the present context, however, suffice it to say that the appropriate descriptive generalisation covering these cases states that the predicate of a SC in adjoined position resists movement. In the light of this generalisation, the grammaticality of (84) is problematic for an analysis of prepositional complex particle constructions according to which the transitive PP is the predicate of an adjunct-SC.[41]

With respect to the two remaining strategies (ii) and (iii), note that adopting either one of these mechanisms to satisfy PP's external θ-role in (79b) runs the risk of forfeiting at least part of the motivation for assuming a SC analysis of subject-predicate relationships. Consider, by way of exemplification, a copula construction like (88):

(88)   John is intelligent.

The SC analysis would assume that *John* in (88) originates in the subject position of a SC in the complement of the copula, being raised to SpecIP in the course of the derivation (for Case reasons). Suppose, however, that the external θ-role of the adjective *intelligent* were capable of "making its way" to SpecIP directly, via either of the two strategies mentioned above. Then *John* could be base-generated in SpecIP, and the copula would feature a "bare" (i.e. non-SC) AP complement. In effect, adopting either one of the mechanisms expounded above would result in an analogue of a Williams (1980, 1994) type Predication analysis, and would be incompatible with the spirit of the SC analysis. Since I subscribe to the latter, it is evident that I cannot embrace "repair strategies" (ii) and (iii) that could allow proponents of (79b) to steer clear of a Theta Criterion violation. This being the case, it is also obvious that an analysis of prepositional complex particle constructions along the lines of (79b) is not available.

In all fairness, however, I should mention here one apparent piece of evidence against treating the post-particle PP in prepositional complex particle constructions as a SC predicate. The evidence concerns Dutch PP-extraposition.

Dutch is an SOV language (Koster 1975; but cf. Kayne 1993b, Zwart 1993). As such, it generates the complements to the verb to the left of the head at D-structure. All (non-adjunct) PPs, then, originate on the left-hand side of the verb. Some PPs, however, may optionally be extraposed to the right periphery of the clause. Consider the examples in (89) and (90):

---

[40] Not all speakers agree on their ill-formedness (cf. e.g. Hornstein & Lightfoot 1987:27, fn. 4), but this does not affect the point made here, there being absolutely no uncertainty about the status of examples like (84).

[41] In connection with option (i), i.e. the PRO strategy, also recall the discussion in fn. 15, above, on the problems that a PRO approach to the *make out a liar* construction runs into.

(89) a.   dat Jan (*aan taalkunde*) dacht (*aan taalkunde*).
            that Jan (of linguistics) thought (of linguistics)
      b.   dat Jan (*op zijn moeder*) wachtte (*op zijn moeder*).
            that Jan (for his mother) waited (for his mother)
(90) a.   dat Jan het boek (*op de plank*) zette (**op de plank*).
            that Jan the book (on the shelf) put (on the shelf)
      b.   dat Jan het boek (*op de plank*) **neer** zette (*op de plank*).
            that Jan the book (on the shelf) down put (on the shelf)

The application of the Dutch PP-extraposition process known as *PP-over-V*
(Koster 1973) is severely restricted (cf. Hoekstra 1984 for discussion). While
the examples in (89) show that extraposition of non-predicative PPs is free,
prepositional SC predicates such as *op de plank* in (90a) resist being extraposed.
Suppose that on the basis of an investigation of (89) and (90a) we were to come
to the conclusion that Dutch PP-over-V targets all and only PPs that are *not*
predicates of complement-SCs. Then the fact that PP-extraposition is possible
in (90b) (which differs minimally from (90a) in that it contains a particle, *neer*
'down') would lead us to conclude that in prepositional complex particle constructions like (90b), the transitive PP is not a SC predicate. In other words, if
the descriptive generalisation concerning Dutch PP-over-V were to read as in
the above, we would be forced into adopting an analysis of prepositional complex particle constructions of the type in (79b).

At this stage I can only note this potential argument for an analysis along the
lines of (79b) in passing, returning to the proper treatment of Dutch PP-
extraposition more extensively in section 3.11.2. Briefly skipping ahead to that
discussion, however, I would like to point out here that the informal descriptive
generalisation covering Dutch PP-over-V mentioned above is probably inadequate. In particular, it would seem to be overly restrictive, in that a well-
defined class of complement-SC PP predicates turns out to be perfectly capable
of undergoing extraposition in Dutch — PP-over-V fails to apply to all and only
those PPs that are the predicate of a SC in the complement of a verb. The
present analysis of prepositional complex particle constructions is perfectly
compatible with this generalisation, which will be reduced to independent ingredients of the theory in section 3.11.2. Referring the reader to that section for
more discussion of the distribution of Dutch PP-over-V, I conclude here that
this phenomenon does not lend unequivocal support to an analysis of prepositional complex particle constructions based on (79b).

In sum, then, there seems to be no reason to abandon the "uniform D-
structure" approach to the whole set of complex particle constructions propounded in section 2.3.3 in favour of an analysis employing different underlying
structures for the various instances of this construction type. On the contrary,
an account along the latter lines appears to face theoretical problems which our
alternative steers clear of.

2.3.5 An inventory of complex particle constructions

Before leaving the topic of complex particle constructions, I would like to finish section 2.3 by providing what I hope is an exhaustive inventory of the types of sentences that can be built on the template underlying complex particle constructions, repeated in (91) (order irrelevant):

(91) $[_{VP}$ V $[_{SC1}$ $[_{Spec\theta'}$ *ec*] $[_{PP}$ Prt $[_{SC2}$ NP XP]]]]

In each of the following subsections I shall highlight a specific instantiation of XP, considering both English and Dutch example material. It will turn out as we proceed that for every logically possible type of XP, actual existing candidates can be found.

2.3.5.1 Nominal complex particle constructions

From the discussion in section 2.3.3 we are already familiar with an example of the structure in (91) with XP=NP:

(92)   They made John *out* **a liar**.

This is perhaps the least controversial of conceivable candidates for the overall structure in (91). The post-particle NP is unmistakably predicative, hence — given the basic tenets of the SC analysis — a SC predicate, and generating the SC that *a liar* is the predicate of in the subject position of the particle-headed SC (as in Kayne 1985) has been shown to be problematic in several ways — *ergo*: only (91) remains.

It might perhaps be felt that building any sort of syntactic argument on the example in (92) is suspect in view of the fact that (92) is a fairly isolated case which, moreover, seems to be acceptable to a subset of the English speaking community only.[42] In response to such criticism, I would like point out that, while admittedly rare in transitive contexts, nominal complex particle constructions are productive in ergative environments featuring the verb-particle combinations *turn out* and *end up* (cf. Kayne 1985:107; also cf. fn. 45, below):

(93) a.   John turned *out* **a liar**.
      b.   John ended *up* **a linguist**.

In addition, Jackendoff (1977) mentions the particle-verb *grow up* and its transitive counterpart *bring up* as candidates for the template in (91):

---

[42] Especially British English speakers seem on the whole quite uncomfortable with (92).

(94)   a.   John grew *up* a **Catholic**.
       b.   They brought John *up* a **Catholic**.

English nominal complex particle constructions do not have a perfect match in Dutch. Dutch counterparts of sentences like (92) or (94) invariably feature a preposition in front of the boldface NP:

(95)   a.   Ze maakten Jan *uit* <u>voor</u> **leugenaar**.[43]
            they made Jan out for liar
       b.   Jan groeide *op* <u>als</u>/<u>tot</u> **katholiek**.
            Jan grew up as/to Catholic
       c.   Ze voedden Jan *op* <u>als</u>/<u>tot</u> **katholiek**.
            they brought Jan up as/to Catholic

The occurrence of prepositions like *als* 'as' and *tot* 'to' in the Dutch cognates of English complex particle constructions is consistent with the fact that such prepositions also show up in the Dutch counterparts of English secondary predication constructions featuring such verbs as *consider* or *appoint*, which in Dutch typically contain a verbal affix like *be-* (cf. (97)). Hoekstra, Lansu & Westerduin (1987) analyse this verbal affix as a SC head. In chapter 5, this analysis will be taken up in detail, *be-* being analysed as an affixal particle. This being the case, (95) and (97) are entirely on a par as far as their structures are concerned, which helps us understand the uniform appearance of *als/tot* in front of the predicate nominal in these constructions.[44]

(96)   a.   They consider John a fool.
       b.   They appointed him general.

(97)   a.   Ze *be*schouwen Jan <u>als</u> een idioot.
            they BEsee ('consider') Jan as a fool
       b.   Ze *be*noemden hem <u>tot</u> generaal.
            they BEcalled ('appointed') him to general.

2.3.5.2 *Adjectival complex particle constructions*

Complex particle constructions with XP=AP, like their nominal counterparts, have a somewhat limited distribution. Jackendoff's (1977) example instantiating this type is repeated here as (98):

---

[43]   This example is not semantically equivalent to English (92); this is irrelevant in the present context, however.

[44]   I refer to Aarts (1992) for an analysis of markers like Dutch *als/tot/voor* and English *as/for* as lexicalisations of the functional head of SC.

(98)   They painted the barn *up* **red**.

In ergative *turn out* contexts, adjectival complex particle constructions can be found as well:

(99) a.   The weather turned *out* **fine** after all.
      b.   Nothing ever turned *out* **right**.
      c.   John turned *out* **intelligent**.

In section 2.3.3, I consistently (but often implicitly) treated adjectival complex particle constructions on a par with nominal cases, particularly because of the fact that with respect to the particle-placement differential, (98) patterns exactly like (92):

(100)   They made (*⁷*out*) John (*out*) **a liar** (**out*).
(101)   They painted (*⁷*up*) the barn (*up*) **red** (**up*).

The parallelism between (100) and (101) extends to their behaviour under extraction of the predicate of the particle's SC complement:[45]

(102)   *What kind of a liar did they make (*out*) John (*out*)?
(103)   *How red/What colour did they paint (*up*) the barn (*up*)?

The match between nominal and adjectival complex particle constructions follows from the analysis presented in section 2.3.3. In both cases the particle's SC complement is a barrier — it is neither L-marked (the particle not being a lexical element) nor categorially non-distinct from the particle.

Unlike in the case of nominal complex particle constructions, Dutch does have direct cognates of English adjectival complex particle constructions. Some examples are given in (104):

---

[45] Kayne (1985:112) notes that in ergative adjectival complex particle constructions with *end up* or *turn out*, extraction of the adjectival SC predicate is possible (cf. (i)). Kyle Johnson points out to me that the adjectival cases do not seem to differ in this respect from their nominal counterparts with *end up* (cf. (ii)); Joe Emonds, p.c., rejects (ii), however. Exactly how to accommodate this is unclear. Kayne's suggestion that Case Theory is crucially implicated in the restrictions on the extractability of the secondary predicate seems dubious in view of the poor status of the passive counterpart of (102) (cf. (iii)), as Kayne also notes. (The remarks in fn. 53, below, might shed some light on the questions raised by *turn out* and *end up*, if these — in contrast to *make out* — involve raising of the particle's entire SC complement to SpecSC1. I cannot work this out here.)

(i)   a.   How intelligent did he turn *out*?
      b.   How poor did he end *up*?
(ii)   (*)How good a linguist did he finally end *up*?
(iii)   ??What kind of a liar has he been made *out* this time?

(104) a.   dat ze de schuur **rood** *over* hebben geschilderd.
            that they the barn red PRT have painted
      b.   dat ze de schuur **rood** *af* hebben gelakt.
            that they the barn red PRT have varnished
      c.   dat ze de schuur **rood** *bij* hebben geverfd.[46]
            that they the barn red PRT have painted

Though the contrast between the particle constructions in (105) and the particle-less cases in (106) is not as sharp as in English (cf. (103)), Dutch seems to essentially correspond to English with respect to the impossibility of extraction in these complex particle constructions:

(105) a.   ??Hoe rood/Wat voor kleur hebben ze de schuur *over* geschilderd?
            how red/what for colour have they the barn PRT painted
      b.   ??Hoe rood/Wat voor kleur hebben ze de schuur *af* gelakt?
            how red/what for colour have they the barn PRT varnished

---

[46] This example has been adapted from Neeleman (1994:331–32, n. 7). Neeleman disagrees with my claim that the adjectival phrase is a *resultative* secondary predicate, on account of the semantic intuition that 'the act of touching up does not lead to a [red barn]'. Neeleman thus takes the apparent lack of a "holistic" or "totally affected" interpretation of the sentence to indicate that an analysis of adjectival complex particle constructions along the lines of (91) is untenable. But then, by the same token, a resultative approach to (104c) *without* the adjective *rood* 'red' (i.e. *dat ze de schuur bij hebben geverfd*), which similarly lacks (or certainly does not force) a reading in which the entire barn is covered with new paint, would also have to be abandoned. The adjective in (104c) does not seem to play a crucial role here. And in (104a), for instance, the barn does certainly end up all covered with red paint, so Neeleman's objection — if valid at all for (104c) — cannot be taken to apply to the class of adjectival complex particle constructions in general. As a final note in connection with Neeleman's objection to a resultative analysis of the adjectival phrase, let me draw attention to the fact that the extraction data presented in (105) seem tractable only on a (91) based analysis of (104), not on an approach that takes the AP to be some sort of modifier ('with red paint') — such modifiers are normally extractable in Dutch.

In the same note, Neeleman also points out another interesting example of what may seem to be an adjectival complex particle construction, reproduced below as (i). It is unlikely that this is really a case of an adjectival complex particle construction of the general type in (91), though. As Neeleman notes, (i) is presumably an unergative construction, like its adjective-less counterpart *dat de krant afgeeft* 'that the newspaper off-gives (i.e. gives one filthy hands)'. Moreover, *afgeven* also figures in transitive constructions like *dat dat spul een rare lucht afgeeft* 'that that stuff a funny smell off-gives'. Although this hypothesis should have to be investigated in much fuller detail, I tentatively suggest that *zwart* in (i) is the adjectival modifier of a zero-headed NP that functions as the particle's argument — (i) will then be underlyingly analysed as *dat de krant (een) zwart(e kleur) afgeeft* 'that the newspaper (a) black (colour) off-gives'. Analysed this way, (i) is not an instance of (91), but a disguised example of a run-of-the-mill simple transitive verb-particle construction like *dat hij de brief afgeeft* 'that he the letter off-gives (i.e. delivers)'.

(i)   dat de krant zwart afgeeft.
             that the newspaper black off-gives

(106) a.   Hoe rood/Wat voor kleur hebben ze de schuur geschilderd?
            how red/what for colour have they the barn painted
     b.   Hoe rood/Wat voor kleur hebben ze de schuur gelakt?
            how red/what for colour have they the barn varnished

The parallel between English and Dutch adjectival complex particle constructions with respect to the extractability of SC2's predicate suggests that Dutch
assigns complex particle constructions the same underlying structure as do
English and Norwegian. It would of course be quite surprising if things had not
been like this. Since the thematic organisation of complex particle constructions
does not seem to vary cross-linguistically, subjecting these constructions to
different D-structure analyses in different languages would have been flatly
irreconcilable with (a cross-linguistic formulation of) Baker's (1988) UTAH (cf.
chapter 1).

Interestingly, while (105) are predictably deviant, Dutch has a way of questioning the colour which the barn ended up having as a result of the activity
denoted by the verb-particle combination, a possibility which again fits in
directly with the discussion of English complex particle constructions in section
2.3.3. Alongside (104b), Dutch has a semantically equivalent construction in
which the role of the adjective *rood* is played by a PP containing this adjective,
as is shown in (107a). This PP can undergo *wh*-fronting, as in (107b):

(107) a.   dat ze de schuur **in een rode kleur** *over* hebben geschilderd.
            that they the barn in a red colour PRT have painted
     b.   In wat voor kleur hebben ze de schuur *over* geschilderd?
            in what for colour have they the barn PRT painted

The grammaticality of (107b) in contrast to the deviance of (105) is of course
fully in line with our expectations. After all, if the predicate of the particle's SC
complement is categorially non-distinct from the particle, the SC in question is
exempt from barrierhood (by virtue of being a *segment* of the particle-headed
SC). The trace left by *wh*-extraction of PP can hence be properly governed in
accordance with the ECP. In (105), by contrast, an ECP violation is unavoid-
able.

2.3.5.3 Prepositional complex particle constructions

The properties of prepositional complex particle constructions in both English
and Dutch, representative examples of which are repeated here as (108) and
(109), were extensively addressed in sections 2.3.3 and 2.3.4.

(108)   They put (*down*) the books (*down*) on the shelf (*down).

(109)   dat ze de boeken (*neer*) op de plank (*neer*) hebben (*neer*) gezet.
           that they the books (down) on the shelf (down) have (down) put

In the discussion in these sections, it was noted that extraction of the transitive
PP in English prepositional complex particle constructions is possible only if the
particle is *reanalysed* with the verb. This is evident from the fact that the
particle, in such cases, always precedes the subject of the lower SC.

In English, verb-particle reanalysis is *abstract* incorporation, taking place at
LF. In Dutch, overt syntactic particle incorporation is possible. This is shown
by the fact that particles can be part of the verb cluster created by Verb
Raising, as in the variant of (109) in which *neer* 'down' finds itself between
hebben 'have' and *gezet* 'put'. Extraction of the transitive PP in Dutch (109)
does not *require* the particle to be integrated into the verb cluster, however.
That is, (110a), in which *neer* finds itself outside the clause-final verb cluster
hebben gezet, is just acceptable as (110b), in which particle incorporation has
demonstrably taken place:

(110) a.   Op welke plank zouden ze de boeken *neer* hebben gezet?
           on which shelf would they the books down have put
      b.   Op welke plank zouden ze de boeken hebben *neer* gezet?

In view of what I argued with respect to the structure of complex particle
constructions and the restrictions on extraction earlier in this chapter, it is clear,
however, that particle incorporation must have taken place in (110a) as well.
I assume, therefore, that in (110a) the particle does in fact incorporate into the
participle *gezet*, but that it is *stranded* under further movement of the verb later
in the derivation. In particular, I suggest that the complex V^0-node created by
particle incorporation is split up in (110a) (but not in (110b)) as a result of the
excorporation of the verb from the V–Prt complex (cf. Roberts 1991 on excorporation). The relevant part of the structure of (110a) hence reads as in
(111):[47]

(111) $[_{CP}$ PP$_i$ zouden ze $[_{VP1}$ $[_{VP2}$ $[_{SC1}$ $[_{PP1}$ $[_{SC2}$ de boeken $t_i]$ $t_j]]$
           $[_{V2}$ neer$_j$+$t_k]]$ $[_{V1}$ hebben+gezet$_k]]]$

2.3.5.4 To-*infinitival complex particle constructions*

Just like the *make out a liar* construction (92), the corresponding *make out to
be a liar* construction occurs in both transitive and ergative contexts:

---

[47]   I abstract away completely from the irrelevant modal *zouden*, which projects its own VP;
including it in (111) would render this structure unnecessarily complicated.

(112) a.   They made John *out* **to be a liar.**
      b.   John turned *out* **to be a liar.**

In addition, an aspectual construction like (113) probably instantiates the pattern of (unaccusative) complex particle constructions:

(113)   The baby dropped/went *off* **to sleep.**

The example in (113) paves the way for a discussion of verbal complex particle constructions, the only instance of the general schema that I did not pay any attention to in the foregoing discussion.

2.3.5.5 Verbal complex particle constructions

Though the distribution of complex particle constructions in which $X=V$ appears to be limited both lexically and geographically,[48] some dialects of Dutch feature verbal complex particle constructions of the type in (114). Of these examples, (114b) is from the West-Frisian dialect (cf. Pannekeet 1984), and (114c) (cf. Boekenoogen 1897) was recorded in a dialect spoken in the Zaandam area, to the north-west of Amsterdam.

(114) a.   De baby ging **slapen** *heen.*
          the baby went sleep PRT
          'The baby fell asleep straightaway.' or:
          'The baby dropped off to sleep.'   (cf. (113))
     b.   Hai gong **loupen** *heen.*
          he went walk PRT
          'He went walking.'
     c.   Hij ging weer **werken** *heen.*
          he went again work PRT
          'He went to work again.'

As the English translations suggest, verbal complex particle constructions of the type in (114) have an aspectual meaning. The particle essentially seems to contribute a sense of immediacy to the particle-less, and likewise aspectual constructions with simple *gaan* 'go'. This is especially evident from a comparison of (114a) and (115):

---

[48] The Dutch constructions in (114) are roughly found in North-Holland (the north-western part of the country), north of Amsterdam. Naarding (1951) discusses the semantically parallel and geographically more widespread *heengaan en* (and) *V* construction. In section 3.13.2 I shall present data from verb-serialising languages which are further instantiations of the general schema in (91) with $X=V$. In these constructions, however, the position of the particle is left unlexicalised.

(115)   De baby ging slapen.
           the baby went sleep
           'The baby went to sleep.'

In section 2.3.6 I shall turn to an interesting word-order difference between
(114) and (115).

2.3.5.6 On particle recursion

For all category types of the XP node in the basic structural template underlying
complex particle constructions in (91), I have shown that actual examples can
be found in the grammars of English and Dutch, thereby giving an illustration
of the pervasiveness of this structure. There is one logically conceivable instantiation of this template which I have so far ignored: a subset of prepositional
complex particle constructions in which the head of XP is itself a *particle*.
Though quite rare, such multiple particle constructions do actually seem to
exist, as Di Sciullo & Klipple's (1994) examples in (116) show.[49] And Dutch
fairly productively embeds particle-headed SCs under *affixal* particles like *be-*
or *ver-* (cf. also section 3.15.2 and chapter 5, below), as can be seen in (117).

(116) a.   Go *on over* to Grandma's house.   (Di Sciullo & Klipple 1994)
      b.   I'll send the letter *on over* to Grandma's house.
      c.   I'll send *on over* the letter from Grandma.

(117) a.   *af/terug-be*-talen   'off/back-BE-pay'   (pay off/back)
      b.   *door-ver*-binden   'through-VER-bind'   (connect)
      c.   *uit-ver*-groten   'out-VER-make.large'   (enlarge)
      d.   *weg-be*-zuinigen   'away-BE-economise'   (economise away)

There does not seem to be a structural reason for the paucity of constructions
involving particle recursion. Guéron's (1990:162) attempt to derive it from the
claim that particles cannot embed resultative SCs fails in the light of the analysis of such constructions as *They put the books down on the shelf* or *They
painted the barn up red* presented in the above. Particle recursion is structurally
possible (witness (116) and (117)) but rare, for reasons unclear to me.

---

[49] Guéron (1990:162) gives two ungrammatical examples of particle recursion (cf. (i)). Of these,
(ia) is predictably deviant given the analysis of particles as ergative SC heads. And (ib) can be made
fully grammatical by deleting *out*: *She put the book back down*. It is unlikely, though, that this
example represents embedding of one particle under another, *back* presumably being a modifier of
down rather than a head taking *down* as its complement. This use of *back* (basically equivalent to
the adverb *again*) is also frequent in Flemish varieties of Dutch, with the particle *terug* 'back'.

(i)   a.   *She took Bill *out* the book *down*.   (Guéron 1990)
      b.   *She put the book *back out down*.

2.3.6 On the non-lexical status of particles

At this point, let me return to the Dutch examples of adjectival complex particle constructions (104). It is interesting to note that in these examples, in contrast to their particle-less counterparts in (118) and (119), incorporation of the adjective into the verb is impossible, regardless of where the particle is positioned. This is shown by the examples in (120) and (121):

(118) a. dat ze de schuur **rood** hebben geschilderd.
          that they the barn red have painted
   b. dat ze de schuur hebben **rood** geschilderd.
          that they the barn have red painted

(119) a. dat ze de schuur **rood** hebben gelakt.
          that they the barn red have varnished
   b. dat ze de schuur hebben **rood** gelakt.
          that they the barn have red varnished

(120) a. dat ze de schuur **rood** *over* hebben geschilderd.
          that they the barn red PRT have painted
          dat ze de schuur **rood** hebben *over* geschilderd.
   b. *dat ze de schuur *over* hebben **rood** geschilderd.
          *dat ze de schuur hebben *over* **rood** geschilderd.
          *dat ze de schuur hebben **rood** *over* geschilderd.

(121) a. dat ze de schuur **rood** *af* hebben gelakt.
          that they the barn red PRT have varnished
          dat ze de schuur **rood** hebben *af* gelakt.
   b. *dat ze de schuur *af* hebben **rood** gelakt.
          *dat ze de schuur hebben *af* **rood** gelakt.
          *dat ze de schuur hebben **rood** *af* gelakt.

A similar restriction on incorporation turns out to be operative in dialectal Dutch verbal complex particle constructions of the type in (114). Thus, while *slapen* 'sleep' may (in fact must) undergo Verb Raising in (122), it may not in (123), again irrespective of the surface position of the particle.

(122) a. *dat de baby **slapen** is gegaan.
          that the baby sleep is gone
   b. dat de baby is gaan **slapen**.
          that the baby is gone sleep
          'that the baby has gone to sleep.'

(123) a.   dat de baby **slapen** *heen* is gegaan.
           that the baby sleep PRT is gone
      b.   *dat de baby *heen* is gaan **slapen**.
           *dat de baby is *heen* gaan **slapen**.
           *dat de baby is gaan *heen* **slapen**.

While the infinitive in (122) is verbal and must be incorporated into the Tense-
chain (cf. Guéron & Hoekstra 1988; Bennis & Hoekstra 1988), the infinitive in
(123) is a *nominal infinitive*.

Why is it that a particle, regardless of whether it itself undergoes incorporation or not, blocks incorporation into the verb of the head of the particle's
complement? As a first approximation, let us observe that the particle structurally *intervenes* between the prospective incorporate and the incorporating verb,
given the structure of complex particle constructions that I motivated in section
2.3.3. In (124), this structure is reproduced, tailored to the SOV phrase structure of Dutch:

(124) $[_{VP} [_{SC1}$ Spec $[_{PP} [_{SC2}$ NP $[_{XP} (...) X (...)]]$ Prt$]]$ V$]$

XP in (124) does not find itself in the immediate governing domain of the verb.
The particle is a "closer governor", hence may be expected to draw up a
Minimality barrier to the incorporation of X into V.

Notice, however, that it is not immediately obvious that the particle will
count as an intervener if the particle is itself incorporated into the verb. After
all, Baker (1988) argues on the basis of a range of data that incorporation
extends the governing domain of the incorporator (cf. his Government Transparency Corollary, quoted in section 1.2.5, and repeated as (57) above). By
incorporating the particle into V, the V+Prt complex would hence seem to
come to govern the particle's complement, the head of which might then be
directly incorporable into the verb. As an alternative strategy, one might also
consider a successive-cyclic approach, whereby X first incorporates into the
particle, after which the newly formed complex head undergoes further incorporation into the verb. In either case, we might expect incorporation of X into
V in (124) to be licit whenever the particle is also incorporated into V, contrary
to fact. What, then, rules out these two scenarios?

First note that even if the particle incorporates into the verb, we still have to
reckon with the status of the particle's complement as a barrier to outside
government. Particle incorporation does not have any influence on the barrierhood of Prt's complement. In the cases under discussion, (120) and (123), the
particle takes an adjectival and a verbal SC, respectively. Being categorially
distinct from the particle and not L-marked, these count as barriers (cf. section
2.3.3). The "long-distance incorporation" scenario sketched in the previous
paragraph can then of course be ruled out straightforwardly in the specific cases

of (120) and (123): if the prospective incorporates were to skip the particle position on their way to the matrix verb, their traces would fail to be antecedent governed due to the intervention of a barrier (SC2 in (124)).[50]

Suppose, however, that the prospective incorporates first incorporated into the particle position, thereby turning this position into a *lexical* head position, which may then be expected to L-mark its SC complement (cf. Chomsky's 1986 suggestion with regard to the barrier removing effect of V-to-I movement). Suppose, in other words, that the successive-cyclic incorporation strategy were adopted. Then, the ECP could be complied with, the barrierhood of SC2 being voided.

This scenario can nonetheless be blocked by invoking Li's (1990) extension of the scope of the Binding Theory into the domain of heads, which I briefly discussed in chapter 1 (section 1.2.5). A putative successive-cyclic incorporation approach to the constructions in (120) and (123) can then be ruled out as a case of "improper head movement" once we bear in mind that, as argued in section 2.3.3, particles are non-lexical, A'-heads. In the structure in (124), incorporation of X into Prt followed by incorporation into V will then be an illicit case of A-A'-A head-movement, violating Principle C of the (extended) Binding Theory.[51]

---

[50] In section 3.10.2, I shall return to the "long-distance incorporation" scenario in the context of prepositional complex particle constructions, in which the particle's complement is not a barrier. It will be shown that even in these cases, long-distance incorporation is not a theoretical possibility.

[51] Hans Bennis (p.c.) raises the question of how the (extended) Binding Theory allows for V–Prt reanalysis given that, on my assumptions, it involves incorporation of an A'-head into an A-head. In chapter 1, fn. 23 I noted that as the initial trace in such cases does not count as a variable, BT–C effectively rules in A'-to-A movement (unattested in the domain of XP-movement for independent reasons); A-A'-A movement is ruled out, the initial trace in the A-position being a variable.

Though their status as non-lexical prepositions (cf. Van Riemsdijk 1990) seems to me to be sufficient evidence for the A'-status of particles, the proposed A'-status of Prt may not immediately fall out from Li's specific assumptions with regard to the A/A' distinction, given in (i). Since I assume that Prt θ-marks its complement, Prt should qualify as an A-head rather than as an A'-head on these assumptions. Note, however, that (i) is not directly compatible with Chomsky's (1986) suggestion that Infl θ-marks its VP complement either, if (as seems likely, given that it does not incorporate into lexical heads) Infl is an A'-head. Either, as Li (1990:407, fn. 5) suggests, there are different types of θ-roles, some of which do and others do not count for the definition in (i), or θ-marking should not be as crucially implicated in the definition of A/T-positions as it is in (i). That the latter tack is probably correct is suggested by the fact that the original definition on which (i) is based, given in (ii), is untenable in the light of recent developments in the theory according to which subjects are base-generated below SpecIP (cf. Kuroda 1986; Fukui & Speas 1986; Sportiche 1988; Koopman & Sportiche 1988, 1991): while on such a view, SpecIP is *never* a θ-position, it must nonetheless continue to count as an A-position (at least in a significant set of cases).

(i)   A T-position ["θ-related", basically A-position, MD] is a D-structural position to *or from* which a θ-role can in principle be assigned.   (Li 1990:407; original italics)

(ii)   An A-position is a D-structural position to which a θ-role can in principle be assigned.

Thus, both the "long-distance incorporation" scenario and the successive-cyclic strategy for the derivation of examples like (120) and (123) have been eliminated. Since the theory leaves us with no other potential ways of deriving constructions of this type, we are now led to the theoretical conclusion that these cases should be ill-formed. Since this is exactly what they are, this is a desirable result.

Let me finish this subsection with one further empirical illustration of the ban on incorporation across an intervening particle. In English, aspectual constructions like (125a), containing the infinitival marker *to*, alternate with *to*-less constructions such as (125b), provided that the matrix aspectual verb does not bear overt flection (cf. Jaeggli & Hyams 1993; Pollock 1990):

(125) a.   They go to see a movie.
      b.   They go see a movie.

Pollock (1990) argues that in English *to*-less aspectual constructions like (125b), the infinitival verb is obligatorily incorporated into the matrix aspectual verb (at LF, like English particle incorporation). This leads us to expect that once we add a particle to the pair in (125), the alternation should break down. Since the particle blocks verb incorporation, only the variant containing *to* should yield a grammatical output. This expectation is fulfilled, as is shown by the examples in (126) and (127) (cf. (127b) to its Dutch cognate in (123)):

(126) a.   They go *off* to see a movie.
      b.   *They go *off* see a movie.
            *They go see *off* a movie.

(127) a.   The baby always drops *off* to sleep at once.
      b.   *The baby always drops *off* sleep at once.
            *The baby always drops sleep *off* at once.

The ill-formed b-examples in (126) and (127) are analogous to the Dutch V-incorporation constructions in (123), which are likewise ungrammatical. That in Dutch ungrammaticality can be avoided by not incorporating the thematic verb into the verb cluster is due to the fact that Dutch features nominal infinitivals with bare infinitives, lacking the infinitival marker *te*. English, by contrast, has no bare infinitival nominals; instead, English employs *to*-infinitivals to this end. The minimal pair in (128) ((128b) being the literal Dutch translation of English (128a)) testifies to this difference between English and Dutch:

(128) a.   *(*to*) err is human.
      b.   (**te*) vergissen is menselijk.

In aspectual constructions, whenever incorporation of the thematic verb into the matrix aspectual verb is barred, a nominal infinitival is used. For English, this entails that in such cases a *to*-infinitive is the only option.

The blocking effect of a particle on the incorporation of the head of its complement into the verb governing the particle-headed SC, of which I discussed several instantiations in this subsection, can thus be shown to confirm the hypothesis that particles are non-lexical heads, if we adopt Li's (1990) extension of the Binding Theory to heads.[52] [53]

---

[52] The non-lexical status of particles appears to cause problems in the domain of simplex particle constructions like (ia), when we bear in mind that subextraction from the NP following the particle yields a perfectly grammatical result (ib) (in contrast to subextraction from the NP in *pre*-particle position, which follows from Kayne's 1984 Connectedness Condition).

(i)   a.   They looked *up* the information about air pollution.
         b.   What$_i$ did they look [$_{SC}$ *up* [$_{DP}$ the information about t_i]]?

If the particle is non-lexical, hence not an L-marker, then why does (ib) not violate Subjacency, extraction apparently taking place across two barriers (DP and the particle-headed SC, which would inherit barrierhood from DP)? Part of the answer must presumably be sought in the possibility (pointed out to me by Guido Vanden Wyngaerd) that *what* uses SpecDP as an "escape hatch" on its way out (cf. also the deterioration arising if SpecDP is overtly filled: *??What did they look up John's information about?*), though care is needed to ensure that this voids the inherent DP barrier.

[53] If *calm* in the particle verb *calm down* is a deadjectival verb syntactically derived through the incorporation of the base adjective *calm* into an abstract verb (cf. Mulder 1992b; Pesetsky 1993), and if the structure underlying *calm down* is of the type reflected by (91) (cf. (i)), a difficult question arises regarding the way in which *calm* manages to incorporate into the verb across the particle. Both direct and successive-cyclic incorporation being blocked, some other way must be found to manoeuvre the adjective into a position close enough to the verb to enable it to incorporate into it. A way to do this may be to move the entire SC2 to the specifier position of the particle, as depicted in (ii). Then A, being the head of the specifier governed by the verb, can incorporate into V (cf. section 1.2.4 on incorporation from governed specifiers). Moving SC2 to SpecSC1 will create an S-structure configuration which is identical with the base structure that Mulder (1992b: 228) assigns to complex (affixal) particle constructions like *de verf verdunnen* 'to thin the paint', given in (iii), and which also serves as the input to adjective incorporation into V. Notice that Dutch *verdunnen* (with the affixal particle *ver-*; cf. also chapter 5) has a "real particle" variant *uitdunnen* 'out-thin'. Given that I analyse *ver-*, like *uit*, as an ergative SC-head, I would replace Mulder's (iii) with a structure along the lines of (ii); but the two representations share a predication relation (underlying or derived; cf. Chomsky 1993:21 and Mulder & Den Dikken 1992 on S-structure predication in *tough*-movement constructions) between the (affixal) particle and the proposition denoted by SC2. This approach to *calm down* type constructions does not lead to unwanted massive incorporability of the head of SC2 into V in complex particle constructions if the option of raising SC2 to SpecSC1 is appropriately curbed — SC2 may move to SpecSC1 only if it makes semantic sense to have the head of SC1 predicated of a state of affairs (proposition) rather than an individual.

(i)   [$_{VP}$ V [$_{SC1}$ Spec [$_{PP}$ *down* [$_{SC2}$ NP [$_{AP}$ *calm*]]]]]
(ii)   [$_{VP}$ V [$_{SC1}$ [$_{SC2}$ NP [$_{AP}$ *calm*]]$_i$ [$_{PP}$ *down* [$_{SC2}$ t_i]]]]
(iii)   [$_{VP}$ V [$_{SC1}$ [$_{SC2}$ *de verf* [$_{AP}$ *dun*]] [$_{PrtP}$ *ver-*]]]   (adapted from Mulder 1992b:228)

2.4 Simplex particle constructions

After the extensive discussion of the properties of complex particle constructions, the closing section of chapter 2 will now address a number of questions
arising in connection with the analysis of simplex particle constructions of the
familiar type illustrated in (129):

(129) a.   John looked the information *up*.
      b.   John looked *up* the information.

2.4.1 Word-order alternation: The theoretical options

The well-known word-order alternation in the English verb-particle construction
in (129) has given rise to a rich variety of competing analyses in the principles-
and-parameters framework, even if we restrict ourselves to those analyses that
start off on the premise that the particle in these constructions is the predicate
of a SC in the complement of the verb.[54]

Thus, Kayne (1985) opts for an analysis of the pair in (129) according to
which the variant in (129b) is derived from the underlying word order in (129a)
through *extraposition* of the subject NP of the particle-headed SC, as illustrated
in (130a) (where, as in the other examples in (130), triple dots identify the
landing-site of movement). Kayne explicitly rejects an alternative approach to
the alternation in (129) which holds that (129b) is obtained by moving the particle into the verb, this movement operation being an instance of *head incorporation* in the sense of Baker (1988). This analysis is given in (130b). Both approaches take (129a) to represent the base-generated word order, (129b) being
derived from it. Taking the opposite tack, however, one could suggest a third
structure, given in (130c), according to which the particle is *ergative* (cf.
Guéron 1986, 1990; Koopman 1991; also cf. Taraldsen 1983). The word order
in (129a) is then obtained via NP-movement of the particle's complement into
the θ'-subject position of the particle-headed SC.

(130) a.   They looked [$_{SC}$ the information [$_{PP}$ up]] ...

      b.   They [$_V$ looked ...] [$_{SC}$ the information [$_{PP}$ up]]

      c.   They looked [$_{SC}$ [$_{NP\theta'}$ ...] [$_{PP}$ up the information]]

---

[54] Since complex verb approaches to the verb-particle construction have already been discarded (cf.
section 2.2.2, above), I shall not address these in what follows.

2.4.2 Against extraposition

In the account of complex particle constructions (particularly in section 2.3.2), I already pointed out some problems inherent in Kayne's (1985) extraposition approach in that specific domain. In this subsection I shall discuss a direct counterargument to this analysis from the context of simplex particle constructions, partially due to Svenonius (1992).

Svenonius (1992) notes that the rightward NP-movement process that is to be responsible for the derivation of V–Prt–NP word orders is distinct from an apparently highly similar process like Heavy NP Shift, particularly as far as the landing-site of the moved NP is concerned. While Heavy NP Shift positions NPs at the extreme right periphery of VP, to the right of all VP-adjoined adverbial material, the rightward NP-shift rule operative in the derivation of (129b) on Kayne's (1985) assumptions places the NP *before* other VP-contained material. This is evident from an inspection of the examples in (131):

(131) a.   They set the bomb *off* with a transmitter.
      b.   They set *off* the bomb with a transmitter.
      c.   *They set *off* with a transmitter the bomb.

The output in (131c) should be grammatical if rightward NP-shift in particle constructions were parallel to Heavy NP Shift.[55] Also, if rightward NP-shift in particle constructions parallelled Heavy NP Shift, (131b) should be underivable. Since these expectations are not borne out, the conclusion must be that rightward NP-movement in particle constructions targets a position lower than an adjunction position to VP.

Specifically, on the plausible assumption that the instrumental PP in (131) is adjoined to VP, and on the further assumption that maximal projections may adjoin only to other maximal projections (cf. Chomsky 1986, referring to Emonds' 1976 Structure Preserving Hypothesis), there is exactly one potential adjunction site for the rightward-moved NP: it can only adjoin to the particle-headed SC. This, however, is not compatible with Chomsky's (1986:6) hypothesis regarding possible adjunction structures, reproduced in (132). Since the matrix verb in all likelihood assigns a θ-role to its SC complement in a verb-particle construction, this SC qualifies as an argument, and hence is ineligible as an adjunction site for the rightward-moved NP.

(132)   Adjunction is possible only to a maximal projection (hence, X'') that is a non-argument.

---

[55] Of course, (131c) becomes grammatical (in fact, becomes a regular case of Heavy NP Shift) if the clause-final NP is sufficiently "heavy".

In conclusion, then, since the theory provides no place for NP to adjoin to, an extraposition approach to the word-order alternation in the English verb-particle construction along the lines of Kayne (1985) cannot be adopted.[56]

2.4.3 On the locus of particle incorporation

While in the account of the properties of English complex particle constructions the assumption that particles may incorporate into the verb plays an important role, I have assumed that particle incorporation in English does not take place in the overt syntax. Rather, the particle is reanalysed with the verb ("cosuperscripting" or "abstract incorporation"), actual incorporation being postponed until LF. In this subsection I shall present evidence that, although particle incorporation is involved in the account of the word-order alternation in the English verb-particle construction, the particle does not undergo overt-syntactic head movement.

Suppose (129b) were to be derived by physically incorporating the particle into the verb. Surface word order decrees that the particle land in a position to the *right* of the verb stem. Let us assume now that one of the principles governing the well-formedness of morphological constructs is Williams' (1981) Right-hand Head Rule, which defines as the head of a complex X^0-category the right-hand member of the word. Since there is no doubt that the verb is the head of the V+Prt complex, but since the verb is not the right-hand member of this complex X^0-category, right-adjunction of the particle to the verb would result in a violation of the Right-hand Head Rule.

---

[56] Svenonius (1992), while noting that SC is the only place for NP to adjoin to, does not present this as an argument against Kayne's (1985) analysis. Rather, having reached this conclusion and proceeding on the assumption that this is where NP adjoins, he goes on to present the fact that the rightward-moved NP does not license a *parasitic gap*, as shown by the deviance of (i), as evidence against Kayne's proposal.

(i) a. *I cut out a picture with my pocketknife, without really looking at.
     b. *I cut out a picture, without really looking at, with my pocketknife.
     c. *I cut out, without really looking at, a picture with my pocketknife.

This argument does not go through, however. Since for all intents and purposes the adjunct clause containing the parasitic gap is VP-adjoined, (ic) instantiates an impossible case of light NP-adjunction to VP below other VP-adjoined material (viz. the instrumental PP). The examples in (ia,b) are also straightforwardly ungrammatical due to the fact that the head of the "real" A'-chain (*a picture*) does not c-command the parasitic chain, hence is unable to bind the parasitic gap. The ill-formedness of (i) hence does not show that rightward NP-shift in particle constructions is not a regular case of A'-movement; it just shows that its landing-site is below VP, hence below VP-adjoined constituents containing parasitic gaps.

Physical, overt-syntactic particle incorporation hence cannot be responsible for the word order in (129b), on purely theoretical grounds.[57] Empirically, too, support can be adduced to the claim that particles do not physically incorporate into the verb in English. As Emonds (1993:243, fn. 27) observes, verb-particle sequences like *brush off* 'exhibit neither English compound stress (cf. the noun *brush off* and the verb *baby sit*) nor the necessarily stressless ending typical of English inflection'. This latter point is illustrated in (133):

(133) a.　Are your friends *pushin'* the car?
　　　b.　Can your friends *push in* the car?

We may hence safely conclude that English does not feature overt-syntactic particle incorporation.[58] In this regard, English differs from the related VO-languages spoken in Scandinavia, in which left-adjunction of particles to verbs does exist. Thus, Åfarli (1985:89) notes that in Norwegian, particles may surface to the left of the verb stem in passive verb-particle constructions, as in the passive counterparts of the examples in (134), given in (135):

(134) a.　Vi har (*ut*)sparka (*ut*) hunden (*ut*).
　　　　　we have (out)kicked (out) the-dog (out)
　　　b.　Vi har (**av*)klipt (*av*) tråden (*av*).
　　　　　we have (off)cut (off) the-thread (off)
　　　c.　Vi har (**bort*)kjørt (*bort*) avfallet (*bort*).
　　　　　we have (away)driven (away) the-waste (away)
(135) a.　Hunden vart (*ut*)sparka (*ut*).
　　　　　the-dog was (out)kicked (out)
　　　b.　Tråden vart (*av*)klipt (*av*).
　　　　　the-thread was (off)cut (off)
　　　c.　Avfallet vart (*bort*)kjørt (*bort*).
　　　　　the-waste was (away)driven (away)

---

[57] See also Kayne's (1993:27) conclusion that, given his Linear Correspondence Axiom, 'an adjoining head will invariably *precede* the head that it adjoins to' (my emphasis). I abstract away here from recent, Larson (1988) type approaches to English phrase structure according to which the particle might be left-adjoined to the verb, the verb excorporating from the Prt+V complex under head movement to a higher, radically empty V-position. Johnson's (1991) account of particle constructions is similar to this approach. Johnson assumes — cf. section 2.2.2 — that particles are generated as (right-hand!) members of complex V⁰-nodes.

[58] By parity of reasoning, English cannot feature overt-syntactic adjective incorporation either, so that a different analysis will have to be found for cases like *set free NP* or *cut short NP* (for which Déchaine 1993:210-11, for instance, presents a physical incorporation account, on the analogy of her physical incorporation approach to the word-order alternation in the English verb-particle construction). "Abstract incorporation", as in the case of V-Prt constructions, will work only if the "incorporable" adjectives can be argued to be ergative in the sense of Cinque (1990), which is questionable. See Neeleman (1994) for a fundamentally different account. I leave this matter open.

In Swedish, physical particle incorporation is likewise restricted to passives. The examples in (136) are parallel to their Norwegian cognates in (135):[59]

(136) a.   Hunden blev *bort*kord.
           the-dog was away-driven
      b.   Tråden blev *av*klippt.
           the-thread was off-cut

I suggest that (135) and (136) — with the particle in a position to the immediate left of the participle — should be analysed in terms of syntactic incorporation of the particle. In English, this is altogether impossible (isolated cases like *onlooker* and *bypass* presumably not being the output a syntactic incorporation process), while in Norwegian and Swedish it is restricted to passive constructions. Danish is more liberal than its fellow Mainland Scandinavian languages in this regard. While Danish particles normally follow their argument (i.e. only the "outer particle" order is found, not the V-Prt-NP order; cf. (137)), Herslund (1984:44ff.) notes that particle constructions featuring a word-order pattern in which the particle is prefixed to the verb can often be found in Danish, not just in passives but in active contexts as well. This is illustrated in (138):[60]

(137) a.   Han lukkede katten *ud*.
           he let the-cat out
      b.   *Han lukkede *ud* katten.
           he let out the-cat

(138) a.   Han *op*gav sine studier.
           he up-gave his studies
      b.   Han *over*tog forretningen efter sin far.
           he over-took the-shop after his father
      c.   Han *ud*deler billeter.
           he out-deals tickets

While in English particles are never physically incorporated into the verb, and overt particle incorporation is restricted (to a varying extent) in the Scandinavian languages, it is freely possible in Dutch (cf. Bennis 1992a for extensive exemplification) and obligatory in contemporary Romance. In the Romance languages, verbal prefixes (like French *par-* and *entre-*) represent what would be particles in languages like English.

---

[59] Thanks to Clas Garlen and Agneta Taube for providing these examples.

[60] Herslund (1984:44) stresses that particle prefixation is not a productive syntactic process; it is highly lexically conditioned, and there is not normally an alternation between incorporated and unincorporated cases with the same base verb.

It is instructive to note that, as Ménard (1973:265) and Morin & St-Amour (1977:147–48) point out, the particle-like prefix *en(t)*- could occur separated from, and to the right of, the verb in medieval French:

(139)   mais venés *ent* aveuques mi.   (*Aucassin et Nicolette* XL 42)
          but come along with me

That the particle-like prefixes of Romance are relatively independent from the verb is also shown by the fact that, in the history of French and in contemporary dialects (north of the River Loire), clitics can intervene between the verb stem and the prefix *re*-.[61] This is shown in (140a) for a dialect spoken in the north of France (cf. Morin & St-Amour 1977:148–49). Combinations of the clitic *y* and the prefix *re*- seem to prefer the order given in (140b) even in standard French, according to Morin & St-Amour. Even more strikingly perhaps, *re*- could undergo "climbing" to a higher verb in medieval French. This is shown by the examples in (141), from Morin & St-Amour (1977:148) (to which I refer for detailed references):

(140) a.   C'est bien simple, t'as qu'à *re*-lui-demander.
           it is quite simple, you have but to re-him-ask
      b.   Quand est-ce qu'on va *re*-y-aller?
           when is-it that one will re-there-go

(141) a.   Tu me *re*devroies dire ...
           you me re-should tell
      b.   Une dolors ... lor *re*fet lor joie oblier.
           a sadness them re-made their joy forget

Evidence of this sort suggests that, even in the Romance languages, particle-like prefixes originate as independent syntactic elements, undergoing incorporation into a verb in the course of the derivation (cf. also section 5.2.5, below).

Summarising the result of the above discussion, we can say that, while in all languages investigated particles are independent syntactic heads at D-structure, languages vary with respect to the locus and obligatoriness of incorporation. In Romance, syntactic incorporation is generally obligatory, in Dutch it is optional, in Scandinavian it is possible in specific contexts, and in English it is altogether ruled out. If the conclusion that English features no overt-syntactic particle movement is correct, we can now also eliminate an account of the word-order alternation in the English verb-particle construction along the lines of (130b), which is crucially dependent on the existence of syntactic particle movement.

---

[61] Keyser & Roeper (1991) have shown on the basis of English data that the prefix *re*- has much in common with verbal particles. I shall treat it on a par with particles here.

2.4.4 On the ergativity of particles

We are left, then, with the view that particles (at least those taking part in word-order alternations of the English and Norwegian type[62]) are ergative SC heads taking their sole argument *internally*. In this section, I shall first present an argument from the domain of verb-particle idioms in support of this view, and then proceed to investigating a set of apparent counterexamples to it.

2.4.4.1 Verb-particle idioms

A familiar generalisation about idiomatic expressions is that a verb can combine with an object to give rise to an idiom, but a verb normally does not form an idiom together with its subject (cf. Keenan 1976; Marantz 1984). For simple transitive constructions, this is illustrated in (142), where italicisation marks fixedness in the idiom.

(142) a.   NP *V NP* (e.g. John *kicked the bucket*)
      b.   **NP V* NP

In verb-particle constructions, idioms in which the verb, the particle and the "object NP" are all fixed parts of the idiom are typically of the "inner particle" form; i.e. the particle in such idioms typically finds itself in verb-adjacent position, to the left of the "object NP" (on the inevitable exceptions and their status, cf. fn. 63, below). E. Hoekstra (1991:109) presents the following examples of verb–particle–object idioms, where in each case the "outer particle" alternative is not idiomatic (cf. Cowie & Mackin 1993 for several other examples of V–Prt–NP idioms):

(143) a.   John will *bring up the rear*.
      b.   The search party has *given up all hope* (of ...).
      c.   Jeremy *put in a brief appearance*.
      d.   The hedgerows *put forth new buds*.
      e.   Many households *take in lodgers*.
      f.   The authorities *trumped up a case* (against X).

The fact that verb-particle idioms with a fixed "object NP" should only feature the "inner particle" order follows directly from an analysis according to which the "object NP" is generated in the complement position of the particle, as the particle's object.

---

[62]   In section 1.3, above, I briefly hinted at the possibility of analysing genuine intransitive prepositions as *unergative* particles.

Verb-particle idioms are not always of the "inner particle" form, however, as is shown by the following examples ((144a,b) adapted from Guéron 1990; (144c–e) from E. Hoekstra 1991:110), which only allow for the "outer particle" order:

(144) a.   She *stood* the fellow *up*.
     b.   He *let* the girl *down*.
     c.   The government will *see* the crisis *through*.
     d.   The police *moved* the spectators *along*.
     e.   The comedian does not *get* his jokes *across*.

In such "outer particle" idioms, the "object NP" is often *not* fixed (while in examples of the type in (143), it normally is).[63] Viewed from the perspective of the overall generalisation about fixedness in idioms, what this means is that the "object NP" in (144) must be a subject. This condition is met on the present analysis, after NP-raising of the "object NP" into the specifier position of the particle-headed SC has taken place, hence only at S-structure.

While one might perhaps successfully argue that the particles in (144c–e) are unergative rather than ergative,[64] it seems unlikely that the particles *up* and *down* used in the examples in (144a,b) are radically different from their cognates in non-idiomatic, run-of-the-mill particle constructions, for which I have argued at length (especially on the basis of the properties of complex particle constructions involving these elements) that they are ergative. The case of *up* is particularly interesting in this respect. To claim that *up* is unergative in (144a), while in all other contexts, including the V–Prt–NP idioms in (143a,b,f), it must clearly be ergative, would be an entirely *ad hoc* move motivated solely by a desire to state restrictions on idiomatic fixing in D-

---

[63] Generalisations about the restrictions on idiomatic fixing are notoriously difficult to make, exceptions often being abundant. Fraser (1974), in his study of English particle constructions and verb-particle idioms, lists several examples of such idioms in which verb, particle and object are all fixed, but which nonetheless feature the "outer particle" order (V–NP–Prt), sometimes even obligatorily (cf. Fraser 1974:19–20). Although this statement certainly does not cover all problematic cases, it generally seems to be the case that V–NP–Prt idioms in which NP is fixed allow this NP to undergo movement processes (particularly, passivisation) more freely than "well-behaved" V–Prt–NP idioms with fixed NPs. Thus, while *blow off some steam* resists the "outer particle" order, *make up one's mind* does; correlatively, NP-movement is possible in the latter (*Your mind can be made up by no one but you*) but not in the former (**Some steam was blown off at the party*), as Fraser (1970) notes. Idioms allowing for NP-movement to subject position in passives should not be taken to be subject to the claims to be made in what follows. (See also Williams 1994:4.2.2.1 on the (un)analysability of idioms: 'nothing requires that idioms be completely unanalyzable'.)

[64] E. Hoekstra (1991:110–12) essentially takes this tack, by suggesting that these directional particles are adjective-like.

structure terms.[65] A more principled tack to take would seem to be to uniformly analyse *up* as an ergative particle, and to modify the standard view on idiom formation.

That such a modification is called for is suggested entirely independently of the issue at hand by the fact that D-structure subjects, under certain circumstances, do appear to allow for idiomatic fixing. Consider the examples in (145) (cf. Coopmans & Everaert 1988:77 and references cited there).

(145) a.   *De moed zonk hem in de schoenen.*
           the courage sank him in the shoes
           'He lost courage.'
      b.   *De schellen vielen haar van de ogen.*
           the scales fell her from the eyes
           'The scales fell from her eyes.'

In defence of a thematic approach to idiomatic fixing, it is commonly pointed out in the literature that idioms of this type typically involve unaccusative verbs. The fixed subjects of (145) hence do not originate in the verb's external argument position. Notice, however, that on a SC analysis of resultative constructions (cf. T. Hoekstra 1988a for several arguments), the subjects of these idioms are still D-structure *subjects*, not of the verb itself but of the verb's SC complement. In transitive resultative constructions, the SC subject is typically *not* fixed, as Larson's (1988:340) examples in (146) show. This is in keeping with an approach to idiomatic fixing in terms of compositionality of θ-role assignment. The fixedness of the SC subjects in (145), by contrast, is clearly problematic for an account along such lines.[66]

---

[65] Note that I am not claiming that a particular head is (un)ergative once and for all. There certainly are ergativity shifts (cf. Hoekstra & Mulder 1990; chapter 5, below), but these are always *conditioned* by syntactic context: the presence of a SC complement. The examples in (143a,b,f) and (144a) are identical in all respects, however, and hence a difference between them with respect to the (un)ergativity of the particle is unlikely.

[66] Williams (1994:184) criticises this statement, and the role it plays in Larson's (1988) line of argument, with reference to such idioms as the ones listed in (i), saying that '[i]n general, ... there are idioms both of the form *V NP to X* and of the form *V X to NP*, perhaps comparable numbers of each; thus whatever D-structure representation is chosen, there will be discontinuous idioms'. This will no doubt be true; however, the amount of regularity in especially the behaviour of verb-particle idioms renders it legitimate to build at least a weak argument for my analysis on them.

(i)   a.   *pass the baton to* NP.
       b.   *put the moves on* NP.
       c.   *give the lie to* NP
cf.   d.   *de brui geven aan* NP.   (Dutch; Maaike Verrips, p.c.)
            'chuck it (in)'

(146) a. Lasorda *sent* his starting pitcher *to the showers*.
     b. Mary *took* Felix *to the cleaners*.
     c. Felix *threw* Oscar *to the wolves*.

The problems with an approach to idiom formation in terms of compositionality of θ-role assignment (cf. Marantz 1984) are hence twofold: (i) in some contexts, S-structure subjects originating in object position are not fixed; and (ii) in other cases, D-structure subjects (of resultative SCs) are fixed.[67] Rather than stating the restrictions on idiomatic fixing in D-structure *thematic* terms, then, let us consider the possibility of capturing the desired constraints in S-structure *aspectual* terms.

A comparison of the examples in (145) and (146), which are identical in all relevant D-structural thematic respects, will help us find the proper way of stating these restrictions. While in (145), the subject of the resultative SC is raised to matrix subject position, this NP remains *in situ* in the complement of the governing verb in (146). Suppose, then, that this is what renders it impossible for the SC subject in (146) to be idiomatically fixed. This can be made sense of if it is assumed that the subject position of a SC in the complement of a verb denoting (change of) state or location is the canonical structural position of *affected arguments* (cf. also Hoekstra & Roberts 1992; Voskuil & Wehrmann 1990; Hoffman 1991; Hale & Keyser 1992, 1993). The assumption that idiom chunks cannot occupy this position at S-structure may then be related to the plausible claim that idiom chunks cannot qualify as affected arguments — only referential expressions can be affected arguments. Replacing a thematic account of idiomatic fixing with an aspectually based one along these lines, we can then make the appropriate distinction between the examples in (145) and (146), which seem identical in all relevant D-structural respects.

When we now return to the examples of verb-particle idioms, it is easy to see that a configurational approach to affectedness coupled with the unaffected character of idiom chunks yields precisely the desired results. In the "outer particle" idioms in (144) — in contrast to (143) — the NPs sandwiched

---

[67] An additional problem, stemming from the abolition of D-structure in Chomsky (1993), is that the level at which restrictions on idiomatic fixing are traditionally stated is no longer available in the recent minimalist framework. Chomsky (1993:39) states that 'we must assume that idiom interpretation takes place at LF, as is natural in any event'. That idiomatic fixing is not a purely D-structural phenomenon is also stressed by Brame (1984:317), who notes that various English idiomatic constructions 'appear only at the S-structure level' (cf. (i)). Idioms of the type in (i) are not readily amenable to the suggestions to be made in the remainder of this subsection either, however.

(i)   a.   He thinks he has it made in the shade.
     b.   They all have a score to settle.
     c.   Transformationalists don't have a leg to stand on.
     d.   Do you still have a bone to pick?

between verb and particle may not be idiomatically fixed since they find themselves, at S-structure, in the specifier position of a resultative SC, the canonical "affected argument" position.

Clearly, much more can be said about idiom formation, many details of which are still poorly understood. The essential point to note in the present context, however, is that the fact that idioms in which the verb, the particle and the "object NP" are all fixed as a rule feature the particle in verb-adjacent position can be interpreted as an argument in favour of the view, propounded here, that particles are ergative SC heads.

2.4.4.2 An apparent problem

Constructions of the type in (147b,c)/(148b,c), in which the particle appears to take a complement (printed in boldface) other than the "object NP", seem to challenge an approach to particle constructions according to which particles are unaccusative predicates:[68]

(147) a.   They kicked the dog *out*.
     b.   They kicked the dog *out* **the door**.
     c.   They kicked the dog *out* **of the house**.

(148) a.   They snapped the antenna *off*.
     b.   They snapped the antenna *off* **the car**.
     c.   They snapped the antenna *off* **of the car**.

If in (147b,c) *the door* and *of the house* are complements of the particle *out* (cf. Svenonius 1992 for an explicit suggestion to this effect) so that *the dog* in these sentences can only be the particle's subject, while in (147a) *the dog* is the internal argument of the particle (as I have argued above), we are facing a head-on collision with UTAH, given that the θ-role assigned to *the dog* is arguably constant throughout the paradigm in (147).[69] Since, as pointed out in chapter 1, UTAH is conceptually desirable for its significant limitation of the

---

[68] Constructions of the b-type also occur with the particles *down* (*down the garden path*) and *up* (*up the hill*). Wegner & Rice (1988) show that of particle/transitive preposition homonyms the transitive P is generally acquired first by English speaking children, the particle variant coming in at a later stage; but in the case of *down, off* and *up* it is the particle use that comes in earlier than the transitive P use. This suggests that *down, off* and *up* are fundamentally particles; if what is argued in this subsection holds water, they are in fact *always* particles, never true transitive Ps, and their apparent transitive P guises are structurally rather marked (which may explain their late acquisition). For *out* Wegner & Rice do not present similar evidence.

[69] Richard Kayne first drew my attention to the potential problems in the domain of uniformity of θ-assignment caused by paradigms of the type in (147)/(148).

logically possible mappings from thematic structure onto syntactic D-structure, abandoning it in the face of examples like (147) and (148) is not an option. Two strategies remain open to us at this point: (i) to revoke our earlier conclusion that particles in constructions like (147a)/(148a) are unaccusative; or (ii) to argue that even in (147b,c)/(148b,c), the "object NP" originates in the complement of the particle. The latter option implies casting doubt on the complement status of the constituents following the particle in (147b,c) and (148b,c). This is what I shall attempt to do in this subsection.

Let me start out emphasising that the Norwegian counterpart of (147c) presents evidence for the view that the particle in constructions of this type is in fact ergative. The thing to note about Norwegian (149), taken from Åfarli (1985:83), is that the word-order alternation familiar from simplex particle constructions shows up here as well:[70]

(149)   Vi sparka (*ut*) hunden (*ut*) **av huset.**
         we kicked (out) the-dog (out) of the-house

I have argued that particle constructions in which the "object NP" finds itself to the right of the particle (which in its turn occupies a verb-adjacent position) reflect the D-structure order, the "object NP" receiving objective Case in its base position by virtue of the application of verb-particle reanalysis. Given this analysis of the word-order alternation in verb-particle constructions, then, the grammaticality of the "inner particle" variant of (149) lends direct support to the view that *ut* in this example is an ergative particle. By the cross-linguistic UTAH, this conclusion then immediately carries over to English (147c). Similar evidence for the ergativity of the particle is lacking in the case of (147b), whose Norwegian cognate does not exhibit a word-order alternation (Åfarli 1985:83-4):

(150)   Jon sparka (**ut*) hunden (*ut*) **døra.**
         Jon kicked (out) the-dog (out) the-door

Nonetheless, even here there are indications of a somewhat different nature which suggest that the boldface constituent is not the complement of the particle. The evidence in question concerns extraction.

---

[70] The Norwegian cognate of English (147b) (cf. (150), below), to which I briefly turn further below, does not exhibit an alternation of this sort, nor in fact do English (147b,c)/(148b,c). Why this should be so is quite unclear. I leave this issue open.

Guéron's (1990:fn. 3) analysis of (149) as a complex particle construction (cf. (i)) treats *av* as 'from'. Such an analysis would not carry over to English (147c), but it would be appropriate for English *out from the house.*

(i)   [$_{VP}$ sparka [$_{SC1}$ Spec *ut* [$_{SC2}$ hunden av huset]]]

A'-extraction from English and Norwegian PPs with concomitant P-stranding is well known to be widely possible, even if the PPs from which extraction takes place find themselves in adjoined positions:[71]

(151) a.   Who are they looking at?
      b.   Which shelf did they put the book on?
      c.   Who did they send the letter to?
      d.   What did they write this letter with?
      e.   Who was this poem written by/for?
      f.   ?Which innings did they leave the match after?

Interestingly, extraction of the constituent following the particle in the examples in (147b,c) and (148b,c) is impossible. The examples in (152) illustrate this for the cases with *out*:[72]

(152) a.   ?*Which door did they kick the dog *out*?
      b.   *Of which house did they kick the dog *out*?

For Norwegian, judgements are not completely unanimous, but on the whole it seems that extraction of the boldface constituents in (149) and (150) is impossible, irrespective of the position of the particle:[73]

(153) a.   ?*Av huset/[??]Av hvilket hus sparket han (*ut*) hunden (*ut*)?
            of the-house/of which house kicked they (out) dog-the (out)
      b.   *Døra/[?]*Hvilken dør sparket han hunden *ut*?
            the-door/which door kicked they the-dog out

---

[71]   All examples in (151) can be directly transposed to Norwegian. Note with regard to (151f) that not all temporal PPs are transparent. Thus (151f) contrasts with a similar example containing the preposition *during*: *Which innings did they leave the match during?*

[72]   Thanks to Bob Frank for judging these and similar examples, and for checking them with other native speakers as well. Frank notes that while (152b) is "crashingly bad", (152a) is slightly less bad, more or less giving the feel of a fairly bad Subjacency violation, not being quite as bad as an ECP violation. Note also that (152b) can of course be rescued by moving only *which house*, leaving *of* behind to the right of *out*.

[73]   I thank Alma Næss for collecting the judgements. Of the various possibilities in (153), [??]*Av hvilket hus sparket han ut hunden* is (marginally) accepted by many speakers (and is noted to contrast with its "outer particle" counterpart). A complex particle analysis along the lines suggested by Guéron (1990:fn. 3), reproduced in fn. 70 (i), according to which *ut av huset* is analysed as English *out from the house*, makes the desired distinction between inner and outer particle placement; cf. 2.3.3.4 on the restrictions on extraction of SC2's predicate in complex particle constructions. As in English, moving just *huset* while leaving *av* in place to the right of *ut* yields an impeccable result in (153a).

To take the case of (147b) first, if *the door* were a complement of *out*, being Case-marked by it as in run-of-the-mill transitive PPs, no contrast would be expected to be found between a case of *wh*-extraction of this NP and the examples in (151). But (152a) is distinctly worse than a case of extraction from the predicate of a prepositional SC like (151b). Similarly, (152b) contrasts sharply with cases of *wh*-extraction of the prepositional complements of adjectives or nouns, which are grammatical:

(154) a.   Of which car did they repair the brakes?
      b.   Of which solution did they seem most convinced/certain?

This suggests that *out (of) the door* in (147b,c) is not a regular transitive PP, and that *(of) the door* is not the complement of *out*. The same conclusion holds for the Norwegian examples.[74]

This conclusion is sufficient for my purposes. After all, if the post-particle NP/PP in (147)–(150) is not the particle's complement, I am free to claim that in all of (147)–(150), the "object NP" originates in the complement of the particle, and hence that in all of (147)–(150), the particle is an ergative SC head.[75]

---

[74] Åfarli (1985:83) suggests that the deviance of the "inner particle" variant of (150) can be derived from the Case Filter. He analyses *døra* as the complement of *ut*. Since the "inner particle" alternant involves incorporation of *ut* into the verb and since incorporation traces cannot assign Case (cf. Baker 1988; this would seem to be preferable to Åfarli's claim that incorporation does not leave a trace in the case of particle movement), *døra* is not Case-marked in the pertinent variant of (150). Notice, though, that if *døra* were really the Case-marked complement of *ut* in (150), we would be at a loss accounting for the deviance of (153b). After all, nominal complements of Norwegian prepositions are generally freely extractable. To me, (153b) suggests that *døra* is not the Case-marked complement of *ut* (although I shall leave it a moot point where this NP finds itself in the tree), so that the ungrammaticality of the "inner particle" variant of (153) cannot reduce to the Case Filter.

[75] For a pair like *John put the clothes on* and *John put the clothes on the child* no UTAH problems arise if we assume — as seems plausible — that in the former sentence *on* is not a particle but a transitive preposition taking a null (*pro*) object (cf. Koopman 1993:13 on "intransitive Ps" like Dutch *boven* 'upstairs', and section 1.3, above), coindexed with the subject (*John put the clothes on himself*). Collins & Thráinsson (1993:167) zoom in on the above pair to criticise the present analysis of particle constructions, but their point really goes through only with respect to the alternation between *John put on the clothes* and *John put the clothes on the child*. On present assumptions, the "inner particle" construction *John put on the clothes* indicates that *on* is an ergative SC head in this case, so that *the clothes* (rather than *the child* or a [+human] *pro*) would be the internal argument of *on* here. Questions raised in this connection need to be thought through more carefully, also with reference to alternations like *cut NP short/cut short NP* (cf. fn. 58).

2.4.5 On pronouns and word order

There is a difference in English between "inner particle constructions" (displaying V–Prt–NP word order) and "outer particle constructions" (with V–NP–Prt order) in the domain of pronominal objects of the particle. While (155a) is perfect with both full and pronominal NP objects, the V–Prt–NP order is unavailable if the particle takes a pronominal object (cf. Lees 1961; Fraser 1974):

(155) a.   John looked *the information/it* up.
      b.   John looked up *the information/*it*.

The contrast in (155) is traditionally attributed to the weak or clitic-like nature of English pronouns. As soon as the pronoun receives focal stress, or is conjoined with another pronoun, or has deictic force, "inner particle constructions" of the type in (155b) are acceptable, as Bolinger (1971:39–41), Fraser (1974:17) and Johnson (1991), among others, point out:

(156) a.   John threw out THEM!
      b.   John looked up *him and her*.
      c.   John dusted off *that*.

In his extraposition account of the word-order alternation in English verb-particle constructions, Kayne (1985) attributes the deviance of the pronominal variant of (155b) to an apparently more general "weight" constraint on the application of rightward NP-shift (cf. also Oehrle 1976):

(157) a.   In ... $[e]_i$ X NP_i ..., where NP_i binds $[e]_i$ NP_i must be at least as heavily weighted as X.
      b.   Weightings: heavy NP=2, ordinary NP=1, pronoun=0, particle= 1, *right*+Prt=2.

Since weak pronouns are less weighty than particles, they may not be extraposed around a particle.[76]

---

[76] In the next section, we shall encounter another application of Kayne's constraint in (157), concerning particle modification.

Diesing & Jelinek (1993) refute a "weight constraint" approach to particle placement restrictions by pointing out that the indefinite pronoun *one*, which is equally light as its definite counterparts, does not have to shift to the left of the particle, as (i) (their (55)) shows. They account for the obligatoriness of movement of definite pronouns to the left of the particle by introducing an LF constraint forcing definite presuppositional elements to leave VP. Replacing the account to be presented below with Diesing & Jelinek's does not affect the analysis of V–Prt constructions propounded here.

(i)   I picked (up) *one* (up) at the store.

On the present approach to the word-order alternation in (155a,b), the explanation of the ban on pronominal objects in "inner particle constructions" must be sought in the fact that in these constructions, verb-particle reanalysis obtains. The ideal account of the deviance of (155b) with a pronominal object should relate it to other peculiarities of English pronouns. In particular, the most promising line of thought would be to say the ungrammaticality of the pertinent variant of (155b) reduces to whatever is responsible for the ill-formedness of Locative Inversion constructions with a post-verbal pronominal subject NP (cf. (158)),[77] and double object constructions with a pronominal direct object (159):

(158)   Down the hill rolled *the baby carriage/*it*.
(159)   John sent the stockholders (out) *the announcement/[?*]it*.

The example in (158) clearly shows that a mere statement to the effect that weak pronouns are clitics which must be hosted by a lexical verb does not help us out in the general case, since in (158) the pronoun certainly is immediately adjacent to a lexical verb. Apart from begging the question of what it means to say that an English weak pronoun is a clitic, then, an account along such lines would also be insufficiently general.

In chapter 3 of this study, an analysis of Dative Shift will be presented according to which this transformation is an instance of Locative Inversion. This allows for an immediate assimilation of the accounts of the deviance of pertinent variants of (158) and (159). The ill-formedness of (155b) with a pronominal object might now be reduced to that of the pronominal variants of (158) and (159) on the assumption that the "inner particle" word order of English particle constructions arises as a result of the application of Locative Inversion within the confines of the particle-headed SC. Specifically, following a suggestion to this effect in Mulder (1992a), we might argue that, SCs containing functional internal structure (cf. Hornstein & Lightfoot 1987; Den Dikken 1987; T. Hoekstra 1991), the V–Prt–NP order comes about by A-moving the particle phrase into the θ'-specifier position of the functional head "F" (presumably to be identified as Agr; cf. chapter 1) of the verb's SC complement, roughly as in (160):[78]

---

[77] As noted in e.g. Emonds (1976:29) and Rochemont (1986:114). The latter also points out that stressing the pronoun renders examples of the type in (158) grammatical (cf. (156a)).

[78] Mulder (1992a) exploits the Locative Inversion approach to "inner particle constructions" to accommodate the ungrammaticality of *Which money did you pay back the bank?* (Stowell 1981: 342) as a crossover effect (cf. the original paper for details). On the analysis of Dative Shift propounded in chapter 3, however, there is a straightforward way of deriving the deviance of this example as a strong crossover violation without the need to adopt a Locative Inversion approach to "inner particle constructions"; cf. section 4.5.1 for discussion.   (*continued overleaf*)

(160) $[_{VP} V [_{SC} [_{PP} Prt]_i F [NP t_i]]]$

An analysis of "inner particle constructions" along these lines would be incompatible with the overall approach to particle constructions advocated here, since it presupposes that particles are *unergative* SC-heads, taking their only argument externally. Nor is it likely to extend to prepositional and infinitival complex particle constructions with "inner particle" word order. In such constructions, illustrated in (161) and (162), the particle is followed not just by NP but by an additional transitive PP or *to*-infinitival as well. Since this PP/*to*-infinitival must, in view of what was argued earlier in this chapter, be generated in the complement of the particle, it seems impossible to generate complex "inner particle constructions" in a way paralleling the derivation in (160). Nonetheless, the fact that the "inner particle" variants of these complex particle constructions are subject to the same ban on pronominal objects as the simple "inner particle construction" in (155b) (cf. (161b) and (162b)) indicates that any account of the deviance of (155b) with a pronoun should carry over to that of the pertinent variants of (161b) and (162b).

(161) a.   They put *the books/them* down on the shelf.
      b.   They put down *the books/*them* on the shelf.

(162) a.   They made *John/him* out to be a liar.
      b.   They made out *John/*him* to be a liar.

Notice also that even if all of (155b)–(159) were to be analysed in terms of Locative Inversion, we would still beg the question of why Locative Inversion should be inapplicable if the subject of the SC whose predicate is fronted is pronominal.

I would like to suggest that the key towards a comprehensive account of (155b)–(159) is the hypothesis in (163):

Notice that, given (160), we might expect SC predicates to be in general capable of inverting with their subjects within the confines of the SC. Although, adorned with a "heaviness calculus" of the type in (157) (cf. Kayne 1985), this might allow for an approach to Heavy NP Shift in secondary predication contexts in terms of embedded Locative Inversion (cf. (ia,b)), such an account would be insufficiently general since examples like (ic) would have to involve some other type of derivation. A Locative Inversion approach to (ia,b) would hence force a disjoint analysis of the class of Heavy NP Shift phenomena, which does not appear to be empirically motivated. More importantly, unequivocal cases of Locative Inversion in ECM contexts turn out to be ungrammatical (in the absence of further A'-movement of the inverted predicate): sentences such as *I saw down the hill roll the baby carriage* are ungrammatical (cf. Bresnan 1990; Den Dikken & Næss 1993).

(i)   a.   I would consider *foolish*_i/*a fool*_i [anyone who wants to marry Sue] t_i.
        b.   I put *on the top shelf*_i [all the books on cold nuclear fusion] t_i.
        c.   I saw again yesterday [my favourite uncle from Cleveland].

(163)   Weak pronouns cannot be Case-marked via Case transmission along
             a chain; they must stand in a direct relationship of Spec-Head
             agreement with an Agr head.[79]

With the aid of (163), the ungrammaticality of the pronominal variants of
(155b)–(159) can be accommodated as follows.

The Locative Inversion and Dative Shift examples in (158) and (159) both
involve fronting into a Case position of the predicate of the SC with a Case-
dependent subject NP. Along the lines of Hoekstra & Mulder's (1990) analysis
of Locative Inversion, the Case assigned to the fronted SC predicate will find
its way to the Case-needy SC subject via the chain of identical indexations con-
necting the fronted predicate, its trace and (via Specifier-Head agreement) its
subject. The post-verbal subject of a Locative Inversion construction and the
direct object of a Dative Shift construction hence receive Case via transmission
along a chain. Hypothesis (163) now ensures that pronominal post-verbal subjects or objects are impossible in (158) and (159).

In "inner particle constructions", Case is made available to the post-particle
NP, which stays *in situ*, through reanalysis of the particle with the verb.
Reanalysis, an abstract instance of head incorporation, creates a chain extending
the governing domain of the incorporating verbal head. Along this chain, the
Case feature assigned by V finds its way to the Case-dependent NP in the
complement of the incorporated/reanalysed particle. As in the case of the
Locative Inversion and Dative Shift examples in (158)–(159), then, the Case-
needy NP is licensed via Case transmission, which is why pronominal objects
are excluded in "inner particle constructions".[80]

---

[79] Johnson (1991) arrives at a similar conclusion, likewise forcing Case-driven A-movement for
pronouns but not for full NP objects. Also cf. Holmberg (1993:33, 37).

[80] As is pointed out in Holmberg (1986:200ff.) and Josefsson (1992), Swedish particles precede
their arguments even when the argument is a weak pronoun (cf. (i)). In this respect Swedish differs
from the other Scandinavian languages, as well as from English.

(i)   a.   *Jag skrev *det* upp.
             I wrote it up
       b.   Jag skrev upp *det*.

This is unexpected from the present perspective. The key to a (tentative) explanation for these
Swedish facts is the fact (noted by Josefsson 1992) that in Swedish, but in none of the other
Scandinavian languages, weak pronouns can (depending on poorly understood lexical and contextual
factors) be found between the finite verb in Comp and the subject in SpecIP, as in the following
examples from Josefsson (1992:66):

(ii)   a.   Av den enkla anledningen skadade *mig* rånaran inte det minsta.
             for that simple reason hurt me the-robber not the least

In "outer particle constructions", by contrast, the Case-dependent NP will raise from its base-position in the complement of the particle to a position in which it can pick up Case. Given (163), the landing-site of pronouns in these constructions must be a position in which the pronoun entertains a Spec-Head agreement relationship with some Agr head. If SCs are analysed as AgrPs (one of the options considered in section 1.2.8, above), the specifier position of the SC may qualify as a suitable landing-site for pronouns. Alternatively (and more generally also for non-particle constructions containing a pronominal object like *They found it*), we may assume that the object originates in a position to which Case is not directly assigned. This will be a consequence of recent proposals (cf. Chomsky 1991, 1993; Vanden Wyngaerd 1989; Johnson 1991) to the effect that structural objective Case is assigned by some functional head (AgrO) under Specifier-Head agreement much like the way in which nominative Case is assigned. The Case-dependent object pronoun then undergoes A-movement to the specifier position of the Case-assigning AgrO, meeting the demands of (163).

The hypothesis in (163) can be seen to be operative outside the domain of constructions involving particles, double objects or Locative Inversion as well.[81] Kayne (1989) discusses a variety of English (spoken mainly in the New York area) in which, in *wh*-movement constructions of the type in (164), singular subjects may fail to show agreement with the finite verb (cf. Kimball & Aissen 1971 for original data and discussion):

(164)   The people who Clark *think* are in the garden.

Kayne argues that in constructions of this type, the finite verb shows agreement with the *wh*-phrase in SpecCP as a result of Agr-to-C raising having taken place. Agr, then, is not coindexed with the subject in SpecAgrP in these con-

---

(ii)   b.   På stationen mötte *honom* morfar och mormor med en fin present.
                   at the-station met him grandpa and grandma with a nice present

Josefsson (1992) argues that in examples such as these, the weak pronoun is a clitic head which adjoins to Comp. Suppose, then, following Josefsson, that weak pronouns in Swedish are consistently to be analysed as heads. This assumption may now be exploited to explain the data in (i), if we base ourselves on the analysis of particle constructions presented in this study. If particles are heads, we expect them to block head movement across them (even if — as always in Swedish — the particle is reanalysed with the verb; cf. 3.10.2, below, for discussion). The ill-formedness of (ia) then follows from the ECP (Minimality). In (ib), the pronoun cliticises to the particle. The absence of examples of the type in (ii) from other Scandinavian languages may be taken to suggest that in these languages weak pronouns are NPs undergoing (obligatory) NP-movement to the specifier of an Agr head (cf. (163)). With this assumption we then also immediately accommodate the contrast between the grammatical Swedish particle construction in (ia) and its ungrammatical counterparts in the other Scandinavian languages and English.

[81]   Thanks to Teun Hoekstra for noting the relevance of Kayne (1989) in this context.

structions. Now the fact that variants of (164) with *pronominal* subjects (cf. (165)) are 'appreciably worse' than (164) can be accommodated, Kayne suggests, on the assumption that pronouns must be coindexed with Agr. The contrast between (164) and (165), then, is another instance of the generalisation expressed in (163).

(165)   *The people who (s)he *think* are in the garden.

An apparent problem for the hypothesis in (163) is the fact that post-verbal subjects in Romance free inversion constructions can be pronominal, as is shown the Italian example in (166) (taken from Burzio 1986:103):

(166)   Arriva Giovanni/*lui*.
         arrives Giovanni/he

If, in free inversion constructions, nominative Case is transferred to the post-verbal subject in VP-internal position, the fact that (166) with a pronominal post-verbal subject is grammatical would seem to run counter to what (163) leads us to expect. That the problem is merely apparent, however, is evident from the fact that post-verbal pronouns in inversion constructions of this type are always *emphatic* pronouns.[82] Emphatic pronouns pattern with full NPs, as is also evident from the contrast between (155b) and (156a), above. The hypothesis in (163) governs the distribution of *weak* pronouns only.

We have seen in this section that with the aid of the hypothesis that pronouns must be Case-marked directly rather than via Case transmission along a chain, the fact that the surface distribution of pronouns is restricted in various ways cross-linguistically can be made to fall out from the analysis. In particular, I showed that the hypothesis in (163) allows us to generalise over the English examples in (155b)–(159), all of which involve Case transfer through a chain.

---

[82] This is supported by the fact that in Fiorentino and Trentino, two dialects of Italian discussed in Brandi & Cordin (1989) which feature a class of subject clitics, post-verbal pronominal subjects always have the form of *tonic* pronouns rather than of subject clitics (thanks to Maria Teresa Guasti for drawing my attention to these data):

(i)   Tu vieni te.   (Fiorentino)
         you(CL) come you(tonic pron)

Burzio (1986:sect. 2.3) in fact fully divorces the analysis of (166) with an emphatic pronoun from that of (166) with a full NP subject, pointing to some interesting differences concerning locality between the two cases. He argues that (166) with a pronominal subject involves emphatic subject doubling, analysing it as the null-subject counterpart of (ii):

(ii)   Giovanni/*pro* arriva *lui*.
         Giovanni/*pro* arrives he

2.4.6 Particle modification

In section 2.2.2, I briefly touched upon the issue of particle modification by adverbs such as *right* and *straight* to argue against an analysis of the verb-particle construction according to which the particle is base-generated as part of a complex verb. In this subsection I would like to return to the question of particle modification, with particular reference to the fact that its distribution is restricted in an interesting way, as the contrast in (167) illustrates:

(167) a.   They looked the information (**right**) *up*.
     b.   They looked (***right**) *up* the information.

Whenever the particle precedes the "object NP", modification of the particle by *right* is impossible.[83] Since particle modification plays a criterial role in the analysis of Dative Shift to be developed in chapter 3, it is appropriate to end the present chapter on particle constructions with a discussion of the theoretical roots of the restrictions on particle modification.

Kayne (1985:127) relates the deviance of (167b) to that of the pronominal variant of (155b), above, and captures it with the aid of the constraint in (157), repeated here:

(157) a.   In ... $[e]_i$ X NP_i ..., where NP_i binds $[e]_i$ NP_i must be at least as heavily weighted as X.
     b.   Weightings: heavy NP=2, ordinary NP=1, pronoun=0, particle= 1, *right*+Prt=2.

Since in (167b) the post-particle NP is an ordinary NP weighted 1, and the *right*+Prt combination is weighted 2, this example violates the constraint in (157a), whence its ungrammaticality.

An account of the deviance of examples like (167b) along these lines seems somewhat impressionistic. Why is *right*+Prt weighted 2 rather than, say, 1.5 or 3? And even if, as seems intuitively not unlikely, *right*+Prt is weightier than just a bare particle, why does the increased weight of a modified PP have no effect on regular cases of Heavy NP Shift (as Svenonius 1992, from whose paper the examples in (168) are taken, notes)?

(168) a.   Darwin sent to London every bug he caught.
     b.   Darwin sent **right** to London every bug he caught.

---

[83] The same goes for other particle modifiers, such as *straight*, *way*, *all* and *the hell/heck*. I shall confine myself to *right* here.

If a bare particle is weighted 1, then surely a full transitive PP must be more heavily weighted. After all, an ordinary NP may not be extraposed across a transitive PP (cf. *Darwin sent to London a bug*). Let us assume that only whole integers are used in weighting constituents. Then transitive PPs will be weighted (at least) 2. Since modification by *right* increases the weight of a bare particle by (at least) one full integer, let us furthermore assume that this is what *right* modification generally does. If so, *right to London* in (168b) will be weighted (at least) 3, while the extraposed heavy NP is weighted 2. We are led to expect, then, that (168b) should violate the constraint in (157a), and should hence be ill-formed, contrary to fact.

Its failure to account in any insightful fashion for the effect of *right* modification on particle placement can now be added to our earlier conclusion that Kayne's (1985) extraposition approach to the word-order alternation in the English verb-particle construction faces other non-trivial problems as well. Let us then turn to the alternative analysis.

On our assumptions, the word order in (167a) comes about by NP-movement of the "object NP" into the θ'-specifier position of the particle-headed SC. In (167b), on the other hand, the "object NP" remains *in situ* in the complement position of the particle. It is allowed to stay in this position since, as a result of reanalysis of the particle with the verb, objective Case can be assigned to the NP. The ungrammatical (167b) with *right* is different from the acceptable (167a), then, precisely in that reanalysis of verb and particle takes place in the former but not in the latter. It seems plausible to hold verb-particle reanalysis responsible for the deviance of the pertinent variant of (167b):

(169)   Particle modification is impossible if V–Prt reanalysis has occurred.

Verb-particle reanalysis, as argued above, is an instance of the general schema of head incorporation. The roots of the generalisation in (169) should hence be sought among independently known constraints on head movement. One of these clearly is that incorporation may only adjoin heads to other heads, hence only takes *bare* heads (i.c. bare particles) as its input. Notice, however, that incorporation of the bare head with *stranding* of the modifier would appear to be a theoretical option, exploited extensively in cases of noun or verb incorporation (cf. Baker 1988 for discussion). English particle incorporation apparently disallows modifier stranding, and in this respect patterns with adjective incorporation in Chinese (cf. (170); Sybesma 1991). Why do some cases of head incorporation freely allow for stranding of adverbial modifiers while others do not?

(170)   Zhang San ku *shi* shoujuan (**hen**) *t*.
         Zhang San cry wet handkerchief (very)
         'Zhang San cried the handkerchief (*very) wet.'

Notice first that the complexity of the stranded modifier is relevant to the issue at hand. In Dutch particles can be modified by a variety of adverbial elements: bare adverbs like *pal* or *vlak*, which semantically correspond with English *right*, or adverbial phrases such as *twee meter* 'two metres' (cf. Bennis 1991). It seems that while phrasal modifiers of the latter type may freely be stranded under particle incorporation, adverbial atoms like *pal* may not (or in any event not very felicitously):[84]

(171) a.   dat Jan de bal **pal/vlak/twee meter** *over* heeft geschoten.
            that Jan the ball right/id./two metres PRT has shot
      b.   dat Jan de bal *[?]**pal/*vlak/twee meter** heeft *over* geschoten.
            that Jan the ball right/id./two metres has PRT shot

Like *pal* and *vlak* are the adjectival degree modifiers *erg* and *zeer* 'very' (cf. Chinese *hen*), which likewise resist being stranded by incorporation of the head that they modify (cf. T. Hoekstra 1991):

(172) a.   dat Jan de auto **erg/zeer** *vol* wil tanken.
            that Jan the car very/id. full wants tank
      b.   *dat Jan de auto **erg/zeer** wil *vol* tanken.
            that Jan the car very/id. wants full tank

In view of these comparative data, our initial generalisation in (169) can be extended in the following fashion:

(173)   Stranding of bare modifiers under incorporation is impossible.

One possible way of deriving this generalisation would be to suggest that the restrictions on modifier stranding are related to the level at which the modifier is attached: to the maximal projection of the incorporated head, or to the X^0 itself (cf. Den Dikken 1991a). If English *right*, Chinese *hen* and the Dutch bare modifiers in (171)–(172) are X^0-adjuncts, the ill-formedness of (167b), (170), (171b) and (172b) with the pertinent modifiers inserted can be made to follow from an assumed ban on stranding of X^0-adjuncts under incorporation of X.

---

[84] Also cf. Koopman (1993), who follows the account of modifier stranding to be outlined below, and who accepts my judgements on (171b) rather than Bennis' (according to which stranding of *pal* and *vlak* is not unacceptable). Neeleman (1994:67, n. 10) suggests a different explanation for the contrast between bare and phrasal modifiers seen in (171b), pointing out that the latter can be VP-modifiers (as in *dat de politie de verdachte drie kilometer heeft gevolgd* 'that the police followed the suspect for three kilometres', where the adverbial *drie kilometer* is paraphrasable as 'over a stretch of three kilometres'). However, it seems highly unlikely that in (171b) *twee meter* is a VP-modifier — telic VPs like *de bal overschieten* 'the ball over-shoot' are not modifiable by phrases like *twee meter*, which in their function as VP-modifiers typically modify atelic VPs (activities).

On Baker's (1988) assumptions, this could in turn be viewed as an immediate consequence of the general prohibition on word-internal traces. Recent research (cf. Roberts 1991; Guasti 1991, 1993) suggests, however, that movement from within complex X^0-categories (called *excorporation*) may not be barred in general. Some qualification may hence be in order here. Guasti (1991) formalises the restrictions on excorporation in terms of Rizzi's (1990) Relativised Minimality, extended as in (174). With the aid of the requirement that putative cases of excorporation meet the condition in (174), it seems that all and only grammatical instances of excorporation are accommodated.

(174)   *Relativised Minimality*

X ß-governs Y iff there is no Z such that:

(i)   Z is a base position;

(ii)   Z is ß-G(overnment) T(heory) compatible with Y;

(iii)   Z c-commands Y but it does not c-command X.

where $ß = \{A, A', X^0, X^{-1}\}$

Let us investigate the repercussions of (174) for the ungrammatical cases of modifier stranding under incorporation in (167b) and (170). First note that English *right*, Chinese *hen* 'very' or Dutch *pal, vlak* 'right' and *erg, zeer* 'very' are unlikely to be X^{-1} elements: these modifiers have no affixal properties, they just seem to be bare heads. English and Dutch particles, and Chinese and Dutch adjectives do not have X^{-1} properties either — they are bare heads which (optionally) undergo incorporation into V. Both the incorporates and their modifiers, then, are of the category type X^0. Movement of X^0 across an intervening (i.e. c-commanding) element of the X^0 type is disallowed by (174). Hence even if the theory of head movement should be modified along the lines of (174) to allow for some cases of excorporation, we continue to be able to rule out English (167b) and Chinese (170) as violations of (Relativised) Minimality on the assumption that the stranded modifiers in these examples are X^0-elements adjoined to the 0-level projections of the incorporates.

Notice, though, that in order for the ill-formedness of (167b) (and (170)) to follow from (Relativised) Minimality, we need assume no more than that *right* (and the Chinese and Dutch adverbs of the same type) are X^0-elements c-commanding the prospective incorporate — assuming that these X^0-elements are adjoined to the 0-level projection of the incorporate is just one out of three potential ways of giving this idea shape. One alternative would be to assume that modifiers like *right* are 'bare heads that adjoin to P'' (cf. Svenonius 1992). This scenario seems somewhat less attractive in view of the fact that involves an otherwise unmotivated inflation of the number of possible phrase structure configurations, base-adjoining a head to a non-head.

The third conceivable strategy, which is perhaps the most felicitous of all, consists in the assumption that modifiers like *right* are heads of an independent projection between the incorporator (V) and the incorporate (Prt), taking the particle's projection as their *complement* (cf. Koopman 1993, who takes bare modifiers like Dutch *pal* to be Deg(ree)-type heads):

(175) $[_{VP}$ V $[_{SC}$ ... $[_{XP}$ $[_X$ *right*$]$ $[_{PP}$ Prt$]]]]$

The choice between the three scenarios sketched in the preceding discussion is irrelevant in the present context. What should be borne in mind is simply that the descriptive generalisation concerning English particle modification given in (169) can be made to follow (in at least three slightly different ways) from the analysis of the word-order alternation in the English verb-particle construction presented in this chapter, on the plausible assumption that modifiers like *right* are X^0-elements c-commanding the particle. That the ban on particle modification in "inner particle" constructions can be made to fall out from independent principles governing the application of head incorporation supports an analysis of the word-order alternation in verb-particle constructions in terms of particle movement (specifically, reanalysis or LF incorporation) like the one propounded here.

2.5 Conclusion

The focus of this chapter has been an in-depth case study of the intricate cluster of properties of several types of English complex particle constructions with regard to particle placement and extraction. The prime theoretical results concerning the analysis of particle constructions in general are summarised in (176). The structure of complex particle constructions that they give rise to is repeated here as (177) (= (45)).

(176) a.   Particles are independent *SC heads*.
      b.   Particles are *ergative* prepositions.
      c.   Particles are *non-lexical* prepositions.

(177) $[_{IP}$ NP $[_{VP}$ V $[_{SC1}$ $[_{Spec\theta'}$ *ec*$]$ $[_{PP}$ Prt $[_{SC2}$ NP Pred$]]]]]$

The structure in (177) will serve as the foundation on which to build analyses of triadic constructions and Dative Shift (chapter 3) and transitive causative constructions (chapter 5).

3

Particles and the Dative Alternation

3.1 Introduction

With the conclusions drawn in chapter 2 in mind, I now proceed to an analysis of the so-called DATIVE ALTERNATION, the relationship between prepositional dative and double object constructions, illustrated in (1):

(1) a.   John sent a package to Bob.   (dative construction)
       b.   John sent Bob a package.   (double object construction)

The constructions in (1a,b) have each individually given rise to a wide variety of structural analyses. Some of these posit an explicit transformational relationship between (1a) and (1b) while others strongly oppose the existence of such a relationship.

In this chapter, I would like to approach the analysis of examples like (1a,b) from the point of view of similar constructions containing a verbal particle, *off* in (2):

(2) a.   John sent a package *off* to Bob.
       b.   John sent Bob *off* a package.

The properties of particle constructions like these will be shown to yield new insights into the structure of dative and double object constructions, and their relationship. The behaviour of triadic particle constructions argues for the postulation of a *transformational relationship* between dative and double object constructions, the latter being derived from the former, but it militates against Larson's (1988) influential implementation of this relationship, as I shall show in section 3.2.

Setting aside a Larsonian approach to the dative alternation, I then proceed to presenting evidence for an analysis of Dative Shift involving movement of the dative PP around the direct object, to the subject position of the particle-headed SC — a movement operation identical in nature with Locative Inversion. This analysis shares with Kayne's (1984) the view that the indirect object is *always* contained in a PP, whose head is empty in double object constructions.

111

In the course of the development of the analysis of the dative alternation on the basis of the properties of triadic verb-particle constructions, we shall see the need to introduce abstract structure — structure projected by abstract heads — into the tree. Coordination facts discussed in section 3.7 will give occasion to the inclusion of an empty token of the copula *be* in the structure of triadic constructions. It is this empty verb which will be argued to *incorporate* the empty head of the fronted dative PP in the double object construction. This is illustrated in (3), the analysis of double object particle constructions defended here:

(3) $[_{VP}$ V $[_{SC1}$ Spec $[_{VP}$ $[_{V}$ BE$+$P$_{\emptyset/j}]$ $[_{SC2}$ $[_{PP}$ t_j $Go]_i$ $[_{PP}$ Prt $[_{SC3}$ *Th* $t_i]]]]]]$

This structure also hands us the tools for a *decompositional* approach to the possessive verb *have*, which will be denied primitive lexical status and will instead be argued to be the suppletive lexicalisation of the complex head resulting from incorporation of the dative preposition into the copula *be*.

After developing the analysis of triadic constructions on the basis of particle constructions of the type in (2) (section 3.9) and identifying the structural triggers for PP-movement in the double object construction (section 3.10), the account will be carried over to particle-less dative and double object constructions. I shall present evidence to the effect that, even though an overt reflex of it is lacking, the structure of triadic constructions without a verbal particle also features a projection of a (zero) particle. Apart from the fact that the analysis of Dative Shift to be developed in this chapter leads us to postulate this abstract layer of structure, evidence from the domain of PP-placement in Dutch and Chinese dative constructions will be presented in support of the inclusion of an empty particle in the structure of particle-less triadic constructions.

The final sections of this chapter address a number of further issues arising in connection with the analysis of the dative alternation.

3.2   Why Larson's analysis of Dative Shift fails: Evidence from triadic verb-particle constructions

The analysis of Dative Shift has been and still is a matter of lively debate in the generative literature. It has attracted much recent attention, particularly in the wake of Larson's (1988) influential approach to triadic constructions, which — like the present analysis — postulates a transformational relationship between dative and double object constructions, deriving the latter from the former. In view of the important role that Larson's overall proposals have come to play in the literature, I shall open my discussion of triadic constructions by outlining and rejecting Larson's analysis, with specific reference to particle constructions. Readers already convinced that this analysis is inadequate or not specifically interested in my critique of it may wish to move on straightaway to section 3.3.

Larson assigns prepositional dative constructions a D-structure of the type in (4). In the course of the derivation, the lexical triadic verb, which is base-generated in the lower V^0-position, undergoes head movement into the higher V-slot, which is base-generated empty.

(4)

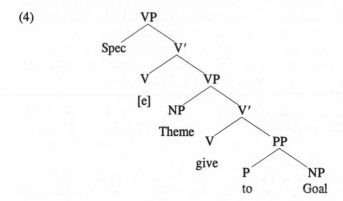

The double object construction is derived from the structure in (4) via *passivisation* of the lower VP, resulting in dethematisation of SpecVP, absorption of the dative preposition, concomitant movement of the Goal to SpecVP for Case reasons, and adjunction of the Theme NP to V'. This is depicted in (5):

(5)

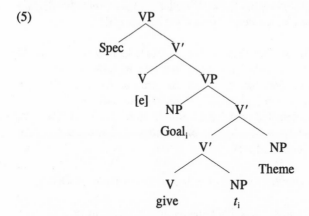

In the structure in (5), the Goal receives objective Case from *give* after raising of *give* to the higher V-slot, while the Theme is taken to be Case-marked by the lowest V' in the structure, which, in keeping with (6), is *reanalysed* as V. After reanalysis, 'the outer NP complement ... is the sister of a complex predicate whose category is V — a complex transitive verb' (Larson 1988:359–60). In this configuration, objective Case is assigned to the Theme.

(6)   *V' Reanalysis*
         Let α be a phrase $[_{V'} \ldots]$ whose θ-grid contains one undischarged
         internal θ-role. Then α may be reanalysed as $[_V \ldots]$.

The concept of V' Reanalysis is used for a variety of purposes in Larson's
work. One is to accommodate the word-order alternation in the English verb-
particle construction (to which I shall turn shortly), another is to account for
Heavy NP Shift phenomena in terms of what he refers to as Light Predicate
Raising. The line of the argument against a Larsonian approach to triadic constructions dictates that the latter application of V' Reanalysis be addressed first.

Larson's use of recursive VP representations and V' Reanalysis gives him an
opportunity to rethink the analysis of Heavy NP Shift phenomena, and to propose that, rather than involving rightward movement of the heavy NP, Heavy
NP Shift involves the "intraposition" of the verb and the constituent(s)
preceding the heavy NP. Concretely, a Heavy NP Shift construction like (7a)
would be derived from the underlying Larsonian structure in (7b) by reanalysis
of the V' in whose specifier position the heavy NP finds itself, and raising of
this reanalysed V'/V^0 to the head of the higher VP-shell, as shown in (7c):

(7)   a.   John gave to Mary yesterday his entire collection of Blaeu maps.
      b. $[_{VP}$ John $[_{V'}$ *ec* $[_{VP}$ $[_{NP}$ his entire collection of Blaeu maps] $[_{V'}$ *ec* $[_{VP}$
           $[_{PP}$ to Mary] $[_{V'}$ give $[_{AdvP}$ yesterday]]]]]]]]
      c. $[_{VP}$ John $[_{V'}$ $[_{V^\circ}$ **give**$_i$ $[_{VP}$ $[_{PP}$ **to Mary**] $[_{V'}$ t_i $[_{AdvP}$ **yesterday**]]]]$]_j$ $[_{VP}$
           $[_{NP}$ his entire collection of Blaeu maps] $[_{V' \to V^\circ}$ t_j]]]]

An important point to emphasise here is that, in order to be able to analyse
Heavy NP Shift uniformly in terms of Light Predicate Raising, Larson must
assume that adverbial modifiers like *yesterday* 'are not the outermost adjuncts
of V but rather its innermost complements' (Larson 1988:346, fn. 11).[1]

With this conclusion about the position of adverbs in mind, let us now turn
to the Larsonian representation of a double object construction containing the
clause-final adverb *yesterday*, like (8):[2]

(8)   John gave Mary his entire collection of Blaeu maps yesterday.

The Larsonian structure underlying this construction reads as in (9):

---

[1]   In the example at hand, this causes the dative PP to be generated in the specifier position of the
lowest VP rather in the "innermost complement position". This is unproblematic for UTAH if, as
Larson (1990) acknowledges, a relativised, θ-hierarchical UTAH is adopted; cf. section 1.2.6.

[2]   I confine my attention here to a double object construction not involving Heavy NP Shift, for
reasons that will become clear as we proceed.

(9)

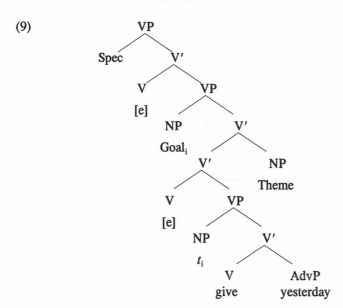

I assume — as seems inescapable in the light of uniformity of θ-role assignment — that the V' to which the Theme is adjoined is the one whose specifier it occupied in the corresponding prepositional dative construction (but nothing crucial changes if the relevant V' should turn out to be the lowest V'). Now notice that, given Larson's assumption that the Theme in a double object construction is *right*-adjoined to V', (9) will *not* in fact yield the word order reflected in (8); instead, it will give rise to a word order featuring the Theme in clause-final position — a "Heavy NP Shift" pattern.

It does not seem crucial, however, that the Theme should be right-adjoined to V' on Larson's assumptions. Let us modify Larson's analysis, then, by *left*-adjoining the Theme to V'.[3] With the Theme left-adjoined to V', the word order in (8) can be derived by raising the verb to the head position of the outermost VP-shell in (10).[4]

---

[3] Left-adjunction would also be more in line with Kayne's (1993b) "antisymmetry" hypothesis. Bowers (1993:639-40) has an independent motive for considering the possibility of a Larsonian analysis with left-adjunction of the Theme; he dismisses this option, but on inadequate grounds, misconstruing Larson's overall framework in the process (by wrongly suggesting that Larson treats adverbs as adjuncts).

[4] Note that, if reanalysis of the V' to which the Theme is adjoined were to be obligatory in double object constructions (cf. Larson 1988:359-60), we would wrongly derive an ungrammatical word order in which *yesterday* immediately precedes both objects. Let us assume, then, that V' Reanalysis is *not* in fact forced by Case considerations in double object constructions. How a structure with a left-adjoined Theme could generate the Heavy NP Shift construction *John gave Mary yesterday his entire collection of Blaeu maps* is quite unclear; cf. double object particle constructions, below.

(10)

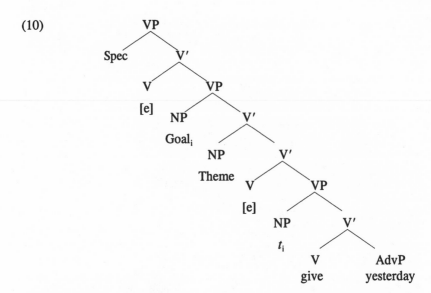

With this interim conclusion in mind, let us now leave the topic of double object constructions for a moment, and consider Larson's (1989) treatment of particles, in order to work our way towards double object particle constructions, which make the case against a Larsonian approach to Dative Shift.

Larson (1989:fn. 11) suggests that verb-particle constructions like *look up, throw out* and *smash in* can be looked upon as constituting a basic V', harbouring the "object NP" in its specifier. This is represented in (11a), which, after V-movement to the head of the VP-shell, straightforwardly yields the word order of an "outer particle construction". The alternative "inner particle construction" can then be obtained from (11a) by optionally *reanalysing* V' as V^0 and raising this complex V^0 to the higher V position, as shown in (11b):

(11) a.   [$_{VP}$ Spec [$_{V'}$ [$_V$ *ec*] [$_{VP}$ NP [$_{V'}$ V [$_{PP}$ Prt]]]]]
      b.   [$_{VP}$ Spec [$_{V'}$ [$_{V°}$ V [$_{PP}$ Prt]]$_i$] [$_{VP}$ NP [$_{V'→V°}$ t_i]]]]

Larson (1989) thus treats particles on a par with other resultative secondary predicates, and essentially follows the path defended in chapter 2 of this study. Given Larson's overall assumptions on phrase structure and the representation of triadic constructions, however, doing so causes him severe trouble accounting for the properties of triadic verb-particle constructions. Let us see first of all what the empirical facts in this domain come down to.

In chapter 2 I already discussed the particle placement possibilities in prepositional dative constructions, noting that both verb-adjacent and medial particle placement yields grammatical results but that it is impossible for the particle to be positioned to the right of the dative PP:

(12)   John sent (*off*) a package (*off*) to Bob (*off).

In double object particle constructions, placing the particle between the two objects is fine and clause-final particle placement is deviant for all speakers (cf. section 3.15.2 for some qualification, irrelevant here), but judgements vary on the acceptability of verb-adjacent particle placement, as Emonds (1976:82–83) notes, some speakers accepting it while others reject it outright, still others making a distinction here between *to*-dative and *for*-dative related double-object constructions (and accepting it only in the former case):

(13)   John sent (%*off*) Bob (*off*) a package (*off).

The fact that there is disagreement among speakers with respect to the status of *John sent off Bob a package* is not directly relevant in the present context. What matters is that medial particle placement in double object particle constructions is consistently judged acceptable while verb-adjacent particle placement is not.

Let us now proceed to considering the Larsonian analyses of triadic verb-particle constructions (bearing in mind that what follows is based on constructed representations faithfully implementing the Larsonian machinery). An analysis that generates the particle in the "innermost complement" position would clearly be at a loss accommodating the ungrammaticality of (12) with clause-final particle placement — the clause-final position would effectively be the base position of the particle on such an approach. So let us assume a potentially more promising analysis which generates the dative PP in the "innermost complement" position and places the particle's projection in the specifier position of the most deeply embedded VP:

(14) $[_{VP}$ Spec $[_{V'}$ *ec* $[_{VP}$ Theme $[_{V'}$ *ec* $[_{VP}$ $[_{PP}$ Prt] $[_{V'}$ V $[_{PP}$ P Goal]]]]]]]

The Dative Shifted counterpart of this structure — with the Theme NP left-adjoined to the V' whose specifier position it occupies in (14), in accordance with the above — then reads as in (15), overleaf. In this structure, successive cyclic raising of *send* to the highest V-node will yield a word order featuring the particle in sentence-final position, which is ungrammatical (except under circumstances discussed in section 3.15.2). The alternative derivation involving reanalysis of the V' containing the verb and the particle would yield verb-adjacent particle placement, which is not consistently accepted by all speakers. The only word order that all speakers of English readily accept, featuring medial particle placement, is precisely the pattern that the structure in (15) can*not* derive — there is no way in which the particle can be manoeuvred into a position right between the two objects.

(15)

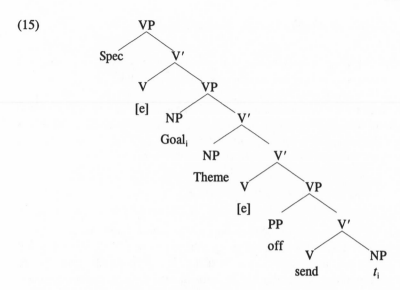

It seems clear, then, that a Larsonian approach to the dative alternation cannot accommodate the properties of triadic constructions featuring a verbal particle.[5] In what follows, I shall develop in detail an empirically more adequate alternative analysis of triadic constructions.

---

[5]   Notice that I have arranged the argument in such a way as to give the Larsonian framework the utmost benefit of the doubt, modifying it on points that would otherwise have trivially ruled out such an approach. But for those readers who are not convinced that *right*-adjunction of the Theme to V' in double object constructions should be replaced with *left*-adjunction to V', let me point out that even if one continues to use right-adjunction (and hence runs into problems in a case like (8)) the case against Larson's Dative Shift analysis can still be made, albeit somewhat differently. With the Theme right-adjoined to V' in (15), medial particle placement is unproblematic. But so is verb-adjacent particle placement (derivable via V' Reanalysis), which is not accepted by all speakers. Larson would hence minimally have to identify some sort of restriction on V' Reanalysis in double object particle constructions.

Also note that, in order to allow Larson to correctly rule out (12) with clause-final particle placement, I have chosen to base myself on the base structure in (14), in which the particle is generated higher than the dative PP. While this structure has no trouble accommodating medial particle placement in a prepositional dative construction, it has serious difficulty deriving the grammatical V–Prt–NP–PP order. Applying V' Reanalysis in (14) will not do, so some other means of manoeuvring the particle into verb-adjacent position will then have to be found. (Switching the relative positions of the particle and the dative PP in (14) creates problems of its own, which I shall not go through here.)

All in all it seems clear that no matter what approach to triadic particle constructions consistent with Larson's overall assumptions is taken, these constructions cause havoc in one way or another. Coupled with the unrestrictiveness of the Larsonian framework (which is particularly evident from the fact that it can give rise to quite a few potential analyses of triadic particle constructions, as the discussion in this footnote has shown), this makes it clear that the case against Larson's (1988) analysis of Dative Shift based on the properties of triadic V–Prt constructions stands firm.

3.3 The predicativity of the dative PP

The point of departure on my journey towards a new analysis of triadic constructions and Dative Shift is the observation that fronting of the dative PP in a passive prepositional dative construction may trigger the stylistic inversion process known as Locative Inversion (cf. section 2.2.1), henceforth to be referred to as Predicate Inversion (since it targets a wider range of phrases than just locative PPs):[6]

(16) a. *To Bob* was sent (*off*) a package.
     b. *To Mary* was given a/the/that book.

Recall from the discussion in section 2.2.1 that Predicate Inversion applies to predicates of complement-SCs only. This follows from Hoekstra & Mulder's (1990) analysis of Predicate Inversion according to which this phenomenon involves movement of the predicative PP into the θ'-specifier position of the matrix IP, as depicted in (17):

(17) $[_{IP}$ PP$_i$ Infl $[_{VP}$ V $[_{SC}$ NP$_i$ $[_{PP}$ $t_i]]]]$

The post-verbal NP in Predicate Inversion constructions receives nominative Case, as is evident from the fact that it determines number agreement with the finite verb. Nominative Case is transferred to the post-verbal NP in the following fashion. The fronted PP is assigned nominative Case in its S-structure position, under Specifier-Head agreement with Infl. Via the chain of identical indexations between this PP, its trace in the predicate position of SC, and its specifier (via Spec-Head agreement, which also involves indexation), this Case eventually finds its way to the post-verbal subject NP of the clause. Notice that

---

[6] The empirical question of whether dative PPs can trigger Predicate Inversion has received no unequivocal answers in the literature. Phillips (1993:181) and Pesetsky (1994) agree with the judgements given by the various native speakers of different varieties of English that I have consulted and reported in (16); their examples of Predicate Inversion applied to dative PPs are reproduced in (ia,b). But Levin & Rappaport Hovav (1992), while stating (on p. 225) that verbs expressing an event structure 'consisting of a process and a resulting state' (to which triadic verbs belong on the analysis presented here) are eligible for Predicate Inversion in passives, nonetheless report that their example (ic) is ungrammatical. They claim that *sell* belongs to the class of transitive verbs that 'cannot be viewed as having a lexical semantic representation that embeds a state or existence' (p. 227). I disagree with Levin & Rappaport Hovav, both theoretically (cf. also section 1.2.8, above) and empirically, and will proceed on the premise — sustained by all speakers that I have consulted over the years — that Predicate Inversion in prepositional dative constructions is grammatical.

(i) a. *To Gillian* was left the bulk of her aunt's estate.   (Phillips 1993:181)
     b. *To John* was given a new book   (Pesetsky 1994:3)
     c. **To the tourists* were sold the most garish souvenirs. (L&RH 1992:227)

the crucial link between the trace of the fronted PP and the Case-dependent post-verbal NP can only be established by the existence of a Spec-Head agreement relationship between them. Since such a relationship only holds between a subject and its predicate, it now follows that a Case Filter violation ensues whenever a PP which is not part of the SC is moved to SpecIP, hence that Predicate Inversion may affect predicative phrases only.

On the further assumption that the SC is the sole locus of subject-predicate relationships in the theory (cf. section 1.2.8), we may now provisionally conclude, given that (16) is grammatical, that the dative PP in prepositional dative constructions is at least part of a SC predicate. This still leaves us with two logically possible analyses: either (i) the dative PP is itself a SC predicate, or (ii) the dative PP is the complement of an empty SC head, the projection of which undergoes movement to SpecIP in dative Predicate Inversion constructions like (16).

Recall at this point the discussion in section 2.3.4, about a possible alternative to the analysis of prepositional complex particle constructions proposed in chapter 2. This alternative would consist in assuming that the transitive PP in such complex particle constructions is not itself the predicate of a SC, but rather the complement of a predicative particle. The derivation of Predicate Inversion constructions like (17) would then involve fronting of the projection of the particle, the head (i.e. the particle) undergoing prior (overt-syntactic) incorporation into the verb, as in (19):

(18)   On the table were put down some books.

(19) $[_{PP1} \ t_i \ [_{PP2}$ on the table$]]_j$ were [put$+down_i$] $[_{SC}$ some books $t_j]$

My objections to this analysis were twofold. First, the account is critically dependent on the existence of overt-syntactic particle movement in English, against which I presented evidence in section 2.4.3. Secondly, and more importantly, an analysis along these lines runs into problems with the Theta Criterion in establishing the relationship between locative resultatives with and without a verbal particle. In constructions lacking a particle, there is no doubt that the locative PP is responsible for θ-role assignment to the "locatum". This is particularly evident from the fact that in Dutch this PP resists undergoing PP-over-V, as shown in (20a). Failure to undergo extraposition is an unambiguous indication that the PP in question is a SC predicate (cf. Hoekstra 1984). In similar cases with a verbal particle, on the other hand, the locative PP has somehow forfeited its predicativity, apparently no longer assigning an external θ-role. While this may seem to be supported by the fact that in these cases, PP-over-V is possible (cf. (20b)), the hypothesis that one and the same PP in roughly identical contexts vacillates between being predicative and being argumental is incompatible with the clause of the Theta Criterion stating that a predicate that has a θ-role to assign must assign it.

(20) a. dat Jan het boek (*op de plank*) zette (**op de plank*).
          that Jan the book (on the shelf) put (on the shelf)
     b. dat Jan het boek (*op de plank*) **neer** zette (*op de plank*).
          that Jan the book (on the shelf) down put (on the shelf)

In the case of locative resultatives of the type in (20), the PP's resistance to PP-over-V in the particle-less construction clearly prevents us from assuming that the locative PP is non-predicative throughout. Consider next, however, the case of prepositional dative constructions. As (21) shows, the dative PP is extraposable irrespective of the presence of a lexical particle:

(21) a. dat Jan het boek (*aan Marie*) gaf (*aan Marie*).
          that Jan the book (to Marie) gave (to Marie)
     b. dat Jan het boek (*aan Marie*) **terug/weg** gaf (*aan Marie*).
          that Jan the book (to Marie) back/away gave (to Marie)

The paradoxical outcome of a comparison of English (16) and Dutch (21) seems to be that in Dutch the dative PP apparently never qualifies as a complement-SC predicate, while in English the very same PP passes the Predicate Inversion test for predicativity.

One way to go about solving this paradox might be to assume that the dative PP is in fact never a SC predicate. The facts of Dutch PP-over-V then fall out without further ado. The grammaticality of English (16) may be reconciled with the hypothesis by assuming that the structure of "bare" dative constructions features an *empty particle*, whose projection undergoes movement to SpecIP in Predicate Inversion constructions of the type in (16), as in (22):

(22) $[_{PP1} \emptyset [_{PP2}$ to Mary]]$_j$ was given $[_{SC}$ a/the/that book $t_j]$

An analysis along these lines, which is adopted in Mulder (1992a,b), steers clear of a collision with the Theta Criterion, dative PPs being uniformly non-predicative. Notice, however, that the other objection to an analysis of this type raised in section 2.3.4, that it is contingent on the existence of overt-syntactic particle movement in English, still stands. The evidence against syntactic particle incorporation in English presented in section 2.4.3 thus casts doubt on such a proposal. Moreover, an account of dative constructions based on these premises would be incompatible with the analysis of Dative Shift to be presented and motivated in the remainder of this chapter. To the extent that this latter analysis is successful, it counts as an additional objection to a uniformly non-predicative approach to dative PPs.

Finally, notice that on an analysis of prepositional dative constructions according to which the dative PP is never itself predicative, the subject of the verb's SC complement (i.e. the Theme NP) is θ-marked by the projection of the particle, which may be empty or overt. It seems rather counterintuitive to deny a contentful and overt element like the dative preposition the ability to assign an external θ-role, and to assume instead that — in dative constructions lacking a verbal particle — the prime responsibility for θ-marking the Theme NP resides with a zero element.[7]

In what follows, I shall therefore assume the hypothesis in (23a), and adopt an analysis of triadic constructions according to which the verb takes a propositional (SC) complement; it is the dative P that is responsible for the assignment of the Theme θ-role (to its subject) and the Goal θ-role (to its complement), as codified in (23b):[8]

---

[7] Note that my claim here is *not* that empty heads could not be θ-markers — they certainly can select a dative SC complement in the analysis of triadic constructions developed in this chapter.

[8] Kayne (1993b:39) derives the SC analysis of prepositional dative constructions from his Linear Correspondence Axiom, according to which putative structures in which either both the Theme NP and the dative PP are sisters of the verb or the Theme NP forms a constituent with the verb to which the dative PP is adjoined are excluded, so that only the SC scenario remains. Déchaine (1993:228ff.) and Bowers (1993:636, (109a)) agree that dative PPs are syntactic predicates; Reinhart & Reuland (1993) deny all P-types syntactic predicatehood by definition (also cf. chapter 2, fn. 2), which seems untenable in the light of the Predicate Inversion data. Reinhart & Reuland distinguish between locative and dative Ps by claiming that the former but not the latter are *semantic* predicates, on the basis of the binding facts in (i), which their Binding Theory accommodates with the aid of the assumption that all three arguments in (ia) receive their θ-roles from the same θ-role assigner (the verb) while in (ib) the locative P *over* is a semantic predicate of its own. Then (ia) with *him* is bad since the predicate (*explain*) is reflexive (given that two of its arguments are coindexed) but fails to be reflexive-marked (since *him* is not a reflexive-marker); (ib) is fine with *him* coindexed with the subject since it contains two predicates, neither of which is reflexive.

(i)   a.   John$_i$ explained Bill to {*him$_i$/himself$_i$}.
         b.   John$_i$ rolled the carpet over {him$_i$/himself$_i$}.

I disagree with Reinhart & Reuland that the distinction between (ia,b) should be made in thematic terms, by denying dative Ps θ-role assigning potential. In my view, both locative and dative Ps are θ-assigning heads. The analysis to be presented might accommodate (i) by assuming that in P-dative constructions, Dative Shift obtains at LF (cf. also Hornstein 1994:471 for antecedent-contained deletion facts which may suggest that LF Dative Shift applies in P-dative constructions). Facts of the type in (i) require further study, though, in the light of the following observations (from Pesetsky 1993:fn. 153). For one thing, CFC effects do occasionally show up even in P-dative constructions, if 'the Theme is also an Agent of its own activity', as in (ii). For another, CFC effects can remain absent in contexts in which they are otherwise found, witness the contrast in (iii).

(ii)   *The girls$_i$ sent Bill to each other$_i$'s relatives.
(iii)   a.   *Sue$_i$ made the rocks land on herself$_i$.
         b.   John and Mary$_i$ let the honey drip on each other$_i$'s feet.

An appropriately fine-grained theory of opacity conditions on binding relationships should be able to distinguish between the various examples given above; in the light of the contrast between (ia) (with *himself*) and (ii), however, it seems dubious that such a theory will avail itself of Reinhart & Reuland's suggestion that dative Ps are not semantic predicates.

(23) a.   The dative PP is a SC predicate.
      b.   Triadic verbs take a *propositional* (SC) complement; the Theme and
            Goal θ-roles are assigned by the dative preposition.

The Predicate Inversion examples in (16) support the hypothesis in (23a), and
argue directly against a host of recent approaches to triadic constructions (including Kayne 1984:chapter 7; Baker 1988; Larson 1988; Aoun & Li 1989;
Marantz 1990; E. Hoekstra 1991; Johnson 1991) which neither assign the dative
PP predicative status, nor can have recourse to an alternative strategy of the
type advocated in Mulder (1992a,b).[9] Dismissing such analyses, I now turn to
two crucial observations about double object constructions featuring a verbal
particle which pave the way for the analysis of Dative Shift that will be developed later in this chapter.

3.4 Particle modification and Dative Shift

In section 2.4.6 I addressed the distribution of particle modification in English
on the basis of the contrast in (24), and concluded that the descriptive generalisation covering English verb-particle reanalysis can be stated as in (25):

(24) a.   They looked the information (**right**) *up*.
      b.   They looked (***right**) *up* the information.

(25)   Particle modification is impossible if V–Prt reanalysis has occurred.

With the generalisation in (25) (which, as shown in section 2.4.6, follows
from the theory of head movement on the plausible assumption that the modifier
is an X^0-element) in mind, let us now consider the fact (noted by Oehrle 1976:
192; Carlson & Roeper 1980:150, fn. 12; Kayne 1985:126–27) that it is impossible to modify the particle in a double object construction. That is, (2b)
becomes ungrammatical once we insert *right* in front of the particle *off*:

(26)   John sent Bob (***right**) *off* a package.

The ban on particle modification suggests, in view of (25), that verb-particle
reanalysis is obligatory in double object constructions. The necessity of
reanalysis in double object constructions is further corroborated by a correlation
discussed in the next section.

---

[9] I shall return in section 3.11.2 to the issue of Dutch PP-extraposition (PP-over-V), which seems
to present *prima facie* evidence against (23a). There, the problems raised by PP-over-V in P-dative
constructions will turn out to be only apparent.

3.5 Particle reanalysis: A correlation

Oehrle (1976:230–34) has noted that among English particles, 'we find a set which occurs in the prepositional dative construction but not in the double object construction' (1976:230), and although 'the correlation here is not perfect', it seems to be in general correct that precisely those particles that may not occur in the double object construction also do not allow verb-adjacent placement in the corresponding prepositional dative construction. As Oehrle (1976:233) observes, 'the verb *read* seems to behave precisely along [these] lines [in that] there is a perfect correlation between the possibility of the inside position and the occurrence of the double object construction', as is shown by (27) and (28): the particles *down, in, through* and *up* resist V-adjacent placement in the dative constructions in (27), and precisely they cannot occur in the double object constructions in (28).[10]

(27)   a.   John read *back* the figures to me.
     b.   *John read *down* the announcement to the crowd.
     c.   *John read *in* the figures to the secretary.
     d.   John read *off* the figures to the crowd.
     e.   John read *out* the figures to the audience.
     f.   *John read *through* the figures to the audience.
     g.   *John read *up* the figures to the guest (on the second floor).

(28)   a.   John read me *back* the figures.
     b.   *John read the crowd *down* the announcement.
     c.   *John read the secretary *in* the figures.
     d.   John read the crowd *off* the figures.
     e.   John read the audience *out* the figures.
     f.   *John read the audience *through* the figues.
     g.   *John read the guest (on the second floor) *up* the figures.

From a theoretical perspective, the correlation between a particle's ability to be placed in verb-adjacent position and its ability to occur in a double object construction directly appeals to the notion of verb-particle reanalysis. Only those particles that can be reanalysed with the verb and may hence be V-adjacent in datives, can occur in the double object construction. Again we see that verb-particle reanalysis is obligatory in double object constructions.

---

[10] All examples in (27) have grammatical counterparts featuring the V–NP–Prt–PP order.

3.6 Why obligatory reanalysis?

At first blush, it does not seem at all obvious that V–Prt reanalysis has applied in (26) and (28). For one thing, the verb and the particle are not linearly adjacent (and adjacency is often put forward as a condition on reanalysis). Moreover, there seems to be no obvious motive for the application of V–Prt reanalysis. In (24b), reanalysis is executed for the purposes of Case Theory, in that it enables the NP *the information* to receive Case in its D-structure position. In (26)/(28), on the other hand, the Case Filter is not likely to be responsible for the obligatoriness of reanalysis, as becomes clear from even a cursory inspection of the passive constructions that can be formed on the basis of English double object constructions. While for all speakers of English an indirect object passive such as (29a) is perfectly acceptable, a direct object passive like (29b) is rejected in many varieties of English (cf. the survey in Czepluch 1982). This may be taken to suggest that the verb is not (directly) responsible for the assignment of Case to the direct object in the double object construction (at least in the majority case). Since the ill-formedness of (26) with *right* and the pertinent instances of (28) cuts across all dialects, the need for V–Prt reanalysis is hence unlikely to have anything to do with Case assignment to the direct object (*contra* E. Hoekstra 1991:116).

(29) a. Mary was given a book.
    b. %A book was given Mary.

In an example of *wh*-extraction of the predicate of SC2 in a prepositional complex particle construction such as (30), V–Prt reanalysis is forced by the ECP. In order for the PP *to whom* to be extractable, the verb and the particle must be reanalysed for otherwise PP's trace would fail to be lexically governed (cf. chapter 2 for extensive discussion). The obligatoriness of reanalysis immediately explains the deviance of (30) with *right*.

(30)   To whom did John send (**right**) *off* a package?

Again, however, it is not immediately obvious how the ECP could be the trigger for the application of V–Prt reanalysis in a double object construction like (26) or (28). I would like to argue, however, it *is* in fact the ECP which is responsible for the obligatory reanalysis of verb and particle in (26) and (28). In particular, I argue that the double object construction is derived from the D-structure underlying all triadic constructions via *A-movement of the dative PP*, much as in a Predicate Inversion construction like (31):

(31)   To Bob was sent (**right**) *off* a package.

Here reanalysis is likewise forced by the ECP, and particle modification is ruled out in accordance with (25).[11]

3.7 An empty verb in triadic constructions

Before presenting further details of the analysis of Dative Shift, I should first of all determine what it is that the particle is reanalysed with. Is it the matrix triadic verb, or is it perhaps a lower, abstract verbal head? The following data favour the latter view.

In English simplex verb-particle constructions, the particle may normally be positioned either to the left or to the right of the "object NP" (cf. (32)). In coordination constructions of the type in (33), however, only the "outer particle" alternant yields a grammatical output (cf. Svenonius 1992):

(32) a.   John turned (*up*) the heat (*up*).
      b.   John turned (*down*) the air conditioning (*down*).

(33) a.   John turned the heat *up* and the air conditioning *down*.
      b.   *John turned *up* the heat and *down* the air conditioning.

The ill-formedness of (33b) can be made to fall out from the fact that V–Prt reanalysis must apply here but is prevented from applying in the second conjunct due to the fact that this conjunct contains no verbal head with which the particle can be reanalysed. The data in (33) hence support an analysis of the word-order alternation in the English verb-particle construction in terms of V–Prt reanalysis.

These coordination data moreover yield further insight into the structure of double object constructions. As David Pesetsky (p.c.) has pointed out to me, double object constructions with a lexical particle give rise to the following coordination facts:[12]

(34) a.   ?Whether I send Bill *down* a package or Mary *up* a letter, ...
      b.   *Whether I send Bill *down* a package or *up* a letter, ...

---

[11] Recall that, though NP-movement is exempt from the ECP, A-movement of non-referential constituents continues to be subject to the ECP (cf. chapter 1, section 1.2.3 and fn. 9).

[12] The examples are Pesetsky's; (34a) is grammatical with stress on *Bill* and *Mary*, while (34b) is bad on any intonation.

In sections 3.4 and 3.5 I argued on the basis of *right*-modification and particle placement data that the particle in an English double object construction undergoes obligatory reanalysis. The coordination example in (34a) now leads us to conclude that whatever the particle is reanalysed with is *not* the matrix triadic verb. For if *send* were the verb that *up* in (34) reanalyses with, we would expect both (34a) and (34b) to be ill-formed, contrary to fact. Since V–Prt reanalysis is unquestionably involved in the derivation of the double object construction, but since the matrix triadic verb is apparently not the verb with which the particle is reanalysed, we are led to conclude that double object constructions contain more structure than meets the eye. In particular, the grammaticality of (34a) suggests that double object constructions contain an *empty verb* below the matrix verb, and that it is this empty verb that reanalyses with the particle.

Several options are open to us concerning the nature of the empty verbal head "α". We may follow Larson (1988) (also cf. Johnson 1991 and Bowers 1993 for essentially similar views) in assuming that α is the trace of the triadic matrix verb, or we may assume, following Vikner (1990) and E. Hoekstra (1991), that α is a base-generated contentless empty verb coindexed with the triadic matrix verb, or we may adopt Abney's (1987) suggestion (also cf. Aoun & Li 1989; T. Hoekstra 1991; Mulder 1992a,b) that α is an empty contentful verb with possessive meaning, an empty counterpart of possessive *have*.

This third option immediately accommodates the fact that the Theme and the Goal typically entertain a possessive relationship in double object constructions, the latter being the possessor of the former. That is, in a double object construction like (35a), Mary ends up in possession of the book as a result of the action denoted by the verbal predicate. In prepositional dative constructions, the relationship between the Theme and the Goal is locational, somewhat clumsily expressible in English in terms of a copula construction (cf. (35b)).

(35) a. John gave Mary a book. (→ Mary has a book)
    b. John gave a book to Mary. (→ a book "is" to Mary)

That there is a possessive relationship between the Theme and Goal arguments of a double object construction is apparent from such classic mismatches between dative and double object constructions as (36)–(37) (cf. a.o. Hoekstra 1978; Pinker 1987, 1989; Pesetsky 1993; Tremblay 1991):

(36) a. I sent the package to the boarder.
    b. I sent the package to the border.

(37) a. I sent the boarder the package.
    b. *I sent the border the package.

Since *the border*, in contradistinction to the [+human] *the boarder*, is not a possible possessor, the ill-formedness of (37b) follows straightforwardly from the hypothesis that there is a relationship of possession between the direct and indirect objects in a double object construction. This is further confirmed by Tremblay's (1991) examples in (38):

(38) a.   The revolution gave Romania a new government.
     b.   The revolution gave Mary a new status.
     c.   ?*The revolution gave Mary a new government.

While Romania is a possible possessor of a new government, and Mary may naturally be the possessor of a new status, there can be no relationship of possession between Mary and a new government, whence the deviance of (38c).

On the assumption that the structure of double object constructions contains an empty possessive verb, the contrasts in (37) and (38) may then be related to the parallel contrast in the possessive *have* examples in (39) and (40):

(39) a.   The boarder has the package.
     b.   *The border has the package.

(40) a.   Romania has a new government.
     b.   Mary has a new status.
     c.   ?*Mary has a new government.

In view of these facts, I shall opt for the inclusion of an abstract *have*-type verb in double object constructions, though not directly. Rather than assuming that *have* exists as an independent lexical atom, I would like to suggest — in line with tradition — that main verb *have* is not a primitive verb but the result of incorporation of a dative preposition into the copula *be*.[13] All D-structure tokens of main verb *have*, then, are underlyingly DECOMPOSED into the semantically vacuous copula *be* and the θ-assigning dative preposition *to*. Let us codify these assumptions in (41):

(41) a.   The structure of double object constructions features an empty possessive verb.
     b.   Main verb *have* is underlyingly *decomposed* into BE+TO.

Before proceeding to the analysis of triadic constructions, I shall first motivate the hypothesis in (41b).

---

[13] For a traditional claim to this effect, see Benveniste's (1966:197) statement that '*avoir* n'est rien d'autre qu'un *être à* inversé' ('*have* is nothing else than an inverted *be to*'). Kayne (1993a) presents a decompositional approach to *have* which is similar in spirit to the one outlined here but different in detail.

3.8 Decomposition of main verb *have*

Consider (35) once again. The paraphrases of the Theme–Goal relationships to the right of the arrows suggest that the alternation between dative and double object constructions is parallelled by a similar alternation between possessive *have* constructions and copula constructions containing a dative preposition.

In English, the copular paraphrase of (35b) is fairly clumsy. English virtually exclusively employs the verb *have* to express possession in matrix contexts like (42) (but cf. (47), below). In several languages, however, possessive relationships are expressed in copula constructions featuring a preposition. This is the case in for instance the Slavic languages, as in the Russian example in (42) (Chvany 1975; also cf. Kayne 1984:135).[14]

(42)   Ivan *has* pretty eyes.

(43)   *U* Ivana krasivye glaza.
         P Ivan pretty eyes

In a third group of languages, there is an alternation in the domain of possessive constructions between copula constructions with a dative preposition and sentences with *have*. French is among these languages. Tremblay (1991) argues that in French, dative Case is the unmarked strategy for the expression of possession. The French copula construction in (44a), featuring the dative preposition *à*, is an example of a matrix possessive construction. It alternates with (44b), containing the main verb *avoir* 'have'. Similar alternations are found in (French-based) Haitian creole (cf. (45), from Lumsden 1992), and, as is well known, also in Latin (cf. (46)).[15]

(44) a.   Le livre *est à* Jean.
           the book is to Jean
      b.   Jean *a* le livre.
           Jean has the book

(45) a.   Liv la *se pou* Jan.
           book the is for Jan
      b.   Jan *gen* liv la.
           Jan has book the

---

[14]   The example in (43) features a zero copula, as is common in Russian present tense constructions.

[15]   In languages like English and also Fongbe (a Kwa language spoken in Benin; cf. Lumsden 1992), the *have* construction alternates with a construction in which the possessor is expressed as a DP-contained genitive (cf. English *The book is John's*). I shall not be concerned with these latter constructions; cf. Kayne (1993a) and Tellier (to appear) for relevant discussion.

(46) a.   *Mihi est* liber.
            me(DAT) is book
      b.   *Habeo* librum.
            I-have book

Though mostly expressing possession in matrix constructions with the aid of a possessive verb, English and Dutch occasionally feature an alternation similar to French (44) between a copula construction containing the dative preposition (*to* and *aan*, respectively) and the possessive verb *have* or *hebben*, as in the following pairs of examples:[16]

(47) a.   The choice *is* up *to* you.
      b.   You *have* the choice.

(48) a.   De keus/het woord *is aan* jou.
            the choice/the word is to you
      b.   Jij *hebt* de keus/het woord.
            you have the choice/the word

The alternants in (47a,b) and (48a,b) are not semantically equivalent, just like the alternants of the dative alternation and the *be+to*/*have* alternation in general are not. *Thematically*, however, there does not appear to be any robust dichotomy between the a- and b-examples discussed above (though, given our incomplete knowledge of the nature of θ-roles, this is not easy to prove). Let us assume, then, that the a- and b-examples in alternations of the type in (44), (47) or (48) have a common base structure. In particular, let us hypothesise that the *be+to* construction is a reflection of this underlying structure, and that the possessive *have* construction is derived from it via *incorporation* of the dative preposition into the verb, and concomitant movement of the preposition's complement to subject position.[17] Possessive *have*, then, is the surface, suppletive result of the syntactic amalgamation of the copula and an incorporated dative preposition. The possessive interpretation of *have* constructions (as opposed to *be+to* sentences) can now be captured by noting that in *have* constructions, the possessor finds itself in the subject position of the possession predicate *have* at S-structure.

The alternations in (47) and (48) can be fully recreated in triadic constructions, as shown in (49) and (50):

---

[16] Mulder (1990:24) discusses a Dutch case similar to the one in (48).

[17] The details of the transformation involved will be addressed in detail in the analysis of Dative Shift to be presented below. To deny *have* lexical status throughout would entail arguing that auxiliary *have* is also decomposed. Kayne (1993a) presents a decompositional approach to auxiliary *have*.

(49) a.   John gives/offers the choice to you.

      b.   John gives/offers you the choice.

(50) a.   Jan geeft de keus/het woord aan jou.

          Jan gives the choice/the word to you

      b.   Jan geeft jou de keus/het woord.

          Jan gives you the choice/the word

Here again, the b-example features a possessive relationship between the Goal and Theme arguments, while the a-example does not.[18] This can be captured in a way similar to the semantic difference found in (47) and (48), if we assume that (i) the structure of triadic constructions includes an empty verbal head embedded under the triadic verb, and (ii) the dative preposition is incorporated into this abstract verb in the course of the derivation of the double object construction from the structure underlying all triadic constructions. An analysis of the dative alternation along these lines is developed in the next sections.

3.9 The structure of triadic constructions and the analysis of Dative Shift

I can now proceed to presenting the analysis of triadic constructions and Dative Shift that I shall employ in the remainder of this chapter.[19] Recall from section 3.3 that the dative PP is a SC predicate, responsible for θ-role assignment to the Theme. I shall assume (although, as I pointed out in section 3.8, in the absence of proper understanding of the content of the thematic roles involved in the dative alternation this is by no means easy to prove) that the prepositional dative and double object constructions are *thematically identical*. By Baker's (1988) Uniformity of Theta Assignment Hypothesis, we are then led to the conclusion that the dative and double object constructions have identical underlying structures, hence that Dative Shift must be a transformational rule. In particular, I argue that the structure underlying triadic constructions is that of *complex particle constructions*, enriched with an additional abstract VP. A-movement of the dative PP is responsible for the derivation of the double object construction, and the empty head of this PP is incorporated into the abstract verb heading the triadic verb's SC complement.

The basic assumptions that form the backbone of the analysis are summed up in (51). The structures they give rise to are given in (52).

---

[18]   The a-examples are often somewhat odd: the NPs occupying the *affected argument* position here often are not very suitable affected arguments (cf. 2.4.4.1 and 3.12.2 on affectedness).

[19]   I shall initially confine my attention to triadic constructions with a lexical particle, turning to particle-less dative and double object constructions in section 3.11.

(51) a.   The double object construction is transformationally related to the prepositional dative construction.

b.   The structure underlying dative and double object constructions is as in (52a).

c.   The transformation responsible for the derivation of the double object construction is *PP-movement* into the specifier position of SC2, and on to SpecSC1.[20]

d.   The (empty) P heading the moved dative PP is *incorporated* into the abstract copula heading the triadic verb's SC complement.

(52) a.

b.

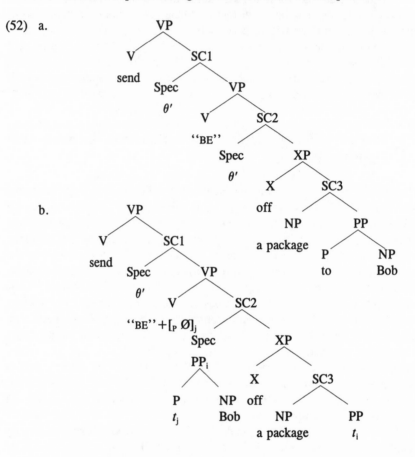

[20]   The additional step from SpecSC2 to SpecSC1 is not pictured in the structure in (52b) (for reasons of perspicuity of the already quite complex structure). This further movement is motivated by the possessive interpretation of Goals in double object constructions (recall that possessive interpretation was given a structural account in section 3.7, (41)), and by Case considerations as well (cf. 3.10.1).

In the following section I shall investigate the motives for movement of the dative PP in the derivation of the double object construction, addressing the issue of Case assignment in double object constructions (3.10.1) and the way in which the empty head of the dative PP in double object constructions is licensed (3.10.2). In section 3.11, I then proceed to the analysis of triadic constructions lacking a verbal particle.

3.10 The motivation for movement

It will be clear that once we analyse the dative alternation in terms of movement of the prepositional predicate of SC3, as in (52), the fact that the particle may not be premodified by *right* in a double object construction reduces to the same factor that rules out examples like (30) or (31) with *right*: the ECP forces V–Prt reanalysis, which is blocked by the presence of an adverbial modifier. Why, though, must there be movement of the Goal in double object constructions? And, more specifically, why must the entire dative PP undergo movement, rather than just the Goal-NP contained in it?

3.10.1 Case Theory

Dative Shift may be viewed as being motivated at least in part by the Case Filter. While in prepositional dative constructions the Theme NP undergoes Case-driven NP-movement, in double object constructions it does not; its predicate, the empty-headed dative PP, moves in its stead, thereby allowing the Theme NP to receive Case *in situ*. Let us see how this happens.

As shown in the structure in (52b), Dative Shift involves movement of the dative PP into the specifier position of the SC embedded under the abstract copula, and incorporation of the dative P into BE. As a result of P-incorporation into BE, which by itself is a non-Case-assigning verb, the head of the lower VP comes to be equipped with a Case feature, which it may then assign to some NP that it governs. The NP in question will be the Theme NP, which is governed by BE+$P_\emptyset$ by virtue of Baker's (1988) Government Transparency Corollary, given the fact that BE is reanalysed with the head of its SC-complement ("X" in (52)). The Goal NP is provided with Case by the matrix verb, which comes to govern it after onward movement of the empty-headed dative PP to SpecSC1. In this way the analysis ensures that both Case-dependent NPs in the double object construction are provided with Case. This is depicted in (53):

(53)
$[_{VP} [_{V1} V1] [_{SC1} [_{PP} t_j NP_{Go}]_i [_{VP} [_{V2} BE+P_{\emptyset j}] [_{SC2} t_i [_{XP} X [_{SC3} NP_{Th} [_{PP} t_i]]]]]]]$

In order that Case can be assigned to the Theme NP in a double object construction, BE must be provided with P's structural Case feature, and in order to bring this about, P must incorporate into BE.[21] In the next subsection we shall see that incorporation of $P_\emptyset$ into BE in its turn forces movement of the entire dative PP across the head of SC2 ("X"), for ECP reasons.

3.10.2 Licensing the empty preposition

In the analysis of triadic constructions presented in this chapter, a key assumption is that even in double object constructions, which lack an overt reflex of it, the dative preposition is structurally present (cf. also Kayne 1984:chapter 7; Czepluch 1982; Haegeman 1986; Baker 1988). I would like to argue that lexical dative prepositions in principle alternate freely with zero counterparts. These empty dative Ps must be licensed, however, which explains the limited surface distribution of these elements.[22] To accommodate the well-known cross-linguistic variation with regard to the positions in which bare dative phrases may turn up, I submit that empty dative prepositions can in principle be licensed in either of two ways:

---

[21] Notice that if the BE + $P_\emptyset$ complex were to assign Case to the Goal (which is *a priori* possible), the Theme would have to move into the governing domain of the matrix verb to pick up Case. Such a scenario is straightforwardly ruled out by economy considerations. A derivation in which the dative PP moves to SpecSC2 and thereby allows the Theme NP to pick up Case *in situ* involves fewer XP-movement chains than one in which the dative PP still moves to SpecSC2 and the Theme NP in addition undergoes Case-driven movement to SpecSC1; since the two derivations are otherwise identical, a Dative Shift scenario involving NP-movement of the Theme is thus less economical than one featuring *in situ* Case assignment to the Theme. Effectively, then, Dative Shift (i.e. movement of the dative PP to SpecSC2) and NP-movement of the Theme NP entertain a mutual "bleeding" relationship — whenever one takes place, the other will not.

This also implies that in a "genuine" double object construction, passivisation with raising of the Theme is ruled out. We thus effectively predict the English type situation in which, on the whole, only Goals raise to subject in double object passives. Languages (and dialects of English; cf. Czepluch 1982) with grammatical double object Theme passives presumably derive these from "covert" prepositional dative constructions, not from Dative Shift constructions (see chapter 4 on the structural ambiguity of double object constructions; cf. esp. the end of section 4.5.2).

[22] In this study I only consider the alternation between lexical and zero P in the context of dative constructions, where it is cross-linguistically most productive. Baker (1988) discusses locative and instrumental applicative constructions, in which (especially if the applicative morpheme is not the spell-out of an incorporated preposition; cf. chapter 5) we also find such alternations. In the European languages, however, locative and instrumental constructions never feature a word-order alternation of the Dative Shift type (cf. *John put the books on the shelf* vs. **John put the books the shelf*). Since there is considerably more variation in the class of locative prepositions (*on, in, under, beneath, between, above* etc.), while there is only one dative preposition in each of these languages, the fact that locative Ps do not alternate with a zero counterpart may be related to the loss of indispensable semantic information that would be its result.

(54)   An empty dative preposition is licensed iff (i) or (ii):
         (i)   [$_P$ Ø] is identified by dative Case morphology;
         (ii)   [$_P$ Ø] is incorporated (at some level) into a verb.

In languages featuring overt Case morphology, like German or Icelandic, the licensing strategy in (54i) is clearly applicable.[23] In these languages, then, the empty head of a zero-headed PP will always be licensed, no matter where the dative PP is positioned. As a result, the empty-headed dative PP may remain *in situ* in a position to the right of the Theme NP, whence the grammaticality of German (55b) and Icelandic (56b) alongside the a-examples exhibiting the familiar Goal–Theme order.[24]

(55) a.   daß der Hans der Maria das Buch gibt.
           that the Hans the Maria(DAT) the book gives
      b.   daß der Hans das Buch der Maria gibt.
           that the Hans the book the Maria(DAT) gives

(56) a.   Jón gaf konunginum ambáttina.
           Jon gave the-king(DAT) the-maidservant
      b.   Jón gaf ambáttina konunginum.
           Jon gave the-maidservant the-king(DAT)

---

[23] In view of the extreme paucity of prepositional dative constructions in German and Icelandic (cf. Sprouse 1989 and Ottósson 1991), it would in fact be plausible to assume that dative Case morphology *realises* P, the dative phrase never actually being empty-headed in these languages. Emonds (1985, section 5.7; 1987) argues explicitly that morphological dative Case on indirect objects in languages like German 'must be ascribed to the presence of an empty, introductory P' (1987:617) which is "alternatively realised" as a dative Case affix.

[24] I assume that in (55b) and (56b), the Goal surfaces *in situ*; cf. Falk (1990), Holmberg (1991) and Collins & Thráinsson (1993) (for Icelandic). Support for this view comes from the fact that in the b-examples (but not in the a-sentences) the Theme may bind a constituent of the Goal, which suggests that the Theme c-commands the Goal (cf. Barss & Lasnik 1986 and also chapter 4, below, on binding asymmetries in double object constructions):

(i) a.   daß man die Gäste$_i$ einander$_i$ vorgestellt hat.   (Müller 1992)
          that one the guests (ACC) each-other introduced has
          'that one introduced the guests to each other.'
     b.   Ég hafði gefið ambáttina$_i$ konungi sínum$_i$.   (Collins & Thráinsson 1993)
          I had given the-maidservant(ACC) king her(REFL)
          'I had given the maidservant to her king.'

Müller (1992) and Ottósson (1991), however, claim that the Goal phrase does not occupy its base position in German and Icelandic double object constructions with Theme–Goal order. I shall address Müller's analysis in section 4.6, below. I cannot account for the fact that the Icelandic Theme–Goal order requires stress on the indirect object and hence is unacceptable with a pronominal Goal.

In languages like English, by contrast, there is no dative Case morphology to effect the licensing of the empty head of the dative PP in double object constructions (i.e. (54i) is inapplicable). These languages may hence only resort to the second licensing strategy: the empty-headed dative PP must be (or must at some point have been) in a position from which its head may incorporate (in syntax or at LF) into the verb.

By moving the entire empty-headed dative PP into the governing domain of the incorporating verb, the structural conditions on incorporation can be met. Recall from section 1.2.4, above, that incorporation of the head of a lexically governed specifier into its governor is both empirically attested and theoretically legitimate. Movement of the dative PP into the specifier of the incorporating verb's SC complement (as depicted in (52b)) hence is a way of complying with the licensing condition in (54ii). What remains to be shown is that if we leave the dative PP *in situ*, incorporation of its head into V is impossible. Once we can show that this is indeed the case, we can *force* the zero-headed dative PP to move in double object constructions in languages lacking overt dative Case morphology (such as English).

At this point, recall the discussion in section 2.3.6 about the blocking effect of an intervening particle on the incorporation of a head in the particle's complement into the verb, instantiated by the ill-formedness of Dutch adjectival complex particle constructions of the type in (57b):

(57) a.   dat ze de schuur **rood** (*over*) hebben (*over*) geschilderd.
            that they the barn red (PRT) have (PRT) painted
      b.   *dat ze de schuur hebben *over* **rood** geschilderd.
            *dat ze de schuur hebben **rood** *over* geschilderd.

In section 2.3.6 I showed that there are two logically possible ways of deriving word orders of the type in (57b): either (i) the particle incorporates into the verb, and the adjective subsequently undergoes "long-distance" head movement across the trace of the particle; or (ii) the adjective first incorporates into the particle, after which the complex head undergoes further incorporation into the verb. Both these scenarios were eliminated for adjectival (and verbal) complex particle constructions. The successive-cyclic strategy (ii) can be ruled out as a case of "improper head movement" in the light of Li's (1990) extension of the Binding Theory into the domain of head movement. The "long-distance" incorporation scenario (i) is straightforwardly eliminable in cases of adjectival (and verbal) complex particle constructions since, irrespective of whether the particle incorporates into the verb or not, its complement is a barrier to outside government for want of L-marking (cf. section 2.3.6 for detailed discussion).

In the triadic cases under current discussion, however, the "long-distance" scenario cannot be rejected simply by invoking the barrierhood of the particle's SC complement. After all, in triadic constructions the particle takes a prepositional SC complement, which is categorially non-distinct from the particle, hence interpretable as a *segment* of the particle's projection, exempt from barrierhood. Even so, "long-distance" incorporation of the empty dative P across the trace of an incorporated (or reanalysed) particle should be barred, for otherwise even languages like English should feature double object constructions with DO–IO order, which they clearly do not (cf. **I sent a book out Mary*). Let us consider the "long-distance incorporation" scenario in some more detail, therefore.

As Baker (1988) points out, it is impossible for the head of a Goal NP to be incorporated into the verb in noun-incorporating languages. The ill-formedness of the Tuscarora example in (58) (cf. Baker 1988:364) testifies to this. In this so-called applicative construction, the incorporated noun *wir* 'child' cannot be understood as the Goal argument:[25]

(58)   *Wa²-khe-yet-*wir*-ahninv²-*θ*.
         'I sold him to the children.'
         (OK as 'I sold the children to him.')

We may actually stay much closer to home illustrating the impossibility of Goal incorporation, when we consider that putative denominal verbs like *to church* in (59a) do not exist in languages like English or Dutch (cf. Hale & Keyser 1992). On the assumption that denominal verbs are derived via incorporation of the base noun into an abstract verb, as argued by Hale & Keyser (1992), the ill-formedness of (59a) is fully analogous to that of Tuscarora (58).

(59) a.   *John *church*ed his money.
      b.   John gave the *church* his money/gave his money to the *church*.

Baker's analysis of double object constructions, like the present approach, takes the Goal NP of triadic constructions to be contained in a dative PP whose head is incorporated into the verb. This analysis of double object (or applicative) constructions can be made to accommodate the structural ill-formedness of (58) and (59), so long as we can ensure that the trace of the incorporated dative preposition blocks antecedent-government of the trace of the incorporated Goal-N. Baker's own Government Transparency Corollary (cf. 1.2.5, (33)) seems to lead one to expect otherwise: incorporation of the intermediate P-head into the verb would turn the latter into the governor of the Goal NP, whose head would then be expected to be incorporable into the verb, the (antecedent-government clause of the) ECP being complied with.

---

[25] The affix *-θ* in (58) is the so-called applicative morpheme. More will be said about applicative constructions and applicative morphemes in chapter 5 of this study. Voskuil (1990) presents several Indonesian counterexamples to Baker's claim that incorporation of Goals is impossible. I shall not be concerned with these here, leaving a potential reanalysis of such examples for future research.

Baker (1988:336–37) prevents the GTC from affecting (i.e. increasing) the possibilities of antecedent-government by modifying the definition of antecedent-government as in (60):

(60)   A is a chain antecedent of B if and only if:
            (i)   A and B are of the same type *T*, and
            (ii)   A and B are chain-coindexed, and
            (iii) there is no category W of type *T* such that the smallest maximal projection containing W is c-commanded by A and has a head which selects some YP, where YP contains or is equal to B.

The revised Minimality condition in (60iii) is crucial in the context at hand. According to this clause of the definition of antecedent-government, the trace of the dative preposition in double object and applicative constructions counts as an intervening category "W" between the incorporating verb "A" and the prospective incorporate "B", the Goal-N. In this way, Baker ensures that putative cases of Goal incorporation are ill-formed.[26]

It is important at this stage to counter Bennis' (1992a) recent proposal that in Dutch particles can incorporate into verb clusters skipping traces of intermediate verbs on the way, which is in conflict with (60iii). Bennis notes that particles in Dutch can surface in several positions within the verbal cluster, as illustrated in (61):[27]

(61) a.   dat ik Jan *op* zou hebben willen bellen.
            that I Jan up would have want call
      b.   dat ik Jan zou *op* hebben willen bellen.
      c.   dat ik Jan zou hebben *op* willen bellen.
      d.   dat ik Jan zou hebben willen *op* bellen.
            'that I would have liked to call John up.'

Of the various options, (61a,d) are uninteresting from the present perspective; it is (61b,c) that interest us here. Let us focus initially on the way in which Bennis derives (61c), with *op* between *hebben* and *willen*. Consider the (conveniently simplified) structure of this construction prior to the application of particle movement, illustrated in (62):

---

[26] Baker (1988:337 and fn. 2) illustrates the relevance of the modification of the definition of antecedent-government given in (60) on the basis of some unrelated data as well. Hence (60) is not motivated solely by restrictions on incorporation.

[27] Not all variants of (61) are equally felicitous to all speakers of Dutch, but none of the particle placement possibilities is rejected outright by all speakers that Bennis consulted.

(62)

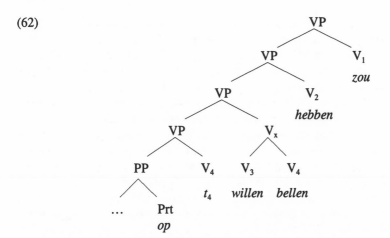

At some point in the derivation of (61c) the particle will have to left-adjoin to the complex V-node labelled "V_x" in (62). Bennis argues that the particle must move into this adjunction position in one fell swoop, crossing t_4, the trace of the verb that governs the particle's projection. This would be in agreement with the theory if t_4 did not count for the purposes of the Minimality condition. Bennis notes that an alternative derivation according to which *op* would first adjoin to t_4, after which the verbal cluster [$_V$ *op* t_4] would undergo Verb Raising, would result in an ill-formed surface result. Since Verb Raising (in contrast to particle incorporation) apparently involves right-adjunction, the result of applying Verb Raising to the complex head [$_V$ *op* t_4] would be the verbal cluster **willen bellen op*, which is ungrammatical. From this Bennis rightly concludes that the particle must move to V_x on its own. But the particular "long head movement" approach that he opts for seems neither forced upon us nor in fact sustainable.

The latter point becomes clear when we consider how Bennis would analyse (61b), with the particle between *zou* and *hebben* (i.e. *dat ik Jan zou op hebben willen bellen*). The difference between this example and the one just discussed lies in the fact that, at the point at which particle incorporation takes place in (61b), the complex verb V_x has undergone further movement, right-adjoining to V_2. This difference is important since in a derivation of (61b) along Bennis' lines the particle would now have to skip both t_4 and the trace of the complex head V_x (raised to V_2) — hence *two* intermediate traces. This time even the Government Transparency Corollary (applied to proper government) would presumably no longer guarantee a legitimate derivation — the complex verb resulting from incorporation of V_x into V_2 will come to govern everything that V_x governed prior to incorporation, but it surely will not extend its governing potential to that of an element incorporated into V_x.[28]

---

[28] I thank Arnold Evers for pointing this argument against Bennis (1992a) to me.

I shall not follow Bennis in assuming massive non-local particle movement in Dutch paradigms of the type in (61), therefore. Instead, one might think of an analysis of an example like (61c) according to which the particle first adjoins to t_4 and subsequently *excorporates* from the complex verbal node, moving up to V_x on its own (cf. Roberts 1991; Guasti 1991, 1993 on the analysis of excorporation).[29] Alternatively, one might even consider giving up a head-movement approach to (61) altogether, and follow Den Besten & Broekhuis' (1992) Verb Projection Raising analysis of this paradigm. The choice between these options (and possibly others which I have not thought of) is immaterial here. The point to bear in mind is that Bennis' (1992a) "long head movement" approach to (61b,c) is presumably not the optimal way to account for these data.

I shall henceforth assume Baker's revised Minimality condition in (60iii). With the aid of this constraint, we may now eliminate the "long-distance incorporation" scenario for the licensing of empty heads of *in situ* dative PPs in languages of the (54ii) class, such as English: (the trace of) the particle intervenes between the incorporator and the prospective incorporate. Since the successive cyclic strategy is also ruled out (improper movement), we may now force empty-headed dative PPs to undergo movement into the governing domain of the incorporating verb in languages of this type. This, then, is why the derivation of double object constructions in languages featuring no overt dative Case morphology must involve movement of the empty-headed projection of the dative preposition, and not just of the NP complement of P.

3.11 Triadic constructions lacking an overt particle

3.11.1 An empty verb and an empty particle

The discussion so far has centred on prepositional dative and double object constructions that contain an overt particle. The emphasis on particle constructions was motivated by the fact that these yield us insight into the analysis of triadic constructions, while particle-less dative and double object constructions are rather less instructive.

When we now turn to these "bare" triadic constructions, several considerations lead us to adopt a structure of the type in (63), which is completely identical with that of triadic constructions with a verbal particle. The tree in (63), like the structure of triadic particle constructions, features three SCs. The top SC is again headed by abstract BE, the bottom one by the dative preposition. The intermediate SC, which in the examples discussed so far contained a lexical particle, has an empty head in "bare" triadic constructions.

---

[29]   Other putative cases of "long head movement", particularly in the languages of the Balkans (cf. Rivero 1991 and references cited there), might be (re)analysed in a similar fashion.

(63)

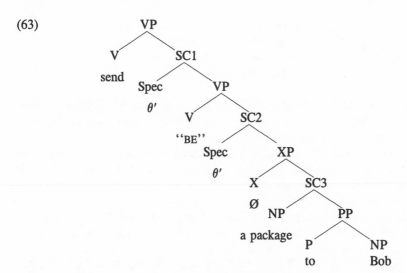

The inclusion in the structure of particle-less triadic constructions of SC3 is motivated by the predicativity of the dative PP, as discussed in section 3.3. The presence of SC1, headed by the abstract copula, is also a consequence of general considerations discussed above. That there are two VPs in the structure of triadic constructions can also be empirically supported on the basis of an interesting peculiarity of Swedish double object constructions in the domain of so-called Object Shift phenomena. I shall briefly address this empirical argument for an empty verb in double object constructions here.

The Scandinavian languages feature a leftward movement process, known as Object Shift (cf. Holmberg 1986; Vikner 1990; and references cited there), whereby objects (in constructions in which verb movement obtains) are moved into a position to the left of adverbial material. In the Mainland Scandinavian languages Object Shift normally affects pronominal objects only. This is illustrated in (64), from Danish (cf. Vikner 1990:289–90):

(64)   I går læste Peter (*den/*bogen*) ikke (*den/*bogen*).
          yesterday read Peter (it/the-book) not (it/the-book)

Interestingly, however, Holmberg (1986:212) notes (also cf. Josefsson 1992: 74, fn. 17) that in Swedish double object constructions, the indirect object may shift across an adverb regardless of whether it is a pronoun or a full NP:

(65) a.   Han gav inte Sara boken.
           he gave not Sara the-book
      b.   ?Han gav Sara inte boken.
           he gave Sara not the-book

(66) a.   Jag visar gärne barnen mina skivor.
           I show gladly the-children my records
      b.   (?)Jag visar barnen gärne mina skivor.
           I show the-children gladly my records

Holmberg (1986:212) observes that the b-examples of (65) and (66) are acceptable, 'more or less marginally, depending on dialect, and certain badly understood contextual conditions'.[30]

The present analysis of triadic constructions recognises *two* verbal projections
in the structure of triadic constructions. Examples of the type in (65b) and (66b)
can be accommodated by this analysis on the assumption that in these cases, the
adverb following the indirect object is adjoined to the VP of SC1 in (63) (headed by the abstract copula). The indirect object (contained in the zero-headed
dative PP which moves to SpecSC1) thus ends up in a position to the left of the
adverb.[31] The special role played by indirect object NPs with respect to the
application of Object Shift in Swedish can hence be accounted for by capitalising on the presence of two VPs in the structure of triadic constructions.

In the tree in (63), SC1 and SC3 hence turn out to be amply motivated. Why,
though, must the tree of "bare" triadic constructions also contain a projection
of a zero counterpart of a lexical particle? Several ingredients of the analysis
of the dative alternation developed in the previous sections conspire to motivate
adopting this additional layer of "invisible" structure. For one thing, just as in
double object constructions containing a verbal particle, the empty-headed dative
PP must be prevented from staying *in situ* in "bare" double object constructions in languages of the (54ii) class (cf. *I sent a book Mary*). In section 3.10.2
the fact that zero-headed dative PPs must move in English-type double object

---

[30] Ouhalla (1991:10) presents similar examples from (British) English, reproduced here in (i). Their
status is not crystal clear; thus Koizumi (1993:125) explicitly reports that his examples in (ii) are
ungrammatical.

(i)   a.   (?)I showed John yesterday the book.   (Ouhalla 1991:10)
       b.   (??)I gave Bill reluctantly the keys.
       c.   (?)I sent Bill last week my photos.
       d.   (?)I sent Mary immediately the parcel.
(ii)   a.   *Mary gave John secretly the book (on Friday).   (Koizumi 1993:125)
       b.   *Amber told Ben quietly the story (in the living room).

[31] The marginality of the pertinent examples might be attributed to a predisposition of adverbs to
be adjoined to the highest VP or to a VP with a lexical head. Also cf. Collins & Thráinsson (1993:
144–45, 149) for a similar problem arising in Icelandic double object constructions featuring Object
Shift of both objects across a sentence adverb. They suggest that sentential adverbials, while preferentially adjoining to the highest VP, 'can marginally adjoin to any VP whose head is in the checking
domain of the matrix T before S-Structure' (p. 149; cf. Chomsky 1993 on the notion "checking
domain").

particle constructions was accounted for by capitalising on the presence of a head position ("X", the position of the particle) intervening between the empty dative P and the verb (abstract BE) that is to license $P_\emptyset$ by incorporating it. Clearly, if this analysis holds water, we should now also include an intervening head between V and P in the structure of "bare" triadic constructions.

If the empty-headed dative PP may not remain *in situ* (in languages employing licensing condition (54ii), such as English), the structure should provide a landing-site for it to move to, in the governing domain of the verb into which the dative preposition must incorporate (i.e. abstract BE). This landing-site must in addition be an A-position, in the light of what was argued with respect to Case assignment in double object constructions in section 3.10.1. The structure of "bare" triadic constructions can only cater for this θ' A-position in the complement of abstract BE if we assume that it contains a projection of an ergative SC-head between abstract BE and the dative SC. The projection in question is XP in (63); the θ' A-position is the specifier of the SC projected from the zero head of XP.

In this way the analysis of the dative alternation ensures that the structure underlying particle-less dative and double object constructions reads as in (63). Clearly, though, if the presence of the empty SC predicate labelled "X" in (63) were motivated solely on theory-internal grounds, the case for the tree in (63) would not be particularly strong. The postulation of an empty SC-head in "bare" triadic constructions is supported, however, by word-order facts from Dutch prepositional dative constructions, which I discuss in section 3.11.2. I then proceed, in section 3.11.3, to presenting word order in Chinese dative constructions as additional evidence for the inclusion of an abstract head within the complement of triadic verbs.

3.11.2 Word order in Dutch dative constructions

As an SOV language, Dutch generates the complements of the verb to the left of the head at D-structure (*pace* Kayne 1993b and Zwart 1993). All prepositional complements, then, originate on the left-hand side of the verb. Some PPs, however, may optionally be extraposed to the right periphery of the clause, by what is commonly referred to as *PP-over-V* (Koster 1973). This PP-extraposition process is severely constrained, as I already pointed out in section 2.3.4, above (cf. Hoekstra 1984 for discussion). Consider the examples in (67) and (68), repeated from section 2.3.4 (also cf. (20a,b), above):[32]

---

[32] Here and elsewhere in this study, whenever examples of optional PP extraposition are presented, the double occurrence of the PP in brackets marks the two possible surface positions of the PP; the brackets should not be taken to mark optionality of the PP. See also fn. 34, below, on the absence of a correlation between extraposability and omissibility in the case of PP-over-V.

(67) a.   dat Jan (*aan taalkunde*) dacht (*aan taalkunde*).
            that Jan (of linguistics) thought (of linguistics).
      b.   dat Jan (*op zijn moeder*) wachtte (*op zijn moeder*).
            that Jan (for his mother) waited (for his mother)

(68) a.   dat Jan het boek (*op de plank*) zette (*op de plank).
            that Jan the book (on the shelf) put (on the shelf)
      b.   dat Jan het boek (*op de plank*) **neer** zette (*op de plank*).
            that Jan the book (on the shelf) down put (on the shelf)

The examples in (67) show that extraposition of non-predicative PPs is free, while (68a) indicates that prepositional SC predicates such as *op de plank* resist being extraposed. Yet it would be wrong to conclude that predicative PPs may not be extraposed at all. As (68b) bears out, once we add the particle *neer* to (68a), right-peripheral PP-placement is rendered possible. Recall that I argued in chapter 2 that in the English counterparts of Dutch prepositional complex particle constructions like (68b), the locative PP is a SC predicate. In particular, I argued that the structure of the English (69) is as in (70a), in which the PP *on the shelf* is predicative, θ-marking *a book*. In the Dutch equivalent of (69), given in (68b), the thematic relationships between the items involved are completely identical with those in the English example. Given the cross-linguistic UTAH, this thematic identity forces us to postulate an analogous D-structure for the Dutch sentence, which then reads as in (70b).

(69)   John put (down) the book (down) on the shelf.

(70) a.   [$_{VP}$ put [$_{SC1}$ θ' [$_{XP}$ down [$_{SC2}$ the book [$_{PP}$ on the shelf]]]]]
      b.   [$_{VP}$ [$_{SC1}$ θ' [$_{XP}$ [$_{SC2}$ het boek [$_{PP}$ op de plank]] neer] zette]

The grammaticality of (68b) with the locative PP *op de plank* in right-peripheral position hence suggests that it would be wrong to categorically deny predicative PPs the possibility of undergoing PP-over-V. The data seem to dictate a descriptive generalisation of the type in (71):[33]

(71)   *Dutch PP-over-V*
           In Dutch, PPs may undergo extraposition *unless* they are the predicate of a SC *in the complement of a verb*.

---

[33] I shall return at the end of this subsection to a way of reducing (71) to independently motivated ingredients of the theory. For the moment, (71) should serve its expository purpose. If (71) is correct, the aspectual Prt *mee* and *door* in (50b)/(51b) of section 1.3 (chapter 1) must be SC-heads taking the SCs headed by the transitive PPs as their complements.

The italicised phrase 'in the complement of a verb' in (71) will ensure that predicative PPs that are not base-generated in the complement position of V (such as the locative PP in (68b)) may undergo rightward movement, while other prepositional SC predicates (the majority case) may not.

With the descriptive generalisation in (71) in mind, now consider the paradigm of prepositional dative constructions given in (72), where, in contrast to the pair in (68), the presence or absence of a lexical particle (or verbal affix, such as *ver-* in (72b)) seems to make no difference as far as PP's mobility is concerned (also cf. (21), above):[34]

(72) a.   dat Jan een brief (*aan Marie*) stuurde (*aan Marie*).
           that Jan a letter (to Marie) sent (to Marie)
      b.   dat Jan een brief (*aan Marie*) verstuurde (*aan Marie*).
           that Jan a letter (to Marie) VERsent (to Marie)
      c.   dat Jan een brief (*aan Marie*) op stuurde (*aan Marie*).
           that Jan a letter (to Marie) up sent (to Marie)
           'that Jan sent a letter (out) to Marie.'

Let me begin by repeating the basic conclusion of section 3.3: the dative PP is a SC predicate. Although the Predicate Inversion argument presented in 3.3 cannot be readily reproduced for Dutch, the conclusion ensuing from it holds with equal force for this language, since the cross-linguistic Uniformity of Theta Assignment Hypothesis prevents us from subjecting thematically identical constructions to different D-structure analyses in different languages. Granting this, I discard any approach to the grammaticality of (72) that holds that the dative PP is extraposable because it is not a SC predicate.

The conclusion that the dative PP in (72) is a SC predicate still does not give us any trouble for the example in (72c), whose D-structure (given the analysis laid out above) reads as in (73):

---

[34] The suggestion that PPs in Dutch are extraposable just in case they are omissible, although valid for the examples in (67), (68b) and (72), where the PPs can be left out, does not go through in general. This is shown by examples such as (ia–c), in which PP can be right-peripheral (in addition, of course, to having the possibility of surfacing in its base position to the left of the verb) but cannot be omitted:

(i)   a.   dat Jan zijn geld toevertrouwde *(aan de bank).
           that Jan his money entrusted (to the bank)
           'that Jan entrusted his money *(to the bank).'
      b.   dat Jan zijn verlies toeschreef *(aan het slechte weer).
           that Jan his defeat ascribed (to the bad weather)
           'that Jan blamed his defeat *(on the bad weather).'
      c.   dat Jan houdt *(van spruitjes).
           that Jan loves of sprouts
           'that Jan loves sprouts.'

(73) $[_{VP} [_{SC1} \theta' [_{VP} [_{SC2} \theta' [_{XP} [_{SC3} NP [_{PP}$ aan Marie]] op]] $V_{\emptyset}]] V]$

In this structure the dative PP is the predicate of a SC that is *not* the complement of a verb. The generalisation in (71) hence correctly permits extraposition
of this PP.

Turning next to (72b), the grammaticality of this example reduces to that of
(72c) once we make the plausible assumption that Dutch verbal affixes such as
ver- (or *be-*), like particles, are SC-heads (cf. Hoekstra, Lansu & Westerduin
1987; Hoekstra & Mulder 1990; chapter 5, below). This suggestion allows us
to explain in a straightforward fashion that prepositional phrases in sentences
containing verbs affixed with *be-, ver-* can freely undergo PP-over-V, not just
in (72b), but also in sentences such as (74):

(74) a.   dat Jan Piet (*tot generaal*) bevorderde (*tot generaal*).
           that Jan Piet (to general) BEadvanced (to general)
           'that Jan promoted Piet to general.'
     b.   dat wij die vrouw (*tot president*) (**ver**)kiezen (*tot president*).
           that we that woman (to president) (VER)choose (to president)
           'that we elect that woman president.'

In all examples of this type, the PP will never be the predicate of a SC in the
complement of a verb, given that the verbal affix performs this part. The fact
that PP-over-V is possible in these sentences hence comes as no surprise in
view of the generalisation in (71). The structure of (72b) is analogous to (73),
the affix *ver-* being generated in the position of the particle *op*, as in (75):

(75) $[_{VP} [_{SC1} \theta' [_{VP} [_{SC2} \theta' [_{XP} [_{SC3} NP [_{PP}$ aan Marie]] *ver*-]] $V_{\emptyset}]] V]$

Finally, there is the "bare" prepositional dative construction in (72a). The
possibility of PP-over-V in (72a) leads me to hypothesise, in view of (71), that
the prepositional dative construction involves more structure than meets the eye.
In particular, in the structure of "bare" dative constructions the dative PP is
not the predicate of a SC in the complement of V, but rather that of a SC
selected by an empty element corresponding to the affix and particle in (72b,c),
as in (76). This structure is fully identical (*modulo* the OV/VO distinction) with
the tree in (63), which the theory led us to adopt.[35]

---

[35] Why there is no such empty particle in the structure of examples such as (68a) is a non-trivial
question which may be answered along the following lines. Recall that the structure of dative
constructions differs from that of locatives not only in the presence of an empty particle but also
in featuring an abstract token of the copula *be*, which was motivated on semantic as well as
syntactic grounds earlier in this chapter. Suppose, then, that *be*'s lexical entry specifies that it
selects (or may select, depending on context) a particle-headed SC complement. Then the difference
between locatives and datives reduces to a lexical property of the copula, an element which is
present only in the latter type of construction.

(76) $[_{VP} [_{SC1} \theta' [_{VP} [_{SC2} \theta' [_{XP} [_{SC3} \text{NP} [_{PP} \text{aan Marie}]] \emptyset]] V_{\emptyset}]] V]$

Postulating zero SC predicates alternating with verbal affixes like *be-, ver-* is necessary outside the realm of dative constructions, too. When we have a closer look at the example in (74b), we see that there the presence of *ver-* is optional. Irrespective, however, of the phonetic realisation of this affix, extraposition of the PP *tot president* is possible. If we were to assume that in the variant of (74b) in which *ver-* is absent, the PP is the predicate of the verb's SC complement, the generalisation in (71) would lead us to expect that PP-over-V should be impossible, contrary to fact. Postulating a zero allomorph of *ver-* in this construction, however, will yield the desired result that the PP *tot president* can always be extraposed in (74b). The alternation between (72a) and (72b) can now be seen to be fully parallel to that between the two variants of (74b). Prepositional dative constructions are hence by no means unique in featuring a zero SC predicate.

The discussion of the placement of PPs relative to the verb in Dutch has shown that the fact that PP-over-V is possible for dative PPs, while in general prepositional predicates of SCs in the complement of a verb may not be so moved, can be construed as evidence in favour of a structure of prepositional dative constructions containing an empty SC-head. I close this subsection by developing an account of the restrictions on Dutch PP-over-V, as stated in the descriptive generalisation in (71).

Let us start out from the following hypotheses concerning the assignment of structural objective Case (for (77a) also cf. section 2.4.5, above):[36]

---

[36] Hans Broekhuis originally suggested to me that the generalisation in (71) might be reducible to Case-theoretic considerations, on the basis of hypotheses of the type in (77). An approach along these lines seems more fruitful than Mulder's (1992a) recent account of the distribution of Dutch PP-over-V in terms of the ECP, of which I include a brief critique in this footnote.

Mulder starts out from the alternative approach to prepositional complex particle constructions discussed and rejected in section 2.3.4, according to which the transitive PP in these constructions is not predicative. He further assumes, crucially, (i) that the structure of SCs is as in (43a) of chapter 1, above, with the external argument being base-generated in the specifier of the predicate head's first-bar projection, (ii) that only maximal projections may undergo A'-movement (while, for quite obscure reasons, non-maximal projections should be allowed to undergo A-movement, as in Predicate Inversion constructions), and (iii) that prior to A'-movement of a predicative phrase, its subject is moved out of the moved phrase (e.g. to the specifier position of a SC-internal functional projection). (I shall exploit some of these ideas in my account of the distribution of PP-over-V as well.) The A'-moved predicative phrase hence contains the *trace* of its subject, which Mulder assumes should meet the demands of the ECP. Consider now the difference in grammaticality between (ia,b) on the one hand — involving PP-over-V and PP-scrambling, respectively — and the grammatical *wh*-movement and topicalisation cases in (ic) (the judgement of (ib) is Mulder's; many speakers, including myself, find (ib) acceptable on a neutral intonation pattern as well):

(i)   a.   *dat Jan het boek zette op de plank.
              that Jan the book put on the shelf   (*continued overleaf*)

(77) a.   Structural Cases are features of functional heads (Chomsky's 1993
             AgrSP and AgrOP).

      b.   In Dutch, structural Case is assigned under Chain government (cf.
             Den Besten 1985) to the deepest V-governed position.[37]

      c.   Extraposed constituents are outside the governing domain of the
             verb, hence cannot be assigned Case in languages in which Case is
             assigned under (Chain) government.

Assume furthermore that, in contradistinction to PP-topicalisation and VP-
internal PP-scrambling, PP-over-V is subject to the condition in (78):

(i)   b.   ?*dat Jan op de plank het boek zette.   (on neutral intonation)
             that Jan on the shelf the book put
      c.   Op {welke/die} plank heeft Jan het boek gezet(?)
             on which/that shelf has Jan the book put

Sentence (ic) is grammatical, Mulder argues, since at LF the *wh*-moved or topicalised PP may be
reconstructed into its base position, whereby proper government of the subject trace can be effectuated. The ECP rules out (ia,b) if PP-over-V and PP-scrambling do not allow reconstruction.
    Notice, however, that it is far from evident that Dutch PP-over-V does not allow for reconstruct-
ion. The variable binding example in (iia) suggests that reconstruction *is* possible in PP-extraposition constructions. Conversely, note that sentence-internal leftward PP-movement is acceptable to
all speakers if a focal stress pattern is imposed on an example like (ib) (which on Mulder's assumptions would imply that leftward focus movement of PPs undergoes reconstruction), and that in such
constructions, reconstruction for binding purposes nonetheless does *not* obtain, as is shown by the
grammaticality of (iib). (Notice that the locative PP in *zetten* 'put' constructions like (iib) does not
undergo PP-extraposition, witness the deviance of (iic).) Finally note that, while the addition of a
particle renders PP-over-V possible, particle insertion has no detectable influence on the applicability of PP-scrambling; that is, for those speakers to whom (ib) seems bad, it is bad regardless of
whether the sentence contains a lexical particle or not; that is, for speakers rejecting (ib), *dat Jan
op de plank het boek neer zette* 'that Jan on the shelf the book down put' is similarly unacceptable,
on a neutral intonation contour.

(ii) a.   dat Jan *elk boek* terug zette op *zijn* (eigen) plaats.
             that Jan every book back put on its (own) place
      b.   dat Jan in *elk boek zijn* (eigen) code zette.
             that Jan in every book its (own) code put
      c.   *dat Jan de code zette in het boek.
             that Jan the code put in the book

[37] This holds true for objective Case as well as nominative Case (cf. Broekhuis 1992). Everything
that is said below with specific reference to objective Case assignment hence carries over, *mutatis
mutandis*, to the passive counterparts of the examples, which exhibit the same PP-over-V effects:

(i)   a.   dat het boek (*op de plank*) werd gezet (**op de plank*).   (cf. (68))
             that the book (on the shelf) was put (on the shelf)
      b.   dat het boek (*op de plank*) werd neer gezet (*op de plank*).
             that the book (on the shelf) was down put (on the shelf)

(78)   PP-over-V of predicative PPs targets not the projection of the prepositional SC predicate, but the entire prepositional SC.

I shall return further below to the roots of this hypothesis, which can be seen to follow from the theory quite naturally.[38] For the moment, let us simply adopt (78) and concentrate on how we can accommodate (71) with the aid of it, in conjunction with the Case-theoretic assumptions in (77).

The subject of a SC in the complement of a Dutch verb is assigned Case in its base position, under (Chain) government by the verb. The subject does not leave the SC to pick up Case in some SC-external position. We may now understand why in constructions featuring a prepositional SC in the complement of the verb PP-over-V is excluded: if SC moved, its subject would incur a Case Filter violation.

Consider now a minimally different case in which the prepositional SC is not the complement of V but of a particle, as is the case in complex particle constructions. Here, the verb does not govern the base position of the Case-dependent subject of the prepositional SC. As a result, Case cannot be assigned under government to this position. The SC subject will hence be forced to undergo Case-driven NP-movement to a position outside the prepositional SC.[39]

Crucially, then, the subject of the SC projected by the transitive PP in a complex particle construction undergoes Case-driven NP-movement, thereby leaving this SC prior to the application of PP-over-V. Extraposition of the prepositional SC in complex particle constructions hence does not result in a violation of the Case Filter. In this way, we can make the appropriate distinction between prepositional SCs in the complement of the Case-assigning verb, and prepositional SCs in the complement of a particle. In general, we can say

---

[38] Though (78) may seem to conflict with the claim that SCs do not undergo movement (also cf. Den Dikken 1987), the account to be presented may avoid this problem with the aid of (80b), below — it is not the prepositional SC itself that undergoes physical movement; instead it is an empty operator associated with the right-peripherally base-generated SC that moves.

[39] The account presented here is a convenient simplification of the full story, which I shall briefly sketch in this footnote (in order not to complicate the discussion in the main text). For ECP reasons (cf. chapter 2), the particle will incorporate into the verb in constructions featuring PP-over-V. We might now expect the Government Transparency Corollary to apply, whereby the verb would come to be able to govern and Case-mark the subject of the prepositional SC *in situ*. I would like to suggest the following account. In Dutch the particle undergoes overt syntactic incorporation into the verb. Dutch verbs move to AgrO to establish the desired connection between it and the place of origin of objective Case (AgrO). AgrO is an inflectional head position which does not accept clusters, by hypothesis (cf. Bennis 1992b). Movement to AgrO hence obligatorily strands the incorporated particle. As a result of this excorporation, the only lexical material present under V^0 will be the particle, a non-verbal element. We may now assume that Case can be transmitted along a *verbal* chain in Dutch, and that the stranded non-verbal particle disrupts this chain. In Dutch, then, particle incorporation and subsequent verb excorporation effectively renders Case transmission under government to the particle's complement impossible.

that PP-over-V of predicative PPs is possible just in case the subject of PP does *not* receive Case in its D-structure position, and is hence forced to leave the extraposed SC prior to the application of PP-over-V, by the Case Filter.

Finally, I return to the statement in (78), derive it from the overall theory, and establish the desired distinction between PP-over-V on the one hand, and *wh*-movement, topicalisation and VP-internal scrambling of PPs on the other. In the latter three cases, movement of predicative PPs is permitted regardless of whether they originated in the complement of a particle or a verb:[40]

(79) a.   Op welke plank heeft Jan het boek (neer) gezet?
            on which shelf has Jan the book (down) put
      b.   Op die plank heeft Jan het boek (neer) gezet.
            on that shelf has Jan the book (down) put
      c.   dat Jan op die plank het boek (neer) heeft gezet.
            that Jan on that shelf the book (down) has put

The starting-point of the discussion will be the restrictive claim in (80a) and the hypothesis in (80b):[41]

(80) a.   Rightward movement does not exist (cf. Kayne 1993b).
      b.   Apparent instances of extraposition are reinterpretable as leftward movement of an empty operator associated with a right-peripherally base-generated constituent.

Dutch PP-over-V is an apparent case of rightward movement. In the light of (80b) I shall reanalyse it as an instance of leftward empty operator movement.[42]

A peculiar property of empty operators is the fact that there are severe restrictions on the positions in which they can be generated. Of particular relevance in the context at hand is the following characteristic of null operators (cf. Tellier 1991; Heggie 1993):

(81)   Empty operators are arguments, not predicates.

---

[40] In fn. 36, quoting Mulder (1992a), I reported judgements on VP-internal PP-scrambling from a dialect different from mine, in which predicative PPs resist undergoing the process. To my mind this is a minority dialect, which I shall ignore here.

[41] I shall not speculate on the nature of the pósition occupied by the right-peripherally generated constituents referred to in (80b); if, as Kayne's (1993b) Linear Correspondence Axiom has it, right-adjunction does not exist, not even in cases of base-adjunction, such constituents cannot be adjuncts.

[42] In section 4.2.7 I shall take up the case of English Heavy NP Shift, another apparent case of rightward movement, and suggest that it, too, can be reanalysed along the lines of (80b).

This can be made to follow from the plausible hypothesis that empty operators are PRO (cf. Jaeggli 1981; Hendrick 1988; Kinyalolo 1991; also cf. Bennis & Hoekstra 1989). Alternatively, we may derive it from Tellier's (1991) theory of Universal Licensing, according to which every XP must be licensed at all levels of representation either by being an argument or by Predication. Both licensing strategies fail in the case of empty operator predicates, the former for perfectly obvious reasons, the latter because 'null categories, since they bear no features, cannot function as predicates at D-structure, and hence are unlicensed' (Tellier 1991:36).

The conjunction of the fact that empty operators cannot be predicates, and our earlier assumption that PP-over-V involves leftward movement of an empty operator associated with the right-peripheral constituent, now yields us the statement in (78). Since topicalisation and VP-internal scrambling of PPs is *overt* leftward movement, not empty operator movement, these processes are not subject to the conditions that I have imposed on PP-over-V. The analysis hence makes the desired distinction between PP-over-V (to which (71) applies) and leftward PP-movement processes (to which (71) does not apply).

After this interlude on Dutch PP-movement restrictions, I now proceed to a further argument for the abstract structure of triadic constructions.

3.11.3 Word order in Chinese dative constructions

Arguing against what has long been the majority view in the principles-and-parameters literature on Chinese (cf. Travis 1984; Li 1985/1990), Mulder & Sybesma (1992) have made a strong case for the view that Chinese is a VO language. Their major arguments for a VO underlying structure in Chinese come from the position relative to the verb of (i) indefinite objects and (ii) SC complements (especially prepositional ones). I shall naturally confine my attention here to (ii).

Though locative PPs may often occur on either side of the verb in Chinese, there is a well-defined interpretive difference between the two alternative word orders. Consider the examples in (82):[43]

(82) a.   Ta   zai   zhuozi-shang   tiao.
           he   at   table-top   jump
           'He is jumping on the table.'
     b.   Ta   tiao   zai   zhuozi-shang.
           he   jump   at   table-top
           'He has jumped onto the table.'

---

[43] Except if explicitly noted otherwise, all Chinese examples are from Mulder & Sybesma (1992). Also cf. Sybesma (1992) for relevant discussion.

The word order in which the PP *zai zhuozi-zhang* is pre-verbal (82a) precludes a resultative interpretation — (82a) means that the referent of *he* finds himself on the table, and is jumping up and down there. A resultative interpretation, according to which the referent of *he* ends up on the table as a result of his jumping, is available only in (82b). On the plausible assumption that resultative constructions involve a SC in the complement of the verb (cf. T. Hoekstra 1988a for extensive discussion), the fact that resultative construal is possible in the Chinese examples in (82) only if the locative PP is in post-verbal position suggests that in Chinese, SC complements are base-generated to the *right* of the verb. The Chinese verb, then, takes its complements to its right, as expected if Chinese is a VO language.

From this perspective it now seems surprising to find that in Chinese *transitive* resultative constructions, a word order in which the resultative SC in its entirety surfaces to the right of the verb is ungrammatical:[44]

(83) a.   *Zhang San leng   shu   diao   le.
           Zhang San throw book   away   LE
      b.   *Ta   nong wode shu   zang.
           he   make my   book   dirty
      c.   *Wo   xie   gangbi she   le
           I   write pen   to-pieces LE

The cause of the ill-formedness of (83) probably lies in the Case Filter, as is suggested by the fact that one way in which these examples can be rescued is by placing the subject of the resultative predicate in pre-verbal position, preceded by the Case-marker *ba* (cf. Sybesma 1992 for detailed discussion), as in (84a):

(84) a.   Zhang San *ba* shu   leng   diao   le.
           Zhang San BA book   throw away   LE
      b.   Zhang San leng   diao   le shu.
           Zhang San throw away   LE book
           'Zhang San threw the book away.'

Alternatively, the sentences in (83) can be made grammatical by incorporating the head of the resultative predicate into the verb, as in (84b). That (84b) is obtained through head incorporation is suggested by the fact that the perfective marker *le* finds itself to the right of *diao* 'away', the incorporate.

Of particular interest to our concerns is the fact that word orders of the type in (83) are not always impossible. There are two conditions under which sentences of this type are acceptable on the surface:

---

[44] The clause-final element *le* in (83a,c) and in other examples to follow is an aspectual marker.

(85)   *[V–NP–Result Predicate], *unless* (i) or (ii):
         (i)   the resultative predicate is a PP and the subject of this PP is
                indefinite;
         (ii)   the sentence contains a *complex verb*.

We need not be concerned with (85i) in the context of this discussion. The second exception to the general ill-formedness of the word-order pattern in (83) is exemplified by a Chinese example like (86):

(86)   Lingdao ti-*sheng*   wo   fuqin   wei   pai-zhang.
         boss   raise-rise   my   father as   platoon-head
         'The boss promoted my father to platoon leader.'

It is plausible to assume, as Mulder & Sybesma (1992) suggest, that *sheng*, the verbal affix, is a SC-head at D-structure undergoing incorporation into the matrix verb in the course of the derivation, much as in Hoekstra, Lansu & Westerduin's (1987) analysis of the Dutch prefixed cognate of Chinese *ti-sheng*, *be-vorderen* 'promote' in (74a), above, and similar complex verbs. On this assumption, the account of the example in (86) can be directly assimilated to that of (84b), which likewise involves incorporation of the head of the transitive verb's SC complement. A descriptively adequate generalisation covering the examples in (84b) and (86) is given in (87):

(87)   In Chinese, a *definite* SC-subject NP may surface to the right of the
         verb iff the head of the verb's SC complement is *incorporated* into V.

That the incorporating head of the verb's SC complement need not be overt is suggested by the example in (88), where, just as in (86), the verb is followed by a definite SC subject (*neige nüren* 'that woman') but where, in contrast to (86), the verb is not physically hosting an affix (cf. Dutch (74b)):

(88)   Women   xuan   neige   nüren   wei   zongtong.
         we   elect   that   woman   as   president
         'We elect that woman president.'

The example in (88) is particularly instructive to the analysis of the word order in Chinese triadic constructions. Consider the examples in (89), taken from Zhang (1990:312–13):

(89) a. Wo   song   le   yi   ben   shu   gei   Li Si.
         I   give   LE   one   copy   book   to   Li Si
         'I gave a book to Li Si.'
     b. Wo   jie   le   yi   zhi bi   gei   ta.
         I   lend   LE   one   twig pencil   to   him
         'I lent a pencil to him.'

Given that the post-verbal NPs in these examples (contrary to what the glosses might suggest) are *definite* NPs, and that — as was argued above — a triadic verb takes a SC complement, the problem posed by triadic constructions of this type is that we seem to find a full complement-SC to the right of the verb, there being no definiteness restriction on the subject of this SC (the Theme NP).[45]

The analysis of the triadic constructions in (89) can be modelled on that of (88). Recall that (88) belongs to the same type of construction as (86), and that for (86) a good case can be made that its derivation involves incorporation of an affixal SC-head into the verb. For (88), an analogous derivation can be assumed, with the difference that in (88) the SC-head that is incorporated into the verb is phonetically unrealised. Similarly, the obstinate triadic examples in (89) are now tractable, if we assume that Chinese dative constructions have a D-structure in which the verb selects a SC whose empty head undergoes incorporation into the matrix verb at S-structure.

Notice that there is a difference between the Dutch data discussed in 3.11.2 and the Chinese facts under current discussion with regard to the implications that they have for the structure of triadic constructions. The Dutch PP-over-V facts specifically require the inclusion of a *non-verbal* head in the structure, intermediate between the "verbal field" and the dative SC. These data, then, argue unequivocally for the presence of "X" in the structure in (63). Consider next the Chinese word-order facts. Mulder & Sybesma (1992) suggest that the theoretical roots of the generalisation in (87) are probably to be sought in Case Theory. The empirical data are consistent with the speculation that the verb in Chinese is unable to Case-mark a SC-subject NP in its complement unless the head of the SC is incorporated into the Case-assigning verb. If this speculation is correct, what the facts about word order in Chinese dative constructions suggest is that the structure of dative constructions should include a zero element which heads the SC whose specifier position is occupied by the Case-dependent Theme NP. This zero element may very well be the abstract copular verb heading the SC complement of the matrix triadic verb; it need not be "X" in (63). I cannot at this point decide between these options. Be that as it may, like the Dutch PP-extraposition data in section 3.11.2, word order in Chinese dative constructions lends support to a structure underlying triadic constructions which is more abstract than the surface output would appear to suggest.

---

[45] Examples of this type are problematic for the "post-verbal constraint" irrespective of whether *gei* (glossed here as a dative preposition) is prepositional (Zhang 1990) or verbal (Li 1985). I shall take no stand on this issue, which is immaterial from my perspective; cf. Sybesma (1992).

3.11.4 Interim conclusion and road map

In my discussion of the structure of triadic constructions so far, I have argued that triadic verbs like *give* select a SC complement headed by an abstract copular verb which in its turn selects a SC whose ergative head may either be empty or lexicalised by a particle or (in Dutch) by a verbal affix. The dative SC finds itself in the complement of this (empty) particle. From this underlying structure, which straightforwardly yields the prepositional dative construction, the double object construction is transformationally derived via movement of the dative PP into the specifier position of the higher SCs.

We have now addressed all of the structural ingredients of the analysis of triadic constructions and Dative Shift defended in this chapter. From this point on I shall be concerned with a range of empirical details arising in connection with the dative alternation, which I shall consider against the background of the analysis proposed. Section 3.12 will first of all address distributional restrictions on the dative alternation, after which section 3.13 focuses on some cases of incorporation in triadic constructions which yield us an additional argument for the particular transformational approach to Dative Shift taken here. In section 3.14 I discuss the analysis of the third, less robustly represented member of the dative alternation paradigm — the *with* construction, instantiated by sentences like *I supplied John with the information*. Section 3.15 then takes us back to particles, the central theme of the book, and discusses some details glossed over so far concerning the distribution of particles in double object constructions. The chapter is closed with a summary of our major findings.

Let me point out here that for the sake of perspicuity of the structural representations to be presented, I have elected to mostly ignore in what follows the layer of structure defined by the abstract copular verb. This is of no consequence to the analysis. The full representations of all triadic constructions do of course contain this additional layer of abstract structure.

3.12 Transformational Dative Shift and distribution

Not all verbs taking part in the prepositional dative construction are eligible for inclusion in a double object construction and *vice versa*, and even if a verb shows up in both constructions, the two variants of the dative alternation often do not have identical semantics. Considerations of this sort might be (and have frequently been; cf. e.g. Oehrle 1976 for a clear example) taken to suggest that it would be wrong to assign common underlying structures to prepositional dative and double object constructions, and to relate them derivationally.

In this section I shall consider some restrictions on the distribution of Dative Shift, and conclude that they do not in any way pose a threat to the analysis proposed above — quite the contrary: they in fact fall out easily from it.

3.12.1 The role played by the (empty) preposition

In a recent in-depth study of the distribution of the double object construction, Pinker (1989) (see also Gropen *et al.* 1989) has laid bare several restrictions influencing the distribution of the construction. As a necessary (though, as we shall see presently, not a sufficient) condition on the grammaticality of the double object construction, Pinker (1989:102) identifies the requirement that verbs fit to take the double object construction must 'involve causation of a change of possession'. All inherently possessive verbs come under this umbrella, but in addition Pinker notes that verbs that do not denote change of possession by way of their inherent lexical semantics may undergo a semantic rule adding the notion of change of possession to their argument structure. A major class of verbs eligible for this semantic rule is formed by the set of *motion verbs*, as illustrated in (90):

(90) a.   John threw the book to Bill.   /   John threw Bill the book.
      b.   John flung the book to Bill.   /   John flung Bill the book.
      c.   John kicked the ball to Bill.   /   John kicked Bill the ball.
      d.   John flicked the coin to Bill.   /   John flicked Bill the coin.

It is not just every verb of motion that may undergo the semantic rule of addition of "change of possession", however. In particular, it turns out that a split in the class of motion verbs must be made along the lines in (91):

(91) a.   Verbs of motion denoting "instantaneous causation of ballistic motion" feature in double object constructions.
      b.   Verbs of motion denoting "continuous causation of accompanied motion in some manner" (i.e. motion that requires "continuous imparting of force") do *not* feature in double object constructions.

Thus, there is a difference between the examples in (90), which feature verbs of motion of the a-type (the agent causes the motion, but the motion continues of its own accord) and hence take part in Dative Shift, and those in (92), involving verbs of "continuous imparting of force" (the agent is involved with the motion throughout the event) and not allowing double object constructions:

(92) a.   John pulled the trunk to Bill.   /   *John pulled Bill the trunk.
      b.   John pushed the trunk to Bill.   /   *John pushed Bill the trunk.
      c.   John dragged the sack to Bill.   /   *John dragged Bill the sack.
      d.   John shlepped the box to Bill.   /   *John shlepped Bill the box.

Pesetsky (1993:section 5.3) has noted that the verbs of the b-type are much more rigid in the preposition they select to mark their Goal argument than are a-type verbs — verbs of "continuous imparting of force" only select *to*:

(93) a.   John {threw/flung/kicked/flicked} NP *at* NP
      b.   *John {pulled/pushed/dragged/shlepped} NP *at* NP.
(94) a.   John {threw/flung/kicked/flicked} NP {*in(to)/on(to)*} NP.
      b.   John {pulled/pushed/dragged/shlepped} NP {*in(to)/on(to)*} NP.

Both the ungrammaticality of (93b) and the facts in (94) (all adapted from Pesetsky 1993:113–14) highlight the b-type verbs' predilection to select *to* as the marker of their Goal. In the case of (93) this is immediately obvious; in (94) this is evident from the fact that while (94a) is ambiguous between a locative and a directional reading for the cases lacking *-to*, in (94b) *-to* must be present in order for a directional reading to arise.

From these facts, Pesetsky (1993:114, (377)) draws the conclusion that:

(95)   A Goal arrived at due to continuous imparting of force must be θ-selected by *to*.   (Pesetsky 1993:114)

This generalisation immediately accommodates the data in (93)–(94), and it carries over to (92) given Pesetsky's (1993) analysis of double object constructions, according to which the Goal in such constructions is not θ-selected by *to*.[46] It is not difficult to ensure, however, that the generalisation in (95) also covers the facts in (92) given the analysis of the dative alternation developed in this chapter. All we need to assume is that the empty counterpart of the dative preposition featuring in the double object construction is lexically underspecified, and does not have the specific lexical semantic features of any of the concrete dative prepositions — an assumption that does not seem unnatural in the light of the emptiness of $P_\emptyset$.

(96) $P_\emptyset$ is lexically underspecified; verbs of continuous imparting of force cannot comply with (95) by taking a PP headed by $P_\emptyset$.

Following Pesetsky's lead, we may thus readily accommodate one potential threat to a transformational approach to the dative alternation of the type presented here.[47]

Another such threat also easily dissolves given the incorporation approach to Dative Shift propounded in this study: the fact that there are restrictions of a morphophonological nature — concerning length (Oehrle 1976) or lexical class (Stowell 1981) — on the applicability of Dative Shift:

---

[46] Pesetsky proposes an analysis of double object constructions according to which it is the Theme, not the Goal (as on present assumptions), that is selected by an empty head, his "*G*".

[47] I refer the interested reader to Pesetsky (1993:section 5.3) for detailed discussion of Gropen *et al.*'s (1989) subtler semantic classification of verbs (not) taking part in double object constructions.

(97) a.   John sent money to Hutus.   /   John sent Hutus money.

      b.   John donated money to Hutus. / *John donated Hutus money.[48]

(98) a.   John showed his car to me.   /   John showed me his car.

      b.   John displayed his car to me. / *John displayed me his car.

Pesetsky (1993:106) suggests that these distributional restrictions on Dative Shift may be the simple (though still not fully understood) effect of some morpho-phonological constraint on zero affixation (of the empty Theme marker "*G*" on Pesetsky's assumptions, of $P_\emptyset$ on mine). If an account of (97)–(98) along such lines holds water,[49] what we have here is another piece of support for the inclusion of an empty head that incorporates into the verb in the structure of double object constructions.

3.12.2 Idioms and affectedness

Distributional effects of the type discussed in section 3.12.1 are one type of potential argument against the postulation of a derivational relationship between prepositional dative and double object constructions. Another is the fact — often noted in the literature (cf. esp. Green 1974; Oehrle 1976) — that there is a clear semantic difference between the two variants of the dative alternation (cf. section 3.8, where I mentioned this semantic distinction in the context of the *be+to/have* alternation). A representative minimal pair is given in (99):

(99) a.   Mary taught linguistics to John.

      b.   Mary taught John linguistics.

Green (1974:157) observes that 'sentence [(99b)] implies or entails that John learned linguistics, while [(99a)] merely states that he was a student of linguistics, and is neutral as to whether his teacher Mary had any success in her efforts'. This meaning difference is even clearer in the pair in (100), of which (100b) is a contradiction:

---

[48] Jim Hurford (p.c.) tells me that double object constructions with *donate* are odd for older speakers, but less so for younger speakers.

[49] See Larson (1988:section 5) for a different account, in terms of recoverability of deletion, an approach that heavily relies on highly specific yet hard to prove thematic distinctions between verbs of the *give* class and verbs of the *donate* class. Larson also discusses the converse of the mismatches under discussion in this subsection: *The judge spared John the ordeal* vs. *The judge spared the ordeal to John*. I have nothing to say about this particular case; but cf. the next subsection for an account of idiomatic constructions only featuring the double object pattern.

(100) a.   In 1955 they taught arithmetic to children, but they didn't teach them anything.

      b.   In 1955 they taught children arithmetic, but they didn't teach anything to them.

Pairs of this type could be claimed to indicate that the two variants of the dative alternation are thematically distinct, so that the Uniformity of Theta Assignment Hypothesis no longer decrees a common base analysis. It seems to me, however, that the semantic difference between dative and double object constructions is not in fact of a *thematic* nature, but rather of an *aspectual* kind, pertaining to the notion of *affectedness*. The Goal-NP is "(totally) affected" by the predicate of the sentence. In fact, as Marantz (1990:4) points out, 'the whole notion of a benefactive involves the concept of affectedness'. As I already suggested in section 2.4.4.1, affectedness can arguably be given a purely configurational account, as is also argued in Tenny (1987), T. Hoekstra (1991), Hoekstra & Roberts (1992), Hoffman (1991), Hale & Keyser (1992, 1993), and — with specific reference to double object constructions — in Marantz (1990). In particular, I advance the hypothesis in (101) (cf. also Voskuil & Wehrmann 1990, whose notion "Theme" corresponds to my "affected argument"):

(101)   The canonical S-structure position for affected arguments is the specifier position of a SC in the complement of a verb denoting (change of) state or location.

With this and what was said in section 2.4.4.1 with regard to idiomatic fixing in mind, we can now also understand why double object idioms typically have a fixed verb and direct object, the indirect object being free (cf. e.g. Marantz 1984; E. Hoekstra 1991:86):

(102) a.   Snakes *give* me *the creeps/shivers*.

      b.   John *gave* linguistics *his all*.

      c.   The boss *gave* him *the chuck/push*.

      d.   John *showed* Mary *the door*.

In section 2.4.4.1 I argued that a thematic approach to idiomatic fixation à la Marantz (1984) should be replaced with an aspectually based, S-structure configurational approach. In essence, idiom chunks resist sitting in affected argument positions at S-structure. Since the indirect object position in a double object construction is an affected argument position, as is evident from the data discussed earlier in this subsection, it now follows that indirect objects in double object idioms must be free. Given a proper understanding of the workings of idiom formation, then, idiomatic fixing does not disconfirm an analysis of double object constructions according to which they are transformationally derived from a deep structure corresponding to prepositional dative constructions.

3.13 Transformational Dative Shift and incorporation

Having cleared away some of the most often heard objections to a derivational approach to Dative Shift, let me now proceed to further bolstering up the case for the particular derivational approach to the dative alternation taken here, focusing on one of the crucial ingredients of the analysis — the incorporation of the head of the dative SC into the verb in the course of the derivation of the double object construction. Two pieces of empirical evidence will be presented in support of this aspect of our account, from Chinese and from triadic serial verb constructions.

3.13.1 Chinese Dative Shift

In section 3.11.3 I noted that word order in Chinese dative constructions constitutes an argument for the inclusion in the analysis of triadic constructions of at least one layer of abstract structure. Chinese not only supports the underlying structure of triadic constructions, however. In this subsection I show that it also provides evidence in favour of the transformational approach to Dative Shift taken in this study.

Chinese, like English, features a dative alternation, as is shown by the examples in (103). In line with the analysis of Dative Shift presented in the above, I assume that (103b) is derived from the dative construction in (103a) by movement of the dative PP, headed by a zero dative preposition which undergoes incorporation into the verb.

(103) a.   Wo   song   le yi   ben   shu   *gei*   Li Si.
         I   give   LE one copy book to   Li Si
         'I gave a book to Li Si.'
     b.   Wo   song le Li Si yi   ben   shu.
         I   give   LE Li Si one copy book
         'I gave Li Si a book.'

The hypothesis that preposition incorporation obtains in the derivation of the double object construction receives direct support from Chinese. Alongside (103b), in which the incorporated preposition is null, we find the example in (104a), quoted from Li (1985:218), in which this preposition is overt and in fact *identical* with the dative preposition occurring in (103a):

(104) a.   Ta   song *gei* le women henduo shu.
         he   send   to   LE us   many   book
         'He sent us many books.'
     b. *Ta   song le *gei* women henduo shu.
         he   send   LE to   us   many   book

That the dative preposition is actually physically incorporated into the verb in (104a) is evident from the fact that the perfect marker *le* obligatorily follows *gei*, the sentence becoming ungrammatical once the relative order of these elements is reversed, as (104b) (also from Li 1985:218) bears out. The Chinese examples in (104) hence lend direct support to Baker's (1988) original claim, taken over in the present account of the dative alternation, that in the double object construction the dative preposition is incorporated into the verb.[50]

3.13.2 Triadic serial verbs and V–V compounds[51]

From the Caribbean via West Africa to the Far East, we find languages, creoles and pidgins featuring the so-called *serial verb construction* (SVC for short), illustrated by the example in (105), taken from Yorùbá, a Kwa language spoken in southwestern Nigeria:[52]

(105)   Bọ́lá   sè   ẹran   tà.
           Bola cook animal sell
           'Bola cooked some meat and (then) sold it.'

Serialising languages throughout the world are remarkably consistent with regard to word order in serial verb constructions whose final verb is *triadic* (henceforth, triadic SVCs). It turns out that in such SVCs it is always the Theme argument that is the "shared argument" (in Baker's 1989b terms), occurring in between the matrix *take* type verb and the triadic verb (in VO serialising languages). The Goal argument never surfaces in this position. The contrast between the Gokana (Benue-Cross) examples in (106a,b) bears this out (cf. Wagner 1985):

(106) a.   mín è   tú   kpá   nẹ̀   pábia.
          child PAST take book give woman
          'The child gave the book to the woman.'
     b. *mín è   tú   pabia nẹ̀ kpá.
          child PAST take woman give book

---

[50] Baker (1988) argues that applicative morphemes in general are spell-outs of incorporated dative prepositions, despite the substantial phonetic discrepancy between the two in languages featuring an applicative alternation. In chapter 5 I shall argue against the view that so-called applicative morphemes are incorporated dative prepositions, arguing instead that these are affixal particles.

[51] The text of this subsection by and large follows Den Dikken (1991b).

[52] For recent GB-theoretical approaches to verb serialisation, cf. Baker (1989b); Déchaine (1990, 1993:chapter 4), and references cited there.

Baker (1989b) accommodates this rigidity of word order in triadic SVCs in *thematic* terms, appealing to a thematic hierarchy in which Theme is higher than Goal (cf. Carrier-Duncan 1985; Larson 1988). I shall argue, however, that it would be wrong to give a thematic account of these data.

This is shown particularly clearly by a comparison of serialising languages like Gokana and Yorùbá on the one hand, and a geographically close and genetically closely related language such as Ìgbo. In Ìgbo, as Déchaine (1990, 1993) points out, triadic serial verb constructions do not surface as SVCs, but come out as V–V compounds instead (cf. (107), from Íhìónú 1988). With Déchaine I assume that the V–V compound is derived by *incorporation* of V2 (the second verb) into V1 from an underlying structure that is analogous to that of triadic SVCs in serialising languages like Yorùbá. The crucial thing to notice about (107a) is that in this example, the Goal *precedes* the Theme, which would seem to suggest that in (107a) the Goal is the "shared object".

(107) a.   Ó   bì-nye-re   Adha akwà.
           he lend-give-ØASP Adha cloth
           'He lent Adha a cloth.'
      b.   *Ó   bì-ri   ákwà   nyé   Ádha.
           he lend-ØASP cloth give Adha

The Ìgbo V–V compound in (107a) is as problematic for Déchaine (1990, 1993) as it is for Baker (1989b). Both would generate the word order *[V1–V2–Theme–Goal] without further manipulation of the structure. Déchaine's suggestion that at S-structure '*ákwà* 'cloth' … is extraposed [in order to be] licensed by Inherent Case' (Déchaine 1990:26; also cf. 1993:311) seems both *ad hoc* and theoretically implausible (cf. Den Dikken 1991b for more discussion).

To me, the Ìgbo triadic V–V compound in (107a) (which is derived by V-incorporation from an underlying serial verb construction) lays bare the inadequacy of a generalisation about word order in triadic SVCs cast in *thematic* terms (such as Baker's 1989b), and indicates that such a generalisation is of a much more surfacy nature than Baker takes it to be. What we should account for is that once the second verb moves, the Goal phrase also moves, as stated in the descriptive generalisation in (108):[53]

(108)   In triadic constructions, whenever incorporation of the embedded predicate takes place, the underlying Theme–Goal order is reversed.

---

[53] Note that Baker's (1988) analysis of triadic constructions, with its ternary branching VPs, can capture this generalisation only by invoking a theoretically suspect linear adjacency condition on incorporation.

An account aimed at capturing this generalisation about surface word order can, of course, never be formulated in terms of θ-role hierarchies. Accordingly, the restrictions on word order in triadic SVCs cannot be looked upon as conditions on "argument sharing" (cf. Baker 1989b), as a result of which the whole concept of argument sharing in SVCs is rendered dubious.

The analysis of triadic constructions and Dative Shift presented in this study, by contrast, provides a natural explanation for the word-order restrictions in triadic SVCs and V–V compounds. All we need assume as a basic premise is that V2 in triadic SVCs is base-generated in the same position in which dative prepositions in languages like English originate, "Y" in the (simplified) tree in (109), and that hence triadic SVCs involve *embedding* (or subordination), not (covert) conjunction (cf. e.g. Stewart 1963) or adjunction (cf. Bickerton & Iatridou 1987; Déchaine 1990, 1993). With V1 under the V node in (109), we then immediately derive the correct word order for Gokana (and Yorùbá), as depicted in (110) (where I assume that the Theme subject of SC2 undergoes no NP-movement into SpecSC1, at least not in Yorùbá, which, as pointed out by Manfredi 1989, features no NP-movement at all).

(109)

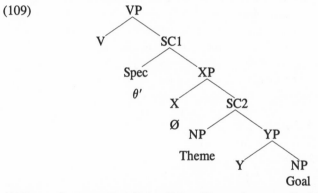

(110)   [$_{VP}$ TAKE [$_{SC1}$ θ' [$_{XP}$ Ø [$_{SC2}$ Theme [$_{YP}$ GIVE Goal]]]]]

On the analogy of the derivation of double object constructions, the Goal–Theme order of Ìgbo triadic V–V compounds can now be viewed as a corollary of the incorporation of V2 into V1. Recall from section 3.10.2 that incorporation of the head of the dative SC into the verb is impossible without prior movement of its projection — the non-lexical head "X" in (109) intervenes between the incorporator and the prospective incorporate. In order to render it possible for V2 in an Ìgbo triadic construction to incorporate into the matrix verb, then, YP in (109) must move into the specifier position of SC1. Since movement of YP transfers the Goal NP into a position to the left of the Theme, the surface word order of an Ìgbo triadic V–V compound is directly accounted for on this approach to Dative Shift. The S-structure corresponding to an Ìgbo triadic V–V compound in (111) bears this out:

(111) $[_{VP} [\text{TAKE} + [_Y \text{ GIVE}]_j] [_{SC1} [_{YP} t_j \text{ Goal}]_i [_{XP} \varnothing [_{SC2} \text{ Theme } [_{YP} t_i]]]]]$[54]

From this analysis of triadic serial verb constructions the conclusion seems to emerge that the difference between serialising languages and non-serialising languages lies in the base position of the *give*-type verb: under the Y-node in the former, and under V in the latter. If this were the right conclusion to draw, it would imply a head-on collision with Universal Alignment or Uniformity of Theta Assignment. It should be borne in mind, however, that the second verb in triadic SVCs (commonly translated as *give*) and the main verb in English type triadic constructions are quite distinct. As V2 in a SVC, this verb performs the role of the dative preposition in languages like English, and assigns the Theme and Goal θ-roles. In many serialising languages, *give* may also occur as V1 in a triadic SVC (cf. the Saramaccan example in (112a); Byrne 1987). In such cases, it is analogous to English type *give*, and assigns the Agent θ-role to the subject and a propositional internal θ-role to its SC complement (which is really all that the main verb in triadic constructions does, given the structure in (109)). In both language types, these latter roles can be assigned by a variety of verbs. Consider, for instance, the Saramaccan paradigm in (112), and the English translations of the examples:

(112) a.   A   *da*   di   moni   da   di   mujee.
            he   give   the   money   give   the   woman
            'He gave the money for the woman.'

    b.   A   *paka*   di   moni   da   di   womi.
            he   pay   the   money   give   the   man
            'He paid the money for the man.'

    c.   A   *sei*   di   wosu   da   di   womi.
            he   sell   the   house   give   the   man
            'He sold the house for/to the man.'

---

[54] It might be asked how YP-movement to SpecSC1 is licit in an Ìgbo triadic construction. After all, the head of YP in Ìgbo is a *verb*, not a preposition, and from the discussion in section 2.3.6 of Dutch aspectual complex particle constructions in which YP in (109) is a VP we know that incorporation of the head of this VP into the matrix verb is impossible, partly due to the fact that the verbal predicate of SC2 in (109) may not escape from the governing domain of "X" by undergoing movement. That YP=VP may not move in Dutch is a consequence of the fact that, in Dutch, this VP is categorially distinct from the head of SC1, "X", a P-type category. As a result, SC2 counts as a barrier (since it is neither L-marked nor interpretable as a segment of SC1), and extraction from it is ruled out by the ECP. In Ìgbo, on the other hand, movement of a verbal YP apparently *is* possible. Notice that this can be made compatible with the analysis on the assumption that "X" in Ìgbo is *not* categorially distinct from V. This is plausible in view of the absence of a separate category P in Ìgbo, verbs expressing what prepositions would in English. This allows us to assume that in Ìgbo triadic V–V compound constructions, SC2 is categorially non-distinct from SC1, hence exempt from barrierhood. Thus, movement of YP=VP in (109) is licit in Ìgbo (but not in Dutch).

With respect to the possible fillers of the V-node in the tree in (109), then, serialising languages are basically similar to English. The principal difference between the two language types lies in the fact that in English, the element responsible for the assignment of the Theme and Goal θ-roles is a preposition (*to*), while serialising languages employ a verb of the *give* type for this purpose. Uniformity of Theta Assignment hence in no way endangers my approach to triadic serial verb constructions.

3.13.3 Conclusion

Among verb serialising languages, there is a dichotomy between languages in which the multiple verbs of a SVC all surface as independent verbs (as is the case in the majority of serialising languages), and a compounding language like Ìgbo, in which all verbs cluster together in a single verbal compound. Both language types feature identical underlying structures, the latter type of language differing from the former solely in that it features overt syntactic *head incorporation*. Chinese, as analysed in section 3.13.1, can be seen as a kind of conjunction of the two language types: its dative marker *gei* can either surface as an independent head, separated from the matrix verb by the Theme NP, or it can incorporate into V.

In triadic constructions, incorporation of the head of the dative SC goes together hand-in-glove with a reversal of the relative order of the Theme and Goal arguments in comparison with the corresponding non-incorporation case. The analysis of triadic constructions and Dative Shift presented in this study (in contrast to Baker's 1988) furnishes an immediate account for this correlation between incorporation of the dative marker and Theme–Goal or Goal–Theme order.

One of the contentions of this section is that a thematic account of the generalisation that in triadic serial verb constructions, the Theme NP consistently precedes the Goal NP is inadequate. I hence challenge Baker's "object sharing" analysis of serialisation. More drastically, Déchaine (1990, 1993) challenges not only Baker's analysis, but the basic generalisation that it aims to capture as well, quoting such Yorùbá triadic constructions as (113) (Baker 1989b:541), which she claims involve Goal sharing:

(113)   Olú bùn   mi ní   owó.
            Olu present me P(RT)/have money
            'Olu presented me with money.'

As the gloss to (113) indicates, the precise categorial status of the element *ní* in triadic constructions of this type is somewhat unclear. Baker (1989b) treats it as a particle (basically, a preposition), while Déchaine (1990, 1993) analyses it as a verb. Oyèláràn (1989) argues that *ní* in (113) is in fact neither P nor V, and he dubs the *ní*-phrase in examples of this type an "antifocus" construction. I shall follow Oyèláràn in not analysing (113) as a run-of-the-mill serial verb construction, whereby (113) becomes uninteresting from the point of view of Baker's (1989b) generalisation.

The example in (113) is interesting in another respect, though. Awóyalé (1988:6) observes that 'transitivity alternations like [(114)] are reminiscent of ... the "locative alternation"', which I illustrate in (115):

(114) a.   Ajé   wọ   aṣọ   fún Olú.
           Aje   wear   clothing give Olu
      b.   Ajé   wọ   Olú ní aṣọ.
           Aje   wear   Olu NI clothing
           both: 'Aje wore an outfit for Olu.'

(115) a.   They loaded the hay onto the wagon.
      b.   They loaded the wagon with hay.

Awóyalé's (1988) connection between (114) (of which (114b) instantiates the same pattern as (113)) and (115) renders it likely that (113) is, as its translation suggests, an example of the *with* alternant of the locative alternation. This example thus forms a natural bridge from the discussion of triadic serial verb constructions to that of triadic *with* constructions like *They provided me with the money*, which are the topic of the next section.

3.14 The *with* construction

So far, the discussion in this chapter has focused on the analysis of the relationship between dative and double object constructions of the type in (116a,b)/ (117a,b). The full paradigm of the English dative alternation also features an additional third member, illustrated in (116)/(117c). In this section I take up the task of analysing this *with* construction.[55]

---

[55] Gropen *et al.* (1989), in their classification of verbs (not) allowing double object constructions, include the entire class of "verbs of fulfilling" ("X gives something to Y that Y deserves, needs or is worthy of"), to which *award* and presumably also *fix up* belong (together with *present, provide, supply, entrust* etc.), in the category of verbs disallowing the double object pattern (cf. also Pesetsky 1993:118, who follows Gropen *et al.* in denying these verbs the double object option). But Kayne (1984:149) observes that some of the verbs of this class 'enter more or less naturally into the "V NP NP" structure', mentioning *supply* as an example. With *award, fix up* and to a lesser extent also *present*, double object constructions are often acceptable as well.

(116) a.   They awarded the prize to us.
   b.   They awarded us the prize.
   c.   They awarded us **with** the prize.

(117) a.   They fixed *up* a date for the boy.
   b.   They fixed the boy *up* a date.
   c.   They fixed the boy *up* **with** a date.

In his discussion of the relationship between the English double object construction in (116b) and the *with* construction in (116c), Kayne (1984:149) notices that 'the two possibilities are quite close semantically'. He speculates that the *with* construction is related to the double object construction in a way similar to the relationship between an *antipassive* construction and an ergative construction in so-called ergative languages, illustrated by the Greenlandic Eskimo pair in (118) (Sadock 1980):

(118) a.   Angut-ip   arnaq   unatar-paa.
      man-ERG   woman(ABS) beat-INDIC:3SG.SUBJ/3SG.OBJ
      'The man beat the woman.'

   b.   Angut   arna-mik   unata-a-voq.
      man(ABS)   woman-MOD   beat-**APASS**-INDIC:3SG.SUBJ
      'The man beat a woman.'

Kayne's (1984) suggestion receives initial support, within the Eskimo language group, from the fact that Eskimo features an alternation very similar to the one found in English (116) (cf. (119), from Johns 1984), and in this alternation, the very same modalis Case is used to mark the "demoted" argument as in the antipassive construction in (118b):

(119) a.   Anguti-up   titiraut   nutarar-mut   tuni-vaa.
      man-ERG   pencil(ABS) child-ALL   give-3SG.SUBJ/3SG.OBJ
      'The man gave the pencil to the child.'

   b.   Anguti-up titirauti-mik nutaraq   tuni-vaa.
      man-ERG   pencil-MOD   child(ABS)   give-3SG.SUBJ/3SG.OBJ
      'The man provided the child *with* the pencil.'

Larson (1988), in his analysis of Dative Shift, proposes a transformational relationship between dative and double object constructions such that the latter is obtained from the former by *passivisation* of the minimal VP containing the Theme and the Goal NPs. Aoun & Li (1989), while disagreeing with Larson in taking the double object construction to be basic, similarly assume Dative Shift to be a detransitivisation operation.

I would like to blend all these insights with Oyèláràn's (1989) analysis of Yorùbá (113), above, as an "antifocus" construction, which Manfredi (1989:26) has interpreted in such a way that "argument demotion" (in Relational Grammar terms) of the passive type is involved in (113). In particular, I would like to suggest that Kayne's (1984) claim that the *with* construction is the result of detransitivisation is essentially correct, but that the pertinent transformation is not antipassivisation but passivisation, adapting a recent suggestion regarding *with* constructions made in Larson (1990:section 3.1).

In concrete terms, I propose that the *with* construction is derived from the structure underlying all triadic constructions (cf. (63), above) via passivisation of the SC headed by the dative preposition. On Larson's assumptions as on mine, passivisation of the dative SC results in the "absorption" of (the phonetic matrix of) this preposition.[56] The (simplified) structure of *with* constructions hence reads as in (120):[57]

(120) $[_{VP}$ V $[_{SC1}$ θ' $[_{XP}$ X $[_{SC2}$ $[_{SC2}$ θ' $[_{PP1}$ $[_P$ Ø$]$ NP$]]$ $[_{PP2}$ *with* NP$]]]]]$

Passivisation of SC2 results in dethematisation of its subject position, which will serve as an intermediate landing-site for the Goal NP which, as a result of passivisation, fails to receive Case *in situ*.

An analysis of *with* constructions in terms of passivisation is especially strikingly supported by the facts of the Austronesian language of Chamorro (Gibson 1980), in which the "demoted" Theme of a *with* type construction bears the same oblique Case as the former subject of a passive sentence, as a comparison of (121) and (122) shows:

(121)   In nä   si tata-n-mami *nu* i   babui.
          1PL.SUBJ-give PN father-Ø-our OBL the pig
          'We provided our father *with* the pig.'

(122)   Ma-dulalak si Jose *nu* i   famagu'un.
          PASS-follow PN Jose OBL the children
          'Jose was followed by the children.'

---

[56] The preposition that is "absorbed" as a consequence of the passivisation process is not in need of licensing (via incorporation). One waý of understanding this is to assume that the preposition is in fact present throughout the syntactic derivation, only failing to get a phonetic matrix at PF — cf. section 4.5.1 for more discussion.

[57] For the sake of concreteness, I assume that the "demoted" Theme is adjoined to SC2. On the analysis of "demoted" arguments in (anti)passive constructions as structural adjuncts, cf. Baker (1988); Baker, Johnson & Roberts (1989).

Similarly, in some dialects of Eskimo the modalis Case used to mark the Theme NP in the *with* construction in (119b) is also employed for the *by*-phrase of passives.[58]

Returning to English, let me point out that since no movement of the dative PP is involved in the derivation of the *with* construction, the analysis leads us to expect that reanalysis of the verb and the "X" node is not obligatory.[59] We hence predict that particles lexicalising "X" in (120) can be premodified by *right*. This prediction is borne out by (123).

(123)   They fixed the boy **right** *up* with a date.

In view of the assumption (cf. fn. 56) that the Case-absorbed dative preposition in the structure in (120) does not need to be licensed by incorporation (hence does not force its projection to move to SpecSC1), we further predict, correctly again, that verb-adjacent particle placement is grammatical in *with* constructions, whereas in double object particle constructions verb-adjacent particle placement is impossible for most speakers (see sections 3.2 and 3.15.1).[60]

(124)   They fixed (*up*) the boy (*up*) with a date.

Finally we may note that the ill-formedness of the putative Predicate Inversion construction in (125) supports the non-predicative status that the present analysis assigns to the *with*-PP.

(125) a.   *With a date was fixed *up* the boy.
      b.   *With a prize was awarded the winning team.

Thus the passivisation approach to the *with* construction (modelled on Larson 1988 but applied to a different construction) is well supported by the facts.

---

[58] Other dialects, however, distinguish between the two; the Case form of the "demoted" Theme in (119b) is always identical with that of the oblique object of an antipassive construction in Eskimo. The present analysis of triadic constructions renders it impossible, however, to derive *with* constructions via antipassivisation.

[59] What moves instead is the NP complement of the head of PP, whose trace is lexically governed by the Case-absorbed P, which — cf. fn. 56 — is non-empty at LF (it only lacks a PF spell-out).

[60] That there is a contrast in this respect between *with* constructions and double object constructions argues against Hale & Keyser's (1993:98) structural assimilation of the two construction types (treating double object constructions as "covert" *with* constructions with an empty token of *with*). Similar remarks apply to Pesetsky's (1993:118) approach to *with* constructions in terms of the empty preposition "*Gwith*", which takes the *with*-PP as its complement. Postulating an empty preposition in *with* constructions furthermore endangers Pesetsky's (1993:106) own account of the morphophonological restrictions on the double object construction (cf. 3.12.1, above).

3.15 Particles revisited

At the end of the previous section I returned to the realm of triadic constructions containing a verbal particle (cf. (123)–(125a)). Coming full circle as it
were, I would like to close this chapter by addressing some further peculiarities
of double object particle constructions.

3.15.1 On the cross-linguistic distribution of
double object particle constructions

Double object constructions containing a verbal particle can be very productively formed in Dutch. With a verb like *give*, a whole range of particles can be
combined to form double object particle constructions, as the (probably non-
exhaustive) list in (126) indicates. This list can essentially be duplicated for
other double object verbs, such as *sturen* or *zenden* 'send'.

(126)   iemand iets {*aan/door/mee/op/terug/toe/weg/ver-*} geven
            somebody something {PRT} give

In English, too, double object particle constructions are quite pervasive. As
Gropen *et al.* (1989:251) note, the construction can even be generalised in spontaneous speech to verbs which do not normally accept it, as the following examples show:

(127) a.   Even if he dribbles me *in* one subject a year, ...
      b.   I put you *out* a big piece.
      c.   We'll credit you *back* the full purchase price.

Children acquiring English also spontaneously produce ditransitive verb-particle
constructions of the V–IO–Prt–DO type (cf. Gropen *et al.* 1989:209):

(128)   Pick me *up* all these things.   (age: 5;2)

Double object particle constructions may hence be taken to be a robust feature
of the grammar of English and Dutch. This is fully in line with our expectations. Since the structure of triadic constructions consistently includes a
position for a verbal particle, it is only natural to expect to find this position
overtly realised in some of these constructions.
    Not all languages are as well-behaved in this respect, however. In particular,
in some languages, particles are basically excluded from occurring in double
object constructions, even though they do productively show up in the corresponding prepositional dative constructions. Thus, Sybesma (1992:90) notes

that in Chinese, the dative construction in (129a), with the particle *zou* 'away' is grammatical, whereas the double object construction in (129b) is ill-formed if it contains *zou*:

(129) a. Ta   ji-(*zou*)-le   yi-ben   shu   gei   Li Si.
　　　　he   send-away-LE   one   book   to   Li Si
　　　　'He sent a book away to Li Si.'

　　　b. Ta   ji-(**zou*)   {le}   gei   {le}   Li Si   yi-ben   shu.
　　　　he   send-away   LE   to   LE   Li Si   one   book

In this regard, Chinese appears to be essentially on a par with the Mainland Scandinavian languages, in which double object particle constructions are non-existent while prepositional dative constructions containing a verbal particle can productively be formed.[61] In Icelandic, though, double object particle constructions do turn out to be found, as the following examples show:[62]

(130) a. Ég gaf (**upp*) Maríu (*upp*) símanúmerið mitt (**upp*).
　　　　I gave (up) Mariu (up) phone number my (up)

　　　b. Í gær hafa þeir sent (**upp*) strákunum (?*upp*) peningana (*upp*).
　　　　yesterday have they sent (up) the-boys (up) the-money (up)

　　　c. Ég hef rétt (**niður*) Jóni ((?)*niður*) hamarinn (*niður*).
　　　　I have passed (down) John (down) the hammer (down)

While I cannot at this point think of any obvious ways of solving the puzzle of why double object particle constructions should be so sparse in some languages,[63] I would like to draw attention to the fact that the placement of the verbal particle *upp* in the Icelandic double object construction in (130a) parallels that of English double object particle constructions, in which, as Emonds (1976) first noted, the canonical position for a verbal particle is likewise between the indirect and direct objects (cf. section 3.2 above):

(131)　　I sent (%*out*) the stockholders (*out*) an announcement (**out*).

---

[61] I thank Alma Næss, Arnfinn Vonen, Christer Platzack and Sten Vikner for trying (in vain) to construct V–IO–Prt–DO constructions in Norwegian, Swedish and Danish, respectively.

[62] Sentence (130a) was constructed for me by Jóhannes Gisli Jónsson (p.c.), the other two examples are taken from Collins & Thráinsson (1993:167–68).

[63] It clearly would not do to suggest that reanalysis of a verb and an overt particle is impossible in these languages, since in Swedish, Norwegian, Icelandic and Chinese, verb-particle reanalysis/incorporation is well known to exist (cf. Åfarli 1985 on Scandinavian; the fact that in Chinese (129a) the particle *zou* surfaces to the left of the perfective marker *le* shows that it is even physically incorporated into the verb).

The fact that "medial" particle placement is the only option which consistently yields a grammatical result in English (131) of course falls out immediately from the analysis of double object constructions presented in this study, reproduced in (132):

(132) $[_{VP} \, V \, [_{SC1} \, [_{PP} \, P_{\emptyset} \, NP_{Go}]_i \, (\ldots) \, [_{XP} \, \{\emptyset/Prt\} \, [_{SC2} \, NP_{Th} \, t_i]]]]$

I have consistently assumed that verbal particles originate in the head position of XP in (132). Since particles do not move in the syntax of English, and since movement of the empty-headed dative PP to the specifier position of the verb's SC complement is obligatory in English double object constructions, we expect there to be precisely one position in which particles can appear in an English double object construction: between the Goal and Theme NPs. This expectation is essentially borne out by the facts.[64]

Neither in English nor in Icelandic does it turn out to be entirely impossible to find particles in sentence-final position in double object constructions, however (cf. Icelandic (130b,c)).[65] In English, especially the particle *back* seems to be fairly comfortable in this position. It is interesting to note, moreover, that the one particle which does occur productively in double object constructions in Mainland Scandinavian is the counterpart of English *back*. Since if *back* were to occupy the X^0 position in the structure of double object constructions in (132), it would never be able to surface clause-finally, it is clear that some special arrangement for this particle must be made. It is not just *back*, though, that is exceptional in this respect, as Icelandic (130b,c) already showed. The following subsection addresses such unexpected double object particle constructions in some more detail, and presents a way of capturing them within the analysis presented.

---

[64]   As was pointed out in section 3.2, and as is also shown by Collins & Thráinsson's (1993) examples in (130b,c) above, verb-adjacent particle placement is not strictly ruled out for all speakers in all contexts (cf. Emonds 1976 and Oehrle 1976 for English). Since I have argued that English (and, as far as I have been able to establish, Icelandic as well) does not have physical syntactic particle movement, the existence of this word-order pattern is potentially problematic for the analysis presented (as well as for Collins & Thráinsson's 1993 alternative, as they note). I can think of several ways of approaching this word order. However, pending further research into the conditions which govern the V-Prt-IO-DO order, I shall not pursue these here.

[65]   Miyara (1983:310) reports that for his English informants, the V-Goal-Theme-Prt order is actually the *preferred* word order in double object particle constructions. A similar impression emerges from Thráinsson's judgements on Icelandic (130b,c) (but cf. Jónsson's (130a)). Much depends here on the specific choice of verb and particle combination, as the discussion to follow makes clear.

3.15.2 Particles in unexpected positions

While clause-final particle placement is generally impossible in double object constructions (cf. (133)), the examples in (134) are acceptable (cf. Oehrle 1976:235; Cowie & Mackin 1993; Johnson 1991; Mulder 1992a):

(133) a. *They sent Bob a package *off*.
     b. *They fixed John a date *up*.
     c. *They handed the children candies *out*.

(134) a. I gave John his books *back*.
     b. Hey, toss me that wrench *up*, will you?
     c. Why don't you send John some of those cigars *over*?
     d. Would you saw me a piece *off*?
     e. Will you sew me a new one *on*?
     f. ?Sam handed her them *down*.
     g. Gary poured me some *out*.

Johnson (1991), from which (134f,g) are taken, suggests that in double object particle constructions, it is possible to find the particle in sentence-final position if and only if both objects are weak pronouns.[66] As the examples in (134a–e) indicate, however, this is not in general correct. In particular, it seems that in constructions in which the particle is especially "predicative", clause-final particle placement is possible.[67] Notice also that, as Gropen *et al.* (1989:217) report, constructions of this type are spontaneously produced by children:

(134) h. I gon' put me all dese rubber bands *on*.   (age: 4;1)

The examples in (134) differ from the "canonical" V–Goal–Prt–Theme cases discussed earlier not only with regard to the surface position of the particle, but with respect to the possibility of particle modification as well, as Mulder (1992a) points out. Thus, while (13), above (repeated here as (135)), is ungrammatical if it contains the adverbial modifier *right*, the particles occurring in (134) may freely be modified, as (136) (from Mulder 1992a) shows:

---

[66] Collins & Thráinsson (1993:170) note that, while they usually find an alternation between clause-final particle placement and medial particle placement, only the former is possible if both objects are pronominal:

(i)   Í gær hafa þeir sent (*upp*) þeim (*upp*) þá (*upp*)   (cf. (130b))
       yesterday have they sent (up) them (up) it (up)

[67] The distinction between verbal particles and predicative particles is Oehrle's. The divide between the two is not always particularly clear, and it seems that one and the same particle may occasionally vacillate between the two types (cf. *up*).

(135)   John sent Bob (*right) *off* a package.

(136) a.   Mike tossed me the wrench (**right**) *up*.

   b.   Sure, I'll send you those cigars (**right**) *over*.

This shows that the sentence-final particles in (136) are not reanalysed with the verb. Since verb-particle reanalysis is obligatory for particles originating in the head position of XP (for reasons outlined in section 3.6), the fact that reanalysis does not obtain in (136) now leads us to conclude that the particles *up* and *over* in these examples do not occupy the head-of-XP position in (132).

If this is not where the particles in (136) and (134) are, then where *are* they? I would like to argue that in constructions of the type in (134), the particle forms a SC together with the Theme NP, and that this SC is base-generated in the *subject* position of the dative SC, as in (137), which represents the structure of (134a):[68]

(137) $[_{VP}$ *give* $[_{SC1}$ $[_{PP}$ $P_{\emptyset}$ *John*$]_i$ (...) $[_{XP}$ $\emptyset$ $[_{SC2}$ $[_{SC3}$ *his books back*$]$ $t_i]]]]$

I shall return in section 3.15.3 and chapter 5 to other constructions in which the dative PP also takes a *propositional* external argument.

For the moment, however, I would like to confine myself to presenting some further evidence in favour of the claim that the clause-final particle in examples of the type in (134) is generated in some position other than the head-of-XP slot. Notice first that the analysis proposed here yields a direct structural reflection of Oehrle's (1976) distinction between verbal (non-predicative) and predicative particles — the former originate under "X", the latter do not.

That predicative particles are not to be generated in the head position of XP in (132)/(137) is further shown by the fact that double object constructions may even include full predicative PPs in clause-final position, as in the following example taken from Jespersen (1965:Vol. III, Ch. XIV):[69]

---

[68]   In (137) I have left the internal structure of SC3 unanalysed, taking no stand on the question of whether the particles heading this SC are ergative or unergative. This is of no consequence to the points made in the present context. The Case-dependent subject of SC3, *his books*, receives Case in the following fashion: there is a coindexation relationship between the fronted dative phrase in SpecSC1 (the position to which V assigns Case), its trace, and SC3 (via Spec-Head agreement); internal to SC3 there is a Spec-Head agreement relation between the particle and *his books*. Via this chain of identical indexations, Case is transmitted to *his books*.

[69]   Haider (1992:18) presents interesting data which might also fall into this category. He notes that (ia) with *off* to the right of the Theme NP is bad unless *off* is followed by the directional PP *to his holiday resort*, and also observes that, contrary to what one might be led to expect, *off to his holiday resort* cannot be fronted as a constituent (cf. (ib)). A possible analysis of (i) built on (137) would generate *off to his holiday resort* under SC3 and would prevent movement of this phrase by invoking the opacity of left-branch constituents (cf. Kayne 1984; also cf. section 3.15.3, below).

(138)   Were I a caliph for a day, I would scourge me these jugglers *out of the commonwealth*.   (Scott A.1.208)

Similar constructions can be found in Dutch, especially — but not exclusively — in double object constructions with datives of *inalienable possession*:[70]

(139) a.   iemand iets *ter inzage* geven
             somebody something for viewing give
       b.   iemand iets *naar het hoofd* werpen
             somebody something to the head throw

Examples of this type show that in a double object construction, the Theme NP can form a SC with a full predicative PP. Given the structure of triadic constructions proposed in this study, this can only mean that the dative SC may have a SC subject, as in the structure in (137).

If, as is claimed here, clause-final predicative particles occupy a different structural position in the tree than non-predicative verbal particles, it should be possible to combine in one single double object construction both a lexical filler of the head position of XP and an additional predicative particle (or some other predicate of the subject-SC in (137)). It does not seem to be possible to use both a verbal particle and a predicative particle in a single clause (cf. e.g. **Could you send me up some cigars over?*), but that this is probably due to some mysterious non-structural cause (cf. also section 2.3.5.6) is shown by the fact that it is indeed possible to lexicalise both X^0 and the predicate of SC3 in (137), as in the following Dutch examples (in which the element lexicalising X^0 is italicised, as before, and the predicative head of SC3 is printed in bold type):

(140) a.   iemand iets **toe**-*be*-delen
             somebody something PRT-BE-deal
       b.   iemand iets **toe**-*ver*-trouwen
             somebody something PRT-VER-trust
       c.   iemand iets **terug/door**-*ver*-kopen
             somebody something back/on-VER-sell
       d.   iemand iets **door**-*ver*-tellen
             somebody something on-VER-tell

(i)   a.   We will send every stockholder a paycheck *off* *(*to his holiday resort*).
       b.   **Off to his holiday resort* we will send every stockholder a paycheck.

[70] Cf. E. Hoekstra (1991:90). That *ter inzage* in (139a) is a SC predicate is suggested by its resistance to PP-over-V (cf. **dat ik je het boek geef ter inzage* 'that I you the book give for viewing'). Note that the SC projected by *ter inzage* does not find itself in the complement of a verb. The descriptive generalisation about Dutch PP-over-V given in 3.11.2 hence does not cover this case; however, the Case-theoretic explanation for it given in that section does, since the SC defined by *ter inzage* contains its Case-dependent subject (as Hans Broekhuis notes).

In Hoekstra, Lansu & Westerduin (1987) (also cf. Hoekstra & Mulder 1990) it is argued that the Dutch verbal affixes *be-, ver-* found in the examples in (140) are affixal particles heading a SC at D-structure and incorporating into the verb in the course of the derivation. These affixes (especially *ver-*) are very common in Dutch double object constructions. It seems plausible that they are generated under X^0. This is suggested by the fact that these affixes are indelible in (140) (while the additional boldface particles in (140c,d) can be freely omitted) — once the *ver-* part of *verkopen* 'sell' and *vertellen* 'tell' is left out, these verbs can no longer take part in a double object construction. The presence of *ver-* hence makes the triadic structure available, which is readily expected if *ver-* is an X^0-element — on the analysis of triadic constructions presented here, X^0 is a crucial ingredient of triadic constructions: since it selects the dative SC, it follows that if X^0 is not there, no dative SC can be present. The dependence of some verbs' ability to have a triadic "argument structure" on the presence of a verbal affix like *ver-* thus suggests that this verbal affix originates under X^0. Since the head position of XP is hence already occupied, the additional (underlined) particles in (140) must be the predicates of SC3 in (137). The examples in (140) thus instantiate a structure of the type in (137) in which both X^0 and the predicate of SC3 have lexical content:[71]

(141) $[_{VP} [_{SC1} [_{PP} P_\emptyset$ *iemand*] (...) $[_{XP} [_{SC2} [_{SC3}$ *iets terug*] $t_i]$ *ver-*]] *kopen*]

With this in mind let me finally return to Mulder's (1992a) observation that clause-final particles in double object constructions (in contrast to their clause-internal counterparts) are freely modifiable by adverbs such as *right* (cf. (136)). This of course follows directly from the analysis: since the clause-final particle does not occupy X^0, it does not have to be reanalysed with the verb, and it is hence free to take on an adverbial modifier. In this regard, clause-final particles are again completely on a par with full predicative PPs in this position, as in (138), which is perfectly fine with *right* in front of *out of the commonwealth*.

---

[71] It is interesting to note that Dutch *terug* in (140c) is just like its English cognate *back* in being base-generated not as the head of XP but as the predicate of the SC in the subject position of the dative SC. This may not be coincidental. After all, in all Germanic languages (with exception of English, which has essentially lost the prepositional part), this directional particle is built up of a preposition and a body-part noun meaning *back* (cf. (i)). There is good reason to assume therefore that *back* type directional particles have evolved from full-fledged directional PPs. That these cannot occupy the X^0 position is clear — they are maximal projections, not heads. Synchronically, it seems that *terug* etc. can be analysed in two ways: they can be "regular" ergative particles as well, as is evident from their incorporability.

(i)	Dutch:	*te* 'at'	+	*rug*	=	*terug*
	German:	*zu* 'at/to'	+	*rück*	=	*zurück*
	Danish:	*til* 'to'	+	*bage*	=	*tilbage*
	English:	(*a*)	+	*back*	=	*back*

Summing up this section, we have seen that there is a difference between verbal and predicative particles (Oehrle 1976), which is manifest in English double object constructions by the fact that the latter may surface in clause-final position, to the right of the Theme NP, while the former may not. This difference can be captured by assuming that verbal particles are invariably generated under X^0 in the structure of triadic constructions, while predicative particles may be the predicate of a SC in the subject position of the dative phrase. Quite independently of the distinction between verbal and predicative particles, dative phrases must be assumed to be capable of taking propositional subjects, as is evident from the fact that full-fledged prepositional secondary predicates may show up in double object constructions (cf. (138)). In the next subsection, and also in chapter 5, we shall encounter additional motives for assuming that dative PPs can have propositional external arguments.

3.15.3 On dative PPs with propositional subjects

A crucial ingredient of my analysis of triadic constructions is the claim that the dative PP is a SC predicate. Against this background, consider the examples in (142):

(142) a.   John seems fond of Mary to me.
     b.   The team seemed ready for the opponent to the coach.

It seems plausible to assume that the *to*-PP in these constructions is a dative PP. This is supported by the fact that the "experiencer" argument in a Dutch *seem* construction of this type surfaces as an indirect object:

(143)   Dat lijkt *mij* leuk.
       that seems me nice

Given that dative PPs are SC predicates, this leaves us little analytical space for the predicative APs in the examples in (142). Since in the corresponding examples lacking a *to*-PP, these APs are the predicates of a SC, assigning a θ-role to the surface subject, there is no denying (given Uniformity of Theta Assignment) that in the examples in (142) as well, this AP projects a SC. It now turns out that, in the light of the analysis of triadic constructions defended here, this SC can only be generated in the *subject* position of the dative PP, as depicted (in an appropriately simplified form, as before) in (144):

(144) $[_{VP}$ *seem* $[_{SC1}$ Spec ... X^0 $[_{SC2}$ $[_{SC3}$ *John fond of Mary*$]$ $[_{PP}$ *to me*$]]]]]$

This analysis is supported in an interesting way by the following observation (due, to my knowledge, to Emonds 1992). While in *seem* constructions lacking an "experiencer" PP, extraction from the predicative AP yields a perfectly grammatical result, extraction from this AP is impossible in the examples in (142):[72]

(145) a.   Who does John seem fond of (*to you*)?
      b.   What opponent did the team seem ready for (*to the coach*)?

(146) a.   Of whom does John seem fond (*to you*)?
      b.   For what opponent did the team seem ready (*to the coach*)?

The deviance of the pertinent variants of the examples in (145) and (146) can, given the analysis in (144), be seen to be an immediate consequence of the fact that the constituent from which extraction takes place is on a *left branch* in the structure.

What we see, then, is that an analysis in terms of a propositional (SC) subject to a dative SC of these *seem+to* constructions, apart from being forced upon us by the theory, yields a straightforward account of otherwise mysterious extraction facts of the type in (145) and (146).[73]

---

[72] Thanks to Kyle Johnson for giving his judgement on these sentences as well. Hans Broekhuis points out that Dutch examples like (i) are fine. A possible explanation capitalises on the fact that here the predicate of the dative SC undergoes movement (Dative Shift or scrambling; cf. chapter 4), which may render its specifier transparent; cf. chapter 5, section 5.3.7.1, on the "priority effect" in French causatives, for further illustration and discussion.

(i)   Waar$_i$ lijkt Jan *jou* niet zo geschikt t_i voor?
               where seems Jan you not so suitable for

[73] The analysis in (144) does not, at first blush, seem to capture the well-known fact that anaphors contained in the surface subject of *seem+to* constructions can be bound by the *to*-PP contained NP:

(i)   Each other$_i$'s pictures seem nice to the children$_i$.

After all, even after reconstruction of the surface subject into the position of the trace in its D-structure position, this NP still is not c-commanded by the prospective binder of the anaphor: from prepositional dative constructions, we are familiar with the fact that the PP-contained Goal cannot bind an anaphor in the Theme NP (cf. (iia)). As Kyle Johnson has pointed out to me, however, the deviance of (iia) vanishes once NP-raising of the Theme NP to subject position in a passive construction takes place (iib). Note that (iib) is structurally on a par with (i), NP-raising from the subject of the dative SC taking place in both examples. The fact that they pattern alike is hence as expected, even though it remains a moot point how the binding facts in (i)/(iib), and the difference between (iia,b) are to be accommodated.

(ii)   a.   *We gave each other$_i$'s pictures to the children$_i$.
        b.   Each other$_i$'s pictures were given to the children$_i$.

The extraction data in (145)–(146) thus lend support to the claim that dative PPs can take propositional subjects, which will be further corroborated in chapter 5. They also suggest that my hypothesis (cf. section 1.2.3, above) that NP-traces are not subject to any conditions on movement and (proper) government is correct. For notice that, even though A'-extraction from the adjectival SCs in (142) is impossible, NP-movement of the subjects of these SCs is perfectly licit. If NP-traces had to obey the conditions imposed on A'-movement, and if — as I just argued — the structure of *seem+to* constructions is as in (144), we would wrongly predict that even (142) should be ill-formed. The grammaticality of these examples now further confirms the view that the distribution of NP-traces is not governed by conditions ruling (A'-)movement.

3.16 Conclusion

The analysis of triadic constructions and Dative Shift has been and still is a matter of lively debate in the generative literature. Emonds (1993:213–14) concisely summarises the history of the debate:

> Just when a structure-preserving [transformational] analysis of [the Dative Shift] rule was justified [in Emonds (1972)], an otherwise productive research strategy (trace theory and subsequently the Projection Principle) was developed [in Chomsky (1975)], but only imperfectly. As a result, the most principled version of transformational syntax seemed unable to explain indirect object movement phenomena and relegated them to the lexicon. Therefore, the research program of formal grammar required some appropriate clarification to again become compatible with a descriptively adequate and comprehensive treatment of indirect objects.

Emonds develops an account in terms of a traceless structure-preserving interchange between the direct and indirect objects, modifying Chomsky's (1981) Projection Principle accordingly. I have presented an analysis which is compatible with the standard principles-and-parameters theory.

In line with the recent return from a predominantly lexicalist approach to the dative alternation (cf. esp. Oehrle 1976) to a derivational analysis (cf. Baker 1988; Larson 1988), I have argued that prepositional dative and double object constructions feature a common underlying structure. In contrast to the currently most popular approach to triadic constructions, represented by Larson (1988) (also cf. E. Hoekstra 1991), which, in Emonds' (1993:215) words, wrongly embraces the 'downplaying or elimination of any central role in syntactic analysis for PP structures, especially covert PPs', the present analysis capitalises on the role played by the dative PP. It is argued that this PP is the predicate of a SC embedded in another SC whose ergative head may either be empty or lexicalised by a particle or (in Dutch) by a verbal affix (*be-, ver-*). This latter SC is in its turn the complement of an abstract copula heading the SC selected by the matrix triadic verb. The double object construction is derived from this underlying structure by movement of an empty-headed dative PP.

The inclusion in the structure of simple, particle-less triadic constructions of no fewer than two abstract SC-heads is motivated by both theory-internal and independent empirical considerations. I shall further support the structure of triadic constructions resulting from this chapter in a discussion of the relationship between dative and transitive causative constructions in chapter 5. There I shall also present additional contexts in which a dative phrase takes a propositional external argument, a configuration of which we encountered two instances towards the end of the present chapter.

In the next chapter, I shall take a closer look at the structure of double object constructions proposed in the above, adducing evidence from the domain of restrictions on movement in favour of the two central ingredients of the analysis of Dative Shift: (i) the assumption that A-movement of the dative PP takes place in the derivation of the double object construction, and (ii) the hypothesis that the Goal NP in a double object construction is governed by an empty dative preposition.[74]

---

[74] It may be felt to be odd that the well-known binding asymmetries in dative and double object constructions, which since Barss & Lasnik (1986) and Larson (1988) have played the most central part in discussions of triadic constructions and Dative Shift (also cf. Pesetsky's 1993 "cascade structures", which are firmly anchored in the claim that all binding asymmetries involve c-command, hence tell us important things about the structural organisation of sentences), have not been addressed in this chapter. The reason for this is that, within the frame of this study, these binding asymmetries are more naturally at home in chapter 4 (section 4.6). I hence refer the reader to chapter 4 for an appraisal of these data.

4

Movement and Structural Ambiguity in Double Object Constructions

4.1 Introduction

The discussion in chapter 3 was primarily concerned with the D-structure representation of triadic constructions, and the nature of Dative Shift. In this chapter, a number of S-structure phenomena associated with double object constructions will be addressed. These will be shown to lend further support to a number of ingredients of the analysis of Dative Shift presented in chapter 3. Some will moreover be seen to constitute arguments for the view that double object constructions are in principle structurally ambiguous between "genuine" Dative Shift constructions and "covert" prepositional dative constructions featuring an empty dative preposition.

4.2 A′-extraction of the double object Goal: Evidence for an empty preposition

In this section I shall be concerned with the restrictions on A′-movement of the double object Goal. It will be shown that, while overt *wh*-movement of the indirect object in a double object construction is generally possible, this constituent resists being the input to EMPTY OPERATOR MOVEMENT. Given a number of independently plausible assumptions, we can derive from this an important argument in favour of the inclusion of an empty dative preposition in the structure of the double object construction (cf. also Kayne 1984; Czepluch 1982).

4.2.1 Restrictions on Goal movement: Introduction to the problem

In the literature on double object constructions, applicatives and Dative Shift, a recurrent theme is the fact that, in many languages, indirect (or applied) objects appear to resist being A′-moved. Since so much attention has been paid to it, and since its weight as an argument for or against a particular analysis of triadic constructions is generally considerable, it is important to first present a concise inventory of the relevant data.

181

Baker (1988:sect. 5.4) reports that in Chichewa, A'-extraction of both dative and benefactive applied (i.e. indirect) objects is impossible, quoting examples of the following type (obtained from Sam Mchombo), featuring long-distance extraction in a relative clause construction, as evidence:

(1)   *Iyi   ndi   mfumu   imene ndi-na-nen-a
         this   is   chief   which 1SG.SUBJ-PAST-say-ASP
         kuti atsikana   a-na-perek-er-a   chitseko.
         that girl   SP-PAST-hand-APPL-ASP door
         'This is the chief that I said that the girl handed the door to.'

(2)   *Iyi   ndiyo mfumu   imene ndi-ku-ganiz-a
         this   is   chief   which 1SG.SUBJ-PRES-think-ASP
         kuti Mavuto a-na-umb-ir-a   mtsuko.
         that Mavuto SP-PAST-mold-APPL-ASP waterpot
         'This is the chief that I think that Mavuto molded the waterpot for.'

Baker takes this to be a structural fact, to be accounted for by the analysis of applicative constructions. In all fairness, however, he admits that 'there are two factors that may conceal what is going on' (1988:293). For one thing, extraction is perfect if the triadic verb shows object agreement with the extracted applied object:

(3)   Iyi   ndiyo mfumu   imene ndi-ku-ganiz-a
         this is   chief   which 1SG.SUBJ-PRES-think-ASP
         kuti Mavuto a-na-*i*-umb-ir-a   mtsuko.
         that Mavuto SP-PAST-OAGR-mold-APPL-ASP waterpot
         'This is the chief that I think that Mavuto molded the waterpot for.'

This, however, is probably irrelevant, no actual extraction taking place in constructions featuring object agreement markers, which typically do not exhibit any island effects.

More importantly, however, the deviant examples in (1) and (2) improve significantly if the applied object undergoes *short* extraction. Baker (1988:293) observes that sentences such as (4) 'are still noticeably deviant, but to a much milder degree ... to the point that they may become essentially acceptable'.

(4)   Iyi   ndiyo mfumu   imene Mavuto
         this is   chief   which Mavuto
         a-na-umb-ir-a   mtsuko.
         SP-PAST-mold-APPL-ASP waterpot
         'This is the chief that Mavuto molded the waterpot for.'

Baker goes on to suggest that it is apparently something about short extraction (e.g. having to do with ease of parsing; cf. Langendoen, Kalish-Landon & Dore 1974; Hornstein & Weinberg 1981) that disturbs the otherwise perspicuous picture, thereby discarding a body of literature on extraction of indirect objects which is restricted in its scope to cases of short extraction, and in which it is observed that grammatical results are obtained.

As I shall argue in this section, however, it would be wrong to set aside short-distance A'-extraction as irrelevant or 'easier to parse or process', hence exempt from whatever blocks long-distance extraction. Notice that the difference between short and long extraction exemplified by the Chichewa examples in (2) and (4) is familiar from English as well (as Baker also notes). Thus, while all speakers of English consistently reject long-distance *wh*-movement of the Goal in an example such as (5b), the corresponding short-distance *wh*-movement construction in (5a) is acceptable to many speakers (cf. Hornstein & Weinberg 1981:77–78):[1]

(5)   a.   %Who did John give a book?
      b.   *Who did Bill think that John gave a book?

In a language as closely related to English as Dutch, on the other hand, there is no noticeable difference between short and long extraction of indirect objects in double object constructions. That is, (6a,b) are both acceptable:

(6)   a.   Wie heeft Jan een boek gegeven?
          who has Jan a book given
      b.   Wie dacht Wim dat Jan een boek gegeven had?
          who thought Wim that Jan a book given had

Notice the oddity of an account of the difference between English and Chichewa on the one hand, and Dutch on the other, phrased in terms of ease of processing or parsing. Why should the Dutch long-distance extraction example in (6b) be any easier to process than its English and Chichewa counterparts? Are speakers of the latter two languages worse parsers than speakers of Dutch?[2]

---

[1]   Also cf. Kurtzman (1989), who reports data obtained from New York City residents.

[2]   Stowell (1981:323–24), Hoffman (1991:225ff.) and Bowers (1993:645) also present evidence against processing/parsing accounts concerning Goal extraction in double object constructions. Hoffman's objections are specifically aimed at Woolford's (1986) "mapping" approach. Bowers points to the non-ambiguity of double object *wh*-movement constructions with two animate objects (such as *Who did John send Mary?*). I refer to the original works for details.

At best, then, we can conclude at this point that there are restrictions on the mobility of double object Goals which, as Marantz (1990:17) also observes, are not universal, but subject to as yet mysterious variation.[3] More insight into the nature of the restrictions on indirect/applied object movement can be gained by considering Dutch and English in more detail. As the next section shows, discussions on indirect object movement are generally blurred by the fact that no distinction is made between overt *wh*-extraction on the one hand, and EMPTY OPERATOR MOVEMENT on the other. Once these are teased apart, a clearer picture emerges.

4.2.2 Overt versus empty operator movement

Even though there is no distinction between long and short *wh*-extraction of indirect objects in Dutch, indirect object movement is not entirely unconstrained in this language. *Tough*-movement and infinitival relativisation of double object Goals generally yields a deviant result (although judgements vary somewhat from speaker to speaker and from case to case):[4]

---

[3]   Thus Chung (1982) notes that in Chamorro (Austronesian; Gibson 1980) there are two ways of questioning object NPs: one in which the clause is nominalised, and one in which nominalisation does not obtain. Only in the first type of question is extraction of the indirect object excluded.

[4]   Two notes on the data are in order. First, let me point out that (7c) is perfectly acceptable on a reading in which *een jongen* 'a boy' is associated with an empty operator in the *subject* position of the infinitival clause ('I am looking for a boy who can send that book'); this is clearly irrelevant to the issues at hand. Secondly, examples like (7b,c) tend to improve (to the point of basically being acceptable) if the direct object is a bare, determinerless NP (ia) and/or part of a V + DO idiom (ib). It is plausible to assume that in such cases the direct object *incorporates* into the verb, the construction being reinterpreted as a simple monotransitive construction with a complex verb. Support for this suggestion comes from the fact that such apparent double object constructions allow for "indirect object" passivisation in spontaneous production (which Dutch otherwise does not allow in double object constructions with two NP objects: *Ze wordt een boek gegeven* 'she is a book given'). This is shown by the example in (ii), taken from Jerôme Heldring's newspaper column on "linguistic errors" made in newspaper/journal articles (*NRC Handelsblad*, 12 October 1993).

(i)   a.   [7]Kleine kinderen zijn leuk om cadeautjes te geven.
              little children are nice COMP presents to give
       b.   [7]Mooie meisjes zijn leuk om het hof te maken.
              beautiful girls are nice COMP the court to make (i.e. to court)
(ii)   Ze wordt bemind, althans: ze wordt het hof gemaakt.
              she is loved, or at least: she is the court made (i.e. courted)

In order to avoid interference from this "reanalysis" effect, my Dutch examples will consistently feature direct object NPs with a definite/demonstrative determiner.

(7) a. Wie heb je dat boek op gestuurd?
         who have you that book up sent
     b. ?*Die jongen is leuk om dat boek op te sturen.
         that boy is nice COMP that book up to send
     c. ?*Ik zoek een jongen om dat boek op te sturen.
         I look-for a boy COMP that book up to send

From the literature on English, we are familiar with an essentially identical pattern. Thus, while there is variation among native speakers of English with respect to the eligibility of indirect objects to undergo short *wh*-extraction (cf. (5a), repeated here as (8a)), the examples of *tough*-movement and infinitival relativisation in (8b,c) are invariably judged ungrammatical by *all* speakers (cf. Hornstein & Weinberg 1981:section 8).

(8) a. %Who did John give a book?   (= (5a))
     b. *Children are not easy to give a book.
     c. *John is not a man to give a book.

And though Larson (1988:356) reports that in Norwegian, the indirect object may undergo virtually all sorts of A'-movement, he nonetheless makes a distinction between overt *wh*-extraction and *tough*-movement, a distinction which — according to my informants — is considerably more robust than the slight contrast that Larson presents. Thus, (9a) is perfect, but (9b), instantiating *tough*-movement of the indirect object, is odd:[5]

---

[5] Speaker variation on the judgement of (9b) may be due (in part) to the effect noted in fn. 4; after all, *blomster* 'flowers' is a bare NP direct object, potentially reanalysable with the verb. It is worth pointing out furthermore that (9b) improves if *det* is inserted, as in (i). In the light of the following discussion, this is expected: (9b) involves empty operator movement of the indirect object, while (i) features IO topicalisation (which, in Norwegian, is not empty operator movement; cf. also p. 190 and fn. 12, below).

(i)   Slike mennesker er *det* hyggelig å gi blomster.
         such men is it nice to give flowers

I also note that, apparently, infinitival relatives featuring indirect object extraction are grammatical in Norwegian (cf. (ii)). The contrast between *tough*-movement and infinitival relativisation might be captured on the assumption that the latter, in Norwegian, does not involve empty operator movement but deletion of the *wh*-phrase in SpecCP (cf. Tellier 1991 on the analysis of some apparent cases of empty operator movement — notably involving relativisation — in terms of *wh*-deletion; also cf. fn. 11, below).

(ii)   Jeg leter etter noen å gi blomster.
         I look for somebody to give flowers

(9)   a.   Hvem sa Marit at hun ga en presang?
           who said Marit that she gave a present
      b.   ⁷*Slike mennesker er hyggelige å gi blomster.
           such men are nice to give flowers

What distinguishes *tough*-movement and infinitival relativisation from overt (short) *wh*-movement is that the former two processes involve EMPTY OPERATOR MOVEMENT. Let us assume, then, that the following generalisation holds:[6]

(10)   Indirect objects can undergo overt *wh*-extraction, but may not undergo EMPTY OPERATOR MOVEMENT.

How do we go about distinguishing between overt *wh*-extraction and empty operator movement in the context of double object constructions? I would like to present the following line of argument. First, I argue that extraction of indirect object NPs from the "indirect object position" in double object constructions is not a theoretical option. Since not all indirect object extraction yields a deviant result, however, I then proceed to arguing that grammatical instances of overt indirect object *wh*-extraction result from *pied-piping* of the (zero-headed) dative PP. This pied-piping strategy is inapplicable in cases of empty operator movement, however, for independent reasons. I spell out the details of an analysis based on this line of argument in the next section.

4.2.3 Analysis

I assume, with Baker (1988), that A'-movement from the indirect object position in double object constructions is structurally impossible. Baker rules this out by appealing to his Non-Oblique Trace Filter in (11), in which a prime role is played by the $[-V]$ trace of the incorporated dative preposition governing the indirect object trace (cf. also Czepluch 1982; Kayne 1984:chapter 9, whose accounts likewise crucially rely on the presence of an empty dative P in the structure of the double object construction).

(11)   *The Non-Oblique Trace Filter*   (Baker 1988:299)
          $*[Op_i \ldots X_j \ldots [\{-V\}_j \ t_i] \ldots]$ at S-structure

---

[6] I shall address the apparent variation among native speakers with respect to indirect object mobility in English short *wh*-questions (cf. (8a)) from the perspective of the generalisation in (10) further below. There I also discuss the difference between short and long *wh*-movement in English, and a number of other construction types.

Taking over Baker's stipulation in (11) is a strategy that is open to me in principle, given that the analysis of Dative Shift presented in chapter 3 is on a par with Baker's in involving incorporation into the verb of the empty dative preposition. In contrast to Baker's overall analysis of triadic constructions, however, it seems possible on the present assumptions to derive (11) from Kayne's (1984) Connectedness Condition. While Baker assumes a flat, ternary branching VP-internal structure for triadic constructions, I have presented an account according to which the dative PP harbouring the Goal NP is moved into a *specifier* position in the derivation of the double object construction. Movement of the NP object of the dative preposition would now involve subextraction from a left branch, in violation of the left branch condition (cf. section 1.2.4, above).[7]

Suppose, however, that we moved the entire dative PP to SpecCP, rather than just P's NP object. Then (11) would be inoperative, and the ECP (involved in the licensing of the P-trace) could be complied with at LF after reconstruction of the dative PP into a V-governed position. This, I claim, is the way in which grammatical instances of overt *wh*-extraction of indirect objects are derived — by *pied-piping* of zero-headed dative PPs.

Pied-piping is *not* an option, however, in the case of empty operator movement. Empirically, this is evident from the ungrammaticality of such putative pied-piping cases as (12b). Theoretically, it straightforwardly follows from the assumption (cf. Jaeggli 1981; Hendrick 1988; Kinyalolo 1991; Bennis & Hoekstra 1989) that empty operators are to be identified as PRO,[8] in conjunction with the PRO Theorem, which decrees that PRO may not be governed at S-structure. Since the zero dative preposition governs its empty operator (i.e. PRO) object, pied-piping the entire dative PP irrevocably entails a violation of the PRO Theorem.[9]

---

[7] It is not immediately obvious whether Chomsky's (1986) *Barriers* theory would accommodate (11) with equal ease. On Chomsky's assumptions the ECP would probably be complied with in cases of extraction of the NP object of the incorporated dative P, the NP's trace being lexically governed by the V+P complex (by the Government Transparency Corollary) regardless of whether P's projection is a left branch constituent or not.

[8] This accords well with Wexler's (1992) claim that children do not have PRO at early acquisitional stages, and do not have empty operators either. (Thanks to Maria Teresa Guasti for bringing this to my attention.)

[9] An alternative account of the inability of empty operators to pied-pipe, which unlike the present suggestion carries over to the fact that the French relative pronoun *dont* is similar in this regard (cf. (i), overleaf) while arguably not being identifiable as PRO, is presented in Pollock (1992). I shall not discuss this analysis here.

(i)   Ce livre, [le premier chapitre *duquel/*dont*] j'ai déjà écrit, ...
        this book the first chapter of which/"dont" I have already written

(*continued overleaf*)

(12) a.   John is not easy [Op_i to talk [$_{PP}$ to t_i]].
      b.   *John is not easy [[$_{PP}$ to Op]$_j$ to talk t_j].

The independently established fact, then, that pied-piping is impossible in cases of empty operator movement allows us to make the desired distinction between overt *wh*-extraction and empty operator movement of indirect objects in double object constructions. Let us sum up the account in (13):

(13) a.   The Goal NP in double object constructions is governed by a zero dative preposition.
      b.   A'-movement of the Goal NP is impossible in Dative Shift constructions (cf. (11)).
      c.   Overt *wh*-extraction of the indirect object in a double object construction involves *pied-piping* of the dative PP.
      d.   Pied-piping of PP under empty operator movement is ruled out (for instance by the PRO Theorem, if empty operator=PRO)
      e.   *Ergo*: There is no grammatical derivation for cases of empty operator movement of double object Goals.

Closing this subsection, let me observe in passing here that the contrast between overt *wh*-extraction and empty operator movement found in the context of indirect object extraction has a direct parallel in the domain of transitive causative constructions. Thus, while overt *wh*-movement of the embedded subject (or "causee") of a transitive causative construction generally yields a grammatical result,[10] empty operator movement of this constituent is typically impossible. The following examples from Dutch and English illustrate this:

What we should also ensure is that the empty operator cannot be the entire dative PP (rather than P's object). This follows from the inability of *Op* to be predicative (cf. 3.11.2, item (81); also cf. Tellier 1991 and Heggie 1993) and from the categorial mismatch that would arise in such an analysis of an example like (12) between the empty operator (PP) and its identifier (NP).

[10] In English, this again appears to be subject to speaker variation. While my informants tend to accept (15a) (also cf. Bowers' 1993:646 examples reproduced in (i), below), Oehrle (1976:244) presents examples of transitive perception verb constructions (whose analysis is assimilable to that of transitive causatives) which he considers ungrammatical (cf. (ii)). In this regard, too, causative/ perception verb constructions seem to be on a par with double object constructions, then.

(i)   a.   Who did you have take out the trash?   (Bowers 1993:646)
      b.   Who did you make do the dishes?
(ii) a.   *Who did you see fight Liston?   (Oehrle 1976:244)
      b.   *Who did you watch cross the street?

(14) a. Wie heb je dat boek laten zien?
          who have you that book let see
      b. ??Die jongen is leuk om dat boek te laten zien.
          that boy is nice COMP that book to let see
      c. ??Ik zoek een jongen om dat boek te laten zien.
          I look-for a boy COMP that book to let see

(15) a. %Who did you let sing (a song)?
      b. ?*Children are not easy to let sing a song.
      c. ?*I am looking for someone to let sing a song.

This naturally leads to a structural assimilation of triadic and transitive causative constructions as far as the status of the Goal and causee NPs is concerned. The data in (14) and (15) can then be made to fall out from the account given for the double object examples in (7) and (8). I merely note this point in passing here, undertaking the desired structural assimilation of the constructions in question in chapter 5.[11]

---

[11] Hans Bennis points out that comparative deletion of indirect objects is perfectly grammatical in Dutch (cf. (i)). This is problematic if comparative deletion involves empty operator movement (cf. Den Besten 1978). Such an account is apparently supported by the fact that prepositional objects may not undergo the process (cf. (iia), from Van Riemsdijk 1977). The example in (iia) is parallel to the parasitic gap construction in (iib), which certainly involves empty operator movement (cf. Chomsky 1986; Mulder & Den Dikken 1992). The deviance of (iib) follows from the fact that while the empty operator bears the feature $[+R]$ (since it is extracted from a PP, and only $[+R]$ elements may be so extracted in Dutch; Van Riemsdijk 1978), its binder is $[-R]$; the resulting clash in R-features rules out (iib), and possibly also (iia).

(i)   Ik heb meer jongens een boek gegeven dan jij een verhaal hebt voorgelezen.
           I have more boys a book given than you a story have read-to

(ii)   a. *Jan heeft meer geld verdiend dan zijn vrouw op gerekend had.
           Jan has more money earned than his wife on counted had
       b. *een boek dat Jan [zonder in te lezen] teruggebracht heeft
           a book that Jan without in to read returned has

Notice, however, that comparative deletion and parasitic gaps diverge in one probably non-trivial respect: while (iib) can be salvaged by turning the binder of the empty operator into a $[+R]$ entity (cf. (iiib); Bennis & Hoekstra 1984), (iiia) is just as ill-formed as (iia). This difference between comparative deletion and "genuine" empty operator movement might be taken to suggest that the former process does not involve empty operator movement. Perhaps it involves *wh*-deletion (cf. Tellier 1991 on relative clause constructions, which, according to her, do not involve empty operator movement; also cf. fn. 5, above).

(iii) a. *Jan heeft *daar* vaker op gezeten dan zijn vrouw in gelegen heeft.
           Jan has there more often on sat than his wife in lain has
       b. een boek *waar* Jan [zonder in te lezen] tegen geprotesteerd heeft
           a book where Jan without in to read against protested has

4.2.4 English topicalisation and relativisation

Hornstein & Weinberg (1981:section 8) note that canonical empty operator movement constructions like *tough*-movement and infinitival relatives are not the only contexts in which indirect object A'-extraction yields a deviant result in English. Topicalisation and *that*-relativisation/clefting of indirect objects are just as bad, as the following examples show:

(16) a. *It is Bill (that) John gave a book.
      b. *Bill likes the man (that) John gave a book.
      c. *Bill, John gave a book.

These constructions can be subsumed under the generalisation in (10) if they are analysed in terms of empty operator movement. For English topicalisation, an analysis along these lines (or in terms of "abstract" *wh*-movement) was first suggested in Chomsky (1977). Such an analysis also seems plausible for English *that*-relativisation, *that* being analysable as a complementiser "agreeing" with an empty operator in its specifier position. In this way, then, the data in (16) reduce directly to the generalisation in (10), which follows from the analysis, as shown in section 4.2.3. Note, incidentally, that in Dutch and Norwegian, topicalisation cannot involve empty operator movement, since topicalisation of indirect objects is perfect in these languages (Norwegian (17b) from Larson 1988:356):[12]

(17) a. Jan zou ik nooit een boek lenen.
          Jan would I never a book lend
      b. Ingen studenter har vi lånt romaner.
          no students have we lent books.

---

[12] This does *not* mean that it must be the topic itself that undergoes physical movement. That is, everything that is said here is compatible with an analysis of Dutch (and perhaps also Norwegian) topicalisation along the lines of Koster (1978b), Weerman (1989:52ff.), Kosmeijer (1993:132) and Zwart (1993:258ff.), which assimilates topicalisation and contrastive left dislocation (cf. (i)) — an analysis for which there is solid evidence. What we cannot assume (in the light of (17a)) is that the covert *d*-word (*die*) moving to SpecCP in topicalisation constructions is an empty operator "proper"; but we are perfectly free to take over an analysis of the type in (i) if we assume that what moves to SpecCP is something other than a true empty operator (cf. Tellier 1991 on relative clause constructions, and fnn. 5 and 11, above).

(i)   [$_{CP}$ Jan [$_{CP}$ (*die*) mag [$_{IP}$ ik niet *t*]]]
               Jan (that) like I not
               'Jan, I don't like (him).'

4.2.5 English long *wh*-extraction

Empty operator movement is definitely implicated in the analysis of *tough*-movement and infinitival relativisation, and an analysis in these terms naturally extends to *that*-relativisation/clefting, as well as topicalisation. What about English long *wh*-extraction, though? This is commonly analysed in terms of successive cyclic movement of a *wh*-operator. In the light of the deviance of English (5b) and what was argued with respect to the restrictions on Goal extraction in section 4.2.4, however, it seems that we should find a way of treating long-distance *wh*-extraction in English (though *not* in Dutch or Norwegian; cf. (6b) and (9a)) in terms of empty operator movement. This section presents such a way.

Thornton (1991) reports on the results of an elicitation test of long-distance *wh*-extraction held among twenty-one English speaking children between the ages of 2;10 and 5;5. Thornton shows that children at these ages use three types of strategies for producing what in adult English would simply be a long-distance *wh*-question:

(18) a. *Regular long-distance* wh-*movement*:
          What do you think that babies drink?
          Who do you think is in the box?
      b. *Medial* wh-*movement or* wh-*copying*:
          What do you think **what** babies drink?
          Who do you think **who** is in the box?
      c. *Partial* wh-*movement*:
          What do you think **where** the froggy lives?

The strategies in (18b,c), while apparently non-existent in adult English, are familiar from the synchronic syntax of adult varieties of German and Romani, a language spoken in (what used to be) Yugoslavia, as McDaniel (1986, 1989) has shown:[13]

---

[13] The dialects featuring (19) are not necessarily identical with those featuring (20). This is irrelevant in the present context. In the examples in (19), *was* and *so* are formally invariant *wh*-scope markers; so is *what* in (18c). A kind of partial *wh*-movement strategy is also employed in Hungarian (cf. Marácz 1989:section 7.5, who refers to it as the "*mit*-strategy"). Note that in (i), the "real" *wh*-phrase remains in the Focus position of the embedded clause, and does not move to the specifier position of the embedded CP.

(i)   *Mit* gondolsz hogy János *kit* láttot?
           what think-you that Janos who saw
           'Who do you think that John saw?'

(19) a. **Was** glaubt Hans **wen** Jakob gesehen hat?   (German)
          what believes Hans whom Jakob seen has
          'Who does Hans believe Jakob saw?'

      b. **So** o Demìri mislinol **kas** i Arìfa dikhla?   (Romani)
          what Demiri thinks whom Arifa saw
          'Who does Demiri think Arifa saw?'

(20) a. **Wen** glaubt Hans **wen** Jakob gesehen hat?
          who believes Hans who Jakob seen has
          'Who does Hans believe Jakob saw?'

      b. **Kas** o Demìri mislinola **kas** i Arìfa dikhla?
          whom Demiri thinks whom Arifa saw
          'Who does Demiri think Arifa saw?'

Arguably, partial *wh*-movement, as illustrated in (18c) and (19), involves syntactic *wh*-movement to the local SpecCP and association (via coindexation) with a scope marker in the higher SpecCP position(s) (cf. also Rizzi 1991). In the present context, I shall not be concerned with this phenomenon. What interests me is the *wh*-copying strategy employed in (18b) and (20). I would like to suggest that what happens in these *wh*-copying constructions is that the *wh*-word in the matrix SpecCP position is base-generated there, like a kind of base topic, while the *wh*-word in the embedded SpecCP in the examples given above is the *spell-out of an empty operator*, bound by the matrix SpecCP filler. This is shown in (21):[14]

(21) $[_{CP}$ *what*$_i$ do you think $[_{CP}$ $[_{Op}$ *what*$]_i$ babies drink $t_i]]$

If this tentative account of *wh*-copying is correct — that is, if the embedded *wh*-word in (18b) and (20) is a spelled-out empty operator — we can establish an immediate link between the *wh*-copying strategy for producing long-distance *wh*-questions, and "genuine" long-distance *wh*-extraction constructions of the type in (18a). The obvious move to make is to suggest that the latter, too, instantiates *wh*-copying, the difference being that the operator moving to the embedded SpecCP remains empty:

---

[14] Note the affinity of the account in (21)–(22) with Chomsky's (1993) "copying (and deletion)" approach to movement. That the analysis in (21) is on the right track is suggested by the fact that complex *wh*-phrase copies are ungrammatical in German and early child English (cf. McDaniel 1986; Thornton 1991). If the medial *wh*-word is the spell-out of an empty operator, which is never complex, the deviance of (i) is as expected. Note that I predict that (i) should improve if the medial *wh* is replaced by a simple *wh*-word. This is in conformity with the facts.

(i)   a. *Wessen Buch glaubst du wessen Buch Hans liest?
          whose book think you whose book Hans reads
      b. *Which smurf do you think which smurf is wearing roller skates?

(22)   [$_{CP}$ *what*$_i$ do you think [$_{CP}$ [$_{Op}$ Ø]$_i$ babies drink *t*$_i$]]

If treating long-distance *wh*-extraction along the lines of (22) stands up to closer scrutiny, what we have found is (i) a truly minimal difference between early child English and adult English with respect to long *wh*-movement (spelling out the intermediate SpecCP element or not), and (ii) an immediate account for the fact that long *wh*-extraction patterns with empty operator movement in the domain of double object constructions.[15]

4.2.6 English short *wh*-extraction

In the above discussion, I have confined my attention to those varieties of English in which short *wh*-extraction of the indirect object in a double object construction is grammatical. I take these to represent the "normal" case (cf. also Baker's 1988:293 observation that in Chichewa, short *wh*-movement yields an essentially grammatical result). Something should be said, however, about dialects or idiolects of English in which no form of *wh*-movement of indirect objects, no matter how local, is acceptable.

In this subsection I can only sketch the outlines of an account of these varieties of English which would be compatible with what was argued in the preceding subsections. Recall that on my assumptions, overt *wh*-movement of indirect objects involves pied-piping of the zero-headed dative PP of which the Goal NP is a part. In accommodating the recalcitrant dialects or idiolects barring all indirect object A'-movement we may now take either of two tacks:

---

[15] Teun Hoekstra points out that David Lebeaux has also proposed that long-distance argument extraction may be analysed in terms of covert *wh*-copying, as in (22). By requiring of the empty operator in this structure that it raise to the SpecCP position nearest to its binder, we can continue to capture the Subjacency effect arising under long-distance argument extraction in English examples like [?]*Which books do you think that Bill wondered why John read?*. In the structure in (i), the empty operator moves to the highest embedded SpecCP, thereby crossing the lowest SpecCP node, which is occupied by the adjunct *wh*-phrase, and causing a Subjacency violation in the familiar fashion:

(i)   [?]*Which books*$_i$ do you think [$_{CP}$ [$_{Op}$ Ø]$_i$ that Bill wondered [$_{CP}$ why John read]]?

The Subjacency effect in the simpler example [?]*Which books do you wonder why John read?* may not follow from (22). An alternative to (22) which does directly capture this effect analyses long-distance *wh*-movement along the lines of the account of short *wh*-extraction presented in section 4.2.6, according to which the *wh*-phrase is a topic associated to an empty operator in the highest SpecCP (cf. (23)). On these assumptions, the structure of *What do you think babies drink?* reads as in (ii):

(ii)   [$_{Top}$ *what*] [$_{CP}$ [$_{Op}$ Ø]$_i$ do you think [$_{CP}$ *t*$_i$ babies drink *t*$_i$]]

(i)   we may try to relate the deviance of short *wh*-extraction of double object Goals to a possible predisposition against pied-piping in general, in the varieties of English in question; or

(ii)   we may seek to assimilate the account of short *wh*-extraction to that of topicalisation, and argue for an analysis in terms of empty operator movement.

Though it is true that some varieties of English rarely use pied-piping, it would probably be too bold a claim to say that in dialects or idiolects in which (8a) (*%Who did John give a book?*) is rejected, pied-piping should be altogether ungrammatical. I therefore opt for (ii).

An assimilation of (short) *wh*-movement to topicalisation would yield an analysis of (8a) according to which the *wh*-word is a base-generated topic associated to an empty operator that undergoes movement to SpecCP:

(23) $[_{\text{Top}}$ *wh*$]$ $[_{\text{CP}}$ Op_i ... $t_i]$

Since English does not allow multiple topicalisation (cf. Chomsky 1977), a topicalisation analysis of *wh*-extraction does not make the undesirable prediction that multiple *wh*-fronting should be possible in English. That is, (24a,b) are on a par:

(24)   a.   *To Mary, a book, John gave.
        b.   *To whom, what did John give?

From languages which do show multiple *wh*-fronting (such as Polish), we know that treating *wh*-phrases as topics is a parametric option that is actually employed in natural language. In view of this, it does not appear to be unreasonable to suggest that the "strict" varieties of English make use of this topicalisation strategy in forming *wh*-questions.

Though an analysis along these lines allows us to capture the English-internal variation with respect to the acceptability of examples like (8a), and hence serves a direct purpose in the context of this study, I am fully aware that (23) may raise more questions than it solves, as future research will tell.[16]

---

[16] One question that arises is why *wh*-fronting should trigger Subject–Aux inversion, while topicalisation (except in cases of negative inversion) does not. It seems plausible to assume that an empty operator is featurally identical with the element it is associated with, and that V-to-C movement is triggered by the presence of some feature in Comp (esp. [+wh]). The difference between topicalisation and *wh*-fronting with regard to Subject–Aux inversion is then relatable to the fact that topics are [−wh] while *wh*-phrases are obviously [+wh].

4.2.7 Heavy NP Shift

Indirect objects in double object constructions consistently resist undergoing Heavy NP Shift, not just in English, but in other languages as well, as the following English and Norwegian examples (from Larson 1988:sect. 3.2) show:

(25) a. *I gave a book my favourite uncle from Cleveland.
      b. *Vi har lånt en bok den hyggelige gutten du kjenner.
          we have lent a book the nice boy you know

Larson (1988) exploits this fact to support his analysis of Dative Shift. In this subsection, I shall first of all evaluate and reject Larson's account of the ban on Heavy NP Shift of indirect objects, and then proceed to accommodating it in the present framework of assumptions.

Larson argues that the ill-formedness of examples of the type in (25) falls out immediately from his V' Reanalysis account of Heavy NP Shift (cf. section 3.2, above, for discussion of V' Reanalysis). Consider the structure of double object constructions prior to verb raising, given in (26):

(26) $[_{VP} \text{ Spec } [_{V'} [_V \text{ e}] [_{VP} \text{ Goal}_i [_{V'} [_{V'} \text{ V } [_{NP} t_i]] \textbf{ Theme}]]]]$

In order to derive (25) via Light Predicate Raising, the boldface V' in (26) should be reanalysed as a bare V. This instance of V' Reanalysis is ruled out by the condition on reanalysis in (27) — after all, this V' is thematically completely saturated as far as the internal θ-roles are concerned; it does not contain an undischarged internal θ-role.

(27)   *V' Reanalysis*
          Let α be a phrase $[_{V'} ...]$ whose θ-grid contains one undischarged internal θ-role. Then α may be reanalysed as $[_V ...]$.

V' Reanalysis being blocked in (26), Larson's Light Predicate Raising approach to Heavy NP Shift correctly rules out (25).

In response to this argument for a Larsonian analysis of Dative Shift, two lines are open in principle: (i) to argue that reanalysing Heavy NP Shift as Light Predicate Raising raises problems within Larson's overall outlook on phrase structure, thereby casting doubt on the basis for the argument for Dative Shift as passivisation; and/or (ii) to argue that the fact that the Goal NP in a double object construction resists undergoing Heavy NP Shift can be accommodated on the analysis of triadic constructions presented in this study without recourse to Light Predicate Raising and the concomitant VP recursion. I shall briefly pursue both lines.

Given that, as pointed out in the previous section, Larson projects adverbial material onto the innermost complement-of-V position, he assigns the structure in (29) to the triadic construction in (28) (cf. Larson 1988:fn. 11 for this tree):

(28)   John wrote a letter to Mary *in the morning*.

(29)

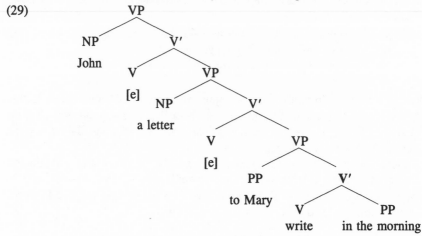

Notice now that the lowest V', printed in boldface in (29), is eligible for V' Reanalysis — the internal θ-roles of *write* are obviously not fully satisfied internal to this V' constituent. Suppose, then, we reanalysed this V' to V and raised it, successive cyclically, to the highest empty V-node. The result would be the ungrammatical (30):

(30)   *John wrote in the morning a letter to Mary.

In general, small clauses containing a lexical subject (like *a letter to Mary* on the analysis of triadic constructions presented in this study) fail to undergo rightward (or, in fact, *any*) movement. Why this is so need not concern us here (cf. Den Dikken 1987 for discussion). The point to note, however, is that on a Larsonian phrase structure of the type in (29), in conjunction with a Light Predicate Raising approach to extraposition, the theory wrongly leads us to expect "SC-extraposition" to be a productive process.

Proceeding to the second line of response, I propose that the ban on "extraposition" of indirect objects can be directly related to what was argued in section 3.11.2, above, with respect to PP-extraposition. There, I based my account of the restrictions on Dutch PP-over-V on the hypotheses in (31):

(31) a.   Rightward movement does not exist (cf. Kayne 1993b).
      b.   Apparent instances of extraposition are reinterpretable as leftward movement of an empty operator associated with a right-peripherally base-generated constituent.

Once Heavy NP Shift, an apparent rightward movement process, is reanalysed in terms of leftward empty operator movement, the deviance of examples like (25), above, immediately reduces to that of other instantiations of empty operator movement affecting indirect objects.

4.2.8 Summary

A'-extraction of the indirect/applied object in a double object/applicative construction is severely restricted, but not as severely as it is often taken to be. While *empty operator movement* of the double object Goal is structurally impossible, (short) overt *wh*-extraction of the indirect object generally yields an acceptable result.

The difference between overt and empty operator movement in the domain of A'-extraction of the double object Goal can be captured on the present analysis of triadic constructions, according to which pied-piping of the dative PP is the only way of A'-extracting an indirect object. Since empty operator movement resists pied-piping for independent reasons, the difference between it and overt *wh*-movement follows.

As in the analyses of Kayne (1984), Czepluch (1982) and Baker (1988), the restrictions on A'-extraction of the double object Goal constitute an important argument for the view that the indirect object in a double object construction is governed by an empty dative preposition.

4.3 A'-extraction of the double object Theme: Structural ambiguity in double object constructions

4.3.1 The problem

In double object constructions throughout the (continental) West-Germanic OV languages it is possible for the indirect and direct objects (in that order) to surface as a pair to the right (cf. (25a)–(27a)) or to the left of a sentence adverb (cf. (25b)–(27b)), or to be split up by a sentence adverb, as in (25c)–(27c):[17]

---

[17] In the examples in (25)–(27), the adverb is italicised. The sentences in (25) are from Dutch, those in (26) from West Flemish, and the examples in (27) are German. I thank Gereon Müller and Matthias Hüning for their judgements of the German data. All West Flemish examples are (adapted) from Haegeman (1991). All Dutch judgements reported are my own; they are consistent with those of other speakers.

(25) a.   dat Jan *waarschijnlijk* Marie het boek geeft.
            that Jan probably Marie the book gives
      b.   dat Jan Marie het boek *waarschijnlijk* geeft.
      c.   dat Jan Marie *waarschijnlijk* het boek geeft.

(26) a.   da Valère *vandoage* Marie da geld geeft.
            that Valère today Marie that money gives
      b.   da Valère Marie da geld *vandoage* geeft.
      c.   da Valère Marie *vandoage* da geld geeft.

(27) a.   daß der Hans *wahrscheinlich* der Maria das Buch gibt.
            that the Hans probably the Maria(DAT) the book gives
      b.   daß der Hans der Maria das Buch *wahrscheinlich* gibt.
      c.   daß der Hans der Maria *wahrscheinlich* das Buch gibt.

Haegeman (1991:4) notes that it is impossible for the direct object in a West Flemish double object construction to undergo A'-extraction if the indirect object *follows* the adverb, while direct object extraction in constructions in which the indirect object *precedes* the adverb is perfectly licit. This is shown in (29). Dutch is exactly like West Flemish in this respect, as the data in (28) bear out.[18] In German, by contrast, direct object A'-extraction is fine irrespective of the position of the indirect object relative to the adverb (30).

(28) a.   *[?]Wat zal Jan *waarschijnlijk* Marie geven?
            what will Jan probably Marie give
      b.   Wat zal Jan Marie *waarschijnlijk* geven?

(29) a.   *[?]Wa goa Valère *vandoage* Marie geven?
            what goes Valère today Marie give
      b.   Wa goa Valère Marie *vandoage* geven?

(30) a.   Was wird der Hans *wahrscheinlich* der Maria geben?
            what will the Hans probably the Maria(DAT) give
      b.   Was wird der Hans der Maria *wahrscheinlich* geben?

The fact that with respect to these Theme extraction data Dutch and West Flemish pattern together and differ from German suggests a possible relationship between these facts and an apparently independent difference between Dutch and West Flemish on the one hand, and German on the other, concerning

---

[18] Throughout, neutral intonation patterns are intended; (28a) improves with heavy focal stress on the indirect object. In this regard there is a perfect correspondence between (28a) and the DO–IO construction in (31b), whose deviant status may likewise be improved by stressing the indirect object. The perfect match between (28a) and (31b) directly follows from, hence lends support to, the analysis to be presented.

the freedom of relative ordering of direct and indirect objects. While in Dutch and West Flemish a "bare" (preposition-less) indirect object may only precede the direct object, the German indirect object may freely occur on either side of the direct object, as I pointed out in section 3.10.2. This is shown in (31)–(33):

(31) a. dat Jan Marie het boek geeft.
      b. *dat Jan het boek Marie geeft.

(32) a. da Valère Marie da geld geeft.
      b. *da Valère da geld Marie geeft.

(33) a. daß der Hans der Maria das Buch gibt.
      b. daß der Hans das Buch der Maria gibt.

In this section I argue that there is indeed a direct connection between the data in (28)–(30) and those in (31)–(33). I shall start out by showing that given the analysis of Dative Shift presented in chapter 3, it is theoretically impossible to apply A'-movement to the direct object in a genuine double object construction. For all grammatical instances of direct object A'-extraction in double object constructions, then, an alternative derivation must be operative. I shall argue that the key to this alternative derivation, as well as to the link between the paradigms in (28)–(30) and (31)–(33), lies in the *structural ambiguity* of double object constructions between genuine Dative Shift constructions and covert prepositional dative constructions with an unrealised dative preposition.

4.3.2 Dative Shift and Theme extraction

In chapter 3 it was argued that Dative Shift involves A-movement of an (empty-headed) dative PP into the θ'-specifier position of the SC headed by an (empty or overt) particle, as in the (appropriately simplified) structure in (34):

(34) $[_{VP} V [_{SC1} [_{PP} P_\emptyset NP_{Go}]_i [_{XP} X [_{SC2} NP_{Th} t_i]]]]$

The A-movement operation by which the dative phrase ends up to the left of the Theme NP is structurally identical with the A-movement operation obtaining in Predicate Inversion constructions of the type in (35) (cf. Hoekstra & Mulder 1990):

(35)   Down the hill rolled the baby carriage.
          $[_{IP} [_{PP} \text{down the hill}]_i ... [_{VP} \text{rolled} [_{SC} \text{the baby carriage } t_i]]]$

In Predicate Inversion constructions, it is impossible to A'-extract the postverbal subject across the fronted locative PP, as the ill-formedness of (36) shows:

(36) a. *Which baby carriage did down the hill roll?
      b. *Which baby carriage did you say that down the hill rolled?
      c. *I wonder which baby carriage down the hill rolled.

The explanation for the deviance of (36) can be found in the Binding Theory, particularly in Principle C (cf. Hoekstra & Mulder 1990; Den Dikken & Næss 1993). For notice that, as a result of the Specifier-Head agreement relationship between them, the A'-moved SC-subject NP bears the same index as the fronted locative PP, the SC-predicate. Now, by fronting the SC-predicate into an A-position, and A'-extracting the coindexed SC-subject across it, we end up with a variable (the trace of the A'-moved SC-subject) which is A-bound within the domain of its maximal chain, by the SC-predicate in subject position. The structure in (37) is in direct violation of Principle C of the Binding Theory (strong crossover), whence the ill-formedness of (36).[19]

(37)   *$[_{CP}$ which baby carriage$_k$ ... $[_{IP}$ $[_{PP}$ down the hill]$_i$ ... $[_{SC}$ t_k t_i]]]
            A'   A   vbl
          (where $i = k$, as a result of Spec-Head agreement within SC)

Recall now that on the present analysis the Dative Shift transformation is structurally identical with Predicate Inversion. Dative Shift, too, involves the A-fronting of a SC-predicate. By the same token, then, Principle C of the Binding Theory will prohibit A'-extraction of the Theme NP in a genuine double object construction:

---

[19] Topicalisation constructions such as (i) apparently instantiate a configuration similar to that in (37), yet do not give rise to a Binding Theory violation. This may be accommodated in the analysis of topicalisation presented in section 4.2.4, above. Assume that *himself* is base-generated in topic position and that an empty operator *with a different index* (that is, k in (ii) $\neq$ i) moves from the position occupied by t to SpecCP. (Since the empty operator is not bound, the constituent containing it, CP, has a variable range and qualifies as a predicate, the base-generated topic being its subject; cf. Mulder & Den Dikken 1992.) No BT-C violation ensues in (ii).

(i)   *Himself, John really hates t.*
(ii) $[_{Top}$ himself$_i$] $[_{CP}$ Op_k ... John$_i$ really hates t_k]

On this analysis, the interpretive link between the anaphor and its binder (both indexed i) cannot be established under c-command at any level of representation. Note, however, that topicalisation constructions are by no means unique in this respect: similar binding problems arise in copular constructions like *Pictures of himself/His pockets are a man's private kingdom*, in which *a man* does not c-command the anaphor/bound variable at any level either (cf. Mulder & Den Dikken 1992).

(Notice that even if — on the topicalisation approach to *wh*-movement sketched in section 4.2.6 combined with the assumptions about indexation in topicalisation constructions made in this footnote — the overt *wh*-phrase in (37) does not bear the same index as the empty operator in SpecCP to which it is associated, the empty operator *is* of course still coindexed with the fronted SC-predicate. The deviance of (36) thus continues to follow from Principle C of the Binding Theory.)

(38) $*[_{CP} \text{Theme}_k \ldots [_{SC1} [_{PP} \text{P}_\emptyset \text{ Goal}]_i [_{XP} \text{X} [_{SC2} t_k t_i]]]]$
       A'   A   vbl
       (where $i = k$, as a result of Spec-Head agreement within SC2)

This may seem to be an unfortunate result in the light of the fact that direct object A'-extraction in what appear to be double object constructions is generally perfectly legitimate. In what follows, however, I shall argue that this theoretical conclusion to which the analysis of Dative Shift gives rise is correct, and has desirable consequences in the domain of the restrictions on direct object A'-extraction in (continental) West Germanic.

4.3.3 Preliminaries: Structural ambiguity

If A'-extraction of the direct object in a genuine Dative Shift construction is theoretically impossible, as I showed above, we need an alternative base for the derivation of those instances of direct object A'-extraction that yield a grammatical result. I would like to argue here that double object constructions are in principle *structurally ambiguous* between genuine Dative Shift constructions, featuring A-movement of the dative PP, and covert prepositional dative constructions in which the empty-headed dative PP is *not* A-moved into SpecSC1 in (34). The latter analysis may now serve as the input to A'-extraction of the Theme NP in a double object construction (where the term ''double object construction'' should be taken as a cover term for both the genuine Dative Shift construction and the covert prepositional dative construction):

(39) Double object constructions are structurally ambiguous between genuine Dative Shift constructions featuring A-movement of the dative PP, and covert prepositional dative constructions with an empty dative P.

(40) A'-extraction of the Theme NP in double object constructions takes the covert prepositional dative construction as its input.

With the aid of (39) and (40), the word-order restrictions on double object constructions featuring A'-extraction of the Theme NP can now be tackled when we further bear in mind that the surface distribution of empty-headed dative PPs is subject to cross-linguistically varying licensing conditions, as we saw in section 3.10.2:

(41) a. An empty dative preposition must be *licensed*.
    b. An empty dative preposition is licensed iff (i) or (ii):
        (i) $[_P \emptyset]$ is identified by dative Case morphology;
        (ii) $[_P \emptyset]$ is incorporated (at some level) into a verb.

Recall from section 3.10.2 that German, which features overt dative Case morphology, selects option (41b.i), while Dutch and West Flemish must resort to the incorporation strategy (41b.ii).

4.3.4 Theme extraction: Analysis

Having reached these conclusions, we are now ready to return to the paradigm in (28)–(30), repeated here for ease of reference:

(28) a. *[?]Wat zal Jan *waarschijnlijk* Marie geven?
           what will Jan probably Marie give
       b. Wat zal Jan Marie *waarschijnlijk* geven?

(29) a. *[?]Wa goa Valère *vandoage* Marie geven?
           what goes Valère today Marie give
       b. Wa goa Valère Marie *vandoage* geven?

(30) a. Was wird der Hans *wahrscheinlich* der Maria geben?
           what will the Hans probably the Maria(DAT) give
       b. Was wird der Hans der Maria *wahrscheinlich* geben?

Direct object A'-extraction is possible only on the basis of the covert prepositional dative construction, for otherwise a Binding Theory violation would ensue. The empty head of the dative PP in covert prepositional dative constructions must be licensed (41a). In German, this condition can be straightforwardly complied with — the presence of overt dative Case morphology in this language can license the empty head of the covert dative phrase *in situ*. This is why, in German, indirect objects can surface to the right of direct objects in double object (*c.q.* covert dative) constructions, and A'-extraction of the double object Theme is unrestricted.

In Dutch and West Flemish, by contrast, the licensing strategy in (41b.ii) must be exploited to meet condition (41a). Incorporation of the empty dative P into V is impossible if the dative PP remains *in situ* — the intervening (overt or empty) particle sets up a minimality barrier (cf. Baker's 1988:337 revised minimality condition quoted in (60iii) of section 3.10.2, above). The empty-headed dative PP must hence be moved into the governing domain of the incorporating verb in order for the zero preposition to be licensed.

In the direct object A'-movement cases at hand, licensing via Dative Shift is clearly unavailable, for otherwise we would end up with a Binding Theory violation, as discussed above. The one remaining licensing mechanism would hence appear to be *scrambling*. I assume that, by adjoining the dative PP to VP, the verb will be capable of incorporating the empty preposition under government, after verb movement to Infl has taken place, by which the verb (in

Infl) comes to govern the VP-adjoined scrambled PP (cf. Rizzi 1990:Ch. 2; and sections 1.2.2 and 1.2.4 of the present study).[20] In order for (41a) to be met in Dutch and West Flemish double object constructions featuring A'-extraction of the Theme NP such as (28) and (29), then, the empty-headed dative PP must be *scrambled*. Since scrambling will move the empty-headed dative PP across the VP-adjoined sentence adverbs, and since scrambling is forced in the constructions at hand, we now have an account for the deviance of the a-examples in (28) and (29), in which scrambling of the zero-headed dative PP has failed to apply.[21]

[20] The licensing condition in (41b.ii) merely requires that the empty preposition incorporates into some verb — it is immaterial, then, that in constructions of the type in (i) the triadic participle does not undergo Verb Raising: the empty dative P can incorporate into the auxiliary, which (at some point in the derivation of (i)) governs the scrambled dative PP.

(i)   Wat zou Jan Marie *waarschijnlijk* gegeven hebben?
           what would Jan Marie probably given have

[21] Two remarks concerning the data must be made at this point. First, as Eric Reuland has pointed out to me, in Dutch temporal adverbs like *gisteren* 'yesterday' and *afgelopen vrijdag* 'last Friday' differ from adverbs such as *waarschijnlijk* 'probably' in that they *can* be positioned to the left of the indirect object in double object constructions featuring Theme extraction:

(i)   Wat heeft Jan *gisteren/afgelopen vrijdag/*waarschijnlijk* Marie gegeven?
           what has Jan yesterday/last Friday/probably Marie given

This must, on the present assumptions, mean that such temporal adverbs are, or in any event can be, adjoined in a position higher than the landing-site of scrambled dative PPs (in contrast to adverbs like *waarschijnlijk*). This makes sense in view of the relationship between temporal adverbs and Tense, a VP-external functional head. The fact that temporal adverbs need not be peripheral to adverbs like *waarschijnlijk* (cf. (iia)) is not necessarily problematic for this hypothesis. Two possibilities arise for the *waarschijnlijk gisteren* order: (a) *waarschijnlijk* is a modifier of the temporal adverb and forms a constituent with it; (b) the temporal adverb may optionally adjoin to VP, below *waarschijnlijk*. To the extent that the two options are semantically distinguishable, it seems to me that (iib) only has the (a)-reading, as predicted by the analysis.

(ii)   a.   dat Jan {*gisteren waarschijnlijk/waarschijnlijk gisteren*} Marie het boek gegeven heeft.
        b.   Wat heeft Jan [$_{AdvP}$ *waarschijnlijk gisteren*] Marie gegeven?

Examples of the type in (iiia), featuring *two* adverbs, show that adverbial adjunction is possible above the position targeted by scrambling. This being the case, one wonders why, in an example containing just a single adverb like (iiib), scrambling cannot have applied ''string-vacuously'', to an A'-position below the adverbial adjunction site. That this must be impossible — if what is argued in this section is correct — is evident from the fact that Theme extraction is impossible in examples like (iiib) (cf. (iiic) and (28a), above). As Teun Hoekstra has pointed out to me, the present account hence needs an additional condition to the effect that, if there is only one adverb in the clause, it is adjoined to the lowest available position. (This condition does not apply to temporal adverbs, which preferentially adjoin to the projection of Tense.)

Notice that A'-extracting the Theme NP across the scrambled dative PP does not yield a Binding Theory violation. Scrambling being an A'-movement process (cf. Bennis & Hoekstra 1984; Den Dikken & Mulder 1991), no configuration results in which the variable left by Theme extraction is A-bound in the domain of its maximal chain. The scrambled PP can actually be looked upon as an intermediate variable in the A'-chain linking the *wh*-operator in SpecCP and the trace in the base position of the Theme. No Theta Criterion violation arises since the three-member A'-chain only contains a single θ-position: the Theme trace.

That it is really the failure of licensing of the empty dative preposition that is responsible for the deviance of (28a) and (29a) is also shown by the grammaticality of the minimally different examples in (42):

(42) a.   Wat zal Jan *waarschijnlijk* **aan** Marie geven?
          what will Jan probably to Marie give
      b.   Wa goa Valère *vandoage* **an** Marie geven?
          what goes Valère today to Marie give

In these constructions the dative P is overt (*aan, an*), and hence no licensing problems arise. These examples indicate in addition that the oddity of (28a) and (29a) is not likely to have a mere prosodic cause.

It is interesting to note that, as Den Besten (1985:fn. 1) observes, 'the ACC–DAT order ... is not completely impossible in Dutch'. While examples such as (31b) are certainly ungrammatical, those in (43), with verbs like *aanbevelen* 'recommend', *aanraden* 'advise, recommend', *afraden* 'dissuade' or *aanbieden* 'offer', are substantially better:

(43) a.   Ik raad dit uitstapje Uwe Majesteit van harte aan.
          I recommend this excursion Your Majesty warmly PRT
      b.   Ik zou dit uitstapje mijn broer willen afraden.
          I would this excursion my brother like-to PRT-dissuade
      c.   Jan zal het boeket de Koningin aanbieden.
          Jan will the bouquet the Queen PRT-offer

As Hans Broekhuis has pointed out to me, Theme extraction in examples of this type, with the Goal to the *right* of an adverb like *waarschijnlijk*, yields a noticeably better result than in run-of-the-mill DAT–ACC double object constructions:

(iii) a.   dat Jan *waarschijnlijk* Marie *vaak* een boek heeft gegeven.
           that Jan probably Marie often a book has given
      b.   dat Jan *waarschijnlijk* Marie een boek heeft gegeven.
           that Jan probably Marie a book has given
      c.   Wat heeft Jan *waarschijnlijk* Marie *?(vaak) gegeven?
           what has Jan probably Marie often given

(44) a.   Wat zal Jan *waarschijnlijk* zijn kinderen afraden?
            what will Jan probably his children PRT-dissuade
      b.   Wat zal Jan *waarschijnlijk* de Koningin aanbieden?
            what will Jan probably the Queen PRT-offer

This is as expected: whenever an empty-headed dative PP is allowed to surface to the right of the Theme NP, extraction of this NP can take place without there being any need for the dative PP to scramble. The examples in (43) and (44) are completely on a par with German (33b) and (30a).[22]

Because, following Kayne (1984), several accounts of double object constructions assume a SC-structure in which the indirect object occupies the SC-subject position at D-structure, it is worth pointing out furthermore that the deviance of Dutch (28a) and West Flemish (29a) is *not* an instantiation of a general ban on A'-extraction of SC-predicates across their *in situ* subjects in these languages. This is shown by the contrast between the double object construction in (45a) and the SC constructions in (45b–d) (where the indefinite nature of the NP following the adverb is held constant throughout in order to render direct comparison possible):

---

[22] It is presumably significant that in all examples of the type in (43) a verbal particle occurs. This might suggest that an overt particle governing the dative PP is a sufficient licenser for PP's empty head (even though it is not a lexical governor), so that the empty-headed dative PP can stay *in situ* in these cases. That particles have some role to play in this connection is also suggested an observation of Haider's (1992:19 and fn. 15). He shows that in German, with verbs like *aussetzen* 'expose', *entziehen* 'take away from', *unterziehen* 'submit to', *unterwerfen* 'subject to' and *zuführen* 'bring to', all of which contain a particle (affixal *ent-* in the case of *entziehen*; cf. chapter 5), the ACC–DAT order in double object constructions is the preferred word order, while verbs like *stellen* 'pose (a question)' have a preference for the DAT–ACC order (cf. (i)–(ii)). Again, we see that the presence of a particle apparently renders it easier for the empty-headed dative PP to remain *in situ*.

(i)   a.   daß er Kinder Gefahren aussetzte.   (Haider 1992:19)
            that he children(ACC) dangers(DAT) exposed
            'that he exposed children to dangers.'
      b.   ?daß er Gefahren Kinder aussetzte.
            that he dangers(DAT) children(ACC) exposed
(ii) a.   daß er Kindern Fragen stellte.
            that he children(DAT) questions(ACC) asked
            'that he asked children questions.'
      b.   ?daß er Fragen Kindern stellte.
            that he questions(ACC) children(DAT) asked

Den Besten (1985:fn. 1) notes that *aanbevelen* 'recommend', *aanraden* 'advise' and *afraden* 'dissuade' do not occur in prepositional dative constructions with *aan* 'to'. This, however, is not the defining characteristic of Dutch verbs allowing for the DO-IO order: *aanbieden*, used in (43c), does combine with *aan*.

(45)   a.   *ˀWat heeft Jan *waarschijnlijk* een meisje gegeven?[23]
            what has Jan probably a girl given
       b.   Aan wie heeft Jan *waarschijnlijk* een boek gegeven?
            to whom has Jan probably a book given
       c.   Op welke plank heeft Jan *waarschijnlijk* een boek gezet?
            on which shelf has Jan probably a book put
       d.   In welk bed heeft Jan *waarschijnlijk* een meisje gelegd?
            in which bed has Jan probably a girl laid

4.3.5 Conclusion

In this section I have argued that the present analysis of Dative Shift, which forces us to adopt a covert dative analysis of double object constructions featuring A'-extraction of the Theme NP, establishes the appropriate link between the paradigms in (28)–(30) and (31)–(33).[24]

The West Germanic Theme extraction data lend support to an analysis of Dative Shift according to which A-movement of the dative PP is involved in the derivation of the double object construction. They further argue that the double object construction is in principle *structurally ambiguous* between a genuine Dative Shift construction and a covert prepositional dative construction.

---

[23] That it is really the application of Theme extraction that renders (45a) ungrammatical is shown by the well-formedness of (i):

(i)   dat Jan *waarschijnlijk* een meisje een boek heeft gegeven.
              that Jan probably a girl a book has given

[24] The account of Theme A'-extraction presented here may also give us the beginnings of an account of the fact that scrambling of both objects in a Dutch double object construction preserves the relative order of the direct and indirect objects (cf. (i)). On the assumption that scrambling involves A'-movement (cf. Bennis & Hoekstra 1984; Den Dikken & Mulder 1991), (ib) must be a covert dative construction featuring scrambling of the Theme NP and the empty-headed dative PP. On the further assumption that multiple A'-movement forms *nested* dependencies (cf. Pesetsky 1982; but cf. Chomsky 1993 on multiple A-movement), we then correctly derive an IO–DO order.

(i)   a.   dat Jan *gisteren* {Marie het boek/*het boek Marie} gegeven heeft.
             that Jan yesterday Marie the book/the book Marie given has
       b.   dat Jan {[$P_\emptyset$ Marie]$_j$ [het boek]$_i$/*[het boek]$_i$ [$P_\emptyset$ Marie]$_j$} *gisteren* t_i t_j gegeven heeft.
             that Jan Marie the book/the book Marie yesterday given has

Questions remain on such an account, however, particularly about the fact that in German double object scrambling constructions with Theme–Goal orders are grammatical (cf. Haider 1992:14). Possibly the impression that (ib) features movements which do not obtain in (ia) is illusory, and the different word-order patterns are the simple result of the possibility of generating adverbial modifiers in different positions; cf. Zwart (1993) for relevant discussion.

4.4   Raising-to-subject and the double object Theme

So far I have concentrated exclusively on the direct object *wh*-movement paradigm in (25)–(27). It is interesting to note, though, that in passives, a fully identical split between Dutch (and West Flemish, which will be ignored in what follows) and German can be discerned:

(46) a.   *$^?$dat het boek *waarschijnlijk* Marie gegeven wordt.
      that the book probably Marie given is
   b.   dat het boek Marie *waarschijnlijk* gegeven wordt.

(47) a.   daß das Buch *wahrscheinlich* der Maria gegeben wird.
      that the book probably the Maria(DAT) given is
   b.   daß das Buch der Maria *wahrscheinlich* gegeben wird.

Unlike in the case of *wh*-extraction of the direct object across the indirect object, the Binding Theory does not lead us to expect ungrammaticality in cases of NP-movement of the double object Theme around the indirect object, if we base ourselves on the structure of genuine Dative Shift constructions in (34), repeated here:

(34) $[_{VP}$ V $[_{SC1}$ $[_{PP}$ P$_\emptyset$ NP$_{Go}]_i$ $[_{XP}$ X $[_{SC2}$ NP$_{Th}$ $t_i]]]]$

I assume (cf. chapter 1) that NP-movement is subject only to Principle A of the Binding Theory. The only requirement that the trace of the Theme NP in a case of NP-movement to subject position based on (34) must meet, therefore, is that it is bound in its governing category. The governing category in question is constituted by SC1, within which the trace of the Theme NP can indeed by bound. Though the Theme NP itself is higher up in the tree, the coindexed dative PP in the subject position of SC1 can act as the binder of the trace in SpecSC2. The structure of the above passive examples is illustrated in (48):

(48) $[_{IP}$ $[NP_{Th}]_k$ ... $[_{VP}$ $[_{SC1}$ $[_{PP}$ P$_\emptyset$ NP$_{Go}]_i$ $[_{XP}$ $[_{SC2}$ t_k $t_i]$ X]] V]]$
                                           (where $k = i$)

The shifted dative PP comes to be an intermediate member of a three-member A-chain (Theme$_i$, PP$_i$, t_i), which is in perfect accordance with the Theta Criterion: the chain contains precisely one θ-bearing element, since the intermediate dative PP is not an argument but a predicate. Unlike A′-extraction, NP-movement across a shifted dative PP hence is not ruled out by the Binding Theory. Why, then, is (46a) ungrammatical?

   Recent research on Case assignment in the (continental) West-Germanic languages (cf. Hoekstra & Mulder 1990; Broekhuis 1991, 1992; Koopman & Sportiche 1991) has shown that in these languages nominative Case is always assigned VP-internally, under (Chain) Government (cf. Den Besten 1985). Movement of the nominative-marked NP will then be an instance of *A'*-movement — either substitution for an A'-type SpecIP position, or in fact scrambling.[25] Once we realise that raising-to-subject is an A'-movement rule in Dutch, the ungrammaticality of (46a) can again be made to follow from Principle C of the Binding Theory, in much the same way as in the case of *wh*-extraction discussed above.[26]

At the same time we avoid a problem that would otherwise arise in the analysis of the grammatical example in (46b). The indirect object in this sentence is a scrambled zero-headed dative PP which, given that scrambling is A'-movement (cf. Bennis & Hoekstra 1984; Den Dikken & Mulder 1991 for relevant discussion), occupies an A'-position. The zero-headed dative PP is coindexed with the Theme NP, by virtue of the Spec-Head agreement relationship internal to the dative SC. A putative case of A-movement of the Theme NP across the scrambled dative PP would hence result in an *improper movement* (A, A', A) chain. Since the output of raising-to-subject is perfectly grammatical (cf. (46b)), however, the conclusion must be that this process must involve A'-movement, in which case the (A', A', A) chain linking the trace of the Theme, the scrambled dative PP and the Theme NP in VP-external position is perfectly well-formed.

---

[25] If the scrambling option is taken, we steer clear of potential problems for this analysis in the domain of binding and crossover, since, as is well known, scrambling is "like A-movement" in this regard (even though it is *not* A-movement; cf. Den Dikken & Mulder 1991, and references cited there, for a summary of the relevant data).

[26] It is worth pointing out in this connection that if the Theme NP remains *in situ* and does not undergo A'-movement, (genuine) Dative Shift is fine (Hans Broekhuis, p.c.), as predicted:

(i)   dat *waarschijnlijk* Marie het boek gegeven wordt.
         that probably Marie the book given is

The logically possible variant of (46a) and (i) given in (ii), on the other hand, seems distinctly odd, though perhaps slightly less so than (46a). There are two potential derivations for this example. The Theme NP in (ii) may either be in its base position, in which case the empty-headed dative PP must be *in situ* as well, and licensing of the empty dative preposition will fail, so that (ii) is predicted to be completely ungrammatical. Or, if the Theme is A'-moved to some VP-external position (SpecIP or adjunct), in which case the zero-headed dative PP can have scrambled to render P-licensing possible, the adverb must be adjoined above the landing-site of the subject. In the latter case, (ii) is predicted to have the same status as sentences of the type in (iii), which feature highly marked adverbial placement between Comp and the subject. It does indeed appear to be correct that (ii) at best has the acceptability status of (iii).

(ii)   ??dat *waarschijnlijk* het boek Marie gegeven wordt.
         that probably the book Marie given is
(iii)   ??dat *waarschijnlijk* Jan morgen komt.
         that probably Jan tomorrow comes

4.5 Interactions of A'-movement and passivisation

Having moved from A'-extraction in double object constructions to passivisation, I now proceed to an inspection of cases in which the application of A'-movement of either the Theme or the Goal in a double object construction is contingent on raising-to-subject of the other NP. Two such cases have been reported in the literature, for English (Stowell 1981) and the Bantu language of Kichaga (Bresnan & Moshi 1990).

4.5.1 A'-extraction of the English double object Theme

Stowell (1981:342) reports that in English double object constructions containing a verbal particle, A'-movement of the Theme NP is impossible, as the deviance (irrespective of the surface position of the particle) of (49) shows:[27]

(49) a.   *Which money did you pay (*back*) the bank (*back*)?
      b.   *This is the announcement which the board sent (*out*) the members (*out*).

The ill-formedness of these examples falls out from the analysis of Dative Shift presented in this study. Given that movement to the ''indirect object position'' instantiates A-movement of the Predicate Inversion type, the theory leads us to expect a Condition C violation in cases of Theme A'-extraction. This is borne out by the particle constructions in (49).[28]

Stowell (1981:342) presents the striking contrast between these examples and the passive sentences in (50) as evidence for his claim that indirect object passives are derived from *to*-dative constructions, not from genuine double object constructions.

(50) a.   Which money was the bank paid *back*?
      b.   This is the announcement which the members were sent *out*.

If (50) were derived from Dative Shift constructions, the contrast between them and the ungrammatical active cases in (49) would be unexpected. If, on the other hand, indirect object passive constructions are really based on covert *to*-dative constructions, the grammaticality of (50) instantiates the generally unrestricted extraction possibilities of Themes in English prepositional dative constructions (*Which money did they pay back to the bank?*).

---

[27] In this section I consistently rely on the grammaticality judgements reported by Stowell.

[28] I shall have more to say later in this section about the fact that in particle-less double object constructions, A'-extraction of the Theme NP is free.

That the examples in (49) are ill-formed is due, Stowell argues, to the fact that for these active constructions, no covert *to*-dative analysis can be assumed. To Stowell, the dative preposition *to* is a dummy Case marker. Since in indirect object passive constructions, *to*'s complement is not dependent for Case on the presence of a dummy Case assigner (since it receives nominative Case in SpecIP after raising-to-subject), it follows that in these constructions, the dative preposition need not be spelled out. Indeed, Stowell argues, it *must* be omitted, just as in NPs of the type in (51b) the dummy Case marker *of* may not be lexically realised, since its presence is superfluous.

(51)   a.   *John was given a book *to*.
       b.   *the city's destruction *of*

In active dative constructions, by contrast, the dative preposition *to* is required to assign Case to the indirect object. For (49), then, a covert dative analysis is unavailable on principled grounds. Since Stowell stipulates that in genuine double object constructions featuring a verbal particle, A'-extraction of the Theme is impossible, and since no alternative "covert dative" derivation is available for (49), it now follows that these examples, in contrast to the passives in (50), are ungrammatical.

My approach to the contrast between (49) and (50) will essentially be in the spirit of Stowell's proposal, with the obvious qualification that the dative preposition will not be analysed as a mere Case assigner, but as a θ-role assigning head. In particular, I follow Stowell in assuming that, in any event in constructions featuring A'-extraction of the double object Theme, indirect object passives are derived from prepositional dative rather than double object constructions. This conclusion is forced upon me by the fact that A'-extraction of the Theme yields a grammatical result in indirect object passive constructions. If, at any point in the derivation of such constructions, A-movement of the dative PP to SpecIP (via all intermediate A-specifier positions) were to obtain, A'-movement of the Theme across this coindexed PP would inevitably result in a violation of Principle C of the Binding Theory (cf. section 4.3, above, for discussion).

Let us make the claim, then, that indirect object NPs can be A-moved to SpecIP from their base position inside an *in situ* empty-headed dative PP. The crucial question that we should now address is how the empty head of this dative PP can be licensed. Recall from section 4.3 that licensing is generally severely constrained. In particular, we found it to be impossible in languages lacking morphological dative Case for the empty dative preposition to be licensed with the dative PP *in situ* — in these languages the zero P can be licensed only by incorporation into V, and incorporation across the non-lexical head governing the dative SC was independently shown to be impossible in chapters 2 and 3. English belongs to this class of languages. Hence licensing the

head of an *in situ* zero-headed dative PP is out of the question. And since Dative Shift is blocked by the Binding Theory (cf. above), and PP-scrambling is impossible in English, there is no grammatical derivation for the examples in (49). In sum, then, failure to comply with licensing condition (41b) is responsible for the ill-formedness of (49).[29]

Why, though, are the examples in (50) grammatical? In these passive constructions, too, licensing of the empty dative preposition will fail, at least *in syntax*. Let us assume, therefore, that in syntax, the head of the dative PP is filled by a dative preposition. Granting this, no licensing problems will ever arise — the dative preposition is present at the level at which the licensing conditions on syntactically empty elements apply. The fact that the dative preposition is not associated with a phonetic matrix at PF can now be related to Stowell's basic insight that in passive constructions, the dative preposition does not have any Case assigning role to play. I assume therefore that since it is not required to be lexically present for the purposes of the Case Filter, the dative preposition will not be assigned a phonetic matrix in passive dative constructions such as (50).[30]

It will be obvious that the suggestion that Case-superfluous dative prepositions fail to receive a phonetic realisation at PF does not wrongly lead us to predict that (49) should be grammatical as well. After all, in these constructions, the dative preposition does have a definite Case-theoretic role to play — it must Case-mark the indirect object NP, and is hence indispensable at PF. In this way the analysis captures the desired distinction between active (49) and passive (50), in much the same way as on Stowell's (1981) original approach.

The one remaining problem to be accommodated is why the presence of a verbal particle should make a difference with regard to the extractability of the double object Theme. That is, why are the examples in (49) ill-formed while the minimally different sentences in (52) are perfect?

---

[29] Multiple *wh*-questions with an *in situ* Theme NP of the type in (49) are grammatical (cf. (i)). This would be problematic if *in situ wh*-phrases had to undergo movement to SpecCP at LF. As Jan Voskuil reminds me, however, D-linked (Pesetsky 1987) *wh*-phrases, of which the *in situ* object-*wh*'s in (i) are instantiations, do not move at LF. And more generally, Chomsky (1993:26) has recently called into question the whole idea of LF *wh*-movement, arguing that '[t]he LF rule that associates in-situ *wh*-phrases with the *wh*-phrase in SpecCP need not be construed as an instance of Move-α. We might think of it as the syntactic basis for absorption in the sense of Higginbotham & May (1981) ... If so, the LF rule need satisfy none of the conditions on movement.'

(i)   a.   Who paid the bank *back* which money?
       b.   Who sent the members *out* which announcement?

[30] Also cf. chapter 3, section 3.14 (esp. fn. 56). In terms of the minimalist programme of Chomsky (1993) this suggestion presumably means that the operation Spell-Out does not apply to non-Case-assigning dative prepositions.

(52) a.   Which money did you pay the bank?
      b.   This is the announcement which the board sent the members.

From what was argued in section 4.3 it is clear that these examples, like the ones in (49) and (50), can only be analysed as covert prepositional dative constructions featuring an empty-headed dative PP. The crucial question, then, is how the empty dative preposition in (52) is licensed. I tentatively suggest that, by way of a last resort, zero dative Ps can be licensed "by default" if they are linearly *adjacent* to the verb. This condition is met in (52), while it is not in those variants of (49) in which the particle precedes the indirect object — hence their ill-formedness. The alternative instances of (49) in which the linear adjacency condition is met are obviously ruled out by the present analysis as well, given that the only way in which the indirect object could have ended up between V and Prt in English is via the application of Dative Shift, which is blocked by the Binding Theory in double object constructions featuring A'-extraction of the Theme NP.

I emphasise that licensing-via-adjacency is a true last resort option. In languages like Dutch and West Flemish, which feature *scrambling* as a syntactic means to meet the licensing constraint on empty dative prepositions, scrambling of the empty-headed dative PP must be exploited in constructions involving A'-extraction of the double object Theme.[31] In this way we can maintain the account of word-order restrictions in West-Germanic double object constructions featuring Theme extraction while at the same time offering a reasonable approach to the well-formedness of the English examples in (52).

In this subsection I discussed one instance of what Stowell (1981:300) has referred to as the 'bewildering array of ... mysteries' displayed by double object constructions — the fact that in English double object constructions containing a verbal particle, A'-extraction of the Theme NP is ruled out unless the indirect object is raised to subject position via passivisation. As before, the licensing

---

[31] Hence, even though in (i), a putative case of PP-over-V applied to an empty-headed dative PP, the empty dative preposition is linearly adjacent to the verb, this does not suffice to make the sentence grammatical.

(i)   *dat Jan een boek wilde geven [$_{PP}$ P$_\varnothing$ zijn moeder].
           that Jan a book wanted give his mother

That PP-over-V (unlike scrambling) does not license the zero dative P by taking it into the domain of the licensing verb can be made to follow from the hypothesis that PP-extraposition does not exist as a movement process (cf. section 3.11.2, above; also cf. Culicover & Rochemont 1990). The clause-final PP in PP-over-V constructions is base-generated in a position that is probably too high for the verb to govern. Alternatively, the fact that the empty P in (i) cannot be incorporated into V can be related to the government directionality parameter, which is set to the left for Dutch V (but cf. Kayne 1993b).

condition on empty dative prepositions is instrumental. The insight offered by the present subsection is that, if dispensable for Case-theoretic reasons, dative prepositions can be present throughout the syntax and fail to receive a phonetic matrix at PF, thereby being immune to the syntactic licensing constraint.

4.5.2 A'-extraction of the Kichaga double object Goal

In the previous subsection we saw that A'-extraction of the Theme in English double object particle constructions is contingent on the application of raising-to-subject to the Goal. In what follows I discuss the mirror-image counterpart of the English data, represented by the Bantu language of Kichaga. In Kichaga (cf. Bresnan & Moshi 1990; Alsina & Mchombo 1990 for data and discussion), relativisation of the double object Goal is normally impossible (cf. English and Chichewa, section 4.2), as the deviance of the applicative relative construction in (53), from Bresnan & Moshi (1990:159), shows:[32]

(53)   *M-kà á-í-lyì-í-à   k-èlyá nyí-ichu.
        1-wife 1 SUBJ-PRES-eat-APPL-FV   7-food COP-1 this
        'The wife for whom he is eating the food is this one.'

I refer to section 4.2, above, for detailed discussion of the restrictions on Goal extraction in double object and applicative constructions.

Kichaga belongs to what Bresnan & Moshi (1990) refer to as the *symmetric* group of Bantu languages: both the Goal and the Theme NP may be raised to subject position in passive benefactive applicative constructions. The following example (Bresnan & Moshi 1990:150) instantiates Theme promotion to subject in Kichaga:

(54)   K-èlyá k-í-lyì-í-o   m-ká.
        7-food 7 SUBJ-PRES-eat-APPL-PASS 1-wife
        'The food is being eaten for/on the wife.'

Now what is interesting to note about Kichaga applicative constructions is that, as soon as the Theme undergoes raising-to-subject, A'-extraction of the Goal becomes possible. The well-formedness of (55) (Bresnan & Moshi 1990:165), which contrasts strikingly with the ungrammaticality of (53), bears this out. A'-movement of the double object Goal in Kichaga is hence contingent on raising-to-subject of the Theme.

---

[32] In the glosses of all Kichaga examples, the numbers are class indicators. The abbreviation "FV" represents the final vowel of Kichaga verbal forms. Other abbreviations are familiar.

(55)   M-kà k-í-lyì-í-ˈó   yí   Mkàfítˈínà.
         1-wife 7 SUBJ-PRES-eat-APPL-PASS COP Mkafitina
         'The woman for/on whom it is being eaten is Mkafitina.'

When we bear in mind what was argued with respect to English in the previous subsection, this *prima facie* baffling property of the syntax of Kichaga
benefactive applicative constructions can in fact be accommodated quite straightforwardly. First recall from section 4.2 that empty operator movement of the
double object Goal (which is plausibly at work in the relative clauses in (53)
and (55)) is generally impossible. Stranding the dative preposition which
governs the empty operator is possible neither *in situ* (for want of a suitable
licenser of P, in languages, like Kichaga, which do not feature overt dative
Case morphology) nor in the landing-site of Dative Shift (cf. the Non-Oblique
Trace Filter, given in (11), above). Hence only pied-piping of the entire dative
PP remains. This, however, is barred by whatever rules out pied-piping in cases
of empty operator movement in general (cf. section 4.2.3, above). In this way,
the deviance of (53) is accommodated.

In view of the line of argument sketched in the previous paragraph, it is
obvious that the way to ensure grammaticality in the case of (55) is to allow the
empty operator Goal to undergo A'-movement of its own accord, without it
having to carry along the projection of the empty dative preposition. Put differently, what we should ensure is that just in case the Theme NP undergoes
raising-to-subject, the empty dative preposition can remain in its D-structure
position. Movement of the Theme should hence facilitate *in situ* licensing of the
zero dative P governing the trace of the empty operator. Recall at this point
what I argued with respect to Theme A'-extraction in English particle-less
double object constructions in section 4.5.1. There I suggested that, in
languages which apart from Dative Shift have no other syntactic means of creating the appropriate structural configuration for P-licensing, zero dative Ps can
be licensed "by default" if they are linearly *adjacent* to the verb, by way of a
last resort option.

This account of English (52) immediately carries over to the Kichaga cases
under current discussion. In the active construction in (53), the last resort option
is clearly inoperative, given that the *in situ* Theme NP intervenes between the
verb and the zero dative preposition (which, as the reader will recall, heads the
predicate of the dative SC of which the Theme is the subject). In the passive
counterpart in (55), by contrast, A-movement of the Theme makes the empty
dative P end up in a position linearly adjacent to the verb. Only in constructions
featuring Theme movement, then, does the last resort strategy allow *in situ*
licensing of the empty preposition governing the trace of the empty operator
Goal. In this way the contrast between (53) and (55) can be reduced to the conditions governing the licensing of empty dative prepositions in non-scrambling
languages like English and Kichaga.

Notice incidentally that if the account of Kichaga (55) presented here holds water, this gives occasion to some scepticism with regard to Baker's (1988) view that applicative morphemes (like Kichaga *i*) are the spell-outs of incorporated dative prepositions. After all, no preposition incorporation obtains in this example; indeed, it could not, since the appropriate structural configuration for the application of incorporation is not met — no Dative Shift can have taken place in (55) since raising-to-subject of the Theme NP obtains. Case-driven NP-raising of the Theme to the nominative subject position bleeds Dative Shift, which likewise is (at least in part) a Case-driven movement operation: by moving a SC predicate into a Case-marked position, the subject of this predicate is provided with Case. Whenever movement of the Theme NP to the nominative subject position takes place, as in passives, Dative Shift will hence be ruled out by Economy (see also the discussion in section 3.10.1, esp. fn. 21). But if Dative Shift is impossible in Kichaga (55), P-incorporation is, too, so that *i*, the applicative morpheme, cannot be an incorporated dative preposition. In chapter 5 I return in more depth to Baker's analysis of applicative morphemes as incorporated dative Ps, arguing that there are other grounds to reject it as well.

4.5.3 Summary

In this section I have addressed two cases of interaction or dependency between passivisation and A'-extraction in double object constructions. I have shown that these can on the whole be made to fall out from the analysis if we capitalise on the constraints governing the licensing of empty dative prepositions. The data have given rise to a slight but not unnatural extension of the licensing mechanisms, to include "default" licensing by linear adjacency to the verb as a last resort option.[33]

---

[33] Since this is not primarily a study of passivisation in double object constructions, I largely ignore questions of detail pertaining to this beyond what was said above. Languages roughly come in two types — "symmetric" ones, in which both objects can raise to subject (e.g. Kinyarwanda, Norwegian), and "asymmetric" ones, in which only one object behaves like a "true" object (e.g. ChiMwiini); cf. Baker (1988, 1989a), Bresnan & Moshi (1990), Rochemont & Keach (1992), and especially Hoffman's (1991) detailed cross-linguistic study of A-movement (a)symmetries in applicative constructions. Languages also typically behave identically in double object and transitive causative constructions (Sesotho being the odd man out in this regard; cf. Machobane 1989). This argues for a structural assimilation of triadic and transitive causative constructions, which will be undertaken in chapter 5.

4.6 German has no Dative Shift

The data of Theme extraction in West Germanic double object constructions discussed in section 4.3 show that, at least in specific contexts, what appear to be
Dative Shift constructions are really concealed prepositional dative constructions. Sections 4.4 and 4.5 were seen to lend additional support to this view. In
this section, I go one step further by arguing, on the basis of binding asymmetries of the type disscussed in Barss & Lasnik (1986), that this covert P-
dative construction is really all there is in German. That is, German features no
genuine Dative Shift. What appears to be Dative Shift is actually A'-scrambling
of a zero-headed dative PP. Thus, I essentially agree with Müller (1992) (from
whose paper all German data to follow are taken) that the movement operation
responsible for ordering the Goal in front of the Theme is *A'*-movement. I diverge from Müller (1992), however, by recognising that this movement operation is scrambling rather than Dative Shift. Once this is assumed, Müller's
account of German double object constructions can be substantially simplified,
and the differences between German on the one hand, and Dutch and English
on the other can be straightforwardly accommodated, without recourse to additional machinery.

4.6.1 Binding asymmetries

Barss & Lasnik (1986) have noted that English dative and double object constructions exhibit binding asymmetries which, as Larson (1988) and others have
argued, involve command.[34] The examples to follow show that in dative
constructions, the Theme can bind an anaphoric expression or bound variable
(contained in the) Goal, while in double object constructions it is the Goal
which can bind the Theme (or Theme-contained element). In both constructions,
these binding relations are asymmetric.

(56) a.   I showed Mary$_i$ herself$_i$ in the mirror.
         b.   *I showed herself$_i$ Mary$_i$ in the mirror.

(57) a.   I showed Mary$_i$ to herself$_i$ in the mirror.
         b.   *I showed herself$_i$ to Mary$_i$ in the mirror.

---

[34] The formulation here is deliberately vague — whether command is really at stake is not an uncontroversial issue (cf. Jackendoff 1990; also cf. the data in fn. 42, below), and even if the binding
asymmetries reported by Barss & Lasnik involve command, it seems that in some cases (particularly
those involving double PP constructions with verbs such as *talk*) minimal c-command is not the
appropriate notion. But cf. Pesetsky (1993) for an entirely different phrase structural representation
("cascade structure") which can reduce all binding asymmetries to c-command.

(58) a.   I gave every worker$_i$ his$_i$ paycheck.
     b.   *I gave its$_i$ owner every paycheck$_i$.

(59) a.   I gave every paycheck$_i$ to its$_i$ owner.
     b.   *I gave his$_i$ paycheck to every worker$_i$.

On the present analysis of triadic constructions, the binding facts of pre-positional dative constructions (cf. (57) and (59)) straightforwardly reduce to c-command asymmetries. In the corresponding double object constructions in (56) and (58), A-movement of the empty-headed dative PP takes place. On the assumption that the zero preposition does not interfere with c-command relation-ships,[35] the indirect object thus comes to asymmetrically c-command the direct object in a double object construction at S-structure. The binding asymmetries in (56) and (58) can then be made to fall out from the analysis on the assumption that A-movement does not undergo reconstruction.[36]

The binding facts in (56)–(59) can be reproduced in their entirety in Dutch (cf. further below for illustration). Interestingly, however, German double object constructions appear to differ sharply from their English and Dutch cognates, particularly with respect to anaphoric binding.

---

[35] As seems plausible given that c-command even seems oblivious to *lexical* prepositions in some cases; notice particularly double PP constructions with verbs like *talk*, in which the NP contained in the *to*-PP can bind an element contained in the *about*-PP (cf. *I talked to every girl$_i$ about her$_i$ mother*).

[36] This assumption, though often made, is not entirely uncontroversial; cf. Belletti & Rizzi (1988) on psych verb constructions. Mulder (1992a) notes that Predicate Inversion, of which Dative Shift is an instance on the present analysis, seems to undergo reconstruction:

(i) a.   Standing next to each other$_i$ were my two brothers$_i$.
     b.   Buried in his$_i$ own basement lies the town's founder$_i$.

When extrapolated to the domain of double object constructions, these data would seem to lead us to expect no binding asymmetries in these constructions, contrary to fact. Note, however, that Den Dikken & Næss (1993) argue for one important difference between "genuine" Predicate Inversion and "covert" Predicate Inversion of the Dative Shift type. While in the latter, the inverted predicate remains in an A-position, in "genuine" Predicate Inversion constructions the fronted predicate undergoes supplementary A'-movement (topicalisation) after touching down in the nominative sub-ject position (also cf. Bresnan 1990). The fronted predicate in "genuine" Predicate Inversion constructions like (i) hence has A'-properties which the fronted beheaded dative PP in Dative Shift constructions lacks. The crucial A'-property in the context at hand is *reconstructability*: since the fronted predicate in (i) is in an A'-position, it may reconstruct into its base position at LF. No reconstruction is possible in Dative Shift constructions, however, since no A'-movement of the fronted predicate takes place there. In this way the binding contrast between Dative Shift and matrix Predicate Inversions such as (i) can be accommodated.

4.6.2 The binding facts of German

Müller (1992) presents a detailed survey of binding asymmetries found in German double object constructions. The sentences in (60) and (61) represent the basic facts as far as anaphoric binding is concerned.[37] Apparently, a dative-marked NP cannot bind an accusative-marked anaphor in German, while an accusative-marked NP *can* bind an anaphor. If, as Müller (1992) suggests, the DAT–ACC word order represents the basic word order of the German Dative Shift construction, the ill-formedness of (61) contrasts strikingly with the acceptability of the English Dative Shift construction in (56a).

(60) a. daß der Arzt den Patienten$_i$ sich$_i$ im Spiegel zeigte.
          that the doctor the patient(ACC) SELF in-the mirror showed
      b. daß man die Gäste$_i$ einander$_i$ vorgestellt hat.
          that one the guests(ACC) each-other introduced has

(61) a. *daß der Arzt dem Patienten$_i$ sich$_i$ im Spiegel zeigte.
          that the doctor the patient(DAT) SELF in-the mirror showed
      b. *daß man den Gästen$_i$ einander$_i$ vorgestellt hat.
          that one the guests(DAT) each-other introduced has

In the domain of variable binding, the German facts are less dramatically different from the data reported for English. A dative-marked quantified expression can be coindexed with a bound variable contained in the accusative-marked NP in a German double object construction, as (62) shows. Whether the alternative example in (63) is grammatical is not quite clear, speakers' judgements varying to a certain extent according to Müller. "Rigid" speakers tend to consider them slightly odd.[38]

---

[37] Franks (1993:523) reports parallel facts for Polish (cf. (i)). This is no surprise in the light of the account presented here, Polish, like German, licensing P$_\emptyset$ by overt dative Case morphology.

(i)   a. Ja przedstawiłem moich przyjaciół$_i$ sobie$_i$.   (Polish)
          I introduced my friends(ACC) self(DAT)
          'I introduced my friends to each other.'
      b. *Ja przedstawiłem moim przyjaciołom$_i$ siebie$_i$.
          I introduced my friends(DAT) self(ACC)

[38] Again the facts of Polish are essentially on a par with those of German. As Franks (1993: 523) notes, 'a possessive pronoun in either argument can be translated into a variable' (cf. (i)). Why German (63) is mildly deviant for rigid speakers is unclear (also on Müller's assumptions).

(i)   a. Ewa przedstawiła każdego gościa$_i$ jego$_i$ sąsiadowi.   (Polish)
          Ewa introduced each guest(ACC) his neighbour(DAT)
      b. Ewa przedstawiła każdemu gościowi$_i$ jego$_i$ sąsiada.
          Ewa introduced each guest(DAT) his neighbour(ACC)

(62)   daß die Gastgeber jedem Mann$_i$ seine$_i$ Tanzpartnerin vorstellten.
         that the hosts every man(DAT) his dance partner introduced

(63)   ?daß die Gastgeber jeden Mann$_i$ seiner$_i$ Tanzpartnerin vorstellten.
         that the hosts every man(ACC) his dance partner introduced

In addition, Müller notes an asymmetry between the DAT–ACC and ACC–DAT word-order patterns with respect to pronominal coreference. While (64a) is grammatical with the dative-marked NP binding the accusative pronoun, (64b), in which the binder bears accusative Case and the pronoun is dative-marked, is ungrammatical:

(64) a.   daß der Arzt dem Fritz$_i$ ihn$_i$ im Spiegel zeigte.
           that the doctor the Fritz(DAT) him in-the mirror showed
      b.   *daß der Arzt den Fritz$_i$ ihm$_i$ im Spiegel zeigte.
           that the doctor the Fritz(ACC) him in-the mirror showed

In this respect, German (64a) differs from both prepositional dative and double object constructions in languages like English or Dutch, as the fact that (65a,b) are both ungrammatical bears out:[39]

(65) a.   *dat de dokter Frits$_i$ hem$_i$ in de spiegel toonde.
           that the doctor Frits him in the mirror showed
      b.   *dat de dokter Frits$_i$ aan hem$_i$ in de spiegel toonde.
           that the doctor Frits to him in the mirror showed.

What the grammaticality of German (64a) suggests, as Müller rightly concludes, is that the dative-marked NP in this example occupies an A'-position. Since Principle B of the Binding Theory constrains A-binding of pronouns, not A'-binding, the well-formedness of (64a) falls out. I take over this aspect of Müller's (1992) analysis of German DAT–ACC double object constructions, taking issue, however, with his claim that the A'-movement operation responsible for ordering the dative-marked phrase before the accusative NP is Dative Shift. In so doing, I immediately rid Müller's analysis of the hybrid notion of "Case-driven A'-movement", which on his assumptions is the proper characterisation of Dative Shift. If German DAT–ACC constructions do not involve Dative Shift at all, there is no need to have recourse to a classification of Dative Shift as "Case-driven A'-movement". Clearly, this is a desirable result.

---

[39] I use Dutch examples here in order to avoid irrelevant problems related to the use of pronouns in English double object constructions. I have no information on Polish with respect to Principle B effects in triadic constructions.

4.6.3 Analysis

In this subsection I would like to argue that the German binding facts summed up in section 4.6.2, and the differences between German on the one hand and English and Dutch on the other fall out immediately from an analysis according to which German DAT–ACC word order in double object constructions comes about via *scrambling* of the empty-headed dative PP on the basis of the ACC–DAT order which, on the present analysis, underlies *all* German double object constructions.

Recall from section 3.10.2 (also cf. section 4.3, above) that dative prepositions in principle alternate freely with phonetically null counterparts. Recall also that languages differ parametrically with regard to the way in which an empty dative preposition is licensed. Dutch and English, I argued, may only license the zero preposition by incorporating it into the verb, at some level of representation. Since incorporation is contingent on prior movement of the empty preposition's projection, this accounts for the ill-formedness of "bare" double object constructions featuring a DO–IO word-order pattern (cf. (67a,b)). In German, by contrast, the presence of overt dative Case morphology accomplishes the licensing of the dative preposition. Quite possibly even, it is this dative Case morphology which actually spells out P^0. Movement of the dative PP is hence not forced, which explains the fact that German (67c) is grammatical (alongside (66c)).

(66) a. John gave Mary the book.
      b. Jan gaf Marie het boek.
      c. Der Hans gab der Maria das Buch.

(67) a. *John gave the book Mary.
      b. *Jan gaf het boek Marie.
      c. Der Hans gab das Buch der Maria.

This being said, let us proceed on our earlier hypothesis that Dative Shift is (at least partially) motivated by considerations of licensing of the zero dative preposition (cf. section 3.10.2). Let us in addition adopt Chomsky's (1991) Economy Principle, according to which unmotivated steps in a derivation are not taken. Then, in languages in which empty dative prepositions are licensed *in situ*, applying Dative Shift will violate Chomsky's Economy Principle if we assume that the essential motivation for Dative Shift is P-licensing (as I have been assuming all along). Languages which license empty dative Ps *in situ*, then, cannot have Dative Shift, if this line of reasoning is correct. Since German, as we saw before, belongs to this class of languages, I hence conclude that the A-movement transformation known as Dative Shift is absent from the grammar of German.

Scrambling and other A'-movement operations are different from Dative Shift in not being *motivated* by considerations of licensing — even though scrambling can be *used* as a means to license zero-headed dative prepositions (cf. section 4.3, above), licensing is not its motivation. While empty-headed dative prepositions hence may not undergo Dative Shift in German, they may perfectly legitimately be scrambled. This, then, will be the way in which dative-marked phrases in German double object constructions can be moved around accusative-marked NPs. The DAT–ACC word order is hence derived from the underlying ACC–DAT order by scrambling, not Dative Shift.

Scrambling is an A'-movement transformation (cf. Den Dikken & Mulder 1991 for discussion). With this in mind, we can now return to the German examples in (64), and particularly to the apparently remarkable well-formedness of (64a). The examples are repeated here:

(64) a. daß der Arzt dem Fritz$_i$ ihn$_i$ im Spiegel zeigte.
         that the doctor the Fritz(DAT) him in-the mirror showed
     b. *daß der Arzt den Fritz$_i$ ihm$_i$ im Spiegel zeigte.
         that the doctor the Fritz(ACC) him in-the mirror showed

That (64b) is ungrammatical falls out immediately from Principle B of the Binding Theory — the pronoun is illegitimately bound by a c-commanding NP occupying an A-position. On the present analysis of German double object constructions, this example, featuring ACC–DAT word order, is on a par with prepositional dative constructions in languages like English or Dutch, which likewise prohibit pronominal coreference in this context (cf. Dutch (65b)).

The grammaticality of (64a) can now be seen to be a consequence of the fact that the DAT–ACC order in German double object constructions is derived via scrambling (hence A'-movement) of the dative phrase. Since Principle B does not rule out A'-binding of pronouns, (64a) is fine.[40]

Notice the simplicity of an analysis of pronominal coreference in double object constructions based the assumption that German has no Dative Shift. Müller (1992), by contrast, must assume (i) that German Dative Shift is A'-movement, which causes him trouble accommodating the difference between German and other Germanic languages (not only in this particular case, but in fact throughout the syntax of double object constructions), and (ii) that the ACC–

---

[40] A question that arises from the perspective of what was argued in section 4.3 is why (65a) is ungrammatical — if, as I argued in 4.3, empty-headed dative PPs can be scrambled in Dutch (and West Flemish), then why cannot scrambling (rather than Dative Shift) have applied in (65a), so that (65a) would be on a par with German (64a)? I suggest that Dative Shift is the canonical way of (creating the appropriate structural configuration for) licensing empty dative prepositions (in languages without dative Case morphology, like Dutch); scrambling (without prior Dative Shift) can be had recourse to only if Dative Shift is unavailable (cf. section 4.3).

DAT construction in (64b) comes about via Dative Shift of the dative NP plus additional scrambling of the accusative NP across the dative, as is illustrated in (68):

(68)   ... [$_{A'}$ *den Fritz*$_k$] [$_{A'}$ *ihm*$_i$] t_k t_i ...   (where $k = i$)

Apart from the fact that it apparently violates Pesetsky's (1982) Path Containment Condition, the representation in (68) does not yield an immediate answer to the question of why (64b) is ungrammatical. After all, after scrambling, the accusative-marked NP finds itself in an A'-position, and should hence qualify as an eligible binder for the pronoun, contrary to fact. Müller solves this problem by invoking an appropriately modified version of Rizzi's (1986) chain formation algorithm (cf. Müller 1992 for details). Since the present analysis dispenses with the somewhat cumbersome derivation in (68) and captures the deviance of (64b) straightforwardly without recourse to a revised chain formation algorithm, it seems superior to Müller's in this respect.

Turning next to anaphoric binding in German double object constructions, let us see how an analysis according to which ACC–DAT reflects D-structure, DAT–ACC being derived by scrambling, captures (60)–(61):

(60)   a.   daß der Arzt den Patienten$_i$ sich$_i$ im Spiegel zeigte.
              that the doctor the patient(ACC) SELF in-the mirror showed
       b.   daß man die Gäste$_i$ einander$_i$ vorgestellt hat.
              that one the guests(ACC) each-other introduced has

(61)   a.   *daß der Arzt dem Patienten$_i$ sich$_i$ im Spiegel zeigte.
              that the doctor the patient(DAT) SELF in-the mirror showed
       b.   *daß man den Gästen$_i$ einander$_i$ vorgestellt hat.
              that one the guests(DAT) each-other introduced has

If (60) represents D-structure, and essentially corresponds to prepositional dative constructions in English or Dutch, the well-formedness of these examples comes as no surprise — compare (60) to English (57a) or Dutch (69a), below. The ungrammaticality of the DAT–ACC sentences in (61) finds a direct parallel in Dutch P-dative constructions featuring clause-internal scrambling of the dative PP. I illustrate this only on the basis of reciprocal constructions (cf. (69b)), the anaphor *zich* being too light to surface to the right of a scrambled PP so that the Dutch PP-counterpart of German (61a) would be ill-formed on independent grounds.[41]

---

[41] Müller's account of the well-formedness of (60) is crucially dependent on the assumption (for which Müller adduces independent evidence) that German anaphoric expressions like *sich* and *einander* do not need to be assigned structural Case. Hence they do not have to undergo "Case-driven

(69) a.   dat men de gasten$_i$ aan elkaar$_i$ heeft voorgesteld.
            that one the guests to each-other has introduced
      b.   *dat men aan de gasten$_i$ elkaar$_i$ heeft voorgesteld.
            that one to the guests each-other has introduced

Scrambling of the dative PP hence apparently cannot create an appropriate configuration for anaphoric binding. This follows naturally given that Principle A of the Binding Theory requires anaphors to be A-bound. This condition is not complied with in (61) and (69b). In this regard, anaphoric binding differs from variable binding, which is possible from A'-positions. This is why, in German, there is no (substantial) contrast between the examples in (62) and (63), repeated here:

(62)   daß die Gastgeber jedem Mann$_i$ seine$_i$ Tanzpartnerin vorstellten.
            that the hosts every man(DAT) his dance partner introduced

(63)   ?daß die Gastgeber jeden Mann$_i$ seiner$_i$ Tanzpartnerin vorstellten.
            that the hosts every man(ACC) his dance partner introduced

These German examples correspond to the likewise grammatical Dutch dative constructions in (70) and (71):

(70)   dat de gastheren aan iedere man$_i$ zijn$_i$ danspartner voorstelden.
            that the hosts to every man his dance partner introduced

(71)   dat de gastheren iedere man$_i$ aan zijn$_i$ danspartner voorstelden.
            that the hosts every man to his dance partner introduced

The fact that there is a virtually perfect match between German (62)–(63) and Dutch (70)–(71) strongly suggests that an analysis of apparent German Dative Shift constructions as dative constructions featuring scrambling of the dative PP is on the right track.

A'-movement'' (i.e. Müller's Dative Shift), but remain *in situ*. If they did undergo Dative Shift, the accusative-marked NP would have to be scrambled across these anaphors, and then the anaphors would wrongly be A'-bound by the scrambled accusative NP. Müller seeks to support this account of (60) by pointing out that once the anaphor is contained in a Case-dependent NP, it does not seem to be as easily bindable by the accusative NP as in (60). Müller quotes the examples in (i) to bear this out. The contrast between (ia,b), if it were real, would be surprising from the present perspective. Matthias Hüning points out to me, however, that (ia,b) do not seem to contrast; in fact, he finds both examples pretty awkward.

(i)   a.   ??daß wir den Fritz$_i$ [einer alten Freundin von sich$_i$] geschickt/gezeigt haben.
            that we the Fritz(ACC) an old friend of SELF sent/shown have
      b.   daß wir den Fritz$_i$ [*zu* einer alten Freundin von sich$_i$] geschickt haben.
            that we the Fritz(ACC) to an old friend of SELF sent have

4.6.4 Summary

German differs from closely related languages like Dutch and English in a number of respects concerning binding in double object constructions. I have argued that an analysis according to which German has no genuine Dative Shift constructions, all DAT–ACC word orders arising through scrambling of a zero-headed dative PP, straightforwardly accommodates the facts of German. It also yields insight into the question as to why German should differ from Dutch and English — in contrast to German, the latter two languages do have Dative Shift. That the grammar of German should lack the Dative Shift transformation can be related to the fact that the presence of overt dative Case morphology can license — or even (''alternatively''; Emonds 1987) realise — the empty dative preposition in a covert P-dative construction. If Dative Shift is viewed as motivated by licensing considerations, Chomsky's (1991) Economy Principle prevents it from applying in languages like German.[42]

---

[42] The binding facts found in Italian triadic constructions are an interesting challenge to the theory. As Maria Teresa Guasti (p.c.) observes, in such constructions the Goal NP, contained in an *a*-phrase, cannot be bound by the Theme NP to its left; by contrast, an anaphoric Theme *can* be bound by the Goal in the *a*-phrase:

(i)   a.   *Ho mostrato Maria$_i$ a se stessa$_i$.
           I-have shown Maria to herself
       b.   Ho mostrato se stessa$_i$ a Maria$_i$.
           I-have shown herself to Maria

One thing that these facts clearly show is that binding asymmetries do not involve linear order (as Jackendoff 1990 contends they do). Instead, c-command must be at stake: the *a*-phrase c-commands the Theme in Italian triadic constructions. This can be effectuated by having the *a*+NP sequence undergo obligatory Dative Shift to the *right*-peripheral specifier position of the VP headed by abstract BE (cf. Bonet 1989; Rosen 1989; Friedemann 1992; Guasti 1993 for the view that Romance VPs have right-peripheral specifiers; but cf. Kayne 1993b for a theory ruling out this option). The interesting question in this context is why Dative Shift should be obligatory in Italian triadic constructions, if *a* is a preposition realising the head of the dative PP. I hypothesise that *a* either does not realise the P-slot of dative phrases after all (but is some sort of prefix on the Goal NP), or is a dependent P that itself needs licensing. The same binding facts recur in Italian transitive causative constructions, which supports a structural assimilation of datives and transitive causatives. In the next chapter, this assimilation will be brought about.

4.7 Conclusion

In the words of Stowell (1981:300), verb-particle constructions and double object constructions, and especially their intersections, 'display a bewildering array of ... mysteries'. It has been the aim of this chapter to show that the analysis of triadic constructions and Dative Shift developed in chapter 3 furnishes accounts for some of these mysteries, especially those concerning movement restrictions in double object constructions. Focusing on the limitations on A'-extraction of the double object Goal in section 4.2, I showed that, while overt (local) *wh*-extraction of the Goal generally yields a grammatical result, even in many dialects of English, Goals consistently resist undergoing empty operator movement. In the spirit of earlier work by Kayne (1984), Czepluch (1982) and Baker (1988), I construed this as an argument for the inclusion in the structure of double object constructions of an empty dative preposition governing the Goal NP.

The licensing restrictions on this empty dative preposition were subsequently shown to yield insight into some hitherto poorly understood constraints on A'-movement of the double object Theme. A'-extraction of the Theme across a Dative Shifted dative phrase being theoretically excluded by the Binding Theory, I argued that double object constructions featuring A'-movement of the Theme NP must be analysed as covert prepositional dative constructions featuring an empty dative preposition.

Pushing the covert dative analysis to its logical limit, I closed this chapter by arguing that this is in fact the sole structure of German double object constructions, Dative Shift being absent from the grammar of German altogether. This claim, firmly embedded as it is in the overall theory of licensing of empty dative prepositions, was shown to shed light on the otherwise quite mysterious differences between German on the one hand, and related Germanic languages like English and Dutch on the other, with respect to binding asymmetries in double object constructions.

5

Affixal Particles in Applicatives and Causatives

5.1 Introduction

In chapter 3 I discussed the analysis of triadic constructions and Dative Shift mainly on the basis of evidence from analytic languages like English. In poly-synthetic languages such as Chichewa (a Bantu language spoken in Malawi), an alternation similar to the English dative alternation is found. Consider the Chichewa examples in (1) (taken from Baker 1988; cf. this work for the original provenance of these examples):

(1) a. Ndi-na-tumiz-a   chipanda cha mowa *kwa* mfumu.
         1SG.SUBJ-PAST-send-ASP   calabash of beer to   chief
         'I sent a calabash of beer to the chief.'
     b. Ndi-na-tumiz-*ir*-a   mfumu chipanda cha mowa.
         1SG.SUBJ-PAST-send-APPL-ASP chief calabash of   beer
         'I sent the chief a calabash of beer.'

In (1a) the Goal NP is preceded by the dative preposition *kwa* and surfaces to the right of the Theme NP, just as in English. In the so-called *applicative con-struction* in (1b), on the other hand, the Goal appears adjacent to the verb, which bears a special affix *-ir-*, the applicative or applied affix. Applicative constructions correspond in all relevant respects to double object constructions in languages like English. The only difference between English and Chichewa lies in the occurrence of a special morpheme in the double object construction of Chichewa.[1]

Baker (1988) presents an analysis of applicative constructions in terms of preposition incorporation (also cf. my analysis of Dative Shift in chapter 3). According to Baker, the applicative morpheme is the spell-out of the incorporat-ed dative preposition. The analysis of English Dative Shift is assimilated to that of applicative constructions, and likewise features preposition incorporation.

---

[1] I shall only discuss *benefactive* applicatives, which are cross-linguistically regular, while locative and instrumental applicatives 'show much less consistency' (Hoffman 1991:121).

The fact that, in Chichewa, there is no obvious phonological relationship between the dative preposition *kwa* and the applicative morpheme *-ir-*, and the fact that, in English, "applicative morphemes" are consistently non-overt are looked upon as peripheral morphophonological idiosyncrasies. 'When X^0 movement applies, it creates a complex structure consisting of more than one X^0 level item. It is then the task of the morphological subcomponent of the grammar to determine what the phonological shape of the combination will be' (Baker 1988:283).

In this chapter I take issue with Baker's (1988) claim that applicative morphemes are incorporated dative prepositions (while I continue to subscribe to a P-incorporation analysis of Dative Shift, as propounded in chapter 3). My focus in the discussion to follow will be on languages which show a systematic homophony of what are usually called their applicative and causative morphemes.[2] In Tetelcongo Nahuatl (Aztecan), for instance, the suffix *-liya* can act as an applicative morpheme and as a causativiser (cf. Tuggy 1987). In this chapter evidence from Indonesian, Sanuma, Dutch and French will be presented as a further illustration of the systematic homophony of so-called applicative and causative affixes. The conclusion ensuing from this discussion will be that these morphemes are *affixal particles* rather than incorporated prepositions or incorporating verbs.[3]

This chapter will be concluded with an investigation of the structure of (transitive) causative constructions, particularly in the Romance languages. The analysis of causatives will be modelled on that of triadic constructions, and will be shown to capture the cross-linguistic correlation between the Case-form of causees (embedded subjects) in transitive causatives and Goal NPs in dative constructions, without the need for special (hence costly) constraints on the selection of "dummy" Case-markers.

---

[2] Marantz's (1990:29) observation that in Kinyarwanda the causative morpheme *-iish* is identical with the instrumental applicative affix ('a situation not uncommon among African languages') may not be very illustrative in this respect, since instrumental applicatives might presumably be analysed as causative constructions (cf. Voskuil 1990 for arguments).

[3] Initial support for this view comes from Shona, a member of the Bantu language family (to which Chichewa also belongs) spoken in Zimbabwe. The Shona applicative morpheme *-ir-/-er-*, apart from showing up in triadic constructions, also behaves like an affixal particle of the Dutch *be-/ver-* type in some cases. This is particularly evident in the following examples (taken from Dale 1981:109), which should be compared to the Dutch renderings of the English verbs *think* and *suspect*, given in (ii), of which the latter contains the affixal particle *ver-* (cf. Hoekstra, Lansu & Westerduin 1987, and sections 5.2.1 and 5.2.4, below):

(i)   a.   funga   'think'
        b.   fung-*ir*-a   'suspect'
(ii)   a.   denken   'think'
        b.   *ver*denken   'suspect'

5.2 Homophony of applicative and causative affixes

5.2.1 The problem from a Dutch perspective

Consider the following two paradigms of constructions:[4]

(2) a. Jan stuurde uitnodigingen voor het feest aan zijn vrienden.
Jan sent invitations for the party to his friends

b. Jan *ver*stuurde zijn vrienden uitnodigingen voor het feest.
Jan VERsent his friends invitations for the party

(3) a. Jan maakte zijn positie op de arbeidsmarkt beter.
Jan made his position on the job market better

b. Jan *ver*beterde zijn positie op de arbeidsmarkt.
Jan VERbettered his position on the job market

The data in (2) and (3) seem to immediately remind one of properties of the languages of the Bantu class. In particular, one might, on the basis of these examples, be led to the formulation of the following descriptive generalisations about Dutch:

(4) a. *ver-*$_1$ = APPLICATIVE affix.
b. *ver-*$_2$ = CAUSATIVE affix.

Apart from the fact that, as things stand, the two affixes *ver-* just postulated seem to have nothing in common beyond their phonological identity, however, the two descriptive generalisations in (4) are empirically insufficient, in view of the additional data in (5) and (6):

(5) Jan *ver*stuurde uitnodigingen voor het feest aan zijn vrienden.
Jan VERsent invitations for the party to his friends

(6) Zijn positie op de arbeidsmarkt *ver*beterde.
his position on the job market VERbettered

---

[4] It has been pointed out to me by several people that they have difficulty accepting examples like (2b) if these contain a *singular* indirect object. This can be accounted for on the basis of the fact that the prefix *ver-* in triadic constructions has *distributive* semantics: a particular direct object is distributed among a group of recipients/beneficiaries. Hans Broekhuis further notes that *versturen*, as opposed to "bare" *sturen* 'send' or the particle verb *toesturen* 'up-send', does not undergo *krijgen* 'get' passivisation. This is true even if the indirect object is a plural NP (cf. *Deze mensen hebben geen uitnodigingen {gestuurd/toegestuurd/*verstuurd} gekregen*). I do not know how to explain this fact.

Apparently, *ver-* can be used *in combination* with the dative preposition (5). If applicative morphemes are spell-outs of incorporated prepositions, as Baker (1988) claims, this would be difficult to reconcile with an analysis of *ver-* as an applicative affix. Furthermore, the claim that *ver-* is a causativiser clashes with the inchoative counterpart of (3b) in (6).[5]

In the face of these considerations, one might go on to extend the generalisations in (4) to the list in (7):

(7)   a. ver_1 = APPLICATIVE affix in double object constructions.
b. ver_2 = ?? in prepositional dative constructions.
c. ver_3 = CAUSATIVE affix in causative constructions.
d. ver_4 = INCHOATIVE affix in inchoative constructions.

The list in (7) is clearly inadequate, though, in at least two obvious respects. For one thing, a classification of *ver-* in double object contexts as an applicative affix renders it extremely difficult to determine what *ver-* is in corresponding prepositional dative constructions (cf. "??" in (7b)). Moreover, postulating such massive and apparently fully accidental homophony as in (7) can hardly be called insightful. In our desire to eliminate accidental homophony in Dutch *ver-* constructions we are strengthened by the fact that this is apparently also found in languages other than Dutch.

5.2.2 The problem from a Sanuma perspective

In Sanuma (a Yanomami language spoken in Venezuela and Brazil; cf. Borgman 1989) causativisation is marked with the aid of the affix *-ma*:

(8)   a.   masita te   amatosi.
dirt   3SG hard
'The dirt is hard.'
b.   masita te   amatosi-*ma*-kö.
dirt   3SG hard-CAUS-FOC
'Make the dirt hard.'

---

[5]   The view that *ver-* is responsible for the causative semantics of (3b) is called into question not only by (6) but also by the causative construction in (i) (featuring the somewhat idiomatic *ver*-less verb *beteren* 'to better') — even if *ver-* is absent, we can still find causative semantics in examples highly similar to (3b).

(i)   Jan beterde zijn leven.
Jan bettered his life

In Sanuma triadic constructions (cf. (9)) the Goal argument is contained in a postpositional phrase. Arguably, these correspond to prepositional dative constructions in languages like Dutch or English.

(9)   ipa   hao-nö   hama   te   niha masulu kökö toto-ki   kite.
       my   father-AG visitor 3SG   to   beads   3DL   give-FOC FUT
       'My father will give beads to the visitor.'

Interestingly, Borgman (1989:51) notes that in Sanuma, '[c]ausation on ditransitive verbs is rare, but there is an instance of it occurring on the verb *toto* "to give" and the resultant meaning with the causative is "to provide" ', as in the following example:

(10)   pö   a-nö   ulu   töpö niha nii   te   toto-*ma*-ö.
      father 3SG-AG child 3PL for food 3SG give-CAUS-CUST
      'The father provides food for the children.'

Borgman restricts himself to just listing the example. It naturally gives rise, however, to some scepticism about Borgman's classification of -*ma* as a causativiser in Sanuma. After all, there is no sense in which -*ma* in (10) adds a supplementary layer of causation to the triadic construction with "bare" *toto* that forms the input to the affixation process: (10) clearly does not mean 'The father made some unspecified causee give the children food'. In a way parallel to the strategy followed in section 5.2.1 for Dutch, the properties of the Sanuma suffix -*ma* might now be represented by the two statements in (11):

(11) a.   -*ma*$_1$ = CAUSATIVE affix in causative constructions.
     b.   -*ma*$_2$ = ?? in triadic constructions.

Again, however, there is no obvious label for one of the uses of the affix under inspection. Moreover, while (7) and (11) might perhaps be defensible in isolation, it will be clear that we cannot get away with postulating multiple cross-linguistic cases of accidental homophony in identical structural environments.[6] In the context at hand, we can make our case against accidental homophony even stronger by considering a third, again completely unrelated language.

---

[6] For the particular case in (7c,d), the causative/inchoative alternation, in English and Hebrew, however, Borer (1991) does postulate double lexical entries for the morphemes involved.

5.2.3 The problem from an Indonesian perspective

Superficial inspection of the distribution of the Indonesian affix *-kan* on the basis of the examples in (12) and (13) may lead to essentially the same conclusion as we initially drew for Dutch *ver-* (cf. (4)), viz. (14):[7]

(12) a. Ali membuka pintu   untuk bapak.
         Ali open   the-door   for   father
     b. Ali membuka*kan* bapak pintu.
         Ali open-KAN   father the-door

(13) a. Ratna tidur.
         Ratna sleeps
     b. Parto menidur*kan* Ratna.
         Parto sleep-KAN   Ratna

(14) a. *-kan*₁ = APPLICATIVE affix.
     b. *-kan*₂ = CAUSATIVE affix.

In view of our previous discussion of Dutch and Sanuma, the two unrelated lexical entries for *-kan* in (14) are already suspect. The case against (14) can be strengthened, however, by a fuller investigation of the Indonesian *-kan* paradigm. As it turns out, *-kan* is like Dutch *ver-* in being usable in triadic constructions *in combination* with the dative preposition *untuk*, as in the example in (15):

(15)   Ali membuka*kan* pintu   untuk bapak.
        Ali open-KAN   the-door   for   father

Finally, consider the role of *-kan* in (16) and (17) (Voskuil 1990:87):

(16) a. Parto menulis nama saya.
         Parto writes name my
     b. Parto menulis*kan* nama saya di agendanya.
         Parto writes-KAN   name my in his-agenda

(17) a. Parto membaca buku itu.
         Parto read   book that
     b. Parto membaca*kan* buku itu.
         Parto read-KAN   book that

---

[7] The discussion in this section is entirely based on Voskuil (1990) (from which all data are taken, and where the interested reader may find references to earlier literature on the subject), though the conclusions drawn are different from his. Voskuil (1993) presents similar data for Tagalog *-an*.

As pointed out by Voskuil (1990:87), and as suggested by the translations of (16b) and (17b) given by him ('Parto writes my name *up* in his agenda' and 'Parto read that book *out* loud', respectively), in these examples the affix *-kan* corresponds to a PARTICLE in languages like Dutch or English. All in all, then, the Indonesian morpheme *-kan* seems to be four-ways ambiguous, much like Dutch *ver-* (but not quite):[8]

(18) a. *-kan*$_1$ = APPLICATIVE affix in double object constructions.
      b. *-kan*$_2$ = ?? in prepositional dative constructions.
      c. *-kan*$_3$ = CAUSATIVE affix in causative constructions.
      d. *-kan*$_4$ = PARTICLE in a 'small but heterogeneous' (Voskuil 1990:87) set of constructions.

5.2.4 Synthesis

In my quest for a synthetic account of *ver-*, *-ma* and *-kan* I would like to capitalise on two observations that were made in the foregoing: (i) Borgman's (1989:51) comments on the semantic distinction between a Sanuma "bare" *toto* construction and the *toto-ma* example in (10) to the effect that "bare" *toto* means just 'give' while the affixation of *-ma* onto this verb results in a semantics that can be appropriately rendered in English by 'provide'; and (ii) the use of Indonesian *-kan* as a particle in (16) and (17).

In the context of (i), a return to Dutch is in order. Consider first the Dutch counterparts of English *give* and *provide*:

---

[8] Here I only consider *-kan*. Indonesian has another transitivising affix, *-i*, whose properties are non-trivially distinct from those of *-kan*, and in some respects resemble those of Dutch *be-* more closely than *-kan*. The semantic contrast in (i) is illustrative in this connection:

(i) a. Parto menidur*kan* Ratna.   (= (13b))
         Parto sleep-KAN   Ratna
         'Parto made Ratna sleep.'
     b. Parto menidur*i* Ratna.
         Parto sleep-I   Ratna
         'Parto slept with Ratna.'

In this pair, *-kan* seems a "real" causativiser, while *-i* is like Dutch *be-* in the Dutch rendering of the example in (ib), *Ratna besliep Parto*. That *-kan* is nonetheless not to be analysed as a causative morpheme is clear from examples like (16b) and (17b); also cf. fn. 11, below. I shall not present an account of *-i*, referring to Voskuil (1990) for extensive discussion.

(19) a.   Jan gaf de kinderen eten.
            Jan gave the children food
      b.   Jan *ver*schafte de kinderen eten.
            Jan VERprovided the children food

The Dutch *provide* construction in (19b) appropriately distinguishes itself from
the *give* construction in (19a) by the presence of the affix *ver-*, which we
already encountered in section 5.2.1. There we saw ourselves forced to an un-
determined representation of one of the instantiations of this affix (cf. *ver-$_2$* in
(7b)) precisely in the context of triadic constructions as well. Let us consider
the earlier Dutch example in (5), repeated here as (20), in some more detail:

(20)   Jan *ver*stuurde uitnodigingen voor het feest aan zijn vrienden.
            Jan VERsent invitations for the party to his friends

Significantly, the affix *ver-* in (20) can be replaced by a PARTICLE, as in (21):

(21)   Jan stuurde uitnodigingen voor het feest *toe/op* aan zijn vrienden.
            Jan sent invitations for the party out/up to his friends

This observation gives rise to the hypothesis that *ver-*, in any event in (20),
belongs to the class of particles. Since in the double object counterpart of (20),
given in (2b) above and repeated as (22), the affix *ver-* also freely alternates
with a lexical particle, as shown in (23), this hypothesis naturally extends to this
example, as well as to the *provide* case in (19b).

(22)   Jan *ver*stuurde zijn vrienden uitnodigingen voor het feest.
            Jan VERsent his friends invitations for the party

(23)   Jan stuurde zijn vrienden uitnodigingen voor het feest *toe/op*.
            Jan sent his friends invitations for the party out/up

It now seems plausible to equate *ver-$_1$* and *ver-$_2$* in (7) and to treat them as
affixal particles. From the *verschaffen* 'provide' construction in (19b) it is then
but a small step to Sanuma *-ma$_2$* in (10), which can also be classified as a particle. Finally, Indonesian *-kan$_1$* and *-kan$_2$*, which correspond directly to Dutch
ver-$_1$ and *ver-$_2$*, can now be treated in an identical fashion, an assumption which
gains additional support from the fact that *-kan$_4$* can be independently shown to
exhibit particle-like behaviour in constructions like (16) and (17), above. Let us
hence reformulate some of our earlier generalisations as follows:

(24) $ver\text{-}_1 = ver\text{-}_2 = \text{-}ma_2 = \text{-}kan_1 = \text{-}kan_2 = \text{-}kan_4 = $ PARTICLE.

We are still in need of the crucial connection between the particle-like tokens of *ver-*, *-ma* and *-kan* for which we have just furnished an account, and the instances of these affixes showing up in causative (and, in Dutch, also inchoative) contexts. Requiring of the theory that it avoid the postulation of cross-linguistic accidental homophony, we should aim for an identification of all the various guises of the morphemes under investigation. Now that we have found a plausible analysis of *ver-*$_{1,2}$, *-ma*$_2$ and *-kan*$_{1,2,4}$, the obvious move to make is to claim that *ver-*$_{3,4}$, *-ma*$_1$ and *-kan*$_3$ are particles as well:

(25)   *ver-* = *-ma* = *-kan* = PARTICLE.

5.2.5 Interlude: Affixal particles in French

While examples of the type in (26) might at first blush be taken to suggest that French prefixes like *en-* combine with verbs to form causative verbs (*en-* turning the unergative verb *dormir* in (26a) into a causative verb in (26b)), an analysis of *en-* as a causative morpheme is defeated by the fact that a basically causative verb like *lever* 'lift' does not receive a doubly causative reading as a result of *en-* prefixation, as shown in (27). Rather than adding the semantics of causation, *en-* prefixation in (27) has the same effect as the addition of the particle *away* has in the English rendering of French *enlever*. The French prefix *en-* is not a causativiser, then, but a particle.[9]

(26)   a.   Marie dort.
              Marie sleeps
        b.   Pierre *en*dort Marie.
              Pierre ENsleeps (makes sleep) Marie

(27)   a.   *lever*   'x cause y to rise'
        b.   *enlever*   *'x cause y to cause z to rise'
                          'x cause y to rise *away* from something'

The apparent causativising effect of *en-* prefixation in (26a) is a side effect of the aspectual function that prefixes of this class (including *a-*, *dé-*, *trans-* and *ex-*) have. This aspectual function is most clearly discernible in pairs of the type in (28), where the distribution of the adverbial phrases shows the effect that the verbal prefix has on the internal aspectual structure of the VP:

---

[9]   All French examples in this section are taken from Di Sciullo & Klipple (1993) (also cf. Walinska de Hackbeil 1986, Lieber 1992, *a.o.*). They treat the French prefixes under discussion as prepositional adjuncts (adjoined either to V⁰ or to VP), not as particles, although they do note several important similarities between particles and prefixes of the French type.

(28) a. Pierre a porté les livres *pendant une heure/²en une heure*.
          Pierre has carried the books for an hour/in an hour
      b. Pierre a *ap*porté les livres *²pendant une heure/en une heure*.
          Pierre a ᴀcarried the books for an hour/in an hour

This aspectual effect brought about by *a*- prefixation is typical of particles as
well (cf. *eat* vs. *eat up*).

One final piece of evidence for the particle status of French verbal prefixes
is their taking part in prepositional complex particle constructions of the type
discussed at length in chapter 2, above. While the French verbs *mener* and
porter normally do not take part in a resultative construction of the type in
(29a), combining them with the verbal prefix *a*- renders these constructions
grammatical, as (29b) shows. The presence of the *de* PP in (29) is apparently
dependent on the presence of the prefix. Put differently, the *de* PP is *selected*
by the verbal prefix. Such selection is naturally accommodated on an analysis
of the prefix as a particle, given the structure assigned to complex particle
constructions in chapter 2, in which the particle selects the additional SC projected by the transitive preposition.

(29) a. *Ils ont mené/porté ce livre de la bibliothèque.
          they have brought this book from the library
      b. Ils ont *a*mené/*ap*porté ce livre de la bibliothèque.
          they have brought this book from the library

There is a variety of evidence, then, to suggest that French verbal prefixes are
affixal particles, just like the Dutch, Sanuma and Indonesian affixes encountered
above, and that they occupy the same D-structural position as the particles discussed in chapter 2.[10]

---

[10] A similar, though less spectacular illustration of the class of affixal particles is offered by the
Slavic languages. These possess a range of prefixes which, like independent particles and the French
prefixes discussed above, have an effect on the event structure of the VP. Two examples (from
Russian and Polish, respectively) are given in (i):

(i)   a.   *pisal* 'write' — *napisal*   'write up'
      b.   *jesc* 'eat'   — *zjesc*   'eat up'

As Walinska de Hackbeil (1989:18) notes, prefixes of this sort also show up in the Polish instantiations of the LOC–MAT alternant of the locative alternation, where Dutch would feature the prefix
be- — an affixal particle (cf. Hoekstra, Lansu & Westerduin 1987, and above). There is good evidence to suggest, therefore, that Slavic verbal prefixes are to be analysed as affixal particles as well.

(ii)   *o*-sypać dachy śniegiem.
           PFX-scatter roofs with-snow

5.2.6 Two central questions for the analysis of causative constructions

In the previous discussion we have encountered several reasons to endorse the conclusion that apparent causativisers like Dutch *ver-* are affixal particles, as stated in (25). This hypothesis gives rise to two important questions, though:

(i)   If affixes like *ver-* are themselves never causativisers, what is it that adds the semantics of causation in causatives featuring these affixes?

(ii)   What is the structural position of affixes like *ver-*, *-ma* and *-kan* in triadic and causative (and inchoative) constructions?

With respect to the former question, we may observe, in view of Dutch, that it would be wrong in any event to claim that it is *ver-* that adds causation in causative *ver-* constructions, since *ver-* also shows up in the inchoative alternants of such causatives (cf. (3b) and (6); also cf. fn. 5, above).[11] It is

---

[11] For Sanuma *-ma* and Indonesian *-kan*, no instances in inchoative constructions are known to me. This need not refute the analysis to be presented if some degree of selection between a governee and its governor can be had recourse to (i.e., the particle may, in some instances, select for a specific governor — a causative verb but not an inchoative verb). That this may be necessary for (some uses of) Dutch *be-* is suggested by the paradigm of the locative alternation with this affix. Consider the data in (i) and (ii):

(i)   a.   Jan hangt de schilderijen aan de muur.
            Jan hangs the paintings on the wall
      b.   Jan *be*hangt de muur met schilderijen.
            Jan BEhangs the wall with paintings
(ii)   a.   De schilderijen hangen aan de muur.
            the paintings hang on the wall
      b.   *De muur *be*hangt met schilderijen.
            the wall BEhangs with paintings

The thing to note is that while the MAT–LOC variant of the locative alternation in (ia) has an unaccusative (inchoative) counterpart (iia), the LOC–MAT alternant with *be-* does not. This is not due to a structural ban on *be-* occurring in inchoative contexts (cf. (6), above). Apparently, in the LOC–MAT alternant of the locative alternation *be-* requires the verb that governs its SC to be causative. Whatever is responsible for this (perhaps this is intimately related to the "totally affected" character of *de muur*, and the discussion of the configurational representation of affectedness in sections 2.4.4.1 and 3.12.2, above) will presumably carry over to Sanuma and Indonesian *-ma* and *-kan* constructions. Note that it clearly would not do to call Indonesian *-kan* a causativiser in all of its uses: examples like (16b) and (17b) are flatly incompatible with this, and so is (iiib), which in no sense is the causative counterpart of (iiia).

(iii)   a.   Kami bicara   tentang soal   itu.
            we   speak   about   problem   the
      b.   Kami membicara*kan* soal   itu.
            we   speak-KAN   problem   the

then plausible to assume that what is responsible for the semantics of causation in *ver-* causatives is an EMPTY CAUSATIVE MATRIX PREDICATE, which will be absent from the structure of the corresponding inchoatives. Some support for this suggestion can be found in the fact that in Indonesian, the "causative" affix *-kan₃* can cooccur with *sebab* 'cause, reason' (cf. Voskuil's 1990:34 example in (30)), which I would like to analyse as an instantiation of the matrix causative predicate which in other contexts (cf. the corresponding (13b)) has no lexical content of its own:[12]

(30)   Itu   *menyebab-kan*   Ratna tidur.
         that cause-KAN   Ratna sleep
         'That made Ratna sleep.'

Turning next to the second question, let us determine the D-structural position of the particle we have postulated. In chapter 2, I presented an analysis of complex particle constructions, the essence of which is that in constructions featuring both a particle (a SC predicate) and a secondary predicate (also a SC predicate), the particle projects an ergative SC in the complement of the verb, and in its turn selects a SC headed by the additional secondary predicate. In chapter 3 I carried over this analysis to triadic constructions, arguing for one additional layer of structure in these cases: a verbal SC between the matrix verb and the particle-headed SC. Given these results, the relevant part of the structure of our Dutch and Sanuma triadic constructions with *ver-*, *-ma* and *-kan*, which instantiate our "complex particle constructions", will read as in (31):[13]

(31) $[_{VP} [_{SC1}$ Spec $[_{VP} [_{SC2}$ Spec $[_{SC3}$ NP PP$_{dative}]$ $[_{Prt}$ *ver-/-ma*$]]$ V$_{\emptyset}]]$ V$]$

         $[_{VP}$ V $[_{SC1}$ Spec $[_{VP}$ V$_{\emptyset}$ $[_{SC2}$ Spec $[_{Prt}$ *-kan*$]$ $[_{SC3}$ NP PP$_{dative}]]]]]$

This structure naturally accommodates the triadic *ver-*, *-ma* and *-kan* constructions. If we can construct an argument in favour of an assimilation of the structure underlying causative constructions to that in (31), we will then also have found a structural slot for the affixal particles occurring in causatives. In particular, if we can model the analysis of causatives on that of triadic constructions, we can generate these affixes in the very same position in both constructions, thereby reaching our ultimate goal. The structure of transitive causative constructions will then read as in (32):

---

[12]   The fact that *sebab* is nominal rather than verbal is not problematic, Indonesian featuring non-verbal matrix predications quite freely (cf. *Itu sebabnya* '(lit.) that [is] cause-its').

[13]   Dutch and Sanuma are head-final languages, Indonesian is a VO language. Directionality plays no role in the discussions to follow, however; henceforth all structures will be of the VO type (also cf. Kayne 1993b on the universality of initial structures with Spec–Head–Complement order).

(32)

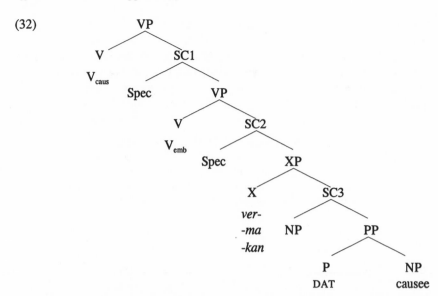

In the next section I shall advance two cross-linguistic generalisations about the relationship between triadic and (transitive) causative constructions which allow us to accomplish a structural assimilation of triadic and transitive causative constructions along the lines of (31)–(32). Before we move on, however, it is perhaps appropriate to insert a caveat to the reader. The structure in (32) will doubtless raise many an innocent eyebrow at first. On their own, the various pieces of evidence specific to causatives to be offered in the following sections would perhaps be insufficiently strong to warrant such a drastic departure from previous approaches to transitive causatives. But in the context of what I have argued in previous chapters with respect to the representation of particle and triadic constructions, and the observations made in the opening sections of the present chapter, the approach reflected in (32) receives substantial support. When we further bear in mind that such an analysis of transitive causative constructions makes a number of subtle empirical predictions (cf. section 5.3.7) which extant analyses on the whole do not, there is much to recommend giving an account along these lines a serious chance.

5.3 The structure of transitive causatives

5.3.1 Two correlations between triadic and causative constructions

It has often been noted that in a wide range of languages, there are clear parallels between triadic and transitive causative constructions. In the following subsections I shall present two important correlations concerning Case.

5.3.1.1 The Case of Goals and causees

There is a strong tendency for the Case borne by the embedded subject (the "causee") of a transitive causative construction to be identical with the Case of the Goal argument in a prepositional dative construction.[14] This is expressed very clearly in Aissen's (1974:29) statement that:

> [i]f a language derives its causative by PR [Predicate Raising; essentially verb incorporation], then if the language does not allow double accusative objects, the subject NP of an embedded transitive verb will appear in some case other than accusative. What case it appears in depends on the case system of the language, but it will be the same case as that assigned to "second" [i.e. indirect] objects.

This can be seen in Romance (cf. (33)), and also in Sanuma, as shown in (34):

(33) a. Jean offrira   des   bonbons *à ses enfants.*
          Jean will-give of-the candies   to his children
          'Jean will give candies to his children.'

      b. Jean fera   manger des   bonbons *à ses enfants.*
          Jean will-make eat   of-the candies   to his children
          'Jean will have his children eat candies.'

(34) a. ipa hao-nö   *hama te   niha* masulu kökö toto-ki   kite.
          my   father-AG visitor 3SG to   beads   3DL   give-FOC FUT
          'My father will give beads to the visitor.'

      b. kamisa-nö *setenapi   te   niha* manasi sa
          1SG-AG   non-Indian 3SG to   guan bird 1SG
          ta-ma-na-ni   ke.
          see-CAUS-EXT-FOC PAST
          'I made the non-Indian see the guan bird.'

GB-analyses of transitive causative constructions (in Romance as well as in polysynthetic languages) generally leave it a mystery why the Case form of the causee of such constructions is identical with that of a Goal in a triadic construction, as expressed in (35):

---

[14] I shall confine myself throughout to causative constructions instantiating Comrie's (1976) "paradigm case" causatives (cf. Marantz's 1984:section 7.2 cases involving Morphological Merger at logico-semantic structure). Not all languages employ causative constructions of this type. I refer to Marantz (1984) and Baker (1988) for extensive discussion of the differences between the various types of causative constructions (also cf. Hoffman 1991). Since I am primarily interested in the relationship between transitive causative and triadic constructions, I shall focus exclusively on "paradigm case" causatives.

(35)   *Cross-linguistic generalisation I*
         The Case form of the causee of a transitive causative construction
         is identical with the Case form of the Goal of a prepositional triadic
         construction.

Marantz (1984) and Baker (1988) both observe the complete regularity of this
correspondence between triadic and transitive causative constructions. Since
they treat the preposition preceding causees as an inserted Case-marker, while
they do not look upon the dative P in triadic constructions in this way, however,
the fact that this correlation exists is purely coincidental from an analytical point
of view.

In her account of Romance causative constructions, Reed (1989) analyses the
preposition preceding the causee as a dummy element, inserted solely for the
purposes of Case assignment. The correlation in (35) is then captured with the
aid of the assumption that the dummy preposition inserted in a particular context
should be thematically compatible with that context (also cf. Reed 1992a:171).
If, however, Case-marking prepositions do not play a thematic role (i.e. do not
have a θ-role of their own to assign), it is difficult to imagine how this
requirement of thematic compatibility can be formulated. A constraint on θ-role
matching is inapplicable: since the dummy preposition is thematically inert,
there is nothing to match the causee's θ-role with. It seems that a requirement
of thematic compatibility can be operative only if one inflates the lexical entry
of dummy Case-markers with a diacritic label specifying the thematic context(s)
with which the non-θ-assigning dummy is compatible. Clearly, this is an undesirable complication.

We might of course modify the account in such a way that, while the causee
continues to receive the external θ-role of the embedded verb, it simultaneously
receives an additional θ-role from the dative preposition, which is not looked
upon as a mere dummy Case-marker. This is Guasti's (1993:98) outlook on the
matter. In this way, the generalisation in (35) can be captured, but at the cost
of a weakening of the Theta Criterion. After all, a single referential expression
must be allowed to receive two θ-roles. And although recent research has
occasionally suggested that multiple θ-role assignment to a single argument
should be condoned under specific circumstances,[15] adhering to as strict a
correlation as possible between θ-roles and arguments is certainly to be
preferred.

[15] See for instance Baker's (1989b) "argument sharing" in serial verb constructions, and also
Carrier & Randall's (1992) analysis of resultatives. Both these proposals are seriously flawed,
however, as shown in Den Dikken (1991b) and section 3.13.2 above for the former, and Den Dikken & Hoekstra (1994) for the latter.

The relationship between Goals and causees of transitive causative constructions is further strengthened by the fact that they pattern together with
regard to binding phenomena. In chapter 4 (fn. 42) I noted that in Italian dative
constructions, an anaphor contained in the *a*-phrase cannot be bound by the
Theme NP to its left, while an anaphor in the direct object position *can* be
bound by the *a*-phrase contained Goal to its right:

(36) a.   *Ho mostrato Maria$_i$ a se stessa$_i$.
           I-have shown Maria to herself
      b.   Ho mostrato se stessa$_i$ a Maria$_i$.
           I-have shown herself to Maria

In this respect, too, transitive causative constructions pattern with dative
constructions. That is, the causee contained in the *a*-phrase can act as a binder
for a reflextive object of the causativised verb, as Burzio's (1986:264) example
in (37) shows:

(37)   Con le minacce fecero accusare se stesso$_i$ a Gianni$_i$.   (cf. (36b))
           with threats they-made accuse himself to Gianni
           'With threats they made Gianni accuse himself.'

Essentially the same point can be reiterated for French, where *à*-phrase contained Goals and causees of transitive causatives can bind (embedded) direct
objects to their right (cf. Pijnenburg 1991:52, 98; also cf. Kayne 1975):

(38) a.   Nixon a donné à Mailer$_i$ un livre à propos de lui-même$_i$.
           Nixon has given to Mailer a book concerning himself
      b.   J'ai fait corriger aux élèves$_i$ les devoirs l'un de l'autre$_i$.
           I-have made correct to-the pupils the homework of each other

A similar binding effect is found in varieties of German. Haider (1990) notes
that in various southern dialects of German, and also in older varieties of the
language (17th–19th centuries), transitive causative constructions with dative
causees are wide-spread. Some examples from dialects of Austrian and Bavarian
German are listed in (39):

(39) a.   Loß   des wai   de eabfi   schöin.   (Waldviertel)
      b.   Loß   dean woe   d'grumbbian schöln.   (Seewinkel)
      c.   Loß   dean weibl   d'eadebfl   schöön.   (Murtal)
      d.   Lou(s) dem wae   de eadöbfi   schöön.   (Bavarian)
           let   this woman(DAT) the potatoes peel

Haider (1990:180) points out that in such causative constructions, the dative causee cannot bind an anaphoric embedded object (cf. (40a), from Haider's dialect of Austrian German, Waldviertel). In this regard, the causee is on a par again with the dative Goal of German triadic constructions, which, as we saw in section 4.6, fails to bind an accusative anaphor (cf. (40b)):

(40) a. *Ea hod den leidn$_i$ si$_i$ an schnobs midbringa lossn.
          he has the people SELF schnaps with-bring let
      b. *Ich habe den Leuten$_i$ einander$_i$ vorgestellt.
          I have the people each-other introduced

What these binding facts from Romance and Germanic show is not only that the causee of transitive causative constructions (of the paradigm case) patterns with Goals of dative constructions, but also that the structural relationship between the causee of transitive causatives and the embedded direct object is identical with that between the Goal and Theme NPs of dative constructions. This sets the stage for a discussion of a second cross-linguistic generalisation about dative and transitive causative constructions.

5.3.1.2 The Case of (embedded) direct objects

Even if the generalisation in (35) could perhaps be captured with the aid of special machinery (*ad hoc* lexical diacritics on dative prepositions, or weakening of the Theta Criterion), the need for a structural assimilation of triadic and transitive causative constructions can no longer be denied, it seems, once a second generalisation covering these constructions is taken into consideration:

(41)   *Cross-linguistic generalisation II*
          The Case form of the embedded direct object of a transitive
          causative construction is identical with the Case form of the Theme
          of a prepositional triadic construction.

An inspection of the Chamorro (Austronesian) triadic and transitive causative examples in (42) and (43) is particularly instructive in this context (cf. Gibson 1980):[16]

(42)   In nä   si tata-n-mami *nu* i   babui.
          1PL.SUBJ-give   PN father-Ø-our OBL the pig
          'We provided our father *with* the pig.'

---

[16] The element glossed as "PN" in (42) is the "proper noun marker" of Chamorro.

(43)   Ha na'-taitai   häm i   ma'estru *ni*   esti na lebbiu.
          3SG.SUBJ-cause-read 1PL the   teacher   OBL this   book
          'The teacher made us read this book.'

The Chamorro example in (42) is commonly translated as an English double object construction. It is more appropriately paraphrased, however, as a *with* construction, as discussed in section 3.14. There I argued, blending insights of
Kayne (1984) and Larson (1990), that the *with* construction in the paradigm of
triadic constructions is derived via passivisation of the SC headed by the dative
preposition. Passivisation results in the absorption of (the phonetic matrix of)
this preposition (*pära* 'to' in Chamorro). Such an approach to (42) is strongly
supported by the fact, noted in section 3.14, that the Case form of the Theme
NP in this triadic example is the same as that of "chômeurs" in Chamorro
passive constructions (Gibson 1980):

(44)   Ma-dulalak si Jose *nu*   i   famagu'un.
          PASS-follow PN Jose OBL the   children
          'Jose was followed by the children.'

If this passivisation analysis of *with* constructions is correct, this has important
repercussions for the structure of transitive causative constructions. This is
shown in the next section, starting out from a comparison of (42) and the causative in (43), in which the embedded object is similarly realised in an oblique
phrase.

5.3.2 Structural assimilation

The oblique Case form of the Theme in the Chamorro triadic example in (42)
can be accounted for in terms of a passivisation approach to *with* constructions.
In Chamorro transitive causative constructions, the embedded object bears the
same oblique Case as the Theme NP in a *with*-construction. How do we accommodate this correlation between Chamorro triadic and transitive causative constructions?
    Notice first that the oblique Case form of the embedded object in (43) clearly
cannot be due to passivisation of the embedded, causativised VP. After all, it
is the embedded *object*, not the embedded *subject*, that is realised obliquely in
(43). Nor is an account of (43) in terms of antipassivisation of the embedded
verb very likely to yield the desired result. Though Chamorro certainly features
antipassivisation (a detransitivisation transformation whereby the object of a
transitive verb is "shunted" into an oblique phrase), the causativised verb in
(43) does not bear the Chamorro antipassive morpheme, *man* in (45):

(45) Man-**man**-bisita i   famagu'un gi as Juan.
      PL-APASS-visit the children OBL Juan
      'The children visited Juan.'

If, then, the oblique Case form of the embedded object in (33) can have resulted neither from passivisation nor from antipassivisation of the embedded verb, and if, as seems likely, the oblique realisation of the embedded object is the result of a detransitivisation operation of sorts (this oblique Case being a typical mark of "chômeurs" in Chamorro), the conclusion ensues that detransitivisation of some *non-verbal* head must have obtained in the derivation of the Chamorro causative in (43). The only candidate available to us seems to be the dative preposition. I would like to argue, then, that in both (42) and (43), the obliquely marked NP is base-generated in the subject position of a dative SC which is detransitivised:

(46) The obliquely marked NP in Chamorro (42)–(43) originates as the subject of a dative SC which undergoes detransitivisation.

Notice that this line of reasoning is virtually compelling. If the basic premises on which the analysis is built hold water (and all were independently motivated earlier in this study), and if the Case identity between the oblique NPs in (42) and (43) is interpreted as not being merely coincidental, the conclusion must be that the embedded object in (43) is the subject of a dative SC at D-structure. The analysis simply forces this conclusion upon us.

That this is in fact a desirable result becomes apparent when we bear in mind that, while I have mostly concentrated on cross-linguistic generalisation II in (41), the analysis of transitive causatives should also capture cross-linguistic generalisation I (35). Notice now that with the analysis of Chamorro (43) just presented, we can immediately accommodate (35) as well. Given that the embedded object of a transitive causative construction originates as the subject of a dative SC, the embedded subject ("causee") will now be base-generated as the object of the dative preposition, just like the Goal in a triadic construction. Thus, the generalisation in (35) is accounted for as well.

5.3.3 The structure

In the previous subsection we established the core part of the desired structural assimilation of triadic and transitive causative constructions, by arguing that the D-structure representation of the latter contains a dative SC just like that of triadic constructions. In chapter 3 I argued that triadic constructions, apart from this core structure, also contain a projection of a (lexical or empty) particle, and an additional verbal projection apart from that of the matrix triadic verb. In particular, I argued that the structure of triadic constructions reads as in (47):

(47)   [$_{VP}$ Vtriadic [$_{SC1}$ Spec [$_{VP}$ V$_{\emptyset}$ [$_{SC2}$ Spec [$_{XP}$ X [$_{SC3}$ Theme [$_{PP}$ P Goal]]]]]]]]

If we are to accomplish a full structural assimilation of triadic and transitive causative constructions, we should hence subject the latter to a basic structure of the type in (48):

(48)   [$_{VP}$ Vcaus [$_{SC1}$ Spec [$_{VP}$ V [$_{SC2}$ Spec [$_{XP}$ X [$_{SC3}$ embedded object [$_{PP}$ P causee]]]]]]]]

In the remainder of this subsection I shall consider the candidates for the various head positions in this structure above the dative preposition. The Sanuma examples in (34), repeated here, may serve as a convenient guide.

(34) a.   ipa   hao-nö   *hama*   *te*   *niha* masulu kökö   toto-ki   kite.
           my   father-AG visitor   3SG   to   beads   3DL   give-FOC   FUT
           'My father will give beads to the visitor.'

     b.   kamisa-nö *setenapi*   *te*   *niha* manasi   sa
           1SG-AG   non-Indian   3SG   to   guan bird 1SG
           ta-ma-na-ni   ke.
           see-CAUS-EXT-FOC PAST
           'I made the non-Indian see the guan bird.'

In section 5.2, I argued that all instantiations of Sanuma *-ma* (along with those of Dutch *ver-* and Indonesian *-kan*) should be treated as affixal particles. In the structure of triadic constructions we found an immediate structural slot for this affix as it occurs in the example in (34a) — the "X" node in (47). The same affixal particle shows up in the transitive causative construction in (34b). This affix, then, is the obvious candidate for the "X" slot in the structure of transitive causatives in (48). In this way we achieve a fully uniform structural treatment of all tokens of Sanuma *-ma* (and, by extrapolation, the other affixes discussed in 5.2 as well).

The SC projected by "X" in (47) and (48) is dominated by another SC, whose verbal head in triadic constructions was argued to be an empty instance of the copula *be*. The postulation of this abstract verbal head was supported in chapter 3 on the basis of evidence of theoretical as well as empirical nature. Yet it might nonetheless be felt that postulating a piece of structure which apparently never surfaces overtly — robustly motivated though it may be — is somewhat of a drawback of the analysis. By taking transitive causatives into account, however, even this potential ground for scepticism can be eliminated, for precisely in these constructions, the intermediate V-position in the structure in (48) does receive a phonetic matrix — it is the base position of the causativised verb. Sanuma *ta* 'see' in (34b), then, originates as the head of the verbal SC embedded under the matrix causative verb, which, in Sanuma, happens to be non-overt. In the French example in (33b), both the lower and the higher V-positions are phonetically realised, by the causativised verb *manger* 'eat' and the matrix causative verb *faire* 'make', respectively.

Now that we have found suitable candidates for all head positions in the structure underlying transitive causative constructions in (48), let me close this section by illustrating this D-structure on the basis of the French and Sanuma examples in (33b) and (34b).[17] The tree in (49), overleaf, is the structure that cross-linguistically underlies all *transitive* causative constructions of Comrie's (1976) "paradigm case" (cf. fn. 14, above).[18]

In the remainder of this chapter, I shall first of all address a number of further issues connected to the structure of transitive causative constructions (sections 5.3.4–5.3.6). I then go on to present two case studies of French causative constructions including a SC or an infinitival CP embedded under the causativised verb (section 5.3.7). The structure of transitive causative constructions developed here will be seen to accommodate the intricate properties of such constructions in an interesting fashion. The chapter is closed by a brief appraisal of some alternative attempts at assimilating the structures of triadic and transitive causative constructions.

---

[17]   As before, I abstract away from irrelevant directionality parameters.

[18]   No necessary claims are made with respect to non-"paradigm case" transitive causatives, such as the ECM causatives of Germanic, which were frequent throughout the history of Romance (cf. Morin & St-Amour 1977; Pearce 1990) and continue to be found in various dialects of French and in literary varieties of the language as well (cf. Poplack 1989; Authier & Reed 1991; Reed 1992a; and references cited there).

(i)   a.   C'était Charlebois qui *faisait leurs élèves signer un contrat*.   (Poplack 1989)
              'It was Charlebois who made their students sign a contract.'
       b.   Rien de plus difficile que de *faire le public revenir* d'un premier jugement hâtif.
              'There's nothing more difficult than making the public go back on their first premature judgement.'   (Gide)

I refer the reader to Abeillé, Godard & Miller (1994) for an HPSG-based "control-*faire*" analysis of *faire* causatives with an accusative clitic causee like *Pierre l'a fait ne pas l'oublier* 'Pierre made him not forget it', and for an inventory of syntactic differences between such transitive causatives and "regular" ones with a dative causee. I also note in this context Mejías-Bikandi & Moore's (1994) demonstration of the fact that, alongside French type *faire à* causatives, Spanish also features transitive causatives which seem more like ECM constructions (and in which the causee may — but need not — surface between the matrix and causativised verbs).

An ECM approach to causatives of the sort mentioned above is *a priori* not implausible, and may be correct for some cases; for others, though, an analysis along the lines of (49) and involving Dative Shift of the PP harbouring the causee (cf. chapter 3 on Dative Shift) may be more adequate (cf. especially — in the light of the discussion in chapter 4 — the resistance of English and Dutch apparent ECM causatives to passivisation on the causee: *John was made sing a song* and *Jan werd een liedje laten zingen*; also cf. the facts discussed in fn. 36, below). I leave the details of an analysis of these constructions as an issue for future research.

(49)

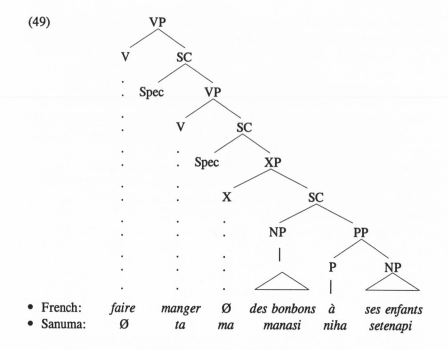

- French: *faire*   *manger*   Ø   *des bonbons*   *à*   *ses enfants*
- Sanuma: Ø   *ta*   *ma*   *manasi*   *niha* *setenapi*

5.3.4 Decomposition of triadic verbs

Before proceeding to further details of the analysis of transitive causative constructions, I slip in here a brief note on the possibility of decomposing triadic verbs into an abstract causative matrix verb and an embedded verb like *have*, as in the Generative Semantics framework.

While in the analysis of triadic constructions I have consistently represented triadic verbs as syntactic and lexical atoms (as I shall continue to do throughout this study), an analysis of causative constructions of the type just presented opens up the possibility that triadic verbs are not in fact atomic, but suppletive spell-outs of the complex head resulting from the incorporation of abstract BE (+TO) into abstract CAUSE.

Since the present analysis could only decompose triadic verbs into CAUSE TO BE(+TO), it would not be subject to a possible objection to decomposing triadic verbs into CAUSE TO HAVE, coming from the domain of double object particle constructions: the inability of *have* to take SC complements headed by a verbal particle (cf. (50b)) renders such a CAUSE TO HAVE approach to the verbs in (50a) dubious.

(50)   a.   They dealt/handed/sent the people *out* lottery tickets.
        b.   *The people have (*out*) lottery tickets (*out*).

Approaches to triadic constructions according to which the matrix verb embeds a verbal SC headed by *have* (cf. Mulder 1992a) might seek to circumvent this problem by adopting a constraint to the effect that non-predicative particles (like *out* in (50)) must be governed by a *telic* verb (Mulder 1992a). Since *have* is not a telic verb, it cannot embed verbal particles (as opposed to *"predicative"* particles, which are not subject to the above constraint: *John has his books back* is perfect; on "predicative" particles, cf. Oehrle 1976 and section 3.15.2, above). Notice, however, that the copula *be* is like *have* in not being telic, yet differs from *have* in being eminently capable of embedding non-predicative particles, which casts doubt on the validity of the telicity condition.

The present approach to triadic constructions assumes — crucially — that the verb heading the matrix verb's SC complement is the copula, and hence does not encounter any problems in connection with (50).

5.3.5 Causatives, possession and affectedness

The analysis of transitive causative constructions presented in (49) is congenial to — though different in fine detail from — a proposal made in Pijnenburg (1991). Pijnenburg, too, assumes that the causativised verb takes a dative SC complement. The difference is that Pijnenburg looks upon the dative phrase not as the predicate of the SC, but rather as its subject. In the light of what was argued with regard to dative PPs earlier in this study, it is clear that the present analysis is to be preferred on general grounds.[19]

In support of assigning French transitive causatives an analysis according to which the embedded object forms a SC together with the dative phrase containing the causee, Pijnenburg notes that the dative causee has all the properties of a dative phrase in triadic constructions. Most interestingly, the same possessive meaning implication holding between the Goal and the Theme in a triadic construction recurs in transitive causative constructions. The following example, from Cannings & Moody (1978:343), illustrates this for causatives:

(51)   Elle a fait obtenir le tableau à Jean-Jacques (puisque ça faisait si longtemps qu'il avait consacré une place sur son mur).
         'She made Jean-Jacques obtain the painting (because he had dedicated a spot on his wall for it for such a long time).'

The *faire à* causative in (51) implies that the painting ends up in Jean-Jacques' possession, just like a triadic construction with *donner* 'give':

---

[19] Though the causee of transitive causatives is not a D-structure subject, it may well be a *derived* subject in some cases (as a result of the application of Dative Shift); cf. the Italian binding facts discussed in 5.3.1.1 against the background of what was suggested in chapter 4, fn. 42.

(52)   Elle a donné le tableau à Jean-Jacques.
            'She gave Jean-Jacques the painting.'

The fact that the semantic relationship between the causee and the embedded
object of transitive causative constructions is the same as that between the Goal
and Theme NPs in dative constructions is a further indication that their structures should be highly similar, a requirement that the present analysis meets.

Another interpretive fact about "paradigm case" transitive causative constructions that the present analysis accommodates directly is Alsina's (1992)
observation (also cf. Ackerman 1994) that in such constructions in Chichewa,
the embedded object is the *affected argument* of the sentence, as shown in (53b)
(where, as in (53a), the affected argument is italicised); in corresponding causative constructions with an objectively Case-marked causee, such as (53a), it is
the causee that qualifies as the affected argument.

(53) a.   Núngu   i-na-phík-íts-a   *kadzidzi*   maûngu.   (Chichewa)
            porcupine S-PS-cook-CAUS-FV   owl-OBJ   pumpkins-OBJ
            'The porcupine made the owl cook the pumpkins.'
     b.   Núngu   i-na-phík-íts-a   *maûngu*   kwá kádzidzi.
            porcupine S-PS-cook-CAUS-FV   pumpkins-OBJ to   owl-OBL
            'The porcupine had the pumpkins cooked by the owl.'

Recall from the discussion on the structural representation of affectedness in
sections 2.4.4.1 and 3.12.2 that affected arguments are S-structure subjects of
small clauses. Given this characterisation of affectedness, the fact that *maûngu*
'pumpkins' in (53b) is [+affected] falls out naturally from the analysis of
"paradigm case" transitive causative constructions with a dative (oblique)
causee given in (32) — the embedded object is a SC-subject on this analysis.
On other approaches to transitive causatives of the "paradigm case", (53b)
would be much less readily compatible — if at all — with the well-motivated
structural account of affectedness offered earlier in this study.[20]

With what was argued in the previous paragraph in mind, we may now also
understand the contrast in (54):

---

[20] Guasti (1993:95) notes that Italian (ia,b) are semantically on a par in that in both the *a*-phrase
contained NP is affected by the caused event. This at once shows that, as expected on the present
analysis, transitive *fare* causatives and triadic *fare* constructions behave completely identically (on
this parallelism, also cf. Herschensohn 1981 for French *faire*), and that the Italian *a*-phrase in
triadic and causative constructions in all likelihood undergoes Dative Shift into the affected argument position (also cf. chapter 4, fn. 42, and examples (36)–(37), above).

(i) a.   Il generale ha fatto pulire le toilette *alla recluta*.
            the general has made clean the toilets to-the recruit
     b.   I ragazzi hanno fatto uno scherzo *al professore*, per divertirsi.
            the boys have made a prank to the professor to amuse-themselves

(54) a. iemand zijn *tanden laten zien*.
        someone his teeth let see

   b. *aan iemand zijn *tanden laten zien*.   (on idiomatic reading)

While (54a) is fine on the idiomatic reading 'to bare/show one's teeth to some-one', in which both verbs and the embedded object are idiomatically fixed, such idiomatic fixing is impossible in (54b), which has the causee contained in a dative PP headed by *aan* 'to'.[21] The non-idiomaticity of (54b) can now be accounted for straightforwardly, given what I argued in section 2.4.4.1 and 3.12.2 about idioms and affectedness. Idioms resist occupying affected argu-ment positions. But as we saw above, the embedded object in a transitive caus-ative with a PP-contained causee occupies precisely this position. It then follows — as required — that idiomatically fixing the embedded object in a "paradigm case" causative construction is impossible.

In the domain of the semantic properties of possession and affectedness, then, the present approach to transitive causative constructions makes precisely the correct predictions.

5.3.6 Ergativisation

On the analysis of transitive causatives advanced here (as on Pijnenburg's 1991), the embedded verb undergoes *ergativisation* — it "loses" its external θ-role and takes a SC complement. As Pijnenburg (1991:123) points out, there is a potential parallel here between causatives and, for instance, French impersonal constructions such as (55), in which the verb *dormir* 'sleep' is likewise "ergativised" (cf. Hulk 1989; Hoekstra & Mulder 1990):

(55)   Il dort un chat au coin de la cheminée.
        it sleeps a cat at-the corner of the mantelpiece

Pijnenburg (1991:124), who confines his attention to French causatives, seeks to relate the "ergativisation" effect to the independently established fact (cf. Den Dikken 1990b; also cf. Guasti 1991, 1993 for Italian) that verb incorpor-ation, or complex predicate formation, takes place in the syntax of French causative constructions. Specifically, he proposes that 'in French causatives, complex predicate formation is the condition allowing for the "external" argu-ment to be mapped onto the small clause dative position' (1991:124). The nature of this connection between complex predicate formation and "ergativis-ation" remains unclear, however. Perhaps a more promising scenario would

---

[21] In Dutch the distribution of transitive causatives with *aan*-marked causees is severely restricted, being found only with perception verbs or *lezen* 'read' embedded under the causative verb. On a literal reading of (54b), this example is fine.

consist in relating the VP-internal projection of the causee to the fact that the embedded subject's *control* over the embedded predicate, although certainly not absent,[22] diminishes in comparison to the subject's control over the same predicate in a non-causativised, root context. The causee is not so much a "volitional agent" as is a matrix subject of an agentive predicate. If "volitional agentivity" is crucially tied up with VP-external realisation (in the case of agentive predicates), the "ergativising" effect of causativisation tallies with the representation of subject-predicate relationships.

In closing this section, let us once again pay a brief visit to Dutch idiom facts. It is interesting to note in connection with "ergativisation" in causative constructions that in complex causative idioms with the verb *laten* (discussed in Coopmans & Everaert 1988) it is often possible for the subject of what would in non-causative contexts be an unergative verb to be idiomatically fixed:

(56) a.   Zij heeft haar *oren laten hangen*.
           she has her ears let hang
           'She listened.'
      b.   Hij heeft *het hoofd laten hangen*.
           he has the head let hang
           'He lost courage.'
      c.   Hij *liet* de *handen wapperen*.
           he let the hands flutter
           'He put his back into it.'

That the base verbs in these examples are unergative in non-causative contexts is evident, among other things, from the fact that their past participles cannot be used attributively in nominals (cf. **het gehangen oor/hoofd* 'the hung ear/ head' or **de gewapperde handen* 'the fluttered hands'), in contrast to past participles of unaccusative verbs such as *vallen* (cf. Hoekstra 1984).

If the tokens of the verbs *hangen* and *wapperen* used in (56) were unergative, however, it would be quite surprising — from the point of view of both the "traditional" thematic approach to idiom formation and the aspectual account presented in sections 2.4.4.1 and 3.12.2 — that the arguments of these verbs can be idiomatically fixed. If, by contrast, these verbs shift to *ergativity* in causative contexts, this follows. The verbs' arguments originate in VP-*internal* position. Since the embedded verbs incorporate into the matrix verb, the

---

[22] In fact, *within* the class of causative constructions, it seems that in French dialects that allow for alternations between dative and accusative (clitic) causees (cf. Authier & Reed 1991; Reed 1992b for recent discussion), it is the dative rather than the accusative that is used if the embedded subject is capable of exerting control over the embedded predicate (i.e. causatives with accusative causees involve "direct causation" while those with dative causees denote "indirect causation"). *All* causees, though, regardless of whether they are marked accusative or dative, presumably exert a smaller degree of control over the event than root subjects.

Government Transparency Corollary ensures that the italicised NPs in (56) receive Case *in situ*, so that at no point in the derivation will they find themselves in the specifier position of a SC in the complement of a verb denoting (change of) state or location — the "affected argument" position from which idiom chunks are barred (cf. 2.4.4.1/3.12.2). The italicised NPs originate and stay in the complement position of the embedded verb, a position which is perfectly legitimate for idiom chunks to appear in. Complex causative idioms of the type in (56) hence support the view that causativised verbs *ergativise*.

5.3.7 Embedding under the causativised verb

In the examples discussed so far, the causativised verb simply takes a single nominal "complement" (or, more adequately in the light of the analysis presented here, a SC with an NP subject). Clearly, though, causativised verbs do not invariably take such simple complements. In this section I consider two constructions which show that the subject of the dative PP accommodating the causee may sometimes be *propositional*.

5.3.7.1 The priority effect in French causatives

Consider what happens when we try to causativise French triadic or transitive resultative constructions of the type in (57) and (58):

(57)   Jean porte ce message à Pierre.
         Jean carries this message to Pierre

(58)   Les étudiants jettent des poubelles sur les passants.
         the students throw of-the dustbins on the passers-by

As Ruwet (1972:225) notes, embedding (57) under *faire* (and not cliticising or otherwise extracting the causee) generally yields a deviant result, even though the example in (59a) is slightly less bad than (59b):

(59)   a.   ??Je ferai porter ce message à Pierre$_{Goal}$ à Jean$_{causee}$.
            I will-make carry the message to Pierre to Jean
       b.   *Je ferai porter ce message à Jean$_{causee}$ à Pierre$_{Goal}$.

The same essentially applies to the examples in (58):

(60)   a.   ?Il a fait jeter des poubelles sur les passants aux étudiants.
            he has made throw of-the dustbins on the passers-by to-the students.
       b.   *Il a fait jeter des poubelles aux étudiants sur les passants.

Though Kayne (1975:265) assigns (60b) a mere ?, Pijnenburg (1991:136) gives it a full asterisk, and notes that the alternative word order in (60a) is somewhat better.[23] [24]

There are two interesting things to note about the causative constructions in (59) and (60). First, they become grammatical if the dative phrase harbouring the causee is extracted, by cliticisation or *wh*-extraction:

---

[23] Baker (1988:193) notes that in Chichewa, (60a) type causative constructions are ill-formed:

(i)　　　　　　*Amayi   a-na-ik-its-a　　　　　mtsuko　pa mpando kwa ana.
　　　　　　　　women SP-PAST-put-CAUS-ASP waterpot on chair   to children
　　　　　　　　'The women made the children put the waterpot on the chair.'

[24] The Romance facts here are rather subtle. Abeillé, Godard & Miller (1994) present a French example of the type in (60) which, on their judgement, freely allows both word orders (cf. (i)); Williams (1994:109) gives an example pair with a preference opposite to the one noted by Pijnenburg (cf. (ii)). And examples of the type in (60b) are fully acceptable in Italian.

(i)　　a.　　Marie fera disposer les livres sur la table aux enfants.　　(Abeillé *et al.* 1994)
　　　　　　Marie will-make set the books on the table to the children
　　　　b.　　Marie fera disposer les livres aux enfants sur la table.

(ii)　　a.　　Jean l'a fait retirer de la table à Pierre.　　(Williams 1994:109)
　　　　　　Jean it-has made remove from the table to Pierre
　　　　b.　　??Jean l'a fait retirer à Pierre de la table.

I shall briefly comment on (ii) and the fact that in Italian the word order in the b-sentences is grammatical, in the light of the analysis to be offered later in this section. (The interested reader may wish to return to this footnote after reading through the rest of 5.3.7.1; the reader not interested in fine details of this sort can skip the remainder of this footnote.)

The thing to note about (ii) is that it features a *cliticised* embedded object. On the assumption that a clitic (which is a head; Kayne 1991a), in contradistinction to an NP-object, is not subject to the demands of the Case Filter (cf. Baker 1988 on incorporated nouns and morphological licensing), the cause of the deviance of the a-examples in (59) and (60) will be absent in (iia). (iib) is ruled out on the same grounds as (59b) and (60b) are; cf. the main text.

The grammaticality of the b-examples in Italian has a different cause. Recall from chapter 4, fn. 42 that there is reason to believe that in Italian triadic constructions, Dative Shift of the *a*-PP obligatorily takes place. In (37), above, I presented evidence to suggest that in transitive causative constructions, too, the *a*-PP undergoes (rightward) Dative Shift. I argue further below that movement of the predicate of SC3 in (65) (i.e. the dative phrase) lifts the barrierhood of SC4, and thus renders rightward movement of the predicate of SC4 (which presumably obtains in the derivation of the b-sentences) possible. Abeillé *et al.*'s judgement of (i) may then be understood if it is assumed that some varieties of French have the Dative Shift properties of Italian. I must leave further questions open. (Note that the French facts in (38) involve "physically" shifted (leftward moved) dative PPs; the examples in (i) in any event do not. Although perhaps suggestive, examples like (38) do not unequivocally show that French has Dative Shift — the fact that the bound elements in (38) are NP-contained, combined with the fact that we know independently that NP-contained anaphors are freer in their distribution that non-NP-contained ones, takes away much of the proving power of examples of this sort.)

(61) a. Je *lui*_{causee} ferai porter ce message à Pierre_{Goal}.
          I to-him(CL) will-make carry this message to Pierre

      b. A *qui*_{causee} feras-tu porter ce message à Pierre_{Goal}?
          to whom will-make-you carry this message to Pierre

(62) a. Il *leur* a fait jeter des poubelles sur les passants.
          he to-them(CL) has made throw of-the dustbins on the passers-by

      b. A *qui* a-t-il fait jeter des poubelles sur les passants?
          to whom has-he made throw of-the dustbins on the passers-by

Secondly, the dative phrase harbouring the Goal in (59) and the directional PP in (60) are extractable only if the causee is moved (via cliticisation) as well. This is what Hulk (1984) has dubbed the *priority effect* (also cf. Aoun 1985: 124–25; Burzio 1986:225–27):

(63)   A *qui*_{Goal} *lui*_{causee} feras-tu porter ce message?
          to whom to-him(CL) will-make-you carry this message

The analysis of causative constructions presented in this chapter provides an account of this constellation of facts. Let us start off by considering the D-structure representation of the examples in (59) and (60) on the present assumptions:

(64)   [_{VP} V_{caus} [_{SC1} [_{VP} V_{emb} [_{SC2} [_{XP} X [_{SC3} [_{SC4} NP PP] [_{PP} P NP_{causee}]]]]]]]

(65)

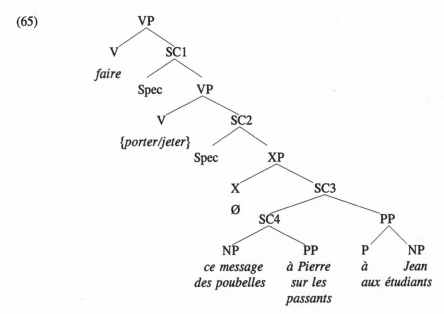

In this structure, the predicate of SC3 (accommodating the causee) takes a *SC subject*, labelled SC4. The predicate of this SC is the secondary predicate embedded in the causativised VP (*à Pierre, sur les passants*).[25]

Notice that this structure (as far as the structure internal to SC3 is concerned) mirrors the analysis that Kayne (1985) assigned to complex particle constructions of the *make out a liar* type, and recall from the discussion of Kayne's proposal in chapter 2 that, even though grammatical at D-structure, SC subjects should somehow be eliminated at S-structure (in order to enable the subject of this SC to receive Case, as Kayne argues). Since in the examples in (59a) and (60a) nothing is done to the D-structure organisation of SC3, these examples are ruled out, as required.[26]

Next consider the b-examples in (59) and (60). These could be derived by extraposing the predicate of the subject-SC. Notice, however, that movement of this PP is subject to a "priority effect" — it is possible only if the predicate of SC3 undergoes movement as well (cf. (63)). The deviance of (59b) and (60b) can be made to fall out from Kayne's (1984) Connectedness Condition. After all, SC4 in the structures above is a left branch constituent. Extraction from it will hence per force violate the prohibition on extraction from a left branch.[27] Hence, (59b) and (60b) are ill-formed.

Why, however, are the examples in (61)–(63) grammatical? The crucial thing to note here is that as soon as the predicate of SC3 is removed from its D-structure position, all that remains of SC3 is its small clausal subject. We may hypothesise that, as a result of the extraction of SC3's predicate, its subject forfeits its configurational subject properties. In general, one finds that, once the predicate is extracted, a SC-subject loses its subject properties. This can be illustrated with the aid of the following piece of independent evidence. Koster (1978a) has observed that full clauses resist occupying subject positions. This is evident, for instance, from the ill-formedness of (66a), in which the finite CP *that we leave* finds itself in the S-structure subject position of the SC projected by *to*. One way of rescuing (66a) is to extract the PP predicate of the SC as a whole (cf. (66b), taken from Kuno 1973:382):

---

[25] A paraphrase of this structure as applied to (60) could read as follows: 'the state of affairs "dustbins on the passers-by" is attributed to the students, and is the result of a throwing event which is brought about by some external causer'.

[26] Why these examples apparently do not deserve a full star is not clear; also cf. fn. 23.

[27] Notice that Kayne (1985) crucially makes use of short rightward movement of the predicate of the subject-SC in his structure of complex particle constructions. As I pointed out in chapter 2, he reconciles this apparent violation of Connectedness by having this predicate adjoin to the "outer" SC. This, however, is incompatible with Chomsky's (1986:6) ban on adjunction to argumental categories. The theory hence rules out movement of the predicate of a subject-SC — correctly, as the French examples suggest. There is one way of avoiding a Connectedness (or ECP) violation, however, as I shall discuss presently.

(66) a.   *I suggested [$_{SC}$ [$_{CP}$ that we leave] [$_{PP}$ to Alex]].
      b.   [$_{PP}$ To Alex]$_i$, I suggested [$_{SC}$ [$_{CP}$ that we leave] t_i].
      c.   *Alex$_i$, I suggested [$_{SC}$ [$_{CP}$ that we leave] [$_{PP}$ to t_i]].

Extracting the SC predicate hence "lifts" CP's subject status; extracting only the complement of *to* leaves the subjecthood of CP intact, as (66c) illustrates.[28]

Returning now to the priority effect found in French causative constructions, we can say that as a result of movement of the dative PP harbouring the causee, the propositional subject of its SC no longer counts as a left branch. It is hence to be expected that SC4's subject can now be reached by an external Case-assigner, and that extraction of the predicate of SC4 is no longer prohibited by the left branch condition, since SC4 is no longer a left branch. In this way, the analysis captures both the well-formedness of (61) and (62), and the "priority effect" illustrated in (63).[29]

5.3.7.2 Causativised verbs with sentential complements

Apart from SC-selecting verbs, we also expect it to be possible to find verbs taking sentential complements embedded in causative constructions. In this sub-section, I shall focus on one such case.

---

[28] Another way of rescuing (66a) is to extrapose CP (cf. *I suggested to Alex that we leave*). That CP does not extrapose in (66b) is evident from the fact that extraposition normally yields a "freezing" effect (cf. Kuno's 1973:382 **Alex, I suggested to that we leave*: extraction from within VP is blocked as a result of CP-extraposition), which is absent in (66b) (witness the grammaticality of PP-extraction).

[29] Note that the analysis correctly predicts the contrast in (i) (see Aoun 1985) — in (ib) *y* originates as the predicate of SC4 in (65), so that (ib) violates the left branch condition; but *y* in (ia) is an adjunct to the causativised VP, moving up into the matrix causative clause without any problems.

(i) a.   Marie *y* a laissé lire ces romans à Paul.
          Marie there-let read those novels to Paul
     b.   *Marie *y* fera mettre ce livre à Pierre.
          Marie there-will make put that book to Pierre

Pijnenburg's (1991:135) account of the "priority effect", which differs from mine in basing itself on a structure in which the dative phrase harbouring the causee is not a SC predicate but a SC subject (cf. (ii)), does not go through. He assumes that (ii) is a multi-segment structure, of which the lower segment (SC2) is a barrier to outside government by the verb. If, however, V L-marks SC1, as Pijnenburg assumes, SC2 will also be L-marked, given that L-marking percolates from a maximal projection to all of its submaximal projections (cf. Chomsky 1986; Lasnik & Saito 1992). The structure in (ii) is also undesirable conceptually since it must assume that an apparently completely saturated constituent such as SC2 can nonetheless be predicated of a subject (the dative PP).

(ii)   [$_{SC1}$ [$_{PP}$ *à* causee] [$_{SC2}$ NP PP]]

Consider the example in (67), featuring the modal verb *vouloir* 'want' embedded under causative *faire*.[30] The first thing to note about this example is
that, given the analysis of transitive causative constructions proposed here, the
infinitival "complement" of *vouloir* in (67) should occupy the subject position
of the dative SC harbouring the causee, as illustrated in (68).

(67)   Ce compte-rendu a fait vouloir lire ce livre à Jean.
            this review has made want read this book to Jean
            'This review made Jean want to read this book.'

(68)   a.   [vp *faire* [sc1 [vp *vouloir* [sc2 [xp X [sc3 [cp *lire ce livre*] [pp *à Jean*]]]]]]]
       b.

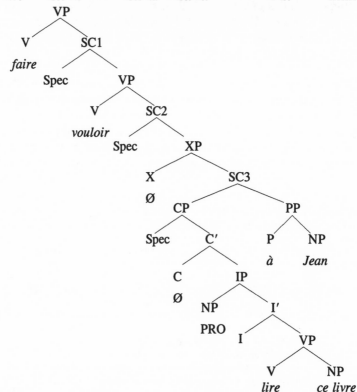

---

[30] Though odd with *volere* 'want', constructions of the type in (67) are also found in Italian, for
instance with the verb *potere* 'be able to' (cf. (i); Maria Teresa Guasti, p.c.). In some of the foot-
notes to this subsection, I shall briefly comment on the properties of this Italian construction, which
can be seen to fall out from the analysis as well.

(i)   Ciò ha fatto poter risolvere il problema a Gianni.
            this has made be-able-to solve the problem to Gianni
            'This has made Gianni be able to solve the problem.'

Is this structure just an artifact of the analysis of causatives, or do we find infinitival subjects of dative SCs in other contexts as well?

Recall from section 3.8 that the expression of possession may vary cross-linguistically. Some languages employ a possessive verb like *have* for this purpose, others express possession in terms of a copula construction featuring a dative preposition. Russian is a representative of this latter group. In Russian, the use of copula constructions containing a dative phrase is not restricted to possessive relations between two NPs. The modal construction in (69) (cf. Schoorlemmer 1991:13) instantiates a *be+to* construction with an infinitival subject of the dative PP:

(69) *Emu* *bylo* kolot' drova.
　　　he-DAT was chop(INFIN) wood
　　　'It was his job/he was able to chop wood.'

This example can be structurally represented as in (70), a structure which corresponds with that of the French causative construction in (68) (*modulo* the presence/absence of a matrix causative predicate).

(70) $[_{VP}$ *bylo* $[_{SC1}$ $[_{XP}$ X $[_{SC2}$ $[_{CP}$ *kolot' drova*] $[_{PP}$ *emu*]]]]]

Though considerably less frequently, constructions of the type in (69) also occur in a language like English. In section 3.8 I pointed out that English occasionally features a *be+to/have* alternation:

(71) a.　The choice *is* up *to* you.
　　 b.　You *have* the choice.

A similar alternation is found in modal constructions resembling Russian (69), as the examples in (72) bear out:[31]

---

[31]　Notice that in the examples in (71a) and (72a), the X^0 position is actually lexically realised by the particle *up*. This supports the view that *be+to* possessive constructions feature a projection of Prt, just like *give* type triadic constructions.

In the corresponding b-examples, however, the particle is obligatorily absent (cf. **You have (up) the choice (up)* and **You have up to do it*): A possible explanation lies in the observation that V–Prt reanalysis is obligatory in the b-examples (for otherwise the trace of the moved PP would fail to be lexically governed; cf. chapter 2). V–Prt reanalysis is an instance of head incorporation. The particle hence oblitagorily becomes part of the complex verb in (71b) and (72b) (but not in the corresponding a-examples), and will "disappear" when this complex head is suppletively lexicalised as *have*. If this suggestion holds water, the obligatory absence of Prt from (71b)/(72b) can be taken to lend further support to the hypothesis that *have* is the suppletive lexicalisation of a copula with an incorporated dative preposition.

(72) a. It *is* up *to* you [to do it].
     b. You *have* [to do it].

What the modal constructions in (69) and (72) show is that dative PPs in non-causative contexts can take propositional external arguments. Nothing now prevents us from adopting an analysis of the French causative construction in (67) as in (68), to which the overall approach to causatives naturally gives rise.

An analysis of (67) along the lines of (68) also gives us a handle on some interesting cliticisation data first noted in Postal (1981:293, fn. 15). Postal notes that while normally, in contemporary standard French, it is impossible to have a clitic object of a verb in the complement of *vouloir* type verbs climb up to the higher verb (cf. (73)), such "long-distance" clitic movement *is* possible if the VP headed by *vouloir* is embedded under causative *faire*, as (74) shows.[32]

(73)   Jean (*le*) veut (*le*) lire.
          Jean it(CL) wants it(CL) read
          'Jean wants to read it.'

(74) a. [?]Ce compte-rendu *l'*a fait vouloir lire à Jean.
          this review it(CL) has made want read to Jean
     b. Ce compte-rendu *le* lui a fait vouloir lire.
          this review it(CL) to-him(CL) has made want read

In accounting for these surprising clitic placement facts on the basis of the D-structure in (68), let us first of all assume, with Kayne (1991a), that clitics are heads undergoing head movement to an adjunction position to an inflectional head. Given these assumptions, the mobility of clitics is expected to be constrained both by the Head Movement Constraint (ECP) and by the presence of a suitable landing-site (i.e. Infl).

Against this background, consider first the standard clitic placement data in French modal constructions presented in (73). French modals select sentential complements, probably CPs (cf. Kayne 1991a for discussion). Internal to the complement of *vouloir*, then, there is a landing-site for the clitic object of the embedded verb. This accommodates the grammatical variant of (73). Clitic climbing out of the embedded CP is impossible, CP inheriting barrierhood from IP, which is a Blocking Category.

Why, then, is clitic climbing rendered possible once the modal construction is embedded in its entirety under causative *faire*? And why is there a contrast between (74a), in which the causee is *in situ*, and (74b), in which the causee

---

[32] I shall clear up the contrast between (74a,b) as we proceed. I thank Réjean Canac-Marquis, Rose-Marie Déchaine, Jean-Yves Pollock, Paul Postal, Johan Rooryck, Mireille Tremblay and Anne Zribi-Hertz for their help with the French examples.

undergoes cliticisation? Recall that I assumed (following Kayne 1991a) that the infinitival constituent embedded under *vouloir* is a CP. Since nothing would lead us to expect otherwise, the null hypothesis is that in *vouloir* constructions embedded under causative *faire*, too, the modal takes a CP complement. Bearing in mind that clitic movement out of this CP is normally impossible, we should now ensure that the VP containing the clitic is freed from this CP in the causative examples in (74), and that freeing this VP is impossible in noncausative (73). The way to set *lire*'s projection free in (74) is to move this VP out of the infinitival CP into some θ'-specifier position in the governing domain of an L-marking element. This specifier is readily provided by the structure in (68) — SpecSC2:

(75) $[_{\text{Infl}}$ $le_j + I^0]$ $[_{\text{VP}}$ *faire* $[_{\text{SC1}}$ $[_{\text{VP}}$ *vouloir* $[_{\text{SC2}}$ $[_{\text{VP}}$ *lire* $t_j]_i$
         $[_{\text{XP}}$ X $[_{\text{SC3}}$ $[_{\text{CP}}$ ... $t_i]$ $[_{\text{PP}}$ *à Jean*]]]]]]]]

Since in order to enable the clitic to climb all the way into the matrix causative clause the VP headed by *lire* must obligatorily be moved in the derivation of (74), this analysis also allows us to capture the contrast between the a- and b-examples of (74). In (75), extraction takes place out of a left branch constituent (CP in (75)). Recall from section 5.3.7.1 that this is normally impossible, *unless*, by movement of the predicate of SC3, its subject can be exempted from its left branch status. In this way I accounted for the "priority effect" found in French causatives of the type in (63) — extraction from the subject of SC3 is possible only if the predicate of SC3 is extracted. The contrast between (74a), in which the predicate of SC3 is *in situ*, and (74b), in which it is cliticised as *lui*, can now be seen to be an instantiation of Hulk's (1984) "priority effect", if the clitic placement data featured by these examples are analysed as in (75).[33]

---

[33] The contrast between (74a,b), though robust in Parisian French (Anne Zribi-Hertz, p.c.), is not reported by all speakers consulted. It remains to be investigated whether these speakers are also more liberal with regard to the "priority effect" discussed in section 5.3.7.1.

Italian exhibits no contrast of the type in (74): both examples in (i) are fine. This follows from what was said in chapter 4, fn. 42 about Italian *a*-phrases. There I suggested, on the basis of binding facts in dative constructions, that the *a*-phrase obligatorily undergoes Dative Shift (to a right-peripheral specifier of VP position). If PP-movement always obtains in datives, and transitive causative constructions are structurally identical with dative constructions in all relevant respects, the impeccability of (ia) (alongside (ib)) follows.

(i)   a.   Ciò *l'*ha fatto poter risolvere a Gianni.
               this it(CL) has made be-able-to solve to Gianni
        b.   Ciò *glielo* ha fatto poter risolvere.
               this to-him(CL)-it(CL) has made be-able-to solve

Why does the clitic climb all the way into the matrix clause, rather than settling for the modal *vouloir*? That intermediate clitic adjunction is barred is shown by the examples in (76), which are unanimously rejected by all speakers consulted:[34]

(76) a. *Ce compte-rendu a fait *le* vouloir lire à Jean.
          this review has made it(CL) want read to Jean
      b. *Ce compte-rendu lui a fait *le* vouloir lire.
          this review to-him(CL) has made it(CL) want read

The ungrammaticality of (76) falls out straightforwardly from the analysis of causative constructions presented here, according to which *faire* does not take a complement containing a projection of Infl. Hence, if Kayne (1991a) is right that clitics in Romance adjoin to an inflectional head, there is no potential landing-site for the clitic in (76).

There *is* a landing-site for *le*, however, in the matrix clause: the matrix Infl node. This position can moreover be reached directly by the clitic provided that, as argued here, the projection of the most deeply embedded verb *lire* undergoes movement into SpecSC2: no barriers intervene between the clitic and its prospective landing-site. The "clitic-climbing" example in (74a) is hence — correctly — predicted to be grammatical.[35]

---

[34] The same holds for the relevant variant of the Italian example in (i) of fn. 30:

(i)   *⁷Ciò ha fatto poter*lo* risolvere a Gianni.
                this has made be-able-to-it(CL) solve to Gianni

[35] There is one other logically possible word-order pattern that has not been addressed so far: the "normal" case involving local cliticisation internal to the infinitival clause embedded under the modal. This is exemplified in (i):

(i)   a. %Ce compte-rendu a fait vouloir *le* lire à Jean.
          this review has made want it(CL) read to Jean
      b. %Ce compte-rendu lui a fait vouloir *le* lire.
          this review to-him(CL) has made want it(CL) read

As the "%" sign in front of these examples indicates, speakers of French are not unanimous in their verdict of these sentences, some accepting them, others rejecting them outright, and yet a third group judging them slightly deviant as compared to the "long-distance" clitic movement example in (74b) in the main text. What this suggests — though I shall not work this out in any detail — is that VP-movement to SpecSC2 is actually the preferred option for some speakers.

5.3.8 Transitive and intransitive causatives

So far we have seen that an analysis of transitive causative constructions modelled on that of triadic constructions (i) yields an account of the cross-linguistic correlation between the Case form of causees of transitive causatives and that of Goals of prepositional dative constructions, (ii) furnishes a structural position for verbal affixes like Dutch *ver-*, Sanuma *-ma* and Indonesian *-kan* in causative constructions, and (iii) captures a number of intriguing properties of French transitive causative constructions.

Naturally, these proposals give occasion to a wealth of questions that I cannot even begin to address within the bounds of this study. For one thing, the discussion in this section is limited to *transitive* causative constructions. One wonders, then, about the structure of intransitive causative constructions, both unergative and unaccusative. In these constructions, the causee is typically not preceded by a dative preposition at S-structure.[36] From the present perspective, intransitive causatives are hence considerably less instructive. A few remarks should suffice in this context.

In the light of my consistent effort to assimilate the structures underlying triadic and causative constructions, the obvious thing to do is to look for as many parallels between the two construction types as can possibly be isolated. From the domain of triadic constructions, we are familiar with triplets of the type in (77):

(77) a. I served the meal to Paul/served Paul the meal.
      b. I served the meal.
      c. I served Paul.

---

[36] Nor should it be assumed to be preceded by a preposition at D-structure. Recall from section 4.2.3, above, that causees of *transitive* causative constructions (in both English and Dutch) pattern with Goals in double object constructions in that they fail to undergo empty operator movement (cf. exx. (14) and (15) of section 4.2.3). I advanced this as an argument for treating causees of transitive causatives as underlyingly PP-contained. Notice now that causees of *intransitive* (unaccusative as well as unergative) causative constructions, unlike causees of transitive causatives and Goals of double object constructions, fairly easily undergo empty operator movement, as Dutch (i) and English (ii) show (compare these with the aforementioned examples from section 4.2.3; thanks to Mika Hoffman for her native intuitions on sentences of the type in (ii)). At no point in the derivation, then, should causees of intransitive causatives be PP-contained.

(i)   a. ?Die meid is leuk om (?²een liedje) te laten zingen.
          that girl is nice COMP a song let sing
      b. Ik zoek iemand om (?²een liedje) te laten zingen.
          I look-for someone COMP a song to let sing
(ii) a. ?Children are not easy to let sing (?*a song).
      b. ??I am looking for someone to let sing (?*a song).

This paradigm can be reproduced for French (cf. (78)). Now a plausible suggestion to make would seem to be that the causative construction in (79b), with an unexpressed causee, corresponds to (78b), while the causative in (79c), in which the embedded verb is intransitive, patterns with the *servir* 'serve' construction in (78c).

(78) a. J'ai servi le repas à Paul.
         I have served the meal to Paul
     b. J'ai servi le repas.
     c. J'ai servi Paul.

(79) a. J'ai fait manger le repas à Paul.
         I have made eat the meal to Paul
     b. J'ai fait manger le repas.
     c. J'ai fait manger Paul.

Although it remains to be investigated how triplets of this type should be analysed, some support for the view that properties of intransitive causative constructions have direct parallels outside the domain of causative sentences comes from the following observations. As Authier & Reed (1991) and others have noted, there exist dialects of French (Québecois, for instance) exhibiting so-called "clitic Case alternations" in causative constructions. Thus, while Standard French intransitive causatives allow only an accusative clitic causee, there are dialects in which (80b), with a dative clitic, is perfectly fine:

(80) a. Ça *l*'a fait patienter.
         this him(ACC) has made wait
     b. Ça *lui* a fait patienter.
         this him(DAT) has made wait

Interestingly, now, Québecois apparently also allows such "clitic Case alternations" outside the realm of *faire*-causative constructions, as the pair of examples in (81) (of which, again, only the a-example is acceptable in Standard French) shows:[37]

(81) a. Je *l*'ai aidé.
         I him(ACC) have helped
     b. Je *lui* ai aidé.
         I him(DAT) have helped

---

[37] The examples in (81) were kindly provided to me by Lisa Reed, who obtained them from Julie Auger, a native Québecois speaker.

This again highlights the fact — capitalised on in the analysis of transitive causative constructions developed in this chapter — that the properties of causative constructions are no isolated quirks of just this sentence type. Although a more thorough execution of this research programme is outside the scope of this study, it will be clear from these examples that the study of causative constructions should not put blinkers on, and must look beyond causatives proper — particularly at triadic constructions, but others as well.

5.3.9 Alternative analyses

Mine is not the only logically conceivable analysis of causative constructions that captures the fact that these tend to correlate with applicative constructions in a number of respects, throughout the languages of the world. Recently, Marantz (1990) has approached the homophony of causative and applicative morphemes from a Larsonian perspective, taking essentially the opposite tack from the one taken here. While I have argued that both causative and applicative morphemes are affixal particles, Marantz suggests that these morphemes are all *verbs*. In this way Marantz reaches a structural assimilation of causative and applicative constructions — cf. (82)–(83); datives are analysed as in (84).

(82)   *Causatives à la Marantz (1990)*

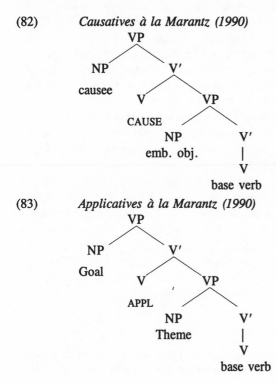

(83)   *Applicatives à la Marantz (1990)*

(84)   *Datives à la Marantz (1990)*

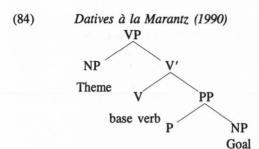

Whatever the merits of Marantz's proposal, it is clear that it does not accomplish nearly as extensive an assimilation of the uses of the various affixes discussed in section 5.2 as does the present analysis.[38] For one thing, the fact that Marantz generates the affixes in question under the higher V positions in (82) and (83) commits him to treating (i) tokens of Dutch *ver-* occurring in inchoative contexts, and (ii) instances of Dutch *ver-* and Indonesian *-kan* appearing in prepositional dative (i.e. non-applicative) constructions as accidentally homophonous to but structurally distinct from the causative and applicative tokens of these morphemes. Moreover, it seems that Marantz could only generalise over, on the one hand, the causative and applicative uses of these Dutch and Indonesian affixes and, on the other, their occurrences as particles on the assumption that particles are verbal elements occupying the higher V positions in the structures in (82) and (83). In chapter 2 I presented evidence against the view that particles belong to the category V. But even if a matrix-V approach to particles in causative/applicative contexts could somehow be defended, particles would have to have some other status in non-causative and non-applicative contexts, from which this higher V position is absent.

All in all, then, Marantz's (1990) assimilatory approach to causatives and applicatives, though already closer to the ultimate goal than Baker's, at best goes only partway towards generalising over all the various tokens of the Dutch and Indonesian affixes *ver-* and *-kan*.

Voskuil's (1990) analysis of Indonesian *-kan* is in a sense in between Marantz's proposal and the approach presented in this chapter. Voskuil, like Marantz, treats all tokens of *-kan* type affixes as verbs, but unlike Marantz he does not assign *-kan* matrix verb status — instead, the affix occupies much the same position as do particles (including *-kan*) in my analysis. Though congenial to the present proposal, Voskuil's treatment of *-kan* still has to contend with the fact that, in examples like (16) and (17) (section 5.2.3), this affix functions as a particle, a non-verbal element if this study is correct.

---

[38]   The same applies to Baker (1991), who carries over his (1989b) analysis of serial verb constructions (including causatives) to Bantu applicative constructions. I shall not address this proposal here.

The fact that so-called applicative morphemes, in languages like Indonesian, are not barred from occurring in non-shifted dative constructions is accounted for on Voskuil's analysis, as on mine. Larson (1988:373-34, and fn. 41) is also aware of the problem that Baker type P-incorporation approaches to applicative affixes face in this respect. In order to avoid it, and to accommodate the general absence of synchronic or diachronic relationships between applied morphemes and prepositions, Larson suggests that these affixes 'are essentially "registration markers" for some particular role like instrument or spatial location' (1988: 373). These "registration markers" are said to 'specify [the verb's] manner or location role' — a property which is typically attributable to particles as well. With the odd concept of "registration marker" understood as "particle", then, Larson's suggestion is tantamount to the central tenet of the present approach to applicative constructions.

5.4 Conclusion

It is often held that Dutch *ver-* is a causativising affix. At the same time, however, *ver-* occurs in contexts in which its presence clearly does not have a causativising effect (inchoatives, triadic constructions and the like). A similar picture arises from an inspection of the distribution of its Sanuma and Indonesian counterparts *-ma* and *-kan*. Only at the cost of proliferation of accidentally homophonous lexical entries for these three affixes can we maintain that these morphemes are causativisers. A more desirable situation would be for all tokens of *ver-*, *-ma* and *-kan* to be listed in the lexicon only once. I have presented an account of constructions featuring these affixes based on the hypothesis that the affixes in question are to be uniformly analysed as PARTICLES.

Analysing some apparently causativising affixes as particles is not to say, however, that there can be no verbal affixes that lexicalise the causative matrix predicate that was postulated in (49). It is perfectly well possible to analyse morphemes that show up only in causative contexts as instantiations of the matrix V-node. An analysis in such terms of affixes that have other, non-causative uses alongside their occurrence in causative constructions is clearly undesirable, however.

Treating APPLICATIVE (or applied) morphemes as particles rather than as spell-outs of incorporated dative prepositions yields us a significant simplification of the analysis of Dative Shift. As I noted in section 5.1, Baker's (1988) P-incorporation analysis of Dative Shift in polysynthetic languages like Bantu can be accepted only if we abstract away from phonological detail. After all, in none of the languages discussed by Baker is there a phonological resemblance between the dative preposition and the applicative morpheme occurring on the verb in Dative Shifted constructions.[39] Moreover, in Baker (1988) an assimilation of the analysis of Dative Shift in polysynthetic languages on the one hand, and languages like English on the other can be accomplished only at the cost of assuming that while in the former languages the preposition incorporating into the verb has a phonetic matrix, in the latter the incorporating preposition is obligatorily void of phonetic content. Once we deny that the applicative morpheme is an incorporated dative preposition, the lack of phonological similarity between the two comes as no surprise. As far as the second problem faced by a P-incorporation approach to Dative Shift is concerned, I have already done away with it by assuming that in *all* languages, the dative PP always has a zero-headed alternant (whose surface occurrence is subject to licensing conditions which may vary cross-linguistically; cf. chapters 3 and 4).

---

[39] Baker (1988) notes that in Kinyarwanda (Bantu; Rwanda) *locative* applicative constructions (though not in other types, including triadic ones), there is a morphological relationship between the independent preposition (*ku, mu*) and the prepositional affix (*-ho, -mo*).

Notice that I am not claiming here that there can never be incorporated dative prepositions with a phonological matrix — the analysis of Chinese Dative Shift offered in section 3.13.1 shows that the Chinese dative preposition *gei* can overtly incorporate into the verb and be realised as part of the verbal complex. For "applicative morphemes", which typically do not have a morphophonological relationship with their dative P counterparts, however, an approach along Baker's (1988) lines is inadequate.

6

Conclusions

Verbal particles, independent or affixal, are numerous and cross-linguistically pervasive. Their distribution and placement are subject to constraints, a proper understanding of which yields insight into the structure of various secondary predicative constructions. Starting out from a detailed analysis of the properties of complex particle constructions, this study has brought forth accounts of triadic constructions and Dative Shift, and the relationship between dative and transitive causative constructions, all of them built on the basic structural template proposed for complex particle constructions.

The foundations of this study are laid in chapter 2, in which the structure of constructions containing a verbal particle and an additional secondary predicate, illustrated in (1), is developed.

(1) a. They made John *out* **a liar**.
     b. They painted the barn *up* **red**.
     c. They put the books *down* **on the shelf**.

The chapter is opened by presenting evidence for the two central tenets of the analysis, the view that particles are small clause (SC) predicates, and that the same holds for the boldface phrases in the examples in (1). Eliminating an analysis of complex particle constructions according to which the SCs projected by the boldface constituents are generated in the subject position of the particle-headed SC (cf. Kayne 1985), chapter 2 proceeds to fleshing out an account built on the premise that the particles occurring in these constructions are *unaccusative* SC heads, taking the additional SC as their complement, as in (2):

(2)   [$_{VP}$ V [$_{SC1}$ Spec [$_{XP}$ Prt [$_{SC2}$ NP {AP/NP/PP/VP}]]]]

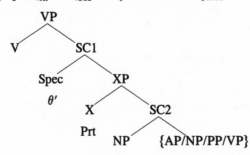

269

Apart from unaccusativity, particles are also ascribed a number of other properties on the basis of the analysis of complex particle constructions. In English, prepositional complex particle constructions are shown to differ from other such constructions with regard to the extractability of the predicate of SC2. Only in the former does extraction of this sort yield a well-formed result, provided that the particle finds itself in verb-adjacent position. This is accommodated on the basis of the structure in (2) with the aid of a small number of instrumental assumptions, which are put to use throughout this study. The essential hypotheses about the nature of particles are listed in (3).

(3)   a.   Particles are *SC heads*.
       b.   Particles are *ergative*.
       c.   Particles are *non-lexical*.
       d.   Particles are *prepositional*.

The non-lexical nature of particles ensures that its complement is, in the general case, a barrier for outside government. Hence, extraction of the predicate of SC2 is excluded in the bulk of English complex particle constructions. On the assumption that particles are prepositional, however, SC2 can be viewed as a *segment* of the particle's projection (hence exempt from barrierhood) if and only if the predicate of SC2 is categorially non-distinct from P. In this way, the transparency of SC2 in (2) to extraction of a prepositional predicate is accounted for.

The premises in (3) have each individually been advanced in earlier literature on particles and prepositions, but they have never, to my knowledge, been combined into a comprehensive analysis of (complex) particle constructions. Kayne (1984, 1985) argues that particles are SC predicates, Guéron (1986, 1990) moreover treating them as unaccusatives. The present study defends Emonds' (1976) original insight that particles are prepositional, rather than verb-like (Guéron 1990) or intermediate between verbs and prepositions (E. Hoekstra 1991). Particles are also argued here to be non-lexical, in the spirit of Van Riemsdijk's (1990) recent identification of a class of "functional prepositions".

The structure of complex particle constructions in (2) forms the backbone of the analysis of triadic constructions and transformational Dative Shift presented in chapter 3. The key observation here is that the dative PP in English prepositional dative constructions can trigger *Predicate Inversion*. The conclusion ensuing from this, that the dative PP qualifies as a SC predicate, immediately eliminates the bulk of recent accounts of triadic constructions and Dative Shift, including Larson's (1988) influential analysis. Effectively confining predicativity to verbal phrases, Larson may only accommodate Predicate Inversion by assigning it an account in terms of fronting of a verbal constituent. However, analysing inversion as VP/V′ fronting in Larson's overall theoretical framework entails massive overgeneration of unattested non-Predicate Inversion constructions.

Chapter 3 argues that triadic constructions, with or without a lexical particle or verbal affix, instantiate a structure which is slightly more elaborate than that in (2), in that it features an additional SC between the particle-headed SC and the matrix verb. This SC is headed by an abstract copular verb. In the derivation of the double object construction from the underlying structure in (4), the dative PP undergoes A-movement (of the type discussed in Hoekstra & Mulder's 1990 account of Predicate Inversion) to the specifier position of SC2. The empty head of the dative PP is licensed by *incorporating* into the abstract copula that governs SC2. The Dative Shift transformation as given shape in this study is illustrated in (5).

(4) $[_{VP}$ V $[_{SC1}$ Spec $[_{VP}$ BE $[_{SC2}$ Spec $[_{XP}$ X $[_{SC3}$ *Th* $[_{PP}$ P *Go*]]]]]]]

(5) $[_{VP}$ V $[_{SC1}$ Spec $[_{VP}$ $[_V$ BE+TO$_j$] $[_{SC2}$ $[_{PP}$ t_j *Go*]$_i$ $[_{XP}$ X $[_{SC3}$ *Th* t_i]]]]]]]

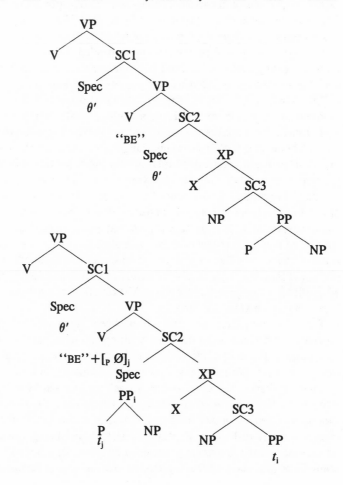

The combination of BE and the incorporated dative preposition TO yields the possessive predicate HAVE, which is denied primitive lexical status in the theory. Though this is not actually undertaken in this study, the analysis of triadic constructions propounded here renders it possible in principle to *decompose* triadic verbs such as *give* into more basic lexical atoms as well.

Two essential ingredients of the analysis of double object constructions are further supported in chapter 4, which addresses a number of S-structure phenomena in this domain. It is well known that, in many languages, A'-extraction of the Goal in a double object construction is not free. On the basis of a comparative investigation of (mainly) English and Dutch, the conclusion is reached that, while empty operator movement of Goals is strictly impossible, overt (short-distance) *wh*-extraction generally yields an acceptable result. This dichotomy between overt and empty operator movement of the double object Goal is explained with the aid of the empty dative preposition governing the Goal NP, in the spirit of earlier work by Kayne (1984), Czepluch (1982) and Baker (1988). The theoretical result that A'-extraction of the double object Goal is possible only by pied-piping the empty-headed dative PP straightforwardly rules out empty operator movement of Goals, since pied-piping under empty operator movement is independently known to be impossible.

That A-movement of the entire (zero-headed) dative PP, in a manner parallel to Predicate Inversion (cf. Hoekstra & Mulder 1990), is involved in the Dative Shift transformation is confirmed by restrictions on A'-movement of the double object Theme in the West-Germanic languages. The analysis of Dative Shift in (5) leads to the theoretical prediction that A'-extraction of the Theme in a genuine Dative Shift construction yields a violation of Principle C of the Binding Theory, and should hence be ruled out. All instances of A'-movement of the double object Theme should hence be derived from *covert* prepositional dative constructions, featuring a non-shifted empty-headed dative PP. This, in combination with the independently established fact that zero-headed dative PPs, if not A-moved via Dative Shift, must be scrambled in Dutch and West-Flemish, while they may stay *in situ* in German, explains the fact that, in Dutch and West-Flemish though not in German, A'-extraction of the double object Theme is contingent on Goal scrambling.

The reason why there is a difference between Dutch and West-Flemish on the one hand, and German on the other with regard to the surface distribution of zero-headed dative PPs lies in the way in which the empty dative preposition can be *licensed*. While in languages lacking an overt Case system (like Dutch and West-Flemish) the zero dative P can only be licensed by being incorporated into a verb, languages with morphological dative Case allow the dative preposition to be licensed *in situ* (quite possibly due to the fact that the dative Case affix effectively realises the P^0 position). Dative Shift being primarily motivated by the need of the empty preposition to be licensed, Chomsky's (1991) Economy Principle leads to the expectation that languages featuring overt dative

Case morphology have no Dative Shift transformation. Instead, all apparent Dative Shift constructions must be covert P-dative constructions in these languages. A case study of German double object constructions shows that this is a desirable corollary of the analysis.

Chapter 5 addresses the oft-noted yet unexplained formal parallel between dative and transitive causative constructions. Arguing first that so-called *applicative* morphemes should not be analysed as spell-outs of incorporated dative prepositions, but as *affixal particles* instead, I go on to show that a structural assimilation of dative and transitive causative constructions on the basis of the template in (4) is both feasible and advantageous. A detailed inspection of a number of hitherto mysterious properties of French causative constructions shows that analysing the dative-marked causee (or embedded subject) of transitive causatives as contained in a predicative dative PP, just as in prepositional dative constructions, makes the right empirical predictions.

A major guiding force in this study has been the Small Clause analysis. As I hope to have shown, this analysis yields fundamental insight into the structure of particle constructions and several other secondary predication constructions, among which most notably triadic constructions and Dative Shift.

References

Aarts, B. (1989) Verb-Preposition Constructions and Small Clauses in English. In *Journal of Linguistics* 25. 277–90.

Aarts, B. (1992). *Small Clauses in English: The Nonverbal Types*. Topics in English Linguistics 8. Berlin: Mouton de Gruyter.

Abeillé, A., D. Godard & Ph. Miller (1994). *The Syntactic Structure of French Causative Constructions*. Paper delivered at the 68th Meeting of the Linguistic Society of America, Boston.

Abney, S. (1987). *The English Noun Phrase in Its Sentential Aspect*. Diss., MIT.

Ackerman, F. (1994). Entailments of Predicates and the Encoding of Causees. In *Linguistic Inquiry* 25. 535–47.

Åfarli, T. (1985). Norwegian Verb Particle Constructions as Causative Constructions. In *Nordic Journal of Linguistics* 8. 75–98.

Aissen, J. (1974). *The Syntax of Causative Constructions*. Diss., Harvard University. (Published 1979, New York: Garland Press.)

Alsina, A. (1992). On the Argument Structure of Causatives. In *Linguistic Inquiry* 23. 517–55.

Alsina, A. & S. Mchombo (1990). The Syntax of Applicatives in Chichewa: Problems for a Theta Theoretic Asymmetry. In *Natural Language and Linguistic Theory* 8. 493–506.

Aoun, Y. (1985). *A Grammar of Anaphora*. Cambridge, MA: MIT Press.

Aoun, Y. & Y.H.A. Li (1989). Scope and Constituency. In *Linguistic Inquiry* 20. 141–72.

Authier, J.-M. & L. Reed (1991). Ergative Predicates and Dative Cliticization in French Causatives. In *Linguistic Inquiry* 22. 197–205.

Awóyalé, 'Y. (1988). Complex Predicates and Verb Serialization. *Lexicon Project Working Papers* 28. MIT.

Baker, M. (1988). *Incorporation. A Theory of Grammatical Function Changing*. Chicago: University of Chicago Press.

Baker, M. (1989a). Elements of a Typology of Applicatives in Bantu. In J. Hutchison & V. Manfredi (eds), *Current Approaches to African Linguistics* 7. Dordrecht: Foris.

Baker, M. (1989b). Object Sharing and Projection in Serial Verb Constructions. In *Linguistic Inquiry* 20. 513–53.

Baker, M. (1991). On the Relation of Serialization to Verb Extensions. In C. Lefebvre (ed.), *Serial Verbs: Grammatical, Comparative and Cognitive Approaches*. Amsterdam: John Benjamins. 79–102.

Baker, M., K. Johnson & I. Roberts (1989). Passive Arguments Raised. In *Linguistic Inquiry* 20. 173–251.

Barss, A. & H. Lasnik (1986). A Note on Anaphora and Double Objects. In *Linguistic Inquiry* 17. 347–54.

Belletti, A. (1990). *Generalized Verb Movement: Aspects of Verb Syntax*. Turin: Rosenberg & Sellier.

Belletti, A. & L. Rizzi (1988). Psych-Verbs and Theta-Theory. In *Natural Language and Linguistic Theory* 6. 291–352.

Bennis, H. (1991). Theoretische aspekten van partikelvooropplaatsing II. In *TABU* 21, 89–95.

Bennis, H. (1992a). Long Head Movement: The Position of Particles in the Verbal Cluster in Dutch. In R. van Hout & R. Bok-Bennema (eds), *Linguistics in the Netherlands 1992*. Amsterdam: John Benjamins. 37–47.

Bennis, H. (1992b). Answers to the questionnaire of the OTS/HIL Workshop on Particle Constructions, Utrecht.

Bennis, H., M. den Dikken, P. Jordens, S. Powers & J. Weissenborn (1994). *Picking up Particles*. Paper delivered at the 19th Boston University Conference on Language Development, Boston.

Bennis, H. & T. Hoekstra (1984). Gaps and Parasitic Gaps. In *The Linguistic Review* 4. 29–87.

Bennis, H. & T. Hoekstra (1988). *The Tense Connection*. Paper delivered at the GLOW Colloquium, Budapest.

Bennis, H. & T. Hoekstra (1989). PRO and the Binding Theory. In H. Bennis & A. van Kemenade (eds), *Linguistics in the Netherlands 1989*. Dordrecht: Foris. 11–20.

Benveniste, E. (1966). *Problèmes de linguistique générale*. Paris: Gallimard.

Besten, H. den (1978). On the Presence and Absence of *Wh*-Elements in Dutch Comparatives. In *Linguistic Inquiry* 9. 641–71.

Besten, H. den (1985). The Ergative Hypothesis and Free Word Order in Dutch and German. In J. Toman (ed.), *Studies in German Grammar*. Dordrecht: Foris. 23–64.

Besten, H. den (1992). Answers to the questionnaire of the OTS/HIL Workshop on Particle Constructions, Utrecht.

Besten, H. den & H. Broekhuis (1992). Verb Projection Raising in het Nederlands. In *Spektator* 21. 21–34.

Bickerton, D. & S. Iatridou (1987). *Verb Serialization and Empty Categories*. Ms., University of Amsterdam.

Boekenoogen, G. (1897). *De Zaansche volkstaal. Bijdrage tot de kennis van den woordenschat in Noord-Holland*. Leiden: A.W. Sijthoff.

Bolinger, D. (1971). *The Phrasal Verb in English*. Cambridge, MA: Harvard University Press.

Bonet, E. (1989). *Postverbal Subjects in Catalan*. Paper delivered at the annual meeting of the Canadian Linguistic Association. Université de Laval, Québec City.

Borer, H. (1991). The Causative-Inchoative Alternation: A Case Study in Parallel Morphology. In *The Linguistic Review* 8. 119–58.

Borer, H. (forthcoming). *Parallel Morphology*. Cambridge, MA: MIT Press.

Borgman, D. (1989). Sanuma. In D. Derbyshire & G. Pullum (eds), *Handbook of Amazonian Languages — Volume 2*. Berlin: Mouton de Gruyter. 15–248.

Bowers, J. (1993). The Syntax of Predication. In *Linguistic Inquiry* 24. 591–656.

Brame, M. (1984). Universal Word Induction vs. Move Alpha. In *Linguistic Analysis* 14. 313–52.

Brandi, L. & P. Cordin (1989). Two Italian Dialects and the Null Subject Parameter. In O. Jaeggli & K. Safir (eds), *The Null Subject Parameter*. Dordrecht: Kluwer. 111–42.

Bresnan, J. (1990). *Levels of Representation in Locative Inversion: A Comparison of English and Chicheŵa*. Ms., Stanford University.

Bresnan, J. & J. Grimshaw (1978). The Syntax of Free Relatives in English. In *Linguistic Inquiry* 9. 331–91.

Bresnan, J. & L. Moshi (1990). Object Asymmetries in Comparative Bantu Syntax. In *Linguistic Inquiry* 21. 147–85.

Broekhuis, H. (1991). Chain Government. In *The Linguistic Review* 6. 297–374.

Broekhuis, H. (1992). *Chain-Government: Issues in Dutch Syntax*. Diss., University of Amsterdam (HIL Dissertations 2).

Broekman, H. & M. den Dikken (1988). The Analysis of Incorporation in Eskimo. In P. Coopmans & A. Hulk (eds), *Linguistics in the Netherlands 1988*. Dordrecht: Foris. 29–38.

Broihier, K., N. Hyams, K. Johnson, D. Pesetsky, D. Poeppel, J. Schaeffer & K. Wexler (1994). *The Acquisition of the Germanic Verb Particle Construction*. Paper delivered at the 18th Boston University Conference on Language Development, Boston.

Büring, D. (1992). Back to the Sixties? In S. Barbiers, M. den Dikken & C. Levelt (eds), *Proceedings of the Third Leiden Conference for Junior Linguists*. 44–58.

Burzio, L. (1986). *Italian Syntax. A Government-Binding Approach*. Dordrecht: Reidel.

Byrne, R. (1987). *Grammatical Relations in a Radical Creole*. Amsterdam: John Benjamins.

Cannings, P. & M. Moody (1978). A Semantic Approach to Causation in French. In *Lingvisticae Investigationes* II:2. 331–62.

Cardinaletti, A. & M.T. Guasti (1991). *Epistemic Small Clauses and Null Subjects*. Paper delivered at ESCOL 1991.

Carlson, G. & T. Roeper (1980). Morphology and Subcategorization: Case and the Unmarked Complex Verb. In T. Hoekstra, H. van der Hulst & M. Moortgat (eds), *Lexical Grammar*. Dordrecht: Foris. 123–64.

Carrier-Duncan, J. (1985). Linking of Thematic Roles in Derivational Word Formation. In *Linguistic Inquiry* 16. 1–34.

Carrier, J. & J. Randall (1992). The Argument Structure and Syntactic Structure of Resultatives. In *Linguistic Inquiry* 23. 173–234.

Chomsky, N. (1970). Remarks on Nominalizations. In R. Jacobs & P. Rosenbaum (eds), *Readings in English Transformational Grammar*. The Hague: Mouton. 184–221.

Chomsky, N. (1973). Conditions on Transformations. In S. Anderson & P. Kiparsky (eds), *A Festschrift for Morris Halle*. New York: Holt, Rinehart & Winston. 232–86.

Chomsky, N. (1975). *The Logical Structure of Linguistic Theory*. Chicago: University of Chicago Press.

Chomsky, N. (1977). On *Wh*-Movement. In P. Culicover, T. Wasow & A. Akmajian (eds), *Formal Syntax*. New York: Academic Press.

Chomsky, N. (1981). *Lectures on Government and Binding*. Dordrecht: Foris.

Chomsky, N. (1986). *Barriers*. Cambridge, MA: MIT Press.

Chomsky, N. (1991). Some Notes on Economy of Derivation and Representation. In R. Freidin (ed.), *Principles and Parameters in Comparative Grammar*. Cambridge, MA: MIT Press. 417–54.

Chomsky, N. (1993). A Minimalist Program for Linguistic Theory. In K. Hale & S.J. Keyser (eds), *The View from Building 20*. Cambridge, MA: MIT Press. 1–52.

Chomsky, N. & H. Lasnik (1977). Filters and Control. In *Linguistic Inquiry* 8. 425–504.

Chung, S. (1982). Unbounded Dependencies in Chamorro Grammar. In *Linguistic Inquiry* 7. 1–37.

Chvany, C. (1975). *On the Syntax of BE-Sentences in Russian*. Cambridge, MA: Slavica Publishers.

Cinque, G. (1989). On Embedded Verb Second Clauses and Ergativity in German. In D. Jaspers, W. Klooster, Y. Putseys & P. Seuren (eds), *Sentential Complementation and the Lexicon*. Dordrecht: Foris. 77–97.

Cinque, G. (1990). Ergative Adjectives and the Lexicalist Hypothesis. In *Natural Language and Linguistic Theory* 8. 1–39.

Collins, C. & H. Thráinsson (1993). Object Shift in Double Object Constructions and the Theory of Case. In C. Phillips (ed.), *Papers on Case & Agreement II. MIT Working Papers in Linguistics* 19. 131–74.

Comrie, B. (1976). The Syntax of Causative Constructions: Cross-Language Similarities and Divergences. In M. Shibatani (ed.), *Syntax and Semantics Vol. 6: The Grammar of Causative Constructions*. New York: Academic Press.

Coopmans, P. & M. Everaert (1988). The Simplex Structure of Complex Idioms: The Morphological Status of *Laten*. In M. Everaert, A. Evers, R. Huybregts & M. Trommelen (eds), *Morphology and Modularity*. Dordrecht: Foris. 75–104.

Cowie, A. & R. Mackin (1993). *Oxford Dictionary of Phrasal Verbs. Oxford Dictionary of Current Idiomatic English (Vol. I)*. London: Oxford University Press.

Culicover, P. & M. Rochemont (1990). Extraposition and the Complement Principle. In *Linguistic Inquiry* 21. 23–47.

Czepluch, H. (1982). Case Theory and the Dative Construction. In *The Linguistic Review* 2. 1–38.

Dale, D. (1981). *Shona Mini-Companion*. Gweru: Mambo Press.

Davis, L. (1984). *Arguments and Expletives*. Diss., University of Connecticut.

Déchaine, R.-M. (1990). *The Syntactic and Semantic Headedness of Serial Verb Constructions*. Ms., University of Massachusetts, Amherst (based on a paper delivered at the 1990 GLOW Workshop, London).

Déchaine, R.-M. (1993). *Predicates across Categories: Towards a Category-Neutral Syntax*. Diss., University of Massachusetts, Amherst.

Diesing, M. & E. Jelinek (1993). The Syntax and Semantics of Object Shift. In *Working Papers in Scandinavian Syntax* 51. 1–54.

Dikken, M. den (1987). Secundaire predicatie en de analyse van small clauses. In *GLOT* 10. 1–28.

Dikken, M. den (1989). *Small clauses als subjecten? Over oppervlakkige discontinuïteit als onderliggend constituentschap en oppervlakkig constituentschap als onderliggende discontinuïteit*. Ms., University of Leiden.

Dikken, M. den (1990a). The Structure of English Complex Particle Constructions. In R. Bok-Bennema & P. Coopmans, (eds), *Linguistics in the Netherlands 1990*. Dordrecht: Foris. 23–32.

Dikken, M. den (1990b). *Verb Incorporation in French Causative Constructions*. Paper delivered at the Giselle Conference, Girona.

Dikken, M. den (1991a). Particles and the Dative Alternation. In J. van Lit, R. Mulder & R. Sybesma (eds), *Proceedings of the Second Leiden Conference for Junior Linguists*. 71–86.

Dikken, M. den (1991b). Serial Verbs, "Object Sharing", and the Analysis of Dative Shift. In F. Drijkoningen & A. van Kemenade (eds), *Linguistics in the Netherlands 1991*. Amsterdam: John Benjamins. 31–40.

Dikken, M. den (1992). *Empty Operator Movement in Dutch Imperatives*. In D. Gilbers & S. Looyenga (eds), *Language and Cognition* 2. 51–64.

Dikken, M. den (1993). *(Affixal) Particles and Argument Structure*. Paper presented at the Universität Stuttgart, June 1993; ms., Vrije Universiteit Amsterdam/HIL.

Dikken, M. den (1994). Predicate Inversion and Minimality. In R. Bok-Bennema & C. Cremers (eds), *Linguistics in the Netherlands 1994*. Amsterdam: John Benjamins.

Dikken, M. den & E. Hoekstra (1994). No Cause for a Small Clause? (Non-)arguments for the Structure of Resultatives. In C.J.W. Zwart (guest ed.), *Groninger Arbeiten zur germanistischen Linguistik* 37. *Minimalism and Kayne's Asymmetry Hypothesis*. 89–105.

Dikken, M. den & R. Mulder (1991). Double Object Scrambling. In J. Bobaljik & A. Bures (eds), *Papers from the Third Student Conference in Linguistics. MIT Working Papers in Linguistics* 14. 67–82.

Dikken, M. den & A. Næss (1993). Case Dependencies: The Case of Predicate Inversion. In *The Linguistic Review* 10. 303–36.

Di Sciullo, A.-M. & E. Williams (1987). *On the Definition of Word*. Cambridge, MA: MIT Press.

Di Sciullo, A.-M. & E. Klipple (1993). *Modifying Affixes*. Paper delivered at WECOL, University of Washington, Seattle.

Emonds, J. (1972). Evidence that Indirect Object Movement is a Structure Preserving Rule. In *Foundations of Language* 8. 546–61.

Emonds, J. (1976). *A Transformational Approach to English Syntax*. New York: Academic Press.

Emonds, J. (1985). *A Unified Theory of Syntactic Categories*. Dordrecht: Foris.

Emonds, J. (1987). The Invisible Category Principle. In *Linguistic Inquiry* 18. 613–32.

Emonds, J. (1992). Answers to the questionnaire of the OTS/HIL Workshop on Particle Constructions, Utrecht.

Emonds, J. (1993). Projecting Indirect Objects. In *The Linguistic Review* 10. 211–63.

Fabb, N. (1984). *Syntactic Affixation*. Diss., MIT.

Falk, C. (1990). On Double Object Constructions. In *Working Papers in Scandinavian Syntax* 14. 67–82.

Frampton, J. (1990). Parasitic Gaps and the Theory of *Wh*-Chains. In *Linguistic Inquiry* 21. 49–77.

Frank, R. (1992). *Syntactic Locality and Tree Adjoining Grammar: Grammatical, Acquisition and Processing Perspectives*. Diss., University of Pennsylvania.

Franks, S. (1993). On Parallelism in Across-the-Board Dependencies. In *Linguistic Inquiry* 24. 509–29.

Fraser, B. (1970). Idioms within a Transformational Grammar. In *Foundations of Language* 6. 22–42.

Fraser, B. (1974). *The Verb-Particle Combination in English*. Tokyo: Taishukan.

Freidin, R. (1992). *Foundations of Generative Syntax*. Cambridge, MA: MIT Press.

Friedemann, M.-A. (1992). On the D-Structure Position of Subjects in French. In S. Barbiers, M. den Dikken & C. Levelt (eds), *Proceedings of the Third Leiden Conference for Junior Linguists*. 155-68.

Fukui, N. & M. Speas (1986). Specifiers and Projection. In *MIT Working Papers in Linguistics* 8. 128-72.

Gibson, J. (1980). *Clause Union in Chamorro and Universal Grammar*. Diss., UCSD.

Gowers, E. (1954). *The Complete Plain Words*. London: Her Majesty's Stationery Office.

Green, G. (1974). *Semantics and Syntactic Regularity*. Bloomington: Indiana University Press.

Grimshaw, J. (1986). A Morphosyntactic Explanation of the Mirror Principle. In *Linguistic Inquiry* 17. 745-50.

Grimshaw, J. (1990). *Argument Structure*. Cambridge, MA: MIT Press.

Grimshaw, J. & R. Mester (1985). Complex Verb Formation in Eskimo. In *Natural Language and Linguistic Theory* 3. 1-19.

Gropen, J., S. Pinker, M. Hollander, R. Goldberg & R. Wilson (1989). The Learnability and Acquisition of the Dative Alternation in English. In *Language* 65. 203-57.

Guasti, M.T. (1991). Incorporation, Excorporation, and Lexical Properties of Causative Heads. In *The Linguistic Review* 8. 209-32.

Guasti, M.T. (1993). *Causative and Perception Verbs: A Comparative Study*. Turin: Rosenberg & Sellier.

Guéron, J. (1986). *Clause Union and the Verb-Particle Construction in English*. Paper delivered at NELS 16; ms., Université de Paris 8.

Guéron, J. (1990). Particles, Prepositions, and Verbs. In J. Mascaró & M. Nespor (eds), *Grammar in Progress*. Dordrecht: Foris. 153-66.

Guéron, J. & T. Hoekstra (1988). Les chaînes-T et les verbes auxiliaires. In *Lexique* 7. 61-85.

Haegeman, L. (1986). The Double Object Construction in West Flemish. In *The Linguistic Review* 5. 281-300.

Haegeman, L. (1991). *Scrambling, Clitic Placement and Agr Recursion in West Flemish*. Ms., Université de Genève.

Haider, H. (1990). Datives in German "ECM"-Constructions. In J. Mascaró & M. Nespor (eds), *Grammar in Progress*. Dordrecht: Foris. 175-85.

Haider, H. (1992). *The Basic Branching Conjecture*. Ms., Universität Stuttgart.

Hale, K. & S.J. Keyser (1992). The Syntactic Character of Thematic Structure. In I. Roca (ed.), *Thematic Structure. Its Role in Grammar*. Dordrecht: Foris. 107-43.

Hale, K. & S.J. Keyser (1993). On Argument Structure and the Lexical Expression of Syntactic Relations. In K. Hale & S.J. Keyser (eds), *The View from Building 20*. Cambridge, MA: MIT Press. 53-104.

Heggie, L. (1993). The Range of Null Operators: Evidence from Clefting. In *Natural Language and Linguistic Theory* 11. 45-84.

Hendrick, R. (1988). *Anaphora in Celtic and Universal Grammar*. Dordrecht: Kluwer.

Herschensohn, J. (1981). French Causatives: Restructuring, Opacity, Filters and Construal. In *Linguistic Analysis* 8. 217-80.

Herslund, M. (1984). Particles, Prefixes and Preposition Stranding. In *Topics in Danish Syntax. Nydanske Studier* 14. Copenhagen: Akademisk Forlag.

Higginbotham, J. (1985). On Semantics. In *Linguistic Inquiry* 16. 547–93.

Higginbotham, J. & R. May (1981). Questions, Quantifiers, and Crossing. In *The Linguistic Review* 1. 41–79.

Hoekstra, E. (1991). *Licensing Conditions on Phrase Structure*. Diss., University of Groningen.

Hoekstra, T. (1978). De status en plaats van het indirekt object. In J. Kooij (ed.), *Aspekten van woordvolgorde in het Nederlands*. Leiden. 40–69.

Hoekstra, T. (1984). *Transitivity. Grammatical Relations in Government-Binding Theory*. Dordrecht: Foris.

Hoekstra, T. (1988a). Small Clause Results. In *Lingua* 74. 101–39.

Hoekstra, T. (1988b). *Parasitic Gaps: A Unified or Composed Chain?*. Ms., University of Leiden. (French translation published in J. Guéron & J.-Y. Pollock (eds), *Linguistique comparée et théorie du liage.*)

Hoekstra, T. (1991). *Small Clauses Everywhere*. Ms., University of Leiden.

Hoekstra, T., M. Lansu & M. Westerduin (1987). Complexe verba. In *GLOT* 10. 61–79.

Hoekstra, T. & R. Mulder (1990). Unergatives as Copular Verbs: Locational and Existential Predication. In *The Linguistic Review* 7. 1–79.

Hoekstra, T. & I. Roberts (1992). *Middle Constructions*. In E. Reuland & W. Abraham (eds), *Knowledge and Language (Vol. II): Lexical and Conceptual Structure*. Dordrecht: Kluwer.

Hoffman, M. (1991). *The Syntax of Argument-Structure-Changing Morphology*. Diss., MIT.

Holloway King, T. (1993). The UTAH and Causation in Russian Psych Verbs. In P. Ackema & M. Schoorlemmer (eds), *Proceedings of ConSole 1*. 115–30.

Holmberg, A. (1986). *Word Order and Syntactic Features in the Scandinavian Languages and English*. Diss., University of Stockholm.

Holmberg, A. (1991). On the Scandinavian Double Object Construction. In H. Sigurðsson (ed.), *Papers from the Twelfth Scandinavian Conference of Linguistics*. 141–52.

Holmberg, A. (1993). Two Subject Positions in IP in Mainland Scandinavian. In *Working Papers in Scandinavian Syntax* 52. 29–41.

Hornstein, N. (1994). An Argument for Minimalism: The Case of Antecedent-Contained Deletion. In *Linguistic Inquiry* 25. 455–80.

Hornstein, N. & A. Weinberg (1981). Case Theory and Preposition Stranding. In *Linguistic Inquiry* 12. 55–91.

Hornstein, N. & D. Lightfoot (1987). Predication and PRO. In *Language* 63. 23–52.

Huang, C.-T.J. (1993). Reconstruction and the Structure of VP: Some Theoretical Consequences. In *Linguistic Inquiry* 24. 103–38.

Hudson, R. (1982). Incomplete Conjuncts. In *Linguistic Inquiry* 13. 547–50.

Hulk, A. (1984). 'Lui' versus 'en' in French Causatives. In *Linguistic Analysis* 13. 253–71.

Hulk, A. (1989). La construction impersonelle et la structure de la phrase. *Recherches linguistiques de Vincennes* 18.

Hyams, N., J. Schaeffer & K. Johnson (1993). *On the Acquisition of Verb Particle Constructions*. Ms., UCLA & University of Massachusetts, Amherst.

Íhìónú, P. (1988). *Serialization and Consecutivization in Ìgbo*. Paper delivered at the 2nd Niger-Congo Syntax and Semantics Workshop.

Jackendoff, R. (1977). *X-bar Syntax*. Cambridge, MA: MIT Press.

Jackendoff, R. (1990). On Larson's Account of the Double Object Construction. In *Linguistic Inquiry* 21. 427–54.

Jaeggli, O. (1981). *Topics in Romance Syntax*. Dordrecht: Foris.

Jaeggli, O. & N. Hyams (1993). On the Independence and Interdependence of Syntactic and Morphological Properties: English Aspectual *Come* and *Go*. In *Natural Language and Linguistic Theory* 11. 313–46.

Jespersen, O. (1965). *A Modern English Grammar on Historical Principles*. London: George Allen & Unwin Ltd./Copenhagen: Ejnar Munksgaard.

Johns, A. (1984). Dative "Movement" in Eskimo. In *Proceedings of the Parasession on Lexical Semantics*. Chicago: CLS.

Johnson, K. (1991). Object Positions. In *Natural Language and Linguistic Theory* 9. 577–636.

Johnson, K. (1992). *Particles*. Paper delivered at the OTS/HIL Workshop on Particle Constructions, Utrecht.

Josefsson, G. (1992). Object Shift and Weak Pronominals in Swedish. In *Working Papers in Scandinavian Syntax* 49. 59–92.

Kayne, R. (1975). *French Syntax. The Transformational Cycle*. Cambridge, MA: MIT Press.

Kayne, R. (1984). *Connectedness and Binary Branching*. Dordrecht: Foris.

Kayne, R. (1985). Principles of Particle Constructions. In J. Guéron, H.-G. Obenauer & J.-Y. Pollock (eds), *Grammatical Representation*. Dordrecht: Foris. 101–40.

Kayne, R. (1989). *Notes on English Agreement*. Ms., CUNY.

Kayne, R. (1991a). Romance Clitics, Verb Movement, and PRO. In *Linguistic Inquiry* 22. 647–86.

Kayne, R. (1991b). *Anaphors as Pronouns*. Paper delivered at LSRL XXI, University of California at Santa Barbara, February 1991.

Kayne, R. (1993a). Toward a Modular Theory of Auxiliary Selection. In *Studia Linguistica* 47. 3–31.

Kayne, R. (1993b). *The Antisymmetry of Syntax*. Ms., CUNY.

Keenan, E. (1976). Towards a Universal Definition of "Subject". In C. Li (ed.), *Subject and Topic*. New York: Academic Press. 303–33.

Keyser, S.J. & T. Roeper (1992). Re: The Abstract Clitic Hypothesis. In *Linguistic Inquiry* 23. 89–125.

Kimball, J. & J. Aissen (1971). I Think, You Think, He Think. In *Linguistic Inquiry* 2. 242–6.

Kinyalolo, K. (1991). *Syntactic Dependencies and the Spec-Head Agreement Hypothesis in KiLega*. Diss., UCLA.

Kiparsky, P. (1982). Lexical Morphology and Phonology. In L. Yang (ed.), *Linguistics in the Morning Calm*. Seoul: Hanshin. 3–91.

Koizumi, M. (1993). Object Agreement Phrases and the Split VP Hypothesis. In C. Phillips & J. Bobaljik (eds), *Papers on Case & Agreement I. MIT Working Papers in Linguistics* 18. 99–148.

Koopman, H. (1991). *The Verb Particle Construction and the Syntax of PPs*. Ms., UCLA.

Koopman, H. (1993). *The Structure of Dutch PPs*. Ms., UCLA.

Koopman, H. & D. Sportiche (1988). *Subjects*. Ms., UCLA.

Koopman, H. & D. Sportiche (1991). The Position of Subjects. In *Lingua* 85. 211–58.

Kosmeijer, W. (1993). *Barriers and Licensing*. Diss., University of Groningen.

Koster, J. (1973). "PP-over-V" en de theorie van J. Emonds. In *Spektator* 2. 294–311.

Koster, J. (1975). Dutch as an SOV Language. In *Linguistic Analysis* 1. 111–36.

Koster, J. (1978a). Why Subject Sentences Don't Exist. In S.J. Keyser (ed.), *Recent Transformational Studies in European Languages*. Cambridge, MA: MIT Press. 53–65.

Koster, J. (1978b). *Locality Principles in Syntax*. Dordrecht: Foris.

Kuno, S. (1973). Constraints on Internal Clauses and Sentential Subjects. In *Linguistic Inquiry* 4. 363–85.

Kuroda, S.-Y. (1988). Whether We Agree or Not. In W. Poser (ed.), *Japanese Syntax. Papers from the Second International Workshop on Japanese Syntax*. Stanford: CSLI.

Kurtzman, H. (1989). Extraction of Indirect Objects. In *Proceedings of ESCOL VI.* 173–81.

Laka, I. (1990). *Negation in Syntax: On the Nature of Functional Categories and Projections*. Diss., MIT.

Lakoff, G. (1970). *Irregularity in Syntax*. New York: Holt, Rinehart & Winston.

Langendoen, T., N. Kalish-Landon & J. Dore (1974). Dative Questions: A Study in the Relation of Acceptability and Grammaticality of an English Sentence Type. In T. Bever, J. Katz & T. Langendoen (eds), *An Integrated Theory of Linguistic Ability*. New York: Crowell.

Larson, R. (1985). Bare-NP Adverbs. In *Linguistic Inquiry* 16. 595–621.

Larson, R. (1988). On the Double Object Construction. In *Linguistic Inquiry* 19. 335–91.

Larson, R. (1989). Light Predicate Raising. *MIT Cognitive Science Center Working Papers*. MIT.

Larson, R. (1990). Double Objects Revisited: Reply to Jackendoff. In *Linguistic Inquiry* 21. 589–632.

Lasnik, H. (1993a). *Lectures on Minimalist Syntax*. Ms., University of Connecticut.

Lasnik, H. (1993b). *Case and Expletives Revisited*. Ms., University of Connecticut.

Lasnik, H. & M. Saito (1984). On the Nature of Proper Government. In *Linguistic Inquiry* 15. 235–89.

Lasnik, H. & M. Saito (1992). *Move Alpha. Conditions on Its Application and Output*. Cambridge, MA: MIT Press.

Law, P. (1991). Verb Movement, Expletive Replacement, and Head Government. In *The Linguistic Review* 8. 253–85.

Lees, R. (1961). *The Grammar of English Nominalizations*. Bloomington, IN: Indiana University Press.

Levin, B. & M. Rappaport-Hovav (1992). *Unaccusativity: At the Syntax–Semantics Interface*. Ms. (November 1992), Northwestern University & Bar Ilan University.

Li, Y. (1990). X^0-binding and Verb Incorporation. In *Linguistic Inquiry* 21. 399–426.

Li, Y.H.A. (1985). *Abstract Case in Chinese*. Diss., USC; revised version published as Y.H.A. Li (1990).

Li, Y.H.A. (1990). *Order and Constituency in Mandarin Chinese*. Dordrecht: Kluwer.

Lieber, R. (1992). *Deconstructing Morphology*. Chicago: University of Chicago Press.

Lonzi, L. (1991). Which Adverbs in SpecVP? In *Rivista di grammatica generativa* 15. 141–60.

Lumsden, J. (1992). *Possession: Substratum Semantics in Haitian Creole*. Paper delivered at the GLOW Workshop on African and Creole Languages, Lisbon.

Machobane, 'M. (1989). *Some Restrictions on the Sesotho Transitivizing Morphemes*. Diss., McGill University.

Manfredi, V. (1989). *Are There Triadic Verbs in Yorùbá?* Ms., Harvard University.

Manzini, R. (1983). *Restructuring and Reanalysis*. Diss., MIT.

Marácz, L. (1989). *Asymmetries in Hungarian*. Diss., University of Groningen.

Marantz, A. (1984). *On the Nature of Grammatical Relations*. Cambridge, MA: MIT Press.

Marantz, A. (1990). *Implications of Asymmetries in Double Object Constructions*. Ms., University of North Carolina, Chapel Hill.

Martin, J. (1991). *The Determination of Grammatical Relations in Syntax*. Diss., UCLA.

May, R. (1985). *Logical Form*. Cambridge, MA: MIT Press.

McCawley, J. (1968a). The Role of Semantics in Grammar. In E. Bach & R. Harms (eds), *Universals in Linguistic Theory*. New York: Holt, Rinehart & Winston. 125-70. (Reprinted in McCawley 1976)

McCawley, J. (1968b). Lexical Insertion in a Transformational Grammar without Deep Structure. In *Papers from the Fourth Regional Meeting of the Chicago Linguistic Society*. 71-80. (Reprinted in McCawley 1976)

McCawley, J. (1976). *Grammar and Meaning*. New York: Academic Press.

McDaniel, D. (1986). *Conditions on* Wh-*Chains*. Diss., CUNY.

McDaniel, D. (1989). Partial and Multiple *Wh*-Movement. In *Natural Language and Linguistic Theory* 7. 565-604.

Mejías-Bikandi, E. & J. Moore (1994). *Spanish Causatives and Indefinites: Evidence for VP Complementation*. Paper delivered at the 68th Meeting of the Linguistic Society of America, Boston.

Ménard, P. (1973). *Manuel du français du moyen-âge*. Bordeaux: Sobodi.

Miller, D.G. (1993). *Complex Verb Formation*. Amsterdam: John Benjamins.

Miyara, S. (1983). Reorderings in English. In *Linguistic Analysis* 12. 271-314.

Morin, Y.-C. & M. St-Amour (1977). Description historique des constructions infinitives du français. In *Montreal Working Papers in Linguistics* 9. 113-52.

Mulder, R. (1990). *An Empty Head for Object Control*. Ms., University of Leiden (abridged version published in *Proceedings of NELS 21*).

Mulder, R. (1992a). Datives and the Particle Alternation. In S. Barbiers, M. den Dikken & C. Levelt (eds), *Proceedings of the Third Leiden Conference for Junior Linguists*. 183-200.

Mulder, R. (1992b). *The Aspectual Nature of Syntactic Complementation*. Diss., University of Leiden (HIL Dissertations 3).

Mulder, R. & M. den Dikken (1992). Tough Parasitic Gaps. In *Proceedings of NELS 22*.

Mulder, R. & R. Sybesma (1992). Chinese is a VO Language. In *Natural Language and Linguistic Theory* 10. 439-76

Müller, G. (1992). In Support of Dative Movement. In S. Barbiers, M. den Dikken & C. Levelt (eds), *Proceedings of the Third Leiden Conference for Junior Linguists*. 201-17.

Müller, G. & W. Sternefeld (1993). Improper Movement and Unambiguous Binding. In *Linguistic Inquiry* 24. 461-507.

Naarding, J. (1951). 'Hij ging en kocht een zevenschot'. In *De Nieuwe Taalgids* 44. 342–44.

Neeleman, A. (1994). *Complex Predicates*. Diss., University of Utrecht.

Neeleman, A. & F. Weerman (1993). The Balance between Syntax and Morphology: Dutch Particles and Resultatives. In *Natural Language and Linguistic Theory* 11. 433–75.

Oehrle, R. (1976). *The Grammatical Status of the English Dative Alternation*. Diss., MIT.

Ormazabal, J. (1994). PRO, Null Case and the Interpretation of Complements. In *Proceedings of NELS 24*. 475–89.

Ottósson, K. (1991). Icelandic Double Objects as Small Clauses. In *Working Papers in Scandinavian Syntax* 48. 77–97.

Ouhalla, J. (1991). *Functional Categories and the Head Parameter*. Ms., Queen Mary and Westfield College, London University.

Oyèláràn, O. (1989). *Transitivity and Antifocus in Yorùbá*. Paper delivered at the 3rd Niger-Congo Syntax and Semantics Workshop.

Pannekeet, J. (1984). *Westfries woordenboek*. Stichting Uitgeverij Noord-Holland.

Pearce, E. (1990). *Parameters in Old French Syntax: Infinitival Complements*. Dordrecht: Kluwer.

Perlmutter, D. & P. Postal (1984). The 1-Advancement Exclusiveness Law. In D. Perlmutter & C. Rosen (eds), *Studies in Relational Grammar 2*. Chicago: University of Chicago Press. 81–125.

Pesetsky, D. (1982). *Paths and Categories*. Diss., MIT.

Pesetsky, D. (1987). *Wh*-in-situ: Movement and Unselective Binding. In E. Reuland & A. ter Meulen (eds), *The Representation of (In)definiteness*. Cambridge, MA: MIT Press. 98–129.

Pesetsky, D. (1993). *Zero Syntax I: Experiencers and Cascades*. Ms. (final version, November 1993), MIT; to appear, Cambridge, MA: MIT Press.

Pesetsky, D. (1994). *Some Long-Lost Relatives of Burzio's Generalization. Developments of Branigan (1992)*. Paper delivered at the OTS/HIL Workshop on Burzio's Generalization, Utrecht.

Pesetsky, D. (in prep.). *Zero Syntax II: An Essay on Infinitives*. Ms., MIT.

Phillips, C. (1993). Conditions on Agreement in Yimas. In C. Phillips & J. Bobaljik (eds), *Papers on Case & Agreement I. MIT Working Papers in Linguistics* 18. 173–213.

Pijnenburg, H. (1991). *Datives in French*. Diss., University of Amsterdam.

Pinker, S. (1987). Resolving the Learnability Paradox in the Acquisition of the Verb Lexicon. *Lexicon Project Working Papers* 17. MIT.

Pinker, S. (1989). *Learnability and Cognition: The Acquisition of Argument Structure*. Cambridge, MA: MIT Press.

Pollock, J.-Y. (1989). Verb Movement, Universal Grammar, and the Structure of IP. In *Linguistic Inquiry* 20. 365–424.

Pollock, J.-Y. (1990). *On Constraining LF V-Movement: Notes on the Comparative Syntax of Aspectual* **Come/Go** *vs.* **Venir/Partir**. Paper delivered at the Going Romance conference, Utrecht.

Pollock, J.-Y. (1992). *Questions in French and the Theory of UG*. Paper delivered at the 15th GLOW Colloquium, Lisbon.

Poplack, S. (1989). The Case and Handling of a Mega-Corpus: The Ottawa-Hull French Project. In R. Fasold & D. Shiffrin (eds), *Language Change and Variation*. Amsterdam: John Benjamins. 411–51.

Postal, P. (1981). A Failed Analysis of the French Cohesive Infinitive Construction. In *Linguistic Analysis* 8. 281–323.

Progovac, L. (1988). *A Binding Approach to Polarity Sensitivity*. Diss., UCLA.

Reed, L. (1989). *A Barriers Approach to the Issues of Complementation and Word Order in French Causatives*. Ms., University of Ottawa.

Reed, L. (1992a). Remarks on Word Order in Causative Constructions. In *Linguistic Inquiry* 23. 164–72.

Reed, L. (1992b). *French Clitic Case Alternations in a Parametric Theory of Grammar*. Ms., University of Ottawa.

Reinhart, T. (1976). *The Syntactic Domain of Anaphora*. Diss., MIT.

Reinhart, T. & E. Reuland (1993). Reflexivity. In *Linguistic Inquiry* 24. 657–720.

Reuland, E. (1983). Government and the Search for Auxes: A Case Study in Crosslinguistic Category Identification. In F. Heny & B. Richards (eds), *Linguistic Categories. Auxiliaries and Related Puzzles* (Vol. I.). Dordrecht: Reidel. 99–168.

Riemsdijk, H. van (1977). On the Diagnosis of *Wh*-Movement. In J. Kegl, D. Nash & A. Zaenen (eds), *Proceedings of the Seventh Annual Meeting of the North Eastern Linguistic Society*. 349–63. (Revised version in J. Keyser (ed.) (1978), *Recent Transformational Studies in European Linguistics*. Cambridge, MA: MIT Press.)

Riemsdijk, H. van (1978). *A Case Study in Syntactic Markedness*. Dordrecht: Foris.

Riemsdijk, H. van (1990). Functional Prepositions. In H. Pinkster & I. Genee (eds), *Unity in Diversity*. Dordrecht: Foris. 229–41.

Rigter, G. & F. Beukema (1985). *A Government and Binding Approach to English Sentence Structure*. Apeldoorn: Van Walraven.

Rivero, M.-L. (1990). *Adverb Incorporation and the Syntax of Adverbs*. Ms., University of Ottawa.

Rivero, M.-L. (1991). Long Head Movement and Negation: Serbo-Croatian vs. Slovak and Czech. In *The Linguistic Review* 8. 319–51.

Rizzi, L. (1982). *Issues in Italian Syntax*. Dordrecht: Foris.

Rizzi, L. (1986). On Chain Formation. In H. Borer (ed.), *Syntax and Semantics* 19. New York: Academic Press. 65–96.

Rizzi, L. (1990). *Relativized Minimality*. Cambridge, MA: MIT Press.

Rizzi, L. (1991). *Argument/Adjunct (A)symmetries*. In *Proceedings of NELS* 22.

Roberts, I. (1988). Thematic Interveners. In *Rivista di grammatica generativa* 13. 111–36.

Roberts, I. (1991). Excorporation and Minimality. In *Linguistic Inquiry* 22. 209–18.

Rochemont, M. (1986). *Focus in Generative Grammar*. Amsterdam: John Benjamins.

Rochemont, M. & N. Keach (1992). *Symmetry, Case, and Agreement in Bantu*. Paper delivered at the GLOW Workshop on African and Creole Languages, Lisbon.

Rooryck, J. (1994). *Prepositions, Functional Projections and Minimalist Case-Assignment*. Paper delivered at the Ninth Comparative Germanic Syntax Workshop, Harvard University.

Rosen, C. (1984). The Interface between Semantic Roles and Initial Grammatical Relations. In D. Perlmutter & C. Rosen (eds), *Studies in Relational Grammar 2*. Chicago: The University of Chicago Press. 38–77.

Rosen, S. (1989). *Argument Structure and Complex Predicates*. Diss., Brandeis University.

Ross, J. (1976). *Constraints on Variables in Syntax*. Diss., MIT.

Rothstein, S. (1983). *The Syntactic Forms of Predication*. Diss., MIT.

Ruwet, N. (1972). *Théorie syntaxique et syntaxe du français*. Paris: Seuil.

Sadock, J. (1980). Noun Incorporation in Greenlandic: A Case of Syntactic Word Formation. In *Language* 56. 300–19.

Safir, K. (1983). On Small Clauses as Constituents. In *Linguistic Inquiry* 14.

Safir, K. (1992). *What's in a Complement?* Abstract of a paper delivered at NELS 23, Ottawa.

Sag, I. (1976). *Deletion and Logical Form*. Diss., MIT. (Published 1980, New York: Garland Press.)

Sag, I. (1982). Coordination, Extraction, and Generalized Phrase Structure Grammar. In *Linguistic Inquiry* 13. 329–36.

Sag, I., G. Gazdar, T. Wasow & S. Weisler (1985). Coordination and How to Distinguish Categories. In *Natural Language and Linguistic Theory* 3. 117–71.

Saussure, F. de (1916). *Cours de linguistique générale*. Paris: Bayot.

Schoorlemmer, M. (1991). *Syntactic Modality in Russian*. Ms., University of Utrecht.

Schultink, H. (1988). Some Remarks on the Relations between Morphology and Syntax in Twentieth-Century Linguistics. In M. Everaert, A. Evers, R. Huybregts & M. Trommelen (eds), *Morphology and Modularity*. Dordrecht: Foris. 1–8.

Speas, M. (1990). *Phrase Structure in Natural Language*. Dordrecht: Kluwer.

Sportiche, D. (1988). A Theory of Floating Quantifiers and Its Corollaries for Constituent Structure. In *Linguistic Inquiry* 19. 33–60.

Sportiche, D. (1992). *Clitic Constructions*. Ms., UCLA.

Sproat, R. (1985). *On Deriving the Lexicon*. Diss., MIT.

Sprouse, R. (1989). *On the Syntax of the Double Object Construction in Selected Germanic Languages*. Diss., Princeton University.

Stewart, J. (1963). Some Restrictions on Objects in Twi. In *Journal of African Languages* 2. 145–49.

Stillings, J. (1975). The Formulation of Gapping in English as Evidence for Variable Types in Syntactic Transformations. In *Linguistic Analysis* 1. 247–73.

Stowell, T. (1981). *Origins of Phrase Structure*. Diss., MIT.

Stowell, T. (1983). Subjects across Categories. In *The Linguistic Review* 2. 285–312.

Svenonius, P. (1992). Movement of P^0 in the English Verb-Particle Construction. In *Syntax at Santa Cruz 1*.

Sybesma, R. (1991). Results in Chinese: Resultatives to an Extent. In J. Bobaljik & A. Bures (eds), *Papers from the Third Student Conference in Linguistics. MIT Working Papers in Linguistics* 14. 271–84.

Sybesma, R. (1992). *Causatives and Accomplishments: The Case of Chinese Ba*. Diss., University of Leiden (HIL Dissertations 1).

Takahashi, D. (1994). Sluicing in Japanese. In *Journal of East Asian Linguistics*.

Taraldsen, T. (1983). *Parametric Variation in Phrase Structure*. Diss., University of Tromsø.

Tellier, C. (1991). *Licensing Theory and French Parasitic Gaps*. Dordrecht: Kluwer.

Tellier, C. (to appear). *The HAVE/BE Alternation: Attributives in French and English*. To appear in *Probus*.

Tenny, C. (1987). *Grammaticalizing Aspect and Affectedness*. Diss., MIT.

Thornton, R. (1991). *Successful Cyclic Movement*. Paper delivered at the GLOW Workshop on syntactic acquisition, Leiden.

Travis, L. (1984). *Parameters and Effects of Word Order Variation*. Diss., MIT.

Tremblay, M. (1991). An Argument Sharing Approach to Ditransitive Constructions. In A. Halpern (ed.), *The Proceedings of the Ninth West Coast Conference on Formal Linguistics*. Stanford: CSLI.

Tuggy, S. (1987). Nahuatl Causative/Applicative in Cognitive Grammar. In B. Rudzku-Ostyn (ed.), *Topics in Cognitive Linguistics*. Amsterdam: John Benjamins. 587–618.

Vikner, S. (1990). *Verb Movement and the Licensing of NP-Positions in the Germanic Languages*. Diss., Université de Genève (2nd version 1991).

Voskuil, J. (1990). *Some Transitivization Processes in Malay*. MA thesis, University of Leiden.

Voskuil, J. (1993). *Verbal Affixation in Tagalog (and Malay)*. Ms., University of Leiden.

Voskuil, J. & P. Wehrmann (1990). *On the Notion "Theme"*. Ms., University of Leiden.

Wagner, D. (1985). Objects in Gokana. In *Studies in African Linguistics* Supplement 9. 304–8.

Walinska de Hackbeil, H. (1986). *The Roots of Phrase Structure: The Syntactic Basis of English Morphology*. Diss., University of Washington, Seattle.

Walinska de Hackbeil, H. (1989). *θ-Government, Thematic Government and Extraction Asymmetries in Zero Derivation*. Centrum voor Wiskunde en Informatica, University of Amsterdam.

Weerman, F. (1989). *The V2 Conspiracy. A Synchronic and a Diachronic Analysis of Verbal Positions in the Germanic Languages*. Dordrecht: Foris.

Wegner, J. & M. Rice (1988). *The Acquisition of Verb-Particle Constructions*. Paper delivered at the American Speech-Language-Hearing Association, Boston.

Wexler, K. (1992). Some Issues in the Growth of Control. In R. Larson, S. Iatridou, U. Lahiri & J. Higginbotham (eds), *Control and Grammar*. Dordrecht: Kluwer.

Williams, E. (1981). On the Notions "Lexically Related" and "Head of a Word". In *Linguistic Inquiry* 12. 245–74.

Williams, E. (1994). *Thematic Structure in Syntax*. Cambridge, MA: MIT Press.

Woolford, E. (1986). The Distribution of Empty Nodes in Navajo: A Mapping Approach. In *Linguistic Inquiry* 17. 301–30.

Wyngaerd, G. Vanden (1989). Raising-to-Object in English and Dutch. *Dutch Working Papers in English Language and Linguistics* 14.

Zaring, L. (1994). On the Relationship between Subject Pronouns and Clausal Arguments. In *Natural Language and Linguistic Theory* 12. 515–69.

Zhang, S. (1990). Correlations between the Double Object Construction and Preposition Stranding. In *Linguistic Inquiry* 21. 312–16.

Zwart, C.J.W. (1993). *Dutch Syntax: A Minimalist Approach*. Diss., University of Groningen.